CW01207424

DUBLIN DOCKLANDS
AN URBAN VOYAGE

DUBLIN DOCKLANDS
AN URBAN VOYAGE

TURTLE BUNBURY

First published in 2009 by Montague Publications Group on behalf of the Dublin Docklands Development Authority.

Copyright © Turtle Bunbury 2009
www.turtlebunbury.com

Commissioning Editor: Carmel Smith.
Co-Editor: Loretta Lambkin.

All rights reserved. No part of this publication may be reproduced, stored in a retrieval system, or transmitted in any form or by any means, electronic, mechanical, photocopying, recording or otherwise, without the prior permission of the copyright holder.

ISBN 978-0-9558155-1-5

Includes Ordnance Survey Ireland data reproduced under OSi
Permit number 8517
Unauthorised reproduction infringes Ordnance Survey
Ireland and Government of Ireland copyright.
© Ordnance Survey Ireland 2008

Cover Image: A true prospect of the north & south Liffey quays in Dublin docklands, drawn from life in the Winter of the year two thousand and five by Brian Lalor, and etched & printed by him at the Graphic Studio Dublin's Green Street East workshops, between Sir John Rogerson's Quay and Hanover Quay.

Set in Gill Sans 9 pt.

Printed and bound in Spain by Estudios Gráficos ZURE S.A.
www.egzure.com

This book was compiled in good faith and with as much care as possible to provide accurate information and honest opinion. The author and publishers do not accept responsibility for any inaccuracies or omissions therein.

Montague Publications Group
39 Upper Fitzwilliam Street, Dublin 2
Tel: +353 1 669 2101 Fax: +353 1 669 2104
www.montaguegroup.ie

This book is dedicated to my parents,
Ben and Jessica Rathdonnell,
who kept my ship firmly pointed
towards the harbour mouth.

Also to my beautiful wife Ally
who guides me through the foggy spells
and our daughter Jemima who tickles me pink
from dawn till dusk till dawn again.

Contents

Introduction

Chapter 1: Custom House Quay

- Streetwise — 34
- The Custom House — 36
- Custom House Characters — 38
- Custom House Quay & the Old Dock — 40
- The Custom House Docks — 42
- *Jeanie Johnston* — 46
- The chq building — 48
- The Crimean Banquet of 1856 — 50
- The Victorian Age — 53
- Seán O Casey Bridge — 54
- Connolly Station & the Iron Horse — 56
- Great Northern Railway — 58
- Sir Isaac Butt Bridge — 60
- The Loopline Railway Bridge — 62
- The 20th Century — 64
- The Guinness Barges — 68
- Talbot Memorial Bridge — 70
- Custom House Docks Development Authority — 72
- International Financial Services Centre — 74

Chapter 2: North Wall

- Streetwise — 80
- The North Lotts Project — 82
- The Industrial Age — 84
- The 20th Century — 88
- Scherzer Rolling Lift Bridges — 90
- The *MV Cill Airne* — 92
- The London & North Western Railway Company — 94
- B&I (The British & Irish Steam Packet Company) — 96
- The 100-Ton Crane & the North Wall Extension — 98
- St. Laurence O'Toole Pipe Band — 100
- The Halpins-Father & Son — 101
- Bindon Blood Stoney — 102
- Sir John Purser Griffith — 103
- St Laurence O'Toole Church — 104
- St Laurence O'Toole GAA Club — 106
- National College of Ireland — 107
- St Laurence O'Toole Girls School — 108
- Luke Kelly — 110
- The Sheriff Street Flats — 112
- Spencer Dock & The Royal Canal — 114
- New Luas Bridge at Spencer Dock — 118
- North Wall Today — 119
- The O$_2$ — 120

Chapter 3: East Wall

- Streetwise — 126
- Creation of a Community — 128
- The 20th Century — 130
- School Boy Strike of 1911 — 131
- Sporting Times — 132
- Splendid Isolation — 138
- Rathborne Candles — 142
- Seán O'Casey — 144
- Seán O'Casey Community Centre — 146
- St. Barnabas Church — 147
- The Building Parson — 148
- Local Heroes — 149
- Wiggins Teape — 149
- Modern Times — 150
- East Point Business Park — 151

Chapter 4: Westland Row & the South Quays

- Streetwise — 156
- City Quay & Townsend Street — 158
- Westland Row — 158
- The Hospital on Lazar's Hill — 160
- Pearse Railway Station — 161
- City Quay-A Potted History — 162
- Sculpture & Chip Shops — 163
- The Brothers Pearse — 164
- The Guinness Ships — 165
- *Asgard II* — 166
- The Gilbert Library & Queen's Royal Theatre — 167
- St Andrew's Resource Centre — 168
- The Hibernian Marine School — 170
- Sir John Rogerson — 172
- The Gasometer — 174
- Sir John Rogerson's Quay — 176
- The Diving Bell — 180
- The Samuel Beckett Bridge — 181

Chapter 5: Grand Canal Docks

- Streetwise — 186
- Grand Canal Docks — 188
- Grand Canal Quay — 191
- Grand Canal Street & Maquay Bridge — 192
- Bolands Mill — 193
- The Boland Garrison of Easter 1916 — 194
- Charlotte Quay — 196
- General Seán MacMahon Bridge — 197
- The Coalmen — 198
- Hanover Quay Gasworks — 200
- Renaissance of Grand Canal Docks — 204
- Grand Canal Square — 206
- U2 - A Docklands Band — 208

Chapter 6: Ringsend & Poolbeg

- Streetwise — 214
- The South Lotts-Streetwise — 218
- The Early Years — 220
- Great South Wall — 224
- Ringsend Cars — 226
- Ringsend's Golden Age — 228
- The Tale Of The Pidgeons — 230
- The Pidgeon House — 232
- Captain William Bligh & *The Ouzel Galley* — 236
- The Pembroke Township — 238
- Ringsend Gasholder — 240
- Ringsend Sport & Community — 242
- Park Life — 244
- The Irish Glass Bottle Factory — 245
- Poolbeg Power Station — 246
- Dublin Docklands Development Authority — 248

Acknowledgements

Bibliography

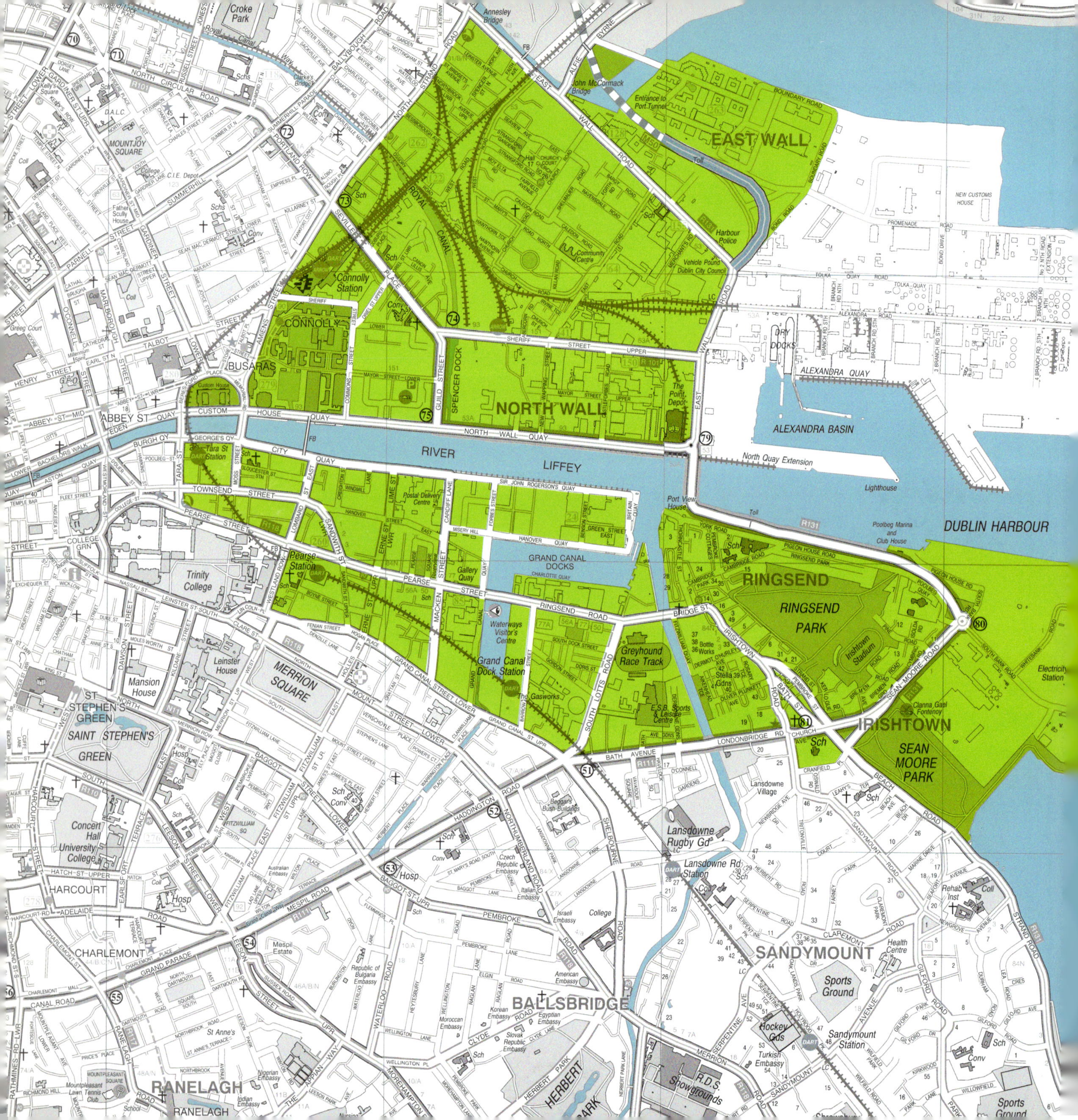
EAST WALL
NORTH WALL
RIVER
LIFFEY
CONNOLLY
BUSARAS
RINGSEND
RINGSEND PARK
IRISHTOWN
SEAN MOORE PARK
DUBLIN HARBOUR
ALEXANDRA BASIN
GRAND CANAL DOCKS
MERRION SQUARE
SAINT STEPHEN'S GREEN
ST STEPHEN'S GREEN
Trinity College
Connolly Station
Pearse Station
Tara St Station
Grand Canal Dock Station
Lansdowne Rd Station
Sandymount Station
Lansdowne Rugby Gd
Greyhound Race Track
Waterways Visitor's Centre
Croke Park
MOUNTJOY SQUARE
Leinster House
Mansion House
Concert Hall University College
HARCOURT
CHARLEMONT
RANELAGH
BALLSBRIDGE
SANDYMOUNT
Sports Ground
Herbert Park
R.D.S. Showgrounds
Custom House
North Quay Extension
Lighthouse
Poolbeg Marina and Club House
Electricity Station
The Gasworks
Harbour Police
Dublin City Council
Vehicle Pound
The Point Depot
Postal Delivery Centre
Gallery Quay
Irishtown Stadium
Mespil Estate
New Customs House
Entrance to Port Tunnel
Clanna Gael Fontenoy
Rehab Inst

CLONTARF

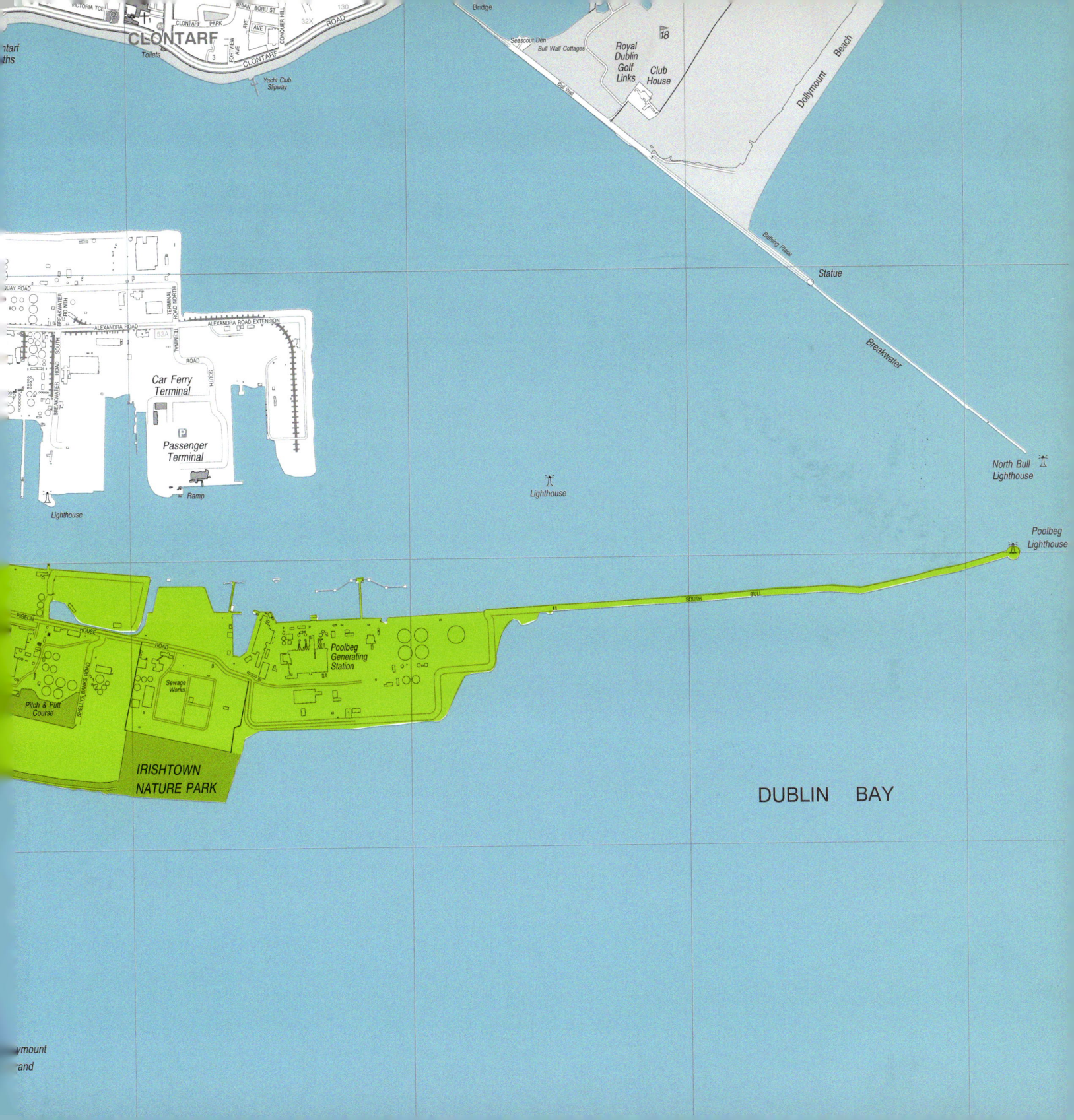

Toilets
Yacht Club Slipway

BRIAN BORU ST
CLONTARF PARK
VICTORIA TCE
FOXFIELD AVE
CONQUER HILL
CLONTARF ROAD
32X
130

Bridge
Seascout Den
Bull Wall Cottages
Royal Dublin Golf Links
Club House
18

Dollymount Beach

Bathing Place
Statue
Bull Wall
Breakwater
North Bull Lighthouse

QUAY ROAD
BREAKWATER ROAD NORTH
TERMINAL ROAD NORTH
ALEXANDRA ROAD
ALEXANDRA ROAD EXTENSION
52A
TERMINAL ROAD SOUTH
BREAKWATER ROAD SOUTH

Car Ferry Terminal

P **Passenger Terminal**

Ramp
Lighthouse
Lighthouse

Poolbeg Lighthouse
SOUTH BULL

PIGEON HOUSE ROAD
SHELLY BANKS ROAD
Pitch & Putt Course
Sewage Works
Poolbeg Generating Station

IRISHTOWN NATURE PARK

DUBLIN BAY

ymount
rand

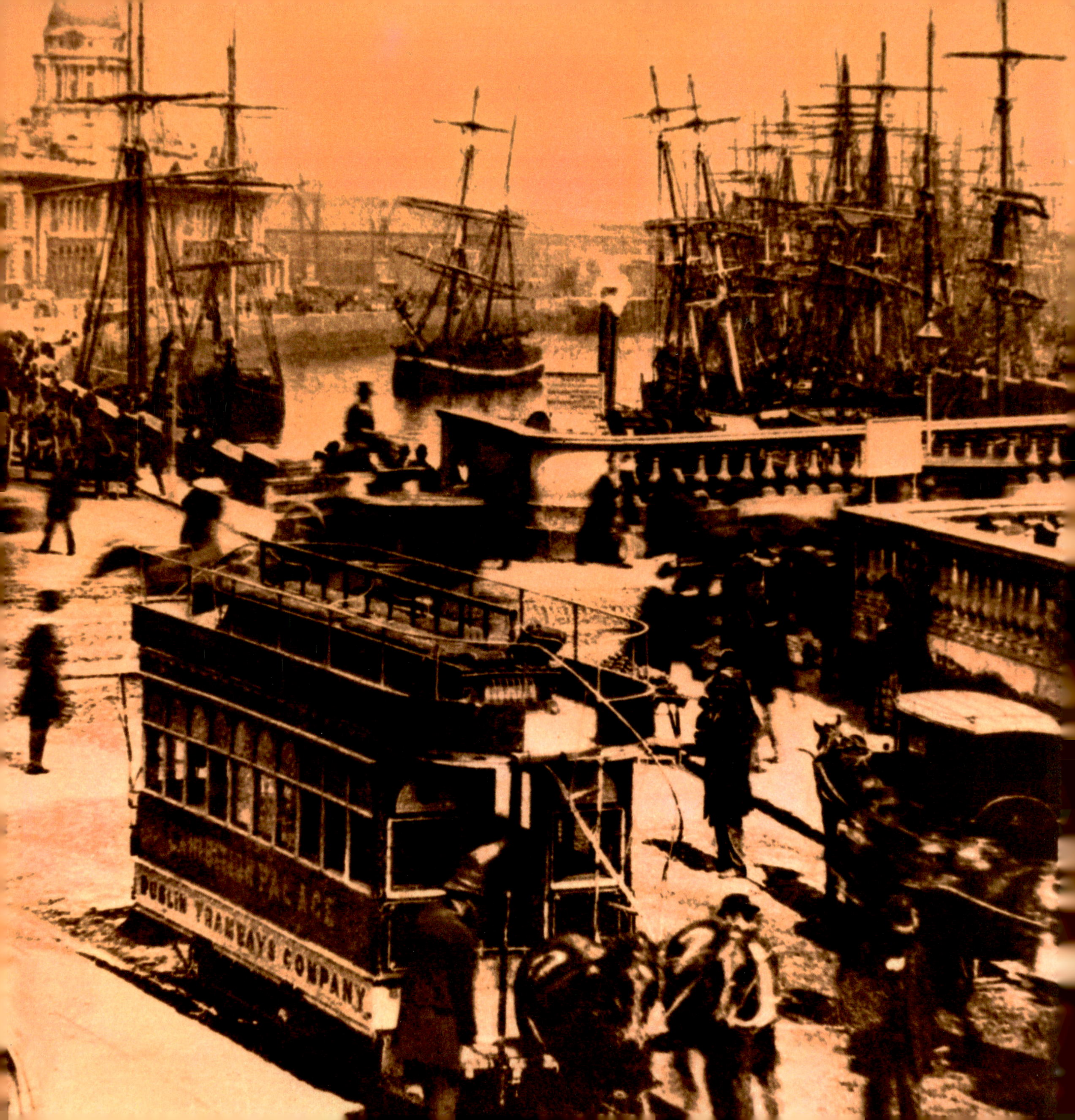
DUBLIN TRAMWAYS COMPANY

Introduction
An Urban Voyage

The old man is standing upon Seán O'Casey Bridge. Beneath him, the strong Liffey waters surge over the same course they have travelled since Turgesius the Norseman's longship passed up this way 1,200 years ago. His eyes move slowly left and right, patiently surveying the shimmering new horizons of the Dublin Docklands. He knew this part of the city well in his youth, he explains. His grandfather was the lock-keeper at the Ringsend Docks beyond Sir John Rogerson's Quay and his mothers' family were dockers for at least five generations. His eyes widen as he conducts me into the past, his hands like wands, his language raw yet magisterial. As we talk, people of every race, creed, fashion, dialect and generation whittle by, left and right, mostly on foot but some on bicycles and others on skateboards. Perhaps it's the sunshine but these faces are excited, smiling, positive, focused. We watch the bumble-bee coloured Liffey ferry make its short progression from the North Wall to Sir John Rogerson's Quay. 'You can forget quick what was here before', he says quietly.

The old man's childhood was set against the backdrop of the North Wall during the 1930s. In those times the quaysides north and south were overrun with people - the brave and the brawny, casuals and button-men, welders and carpenters, farriers and coalmen, gangers and tramps, alcoholics and shawlies, fisher-women, top-hatted gents and hordes of bare-footed children. Between them jostled pie-balled carthorses and skinny donkeys, rickety wagons, rusty black bicycles and the occasional spluttering truck. The air was frequently thick with cold, coal-hued smog. On the river itself, cargo ships, cattle boats, lighters and barges journeyed up and down, while deep voices bellowed out from the Hailing Station, directing skippers to the relevant berth.

Perhaps the most famous vessels were the Guinness ships that moored outside the Custom House. We turn to look at the mighty Custom House, spreading its neo-Classical wings confidently across the waterfront. The old man's father knew some of those who burned the building down during the War of Independence. Our eyes rise to the 16ft statue of Commerce, destroyed in the fire but reconstructed in 1990, which now presides over the city centre from the central dome. When Thomas Banks carved the original Commerce in the 1780s, the Docklands was still in its infancy. Much of the lands now occupied by the North Lotts, East Wall and the Grand Canal Docks comprised a swampy marshland, washed over by the tidal waters of the Liffey, the Tolka and the Dodder rivers twice daily. On the southside, the shoreline ran roughly from Ballsbridge via Grand Canal Street to where Pearse Street Garda station stands today. On the northside, the salty waters swept in as far west as North Strand Road.

During the 17th century, the first major steps were taken to tame the river with the construction of stonewalls, or quays, either side of the Liffey channel. By the 1720s, these walls had extended as far as Sir John Rogerson's Quay on the southside and the North Wall on the northside. A further wall, the East Wall, was constructed up the River Tolka. These three walls - reconstructed, secured and extended over time - form the basis for the present day Dublin Docklands. They enabled the reclamation of substantial lands at the heart of a city about to enter its greatest era of prosperity.

No commercial boom would have been possible without the Docklands. It was here that everything happened. All goods were weighed, taxed, sampled, loaded, unloaded, stored, imported and exported. During the age of imperialism, Dublin's masters concentrated on building the necessary infrastructure to make the Docklands more productive. Completed in 1792, the Custom House marked the start of this new age. It was soon to be joined by ambitious docks and canals on both the north and south sides of the Liffey. Built by the greatest engineers of the age, both the Custom House Docks and the Grand Canal Docks were hailed as pioneering achievements when completed in the decades that immediately followed the opening of the Custom House. However, both were rapidly demoted with the evolution of new merchant ships that were simply too big to access such handsome docks. The Dublin Port and Dock Board eventually responded by commissioning the North Wall Extension and developing new deep-water quays closer to the port itself.

The Victorian architects of Spencer Dock believed they had learned a lesson from these ill-fated Georgian ventures when their new dock opened in the 1870s but it too became swiftly redundant. Indeed, the Royal Canal, through which it linked to the Liffey, was so comprehensively defeated by the evolution of road transport that there was a very serious plan to tarmac the entire thing. Fortunately both the Royal and Grand Canals have survived to the present day. These extraordinary feats of workmanship are now playing a key role in defining the 21st century Docklands as a carefully planned cityscape where businesses, residences, parklands and waterways roll seamlessly from one to the other. The new Royal Canal Linear Park is destined to be a classic illustration of this forward-thinking concept.

The arrival of the railways in the 1840s marked a major evolution of the Docklands as thousands of migrant workers from all across the British Isles poured into Dublin in pursuit of employment. The railway lines carved through the Docklands, separating the East Wall and North

Wall communities. Despite considerable challenges from the roads, the railways have survived to the present day. The handsome Victorian stations at Westland Row and Amiens Street - renamed for Padraig Pearse and James Connolly on the 50th anniversary of the 1916 Rebellion - continue to service thousands of people every day, as do the new stations at Spencer Dock and Grand Canal Dock.

When the old man was a child, he and his friends ran along the quays catching bananas thrown from ships by kindly American sailors. When the tea ships came in, his uncles stuffed their pants full of tea-leaves and waddled home victoriously to their wives. One uncle rarely made it home, preferring the dark, hazy confines of the pub instead. Sometimes the pub was where you collected the wages. If you didn't buy a drink for the man who paid you, you might not be chosen for work the next week. The wives were never happy about the pubs. Many waited by the pub doors to catch their husbands going in or out before the weeks wages were spent on drink. Alcoholism was rife and all the symptoms of abuse and depression that came with it.

The old man's first job was distributing a horse-cart full of coal to the well-to-do homes of Merrion Square and Fitzwilliam Street. His uncle skippered one of the Gas Company coal boats. In those days, the docklands were dominated by colliers, sailing in from England and Wales, laden with black nuggets. Every morning, hundreds of thin, peaky-capped men gathered alongside the docks with large shovels, ready to dig the coal out of the ships and into the waiting trucks and carts. The first electric cranes appeared in Victorian times and astounded people with their ability to do the work of a hundred men. By the time the old man was a teenager, the coalmen were rightly becoming anxious for the security of their jobs; technology was advancing fast. In the 1950s, the coal yards began to abandon carthorses in favour of trucks.

Previous page: An early photo circa 1885 showing tall ships moored outside the Custom House and the horse-drawn tram rumbling down Eden Quay (Photo: The Osman Collection). Opposite Page Left: The Guinness Brewery frequently used the Grand Canal Docks as a storage depot before dispatching their kegs of eagerly awaited stout out into the countryside via the Grand Canal. Opposite Page Right: The locomotive 'Merlin' waiting to leave Amiens Street Station for Belfast in the summer of 1937 (Photo: Charles Friel Collection). Page Left: Dockers at work unloading goods in the North Wall transit sheds. (Photo: Dublin Port Company). Page Right: *The Jeanie Johnson* replica is now a permanent reminder of the mighty tall ships who once sailed in and out of the Dublin Docklands bringing both Irish cargo and adventurous sailors to the farthest reaches of the planet. Next page: The Gasometer on Sir John Rogerson's Quay defined the skyline of the South Docks, marking the extensive terrain of the Dublin Gas Company. This landscape has now been utterly transformed and Sir John Rogerson's Quay is the location of the headquarters of the Dublin Docklands Development Authority. (Photo: Dublin City Council)

In the wake of the Second World War, the Port shifted east and the city began to turn its back on the river. Up until the 1970s, Dublin Port was still the biggest employer in Dublin, providing work for communities north and south through its ships, quays and warehouses. However, the collapse of business in the inner-city Docklands was utterly devastating to those communities who lived there. Much of the North Wall was given over to warehousing, huge sheds racked together like Monopoly pieces, some temporary, others magnificent. The introduction of containerisation to Dublin Port in the 1950s swiftly killed off the need for such warehouses. The glass-fronted chq building at the northern end of Séan O'Casey Bridge is the last surviving warehouse of the Docklands glory days and has lately been restored with award-winning precision and reopened as a state-of-the-art shopping centre. In 1856, this mighty structure hosted close to 4,000 veterans of the Crimean War to a huge banquet.

By the early 1980s, the inner city of Dublin was one of the most depressed, forlorn and dangerous places in the world. It was a harrowing era for anyone who knew the Docklands. The old man closes his eyes when he talks of it. The area was defined by massive unemployment, a serious drop out rate from schools, rising crime, rampant drug use and intense neglect. The landscape became one of abandoned freight yards, dishevelled car parks, poorly surfaced roads, patchy lawns and broken cranes. Once thriving places like the Grand Canal Docks were simply sealed off as no-go areas. When the city bosses tried to resolve the situation, they often did so without sympathy such as with the somewhat ruthless eviction of the residents of the Sherriff Street flats prior to the destruction of those monoliths. The old man well remembers the hey-day of the Sheriff Street flats when another old man, with a clubfoot and a mysterious bag, would clamber to the brown-brick rooftops and scatter conkers for the young 'chiselers' playing below.

Although the regeneration is by no means complete, the extraordinary story of what has happened in the Docklands since the 1980s cannot be overstated. Under the direction of the Custom House Docks Development Authority (CHDDA), the riverside between the Custom House and the North Wall emerged as Dublin's foremost financial district at the very moment that the Celtic Tigers were preparing to take on the world. Less than 20 years ago, the sites of the megalithic green-glass offices of George's Quay and the International Financial Services Centre (IFSC) comprised a car park and a series of warehouses.

However, while CHDDA succeeded in revolutionising Dublin's financial sector, it was not in their brief to consider the communities living around them. In 1997, that changed dramatically when the Dublin Docklands Development Authority was formed. The origins of the Docklands Authority lay in a series of working trips made by members of the Industrial Development Agency (IDA Ireland) to Bill Clinton's United States in 1995 and 1996. All the signs suggested that the wealthy new American technology firms were seeking stylish, low-rent offices, centrally located to attract the finest employees. Nobody wanted to be out in the industrial sticks, in anonymous estates surrounded by out-dated factories. The enormous success of the IFSC had already proved that overseas companies liked being in the centre of Dublin City.

Ruairi Quinn, then Minister of Finance, wondered about the abandoned Bord Gáis site in his own Ringsend constituency. The decontamination of the site might present an enormous environmental and financial challenge, but perhaps it could be made to pay for itself? Quinn consulted Brendan Howlin, then Minister of the Environment, who replied that, as CHDDA's remit was nearing an end, he was proposing to renew it and extend the remit. This would include the entire docklands, excluding the territory of the working port, covering 1,300 acres (526 ha) and extending from East Wall on the northside to Ringsend and Irishtown on the south, running along the Liffey from City Quay and the Custom House right down to the mouth of the river at Poolbeg. It also included what became known as 'the hinterlands', small pockets of Dublin not strictly in the Docklands but where the communities were so destitute that it was deemed both pragmatic and essential to incorporate them into the overall area plan. However, both Howlin and Quinn believed the new authority should have a 'more comprehensive and holistic' attitude than CHDDA.

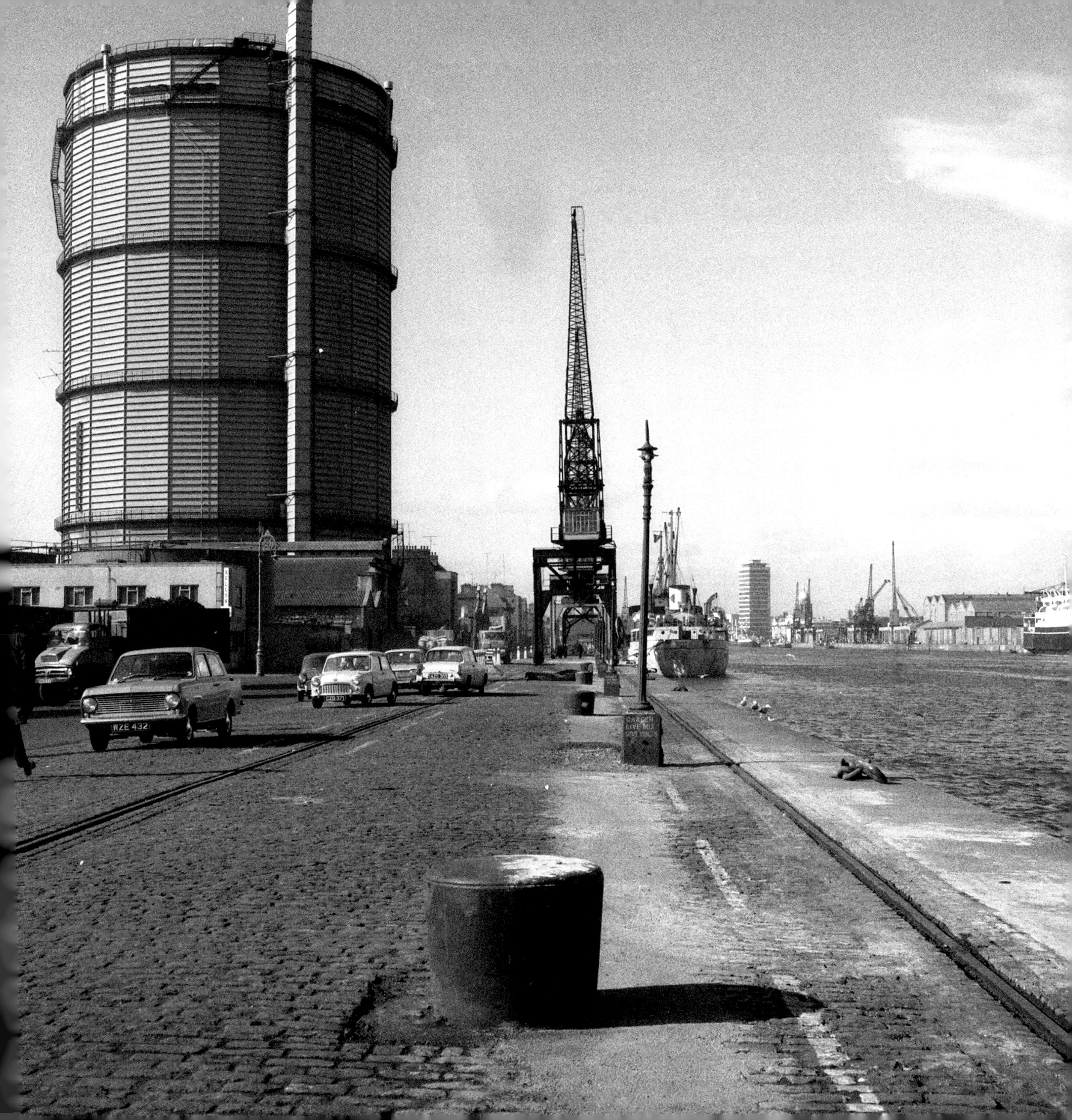
WZE 432

The Dublin Docklands Development Authority

In the 1996 budget, Ruairi Quinn set aside money to commission the Riverrun Consortium, with Murray Ó Laoire Architects as lead consultants, to prepare a Draft Master Plan for the Dublin Docklands. The objective of the 15-year plan was to produce a social democratic model, incorporating integrated, sustainable development that would 'breathe new life' into the area. In what transpired to be a revolutionary approach, the Docklands Authority invited representatives from every part of the Docklands community to contribute to the future planning of the area.

This multi-dimensional think-tank formed the basis of the Docklands Council and comprised 25 people drawn from the unions, local business, political representatives, semi-state bodies and the local community.

Below: The graduation ceremony of the Docklands community representatives at the National College of Ireland in 2006. From left to right: Geraldine O'Driscoll, Mairéad Ní Chíosóig, Willie Dwyer, Anne Carroll, Charlie Murphy, Gerry Fay, Frances Corr, Paul Dolan, Dolores Wilson, Betty Ashe, Seánie Lambe.

Even while the Master Plan was being drafted, land prices across Dublin were soaring. Appointed Chairman of the Docklands Authority in June 1997, Lar Bradshaw believed all haste was required if the Docklands Authority was to stand any chance of success. Bradshaw urged that all debates in the Docklands Council be raised and concluded as quickly as possible. The Master Plan was duly completed in a remarkable six months and made public in November 1997. It recommended a series of specific economic, physical and social regeneration strategies, in tandem with eight detailed local area action plans. The Master Plan's most important conclusion was that economic regeneration would not be feasible unless the local community were in support. Thus, the social and economic agenda became a key priority of the Docklands Authority. The physical regeneration was the second main concern and the continued development of the IFSC was the third.

The 17,500 people who lived in the Docklands in 1997 included a large number of people who had been effectively abandoned by the State since the 1950s. Employment was minimal, education standards were disastrous, self-confidence was shot to pieces and the incidence of crime and drugs was amongst the highest in Ireland. History had shown that new mega-developments in inner cities often just magnified the gulf between the original community and newcomers.

The Docklands Authority was hard-wired for genuine and complete interaction with the local community by the very Act that created it, which stressed that its first duty was to secure the Social and Economic Regeneration of the area. Nonetheless, one of the Docklands Authority's greatest challenges was to convince the community that it was not a gang of smart-dressed shysters trying to steal their homes and pile glass buildings everywhere. 'We walked into the first Council meeting and saw a lot of suits sitting around the table', recalls Charlie Murphy. 'We weren't too used to suits listening to what the local community has to say. I said it to the representative at the time. 'I don't think this is going to work'. 'We didn't really know where to start', says Lar Bradshaw. 'But we didn't want to impose our own false wisdoms so we had to empower those who did know what to do from within the community'. As such, the local community became an intrinsic part of the whole Docklands planning policy, from its architecture and design to its governance and on-going evolution. The Docklands Authority also promised solid investment in local education, housing, leisure, health, childcare, drug treatment and rehab clinics. In time, the community came to accept the Docklands Authority at its word. 'The trust is such that it's no longer a 'them and us' attitude', says Betty Ashe of the St Andrew's Resource Centre on Pearse Street. 'There's just us.'

Twelve years and over five billion Euros worth of investment later, the Dublin Docklands presents a classic case-study for cities across the world to see how an otherwise stagnant rough and tumble inner city landscape can be converted into an intelligent, prosperous and stimulating new quarter. Hand-in-hand with this regeneration has been a remarkable transformation of the educational, housing and social opportunities for the 17,500 inner city residents. This shift permeates everything from the Docklands Authority's education and housing policies to their commendable emphasis on sustainability and public space. Writing in 2005, Ruairi Quinn, one of the pioneers of the entire project, said the Docklands Authority's success had exceeded all his hopes, describing it as 'the epitome of the application of social democratic values at work'.

As confidence is restored in the global economy, many cities across the world will turn to the Dublin Docklands to consider what has happened there. The achievement of all those involved in this resurrection is immense. That follows for the resilient communities who have lived here for generations, for the yellow-hatted builders who physically constructed these new horizons, for the pencil-twirling architects and designers who burnt midnight oil to get their scaled models and master plans as right as possible, for the knuckle-crunching money-lenders who took a chance and invested in the project, for the determined developers who became fired up and kept the wheels turning, for the few politicians who saw the opportunity to breathe new life into the city centre and took it, and for the old and the wise who added their thoughts to the process.

The Face Of The New Docklands

By the 1980s it was all too easy to forget that Dublin was a city built upon a river. In 1999, the Docklands Authority commissioned a River Regeneration Strategy, which provided a comprehensive analysis of what was preventing the river from making a more vibrant contribution to the city. The immediate conclusions of that report resulted in the commissioning of two new bridges linking the north and south waterfronts and clearing the quaysides of the empty warehouses and derelict sheds. The campshires were restored and planted anew with trees and shrubs. The river is no longer a straightforward commercial waterway and is planned to become one of the city's foremost leisure facilities and visitor attractions. Many of the events now staged in the Docklands are river-based while most of the prime development sites are also along the waterfront.

The recent boom in the Irish economy played in favour of the Docklands Authority. It made the creation of a sustainable community seem both plausible and likely. It also meant that the six existing communities explored in this book had the confidence to speak up, to make their presence felt and even to inspire the Docklands Authority through their own unique histories. Each area had its own legacy of entrepreneurs and skills, of adversity and triumph, of spirit and humour. There was still a good deal of soul in the Docklands and that was a social capital the Docklands Authority wished to nurture and develop. As part of the strategy to integrate the community, the Docklands Authority has provided considerable support to initiatives across the six areas. A flurry of new state-of-the-art crèches, football pitches, bingo buses and community halls have been complemented by strategies to calm traffic in residential areas, provide better street lighting and ensure plenty of open-air green parklands.

Today, there are over 23,000 people living and over 40,000 people working in the Docklands everyday. Untold numbers are now also visiting every day. With the development of each campshire and bridge, the opening of every hotel, theatre, shop or restaurant, the creation of every new apartment or office block, the Docklands takes another bold step forward.

Bono described the development of the Dublin Docklands as showing one of the best aspects of 21st century Ireland. In less than a decade, the skyline of Dublin's docklands has been utterly transformed. Where once there were gasometers and cranes, now the riverfront boasts a shimmering collage of glass and block. While many of these new builds are modest in scope, a magnificent burst of landmark structures are due to open in the next two years. A classic example of the Docklands Authority architectural ethos is to be found in the Grand Canal Docks which has attracted considerable praise from across the world. When the Docklands Authority first acquired the derelict, semi-corrugated, coal-stained former Gasworks site at Hanover Quay in 1997, many eyebrows were raised as to their wisdom. Today, that same site boasts some of the most genuinely prestigious office and residential addresses in Dublin City, including a large number of social and affordable units, with the Martha Schwartz designed red poles and green planters lighting the way for the exuberant Studio Libeskind designed Grand Canal Theatre, and the Aires Mateus chequerboard hotel nearby.

Directly across the Liffey from the Docklands Authority's offices on Sir John Rogerson's Quay, the Convention Centre, Dublin, and Samuel Beckett Bridge are also defining a bold new age for the Dublin Docklands. The award-winning Séan O'Casey Bridge has already revolutionised contact between the north and south sides. Irish architects are to the fore with such works as the new Séan O'Casey Community Centre by O'Donnell+Tuomey, Grand Canal Square No 1 by Duffy Mitchell O'Donoghue, Shay Cleary's Altro Vetro, and Urban Projects' Clarion Quay buildings on North Wall. In Mayor Square stands the educational triumph that is the National College of Ireland, providing a huge positive for those in the Docklands seeking better qualifications. The restoration of Stack A into the chq building by Michael Collins Associates has been hailed in highest circles. The developments at both Spencer Dock and the Point Village are also turning heads, not least with the arrival of the Luas line and the opening of The O_2 in the former Point Depot. By 2012, we can expect Harry Crosbie's 40-storey Watchtower and the U2 Tower to stand sentinel over the waterfront. Meanwhile, in East Wall, the new Séan O'Casey Community Centre is fast becoming a beacon for one of the Docklands oldest and most independent minded communities. The combination of cutting edge buildings, public spaces and intelligent, easy access is now billowing out through Ringsend and Irishtown to the Poolbeg peninsula where the former Glass Bottle Company site is destined to become one of Dublin City's foremost visitor attractions in the decades to come.

SUSTAINABLE ENVIRONMENTS

All policies in the Docklands Authority Master Plan are driven by an ambition to create energy efficient, sustainable environments to encourage the best international practices in urban living. These environmental measures include the reuse of grey water, district heating,

Opposite page: At the annual Maritime Festival, visitors get the opportunity to experience the tall ships close up, while foraging along riverfronts lined with market stalls. Below left: The interaction between both residents and visitors on the north and south sides of the River Liffey has never been greater than it is in the 21st century. Below: The production of 'Honk!' was one of the highlights of the Docklands Schools Drama Programme.

high quality low energy cost buildings, well managed open spaces, play spaces for children, cycle lanes, and a specific emphasis on recycling and waste management. An early example of this policy was the Docklands Authority's remediation of the former Bord Gáis site between the Grand Canal Docks and Sir John Rogerson's Quays. They have also promoted clean ups of the Grand Canal, the Royal Canal, the Dodder, the Tolka and the Liffey. New parklands, green spaces and play areas are planned for all new developments from East Wall to the Poolbeg peninsula.

GOOD NEIGHBOURS

The animosity between the northside and southside of the River Liffey has been the subject of much banter down through the years but there was an underlying seriousness to it. The dockers of the two sides would not tolerate one another. Likewise, the parishioners of Westland Row and Ringsend tended to regard one another suspiciously from 'across the brudge', as McMahon Bridge was known. However, a new dawn of communication between the various communities has had an extraordinary impact in bringing people together. The river separates north and south but it also binds them. The new bridges across the river provide a vital and practical means for the bridging of ideologies.

THE LOCAL LABOUR CHARTER.

Unemployment amongst the indigenous Docklands community continues to be high, with the North Wall registering three times the national average. When the Master Plan was being drafted, there were calls from the local community for a guarantee that 10 per cent of all new jobs created in the area would be given to local residents. The implications of this for free market economics were serious. The Docklands Authority felt it would be detrimental to the project and that possible investors would almost certainly recoil. Besides which, they reasoned, the locals would probably be pawned off with undemanding jobs as security men, janitors and such like. The DDDA Council argued that the community should think bigger. Why couldn't they secure jobs as accountants, traders and computer gurus? They had the knack and the aptitude. All they needed were the qualifications. The compromise was the creation of a database on which the details of all participating locals were entered, alongside their level of skill. Educational programmes were put in place for those seeking to gain the necessary qualifications for the higher end jobs. To this day, all incoming companies are invited to consider this list.

THE ARTS

The number of performing arts venues within the Docklands is now extremely impressive. The revamped O2 will provide a massive boost for the North Wall and one can anticipate a good deal of spill-over for the Point Village. Likewise the Studio Libeskind designed Grand Canal Theatre is likely to put the Grand Canal Docks firmly on the international map and will surely tempt some highly rated shows to Dublin. On a community level there are now stages in most areas, including the new 75-seat Pearse Centre on Pearse Street and the new Séan O'Casey Theatre in East Wall. A number of important art galleries have now opened on both sides of the river. The Docklands Authority has also shown a commendable commitment to public sculpture and art, perhaps most notably with the Martha Schwartz design at Grand Canal Square. They also commissioned 'Freeflow', the glass cobble illuminated work by Rachel Joynt along North Wall Quay, and a sequined installation by Martin Richman.

EVENTS GUIDE

The London Docklands suffered greatly because those who worked in the docklands tended to abandon the area the instant they left their office. In Dublin, there has been a noble attempt to ensure that those who work in the Docklands are tempted to stay around the neighbourhood, both after work and during the weekend. The Dublin Docklands has the benefit that six distinctive communities have lived here for at least 150 years. They are also close enough to the city centre for anyone to venture down. In this bustling new quarter, the annual calendar is impressively busy from the St. Patrick's Festival through to the Analog Festival of the summer, the Dublin Fringe Festival in September and the 12 days of Christmas. Increasing numbers are participating in events such as the 'The Docklands Liffey Swim' and 'The Docklands Fun Run'. The summer

Above: The Hanover Quay apartments were one of the areas where the Docklands Authority introduced the pioneering 20% social and affordable housing concept. Pictured here are tenants Martina and Gerard Brennan, Maura Ward and Hubert McCormick with Louise Thompson (BIK Housing Management Co.), Paul Maloney (Docklands Authority) and Lar Bradshaw (Docklands Authority).

months are particularly inviting with the prospect of a dozen or more tall ships floating in the Liffey at the annual Docklands Maritime Festival. During festivals, the campshires and squares come alive with endless stalls selling works of art, magnetic charms, potted plants, wooden toys, tempting hammocks and golden marmalade.

EDUCATION IN THE DOCKLANDS

James Comer was born in 1934 to an impoverished black family living in the inner city of East Chicago, Indiana. The steel and railroad industries that made the city a freewheeling boomtown in the 1920s petered out during his childhood leaving the cityscape derelict and forlorn. Neither of his parents completed any formal education. But they were determined young James and his four siblings would reap whatever they could from the school system. Their mother took a particularly active interest, urging the teachers to bring her kids to the library, to museums, to any place that would help stimulate their minds and build their confidence and self-esteem. She understood that education was the best investment any individual could have. It gave a child the dignity of choice.

Left: The Docklands Gaelic Football and Hurling Academy orchestrates a three day coaching academy for school children in the area every summer. Right: The 5th class of St Laurence O'Toole's Girl School board a bus bound for a cultural visit to the French town of Eu as part of an annual initiative funded by the Docklands Authority.

Fast forward to 2008. James P. Comer, MD, MPH, is the Maurice Falk Professor of Child Psychiatry at Yale University. His considerable achievement has been to develop the Comer Process, or the Comer Whole School Development Programme, a system of education specifically focused on child development in inner-city schools. The programme promotes teamwork between children, parents, teachers and the community at large. Its aim is to improve the lot of each child - socially, emotionally and academically. The programme has been utilized in more than 600 schools in eighty-two school districts across twenty-six states. In 2004, the Dublin Docklands Teachers' Conference opted to run with the programme. This was the first time the Comer Process had been implemented outside the United States.

Perhaps inevitably, the children of inner city Dublin were ignored when industry abandoned the area. As the population declined, many of the old schools closed down. Their pupils moved into the remaining schools, which were already stretched for resources. One of the greatest challenges for the Docklands Authority has been to address the educational situation. When the Authority was created in 1997, the drop-out rate for inner city schools was a staggering 65 per cent while just one per cent went on to Third Level education. For the whole Docklands Social Regeneration project to succeed, those statistics would need to be dramatically reversed. One option was to tackle each school individually. Another was to grab the whole educational bull by the horns and adopt some of the pioneering educational techniques now in motion across the world.

In cooperation with local School Principals, the Docklands Authority decided to address the matter. Formed in 1998, the School Principals Forum was the first event of its kind in Ireland, England, Scotland or Wales. The principals of 25 schools from within the Docklands Area and its hinterland gathered as one body to ponder the situation. The Forum is now an annual event, with over 30 programmes running in the schools represented.

The principals agree that it is vital to incorporate parents as much as possible. Children need the support of adults to maximise their learning potential. James Comer's uneducated mother helped him with his homework and now he's a Professor at Yale. The Docklands Authority offered scholarships to children who completed second level education. The Authority, with the agreement of the principals, funded the Parents in Education (PIE) course, a three-year programme delivered by the National College of Ireland, designed to educate parents and improve their self-confidence.

In addition to the vast array of programming the Docklands Authority also recognized the need to upgrade the schools infrastructure in the area and has begun a programme to build two new schools in Seville Place – St. Laurence O'Toole Primary School for girls and boys, and the St. Laurence O'Toole Special School.

The educational programme has not come cheap for the Docklands Authority but there have been measurable differences. The number of those completing their leaving cert has shot up from 10 per cent to 63 per cent in the past 10 years. 'I think the penny is dropping that the most important thing you can do for your kids is to keep them in school long enough for them to do their leaving cert', says Seánie Lamb of The Inner City Renewal Group. There has also been a marked improvement in the number of Docklands students going on to Third Level, up to 10 per cent by 2005, while the number applying for the Docklands Authority's Third Level scholarships has increased dramatically from nine applications in 1997 to nearly 100 in 2008. Over 140 young Docklanders have attained positions in businesses in the IFSC under the Schools Job Placement programme, and 25 school leavers have been placed in trade apprenticeships in the area. One of the earliest beneficiaries of the Docklands Authority scholarship programme was mother-of-two Karen Dowling who successfully used the scholarship to read law at Trinity College and is now a barrister.

The Docklands Authority has also funded a Psychometric Assessment Programme for each school. As well as addressing the emotional needs of each child, this enables the school to determine if any children are unduly hampered by dyslexia, ADD and such like. These programmes work hand-in-hand with EQ or Emotional Quotient. In the 20th century, a lot of emphasis was placed on one's IQ, or Intellectual Quotient. If your IQ was low, it was assumed you didn't stand much chance of success in this life. However, it transpires that a lot of those with relatively low IQ have done remarkably well. This is attributable to their high EQ. We all have different abilities. Some remember dates, sums, lines and formulas. Others are better with emotional or social skills. Those with high EQ can often empathise with others, remain optimistic in the face of great odds, detach themselves from their emotions in times of pressure and inspire others in times of need. This encouraging development in our understanding of human thought is making an impact on the educational ethos within the Docklands. Many of the Docklands schools are now following the lead of a 2005 programme run by Geetu Bharwaney, one of the world's leading experts in the field of emotional intelligence. It's all about putting the young people into the right gear, to give them the confidence to show off their sassy, gung-ho nature after two generations of defeatism. It is perhaps most apparent in the fields of drama, music and sport where the boys and girls can truly immerse themselves.

In music the schools of the Docklands benefit from the Education and Outreach Programme run by the National Concert Hall. Through this, the children can learn everything from flutes and fiddles to the rhythms of rap. The Performing Arts Academy also provides a useful insight in how to master the arts of dance, drama and singing. The Schools' Drama Programme likewise invites the children to expand their minds by portraying other characters from entirely different walks of life. In 2006, nearly 350 children from the 15 schools involved took to the stage at the Helix for a unique production of the musical *'Honk!,* a contemporary retelling of *'The Ugly Duckling'*.

The Docklands Soccer Academy and the Docklands Gaelic Football and Hurling Academy sees the likes of Niall Quinn, Alan Kelly, Don Givens, Kenny Cunningham, Chris Nichol, Nicky English, Olivia O'Toole, Eoin Kelly, Dessie Dolan and Paul Casey teaching the kids how to play ball. The Docklands Boxing Academy is also popular amongst boys and girls aged twelve to sixteen years, with world lightweight boxing champion Katie Taylor amongst those on hand to show them the ropes.

Pupils become acquainted with the Liffey through the annual Docklands Schools Festival when they race along the river on Dragon Boats and the occasional Tall Ship. During the annual Splashweek, they learn about swimming, sailing, wind surfing and canoeing. Every year, the Authority also sponsors a trip to the French town of Eu (now twinned with North Wall) for fifth class students throughout the Docklands. This provides them with a useful opportunity to practise their French and broaden their horizons, experiencing another way of life first hand.

HOUSING IN THE DOCKLANDS

The history of housing in the Docklands is in itself an extraordinary tale. 300 years ago, there were no houses here with the exception of the small fishing hamlet of Ringsend. Most of the land was underwater with the occasional watchtower, customs outpost and pilgrimage hospice along the waterfront. The reclamation of the North and South Lotts in the 18th century was a largely commercial initiative and there is little record of any residential development before 1780. During the Victorian Age, the industrial magnates who operated the railways, coal-yards, shipbuilding, gasworks, canals and warehouses built many of the terraced rows in North Wall and East Wall for their workers.

The onset of cholera and typhoid in the late 19th century obliged the Pembroke Township to build new and better homes in Ringsend and the South Lotts before the Great War. In the 1920s, the Rev DH Hall inspired a major building programme in East Wall, echoed by Dublin Corporation. A decade later, de Valera's promise to clear the slums resulted in the creation of suburban estates like Kimmage and Whitehall, as well as the East Wall terraces and the infamous Sheriff Street Flats. Elsewhere in the inner city, thousands of families continued to live in the dangerously decrepit and overcrowded tenement houses of Westland Row on the southside and in the crumbling Georgian buildings of the once formidable Blessington estate on the northside.

During the 1950s, there were approximately 22,500 families living in the Parish of Westland Row alone. Most were crammed into the old Georgian tenement houses and run-down mews cottages on the back alleys. Conditions were emphatically sub-standard. In many cases there was one tap and one toilet for four families. 'We lived in a Big House', says Sonny Kinsella, who grew up on Townsend Street. 'Between the parents and the children, there were 54 in the one house, in 10 rooms. Over 1,000 people lived on the street then'. One wonders how any one of them got any sleep with the horse-drawn coal carts rattling down the cobbles outside throughout the night. In June 1963, storm conditions sent a spring tide and heavy rain crashing into Dublin City. A pair of four-storey tenement houses on Fenian Street collapsed, killing two small girls. The tragedy was the catalyst for a hard-line response to the inner city housing crisis. Dublin City Council sent in the demolition men and, north and south of the river, nearly all the tenements came down. The population were scattered amongst new housing schemes in places such as Crumlin, Drimnagh, Ballyfermot, Donnybrook and Ringsend.

By 1970, the massive slum clearances meant the total population of the two parishes of Westland Row and City Quay was little over 6,000. The northside population similarly plummeted from 50,000 to 16,000, with many of those squeezed into the Sheriff Street flats. In the mid-1990s, Dublin Corporation likewise dispatched the 'Sherro' residents to the suburbs, sent the bull-dozers in and the flats came tumbling down. Docklanders still regard these displaced families as 'our people'. Many frequently return to socialize, shop and visit relatives who remained in the area.

One of the pioneering achievements of the Docklands Authority, inspired by the Docklands Council, was the 'Social and Affordable Housing' initiative, subsequently adopted by the Irish government. In order to ensure the local community stood a reasonable chance of buying a house in the area where they grew up, the Docklands Master Plan outlined that 20 per cent of all residential developments in the Docklands Area had to be 'Social and Affordable'. The 'S & A' concept emerged after consultation with London dockers who had expressed horror that the extensive developments along the Thames waterfront in the 1980s meant their own children were unable to afford a house in the area where they were born and reared. As such, the Dubliners were ready when the Docklands Authority sought opinions on local housing policy in 1997. They were determined that the developer would not reap all the benefits. The Docklands Authority concurred and the 20 per cent clause was adopted. This ensures that, by about 2015, the local community can expect to be in ownership of 2,500 new homes in the Docklands. This means that at least 80% of the local community will be able to live and move around within the area where they were born and raised. Administration of all such housing is facilitated by a recently established Housing Trust whose current directors are Seánie Lamb, Gerry Fay, Betty Ashe, William Prentice, Aidan Long, Ciaran McNamara and Gerry Kelly. As representatives of the Docklands community, this board is indicative of the Authority's policy of encouraging the local community to take responsibility for resolving their own issues. Also telling is the fact that the 20 per cent Social and Affordable Housing clause negotiated with the Docklands Authority is now standard in all new housing schemes across Ireland.

The annual Social Regeneration Conference gives everyone an opportunity to air their thoughts on how best to improve the situation for all in the community. In 2007, for instance, the Docklands Authority initiated the Play Space Guidelines to encourage developers to create a specific play area in apartment schemes. Planned public parks such as Chimney Park and the Royal Canal Linear Park also have strong child-friendly cores. The residents of the apartment blocks in North Wall and the Grand Canal Docks are blessed with the revamped campshires and new public spaces such as Mayor Square and Grand Canal Square. Poolbeg promises a whole new green parkland landscape for Dubliners while on-going work at Seán Moore Park and Irishtown Nature Park will ensure they become ever more attractive visitor destinations. Community Centres like the Séan O'Casey Community Centre and the St Andrew's Resource Centre are also playing a vital role in keeping the community spirit alive. After five decades of downtime, the inner city population is rising steadily.

THE FUTURE

The development and regeneration of the Docklands over the next ten years will be guided by the Docklands Authority Master Plan 2008. The main focus areas are social regeneration, economic development, land use, transportation, infrastructure, urban design, arts, culture, tourism and leisure. The Master Plan aims to convert the Dublin Docklands into one of the greatest 'living' urban environments in Europe. Local community leaders and stakeholders will continue to work hand-in-hand with the Docklands Authority to boost the living and working environment throughout the Docklands, and to ensure that this splendid sea-side cityscape becomes one of the unmissable places to visit in Dublin City.

Right: The green and red lights of the Martha Schwartz designed landscape at Grand Canal Square is complimented by Christmas lights on the trees. (Photo: Arco Ardon). Previous Page: A performance at the National Concert Hall during the Docklands Schools Music Programme.

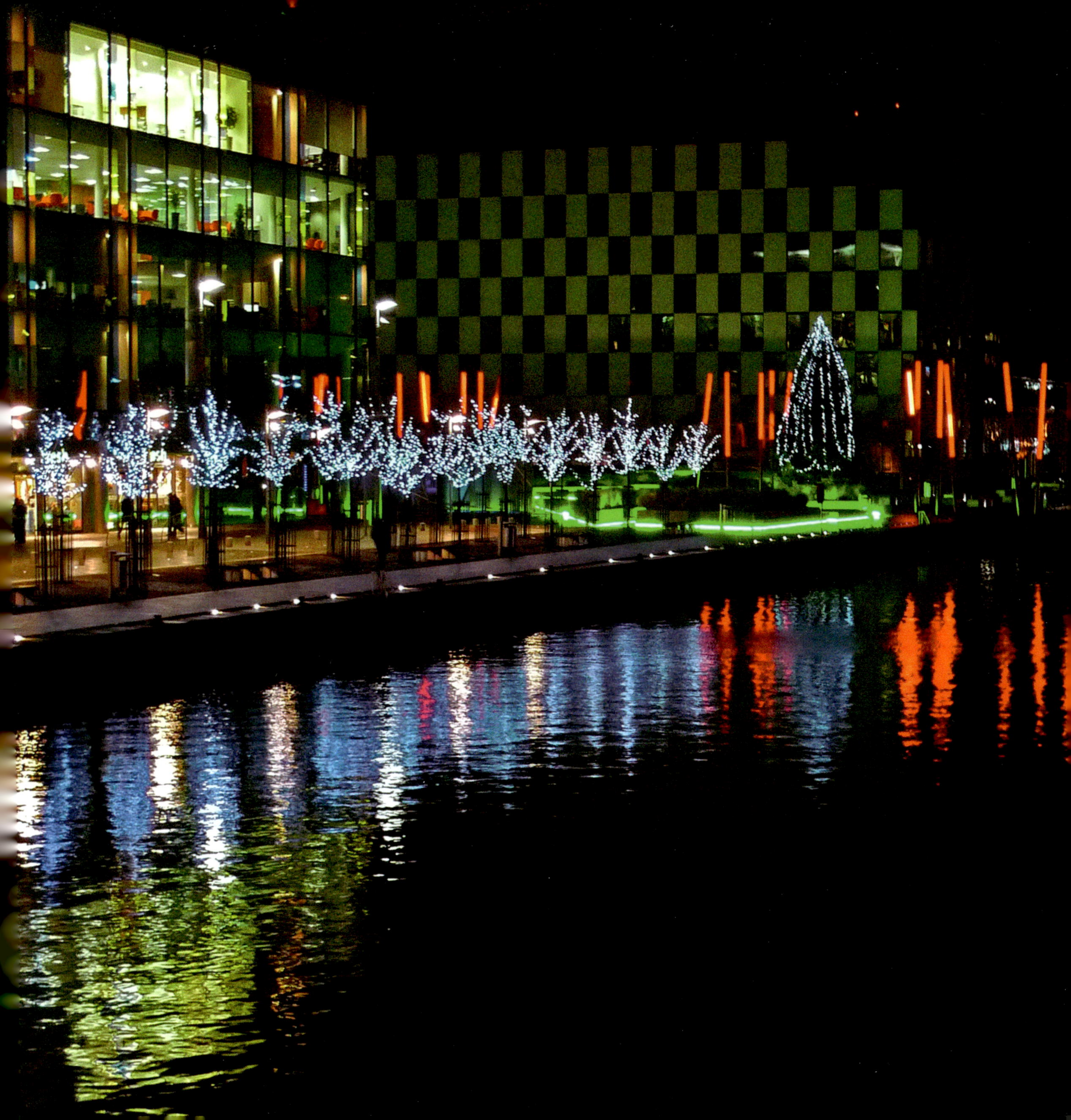

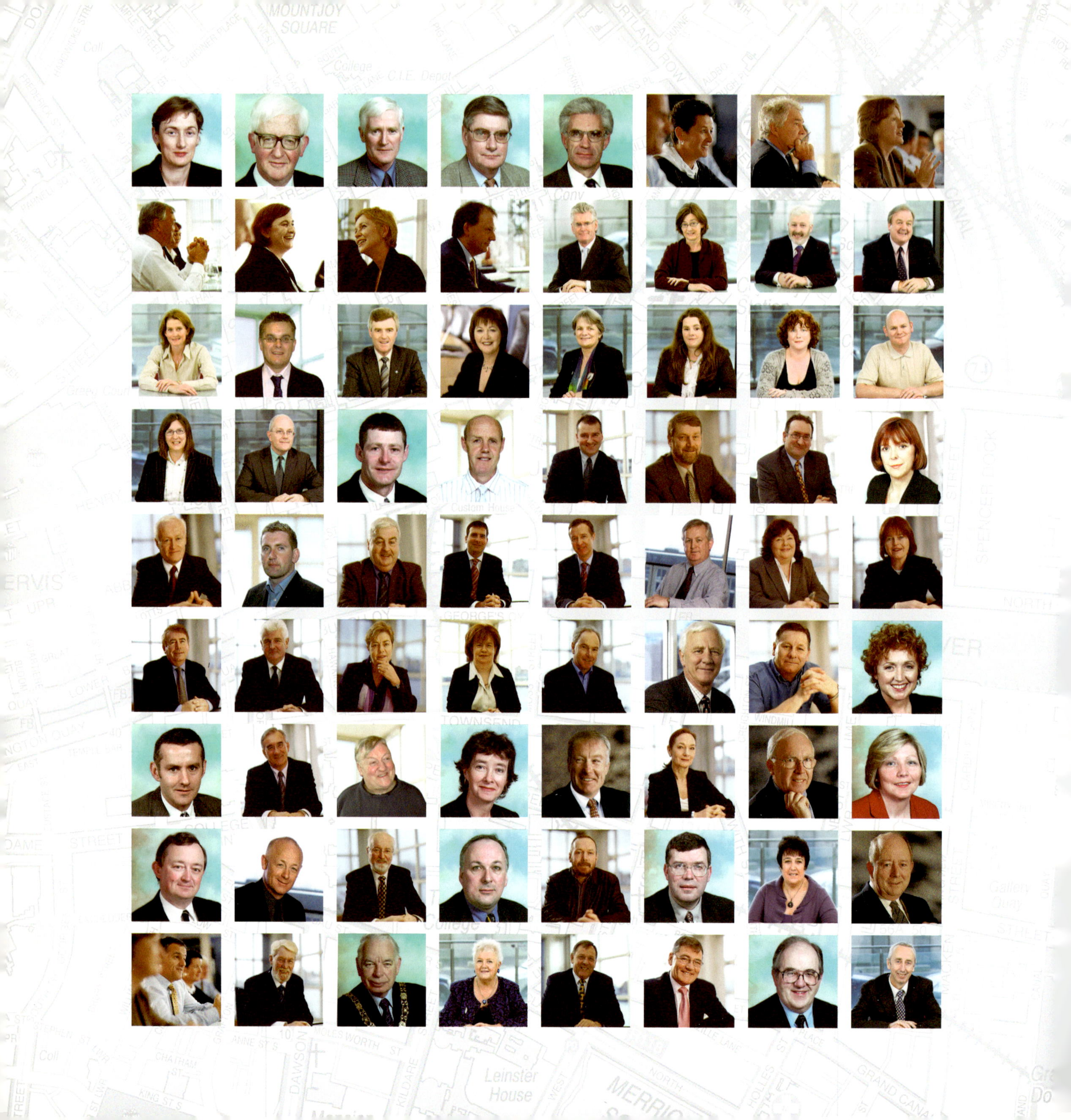
MOUNTJOY SQUARE
Leinster House

Past and present members of the Board and Council of the Docklands Authority

Mary Bergin, Prof PJ Drudy, John Egan, Cyril Forbes, John O'Connor, Joan O'Connor, Sean Fitzpatrick, Mary Moylan, Declan Mc Court, Niamh O'Sullivan, Angela Cavendish, Donall Curtin, Donal O'Connor, Sheila O'Donnell, Niall Coveney, Brendan Malone, Catherine Mullarkey, Mark Griffin, John Tierney, Margaret Sweeney, Fionnuala Rogerson, Deirdre Scully, Oilbhe Madden, Cllr Daichi Doolan, Denise Brophy, Malcom Alexander, Paul Dolan, Colm Treanor, Cllr Gary Keegan, Benny Counihan, Niall Grogan, Cllr Emer Costello, Pat Macken, Cllr Aodhan O'Riordan, John Boylan, Cllr Royston Brady, Michael Conroy, Liam Whelan, Frances Corr, Sandra Gulfoyle, Cllr Joe Costello, Arthur Hickey, Sheena Mc Cambley, Geraldine O'Driscoll, Cllr Tony Gregory, Cllr Tom Stafford, Willie Dwyer, Cllr Mary Mooney, Cllr Ciaran Cuffe, Pat Magner, Gerry Fay, Anne Butler, Bertie Barry, Mary Finan, Finian Matthews, Ann Carroll, Philip Jones, Peter Coyne, John Henry, Cllr Dermot Lacey, Charlie Murphy, Dr Ray Byrne, Dolores Wilson, Brendan Manning, Lar Bradshaw, Seanie Lambe, The Right Honourable Senator Joe Doyle, Betty Ashe, Sean Carey, Enda Connellan, John Martin, Cllr Kevin Humphries

Chapter One
Custom House Quay

Royal Canal Way
Clarke's Bridge
John McCormack Bridge
NORTH CIRCULAR ROAD
R101
MOUNTJOY SQUARE
D.A.L.C.
Kelly's Square
GARDINER ST UPR
BELVIDERE PLACE
RUSSELL STREET
SUMMERHILL PARADE
PORTLAND ROW
SUMMERHILL
BALLYBOUGH
NORTH STRAND ROAD
EAST WALL
ROYAL CANAL
C.I.E. Depot
College
Father Scully House
GARDINER ST MID
GARDINER STREET
PARNELL STREET
SEAN MAC DERMOTT STREET LOWER
RAILWAY STREET
FOLEY STREET
JAMES JOYCE STREET
BUCKINGHAM ST UP
EMPRESS PL
KILLARNEY ST
SEVILLE PLACE
Connolly Station
DART
ARROW
CONNOLLY
SHERIFF STREET
AMIENS STREET
TALBOT STREET
TALBOT PL
STORE STREET
BUSÁRAS
Custom House
MEMORIAL RD
BERESFORD PLACE
MAYOR STREET LOWER
COMMONS STREET
GUILD STREET
SPENCER DOCK
NORTH WALL
NORTH WALL QUAY
CUSTOM HOUSE QUAY
RIVER LIFFEY
O'CONNELL STREET
MARLBOROUGH STREET
HENRY STREET
G.P.O.
Millennium Spire
EARL ST N
ABBEY ST LWR
ABBEY ST MID
EDEN QUAY
BURGH QY
GEORGE'S QY
CITY QUAY
Tara St Station
TARA ST
TOWNSEND STREET
PEARSE STREET
R118
Pearse Station
Trinity College
COLLEGE GRN
WESTMORLAND ST
NASSAU ST
LEINSTER ST SOUTH
LOMBARD ST
SANDWITH ST LWR
SIR JOHN ROGERSON'S QUAY
Postal Delivery Centre
HANOVER QUAY
GRAND CANAL DOCKS
CHARLOTTE QUAY
Gallery Quay
RINGSEND ROAD
Waterways Visitor's Centre
Grand Canal
DAWSON ST
GRAFTON ST
Leinster
Community Centre
CHURCH ROAD
CALEDON ROAD

The Custom House Docks were designed and built on the northside of the River Liffey between 1796 and 1824. The docks and their adjoining warehouses lay just north of Custom House Quay, the walled riverfront that ran from the eastern end of Eden Quay to present-day Seán O'Casey Bridge. The vista is dominated by James Gandon's magisterial Custom House, which opened in 1791. This early neo-classical beauty is considered one of the finest architectural structures in Europe, despite extensive damage suffered during the War of Independence. In 1912, Custom House Quay was officially extended to embrace that part of the North Wall Quay west of Commons Street. In 1987, the Custom House Docks Development Authority was established to redevelop all the lands between Custom House Quay and Sheriff Street, bordered by Commons Street on the east and the Amiens Street/Memorial Road axis on the west. The space between George's Dock and the chq building is now one of Dublin City's most popular outdoor gathering spots, hosting festive nights, market stalls, urban beaches and all-year-round artistic installations. For older generations, Custom House Quay is synonymous with the Guinness ships. In 1978, the construction of the Talbot Memorial Bridge closed off river access to the Custom House. This chapter also embraces the International Finances Services Centre and, by dint of proximity, Connolly Station and the Great Northern Railway.

Custom House Docks - Streetwise

Amiens Street - Named for the Viscount Amiens, the title created in 1777 for the eldest son and heir of the eccentric 1st Earl of Aldborough. Their family home stood on nearby Portland Row close to the Five Lamps.

Beresford Place - Named for the Right Hon John Beresford, 1st Commissioner of the Irish Revenue, who conceived both the Custom House and Carlisle (now O'Connell) Bridge.

Buckingham Street - Named for George Grenville, Marquis of Buckingham, who, having created the Order of St Patrick, went on to become one of the least popular of Ireland's Georgian Viceroys.

Butt Bridge - Named for Sir Isaac Butt, the Donegal barrister who founded the Irish Home Rule movement.

Foley Street - Formerly known as World's End Lane, this was renamed Montgomery Street in 1776, most likely after Barbara Montgomery, wife of the Hon John Beresford. As 'The Monto', this was a notorious haven for prostitution in Victorian times. In 1908 it was renamed after John Henry Foley, creator of the O'Connell Monument, who grew up on the street.

George's Dock - Named for George IV who was scheduled to officially open the dock in 1821 but failed to show up on the day.

Inner Dock - The dock beside George's Dock was originally named Revenue Dock after the Commissioners of Revenue who paid for its construction.

Memorial Road - Constructed on land formerly occupied by the Old Dock, this was named in memory of those members of the Dublin Brigade of the Irish Republican Army who gave their lives during the War of Independence.

North Strand - This marks the approximate high-water tidal shoreline of the Liffey estuary prior to its reclamation by the North Wall in the 18th century.

Portland Row - Named for William Henry Cavendish Bentinck, 3rd Duke of Portland, who relinquished the post of Viceroy to become Prime Minister of Great Britain in 1783.

Store Street - Named for the Custom House stores and warehouses built here in conjunction with the Custom House in the 1780s.

Talbot Memorial Bridge - Named in memory of both the Venerable Matt Talbot and those members of the Dublin Brigade killed in the War of Independence.

Talbot Street - Named for Charles Chetwynd, 2nd Earl of Talbot, who disembarked at the Pigeonhouse in 1817 to take up duties as Viceroy. He left in 1821, spending the remainder of his life at the family home of Alton Towers in England.

Opposite: The Custom House, the International Financial Services Centre and the chq building run along the northern banks of the River Liffey. Immediately east of Connolly Station, the Inner Dock is now home to a residential complex while George's Dock to the east of the IFSC is now a popular outdoor venue The Seán O'Casey Bridge at the bottom right is one of the latest crossings between the north and south sides. (Photo: Peter Barrow). Next page: The Custom House at night. (Photo: Karim Heredia)

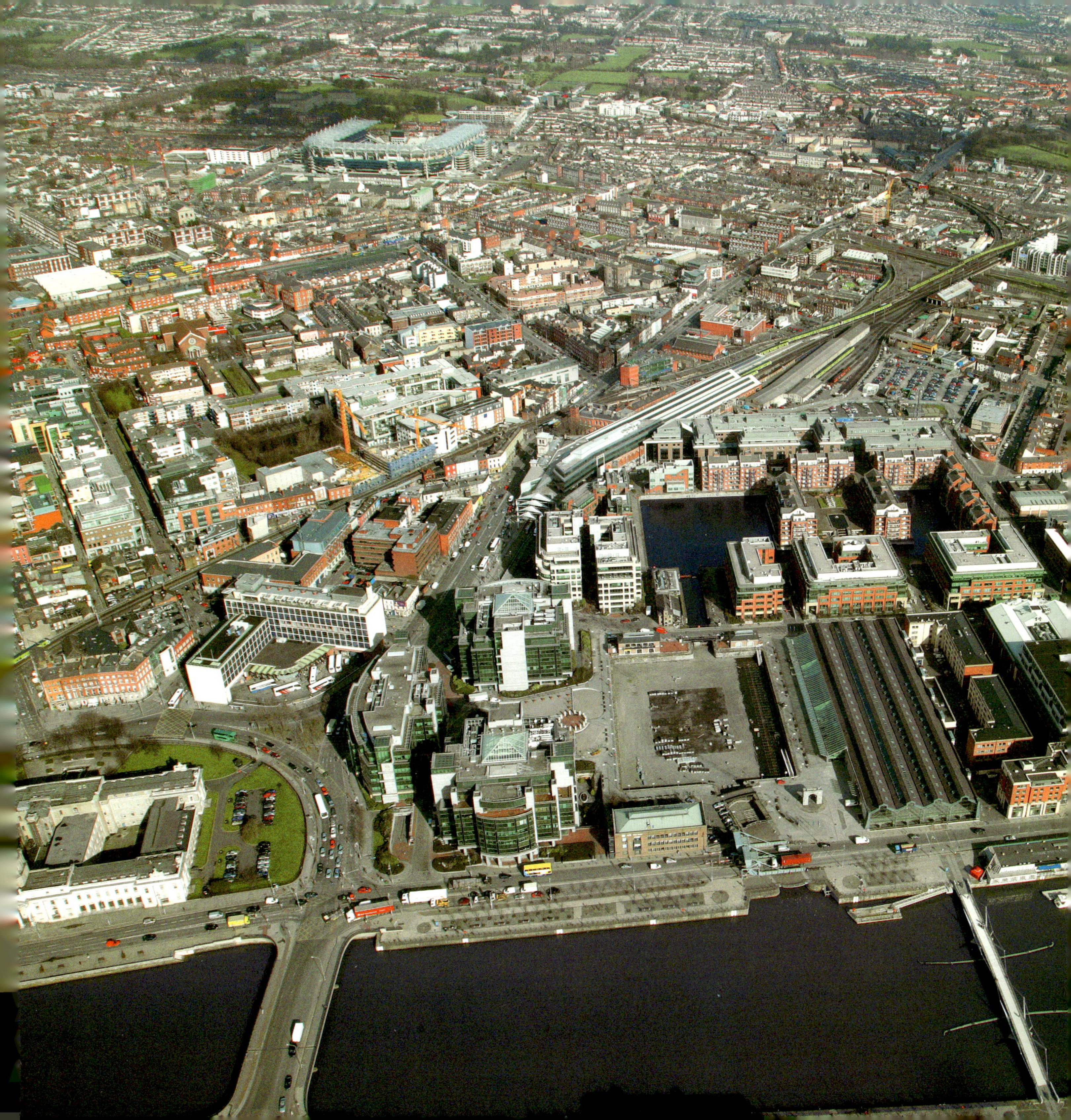

The Custom House

WHEN DUTY CALLS

The concept of 'customs' has hardly changed in 1,000 years. If you're bringing goods into a foreign country, you need to declare them and you probably need to pay a tax. This means paperwork. Back when most goods were carried by water, such formalities took place in a Custom House. If you were exporting or importing merchandise, you had to check in at the Custom House and pay the necessary duties. Dublin has had a Custom House since 1621. By the late 18th century, a new Custom House was deemed necessary. Merchant ships were having tremendous difficulty navigating the rocky bed and tidal waters of the Liffey to access the crowded wharfs of the old Custom House, which stood where the Clarence Hotel is now. Their only option was to load and unload goods onto smaller vessels, a time-consuming and costly performance.

GANDON & BERESFORD

By 1770, a wealthy elite had emerged in Dublin, headed up by the Gardiner and Beresford families. They acquired 'nearly a square mile' of tidal swamp along the north shore of the river, closer to its mouth, where they proposed building a new Custom House. In 1780, the Hon John Beresford was appointed 1st Commissioner of the Revenue. Within a year, he had the go-ahead from London to start construction. He commissioned up-and-coming English architect, James Gandon, for the job. Gandon arrived in Dublin in April 1781 and work began in August. Early spectators went swimming in the foundation trenches. The old guard of the Dublin Assembly were less amused by what they perceived as Beresford abusing his power. Napper Tandy led a mob who smashed down a site fence. Building recommenced soon after and finally, in November 1791, the new neo-classical Custom House opened for business. Its copper dome was visible from miles around. Its Doric exterior was sumptuously enhanced by the innovative use of sculptured keystone heads, representing the Atlantic Ocean and the rivers of Ireland, set above the windows and doors. The building cost £200,000, close to €24 million in today's money. Commissioner Beresford ensured his apartment occupied the best rooms in the house. Wags dubbed it 'Beresford's Ballroom' although, in fairness, Beresford was famed amongst his contemporaries for the considerable devotion he brought to his job.

ABANDONED AND BURNED

By the close of the 18th century, Irish taxpayers were contributing £3.5 million to the British chest, almost exclusively from customs and excise duty. However, the Custom House only enjoyed nine years of prosperity before the Irish Parliament foolishly voted itself out of existence and Dublin's Golden Age came to an end. The building stumbled uncertainly through the 19th century but was dealt a severe blow in 1866 when, despite massive objections, the Loopline Railway Bridge was constructed across the Liffey. This utterly obscured Gandon's masterpiece from the eastward view. Considered a potent symbol of British power, the Custom House was a notorious meeting place for spies and informers. In 1921, 120 Irish Republican Army volunteers attacked the building. It burned for five days. The dome melted, the stonework cracked and many irreplaceable documents relating to Ireland's history were lost to the flames. Five volunteers and two staff members died in the attack. This was one of the last major conflicts before the 1921 truce.

THE RESTORATION

The Irish Free State government commissioned a restoration of the building in the 1920s. Unfortunately, they did not waterproof the dome beneath the parapet properly. Over the ensuing decades, the rusting metal expanded, dislodging some of the stone and allowing more rainwater to seep in, freeze and expand. Three government departments were then located in the building, including that of the Environment. When Ruairi Quinn took office as a Minister of State at the Department of the Environment in 1982, he was appalled by the dilapidated state of the building. In one room, 'two buckets were strategically placed to catch rainwater from a leak in the roof'. Quinn set the wheels in motion for a second restoration which, complimented by the cleaning of the stone exterior, was completed in 1991. The building presently houses the Departments of the Environment, Heritage and Local Government. The revival of Dublin's Docklands over the past 20 years has greatly helped to reinstate the Custom House as one of Dublin's very finest civic buildings.

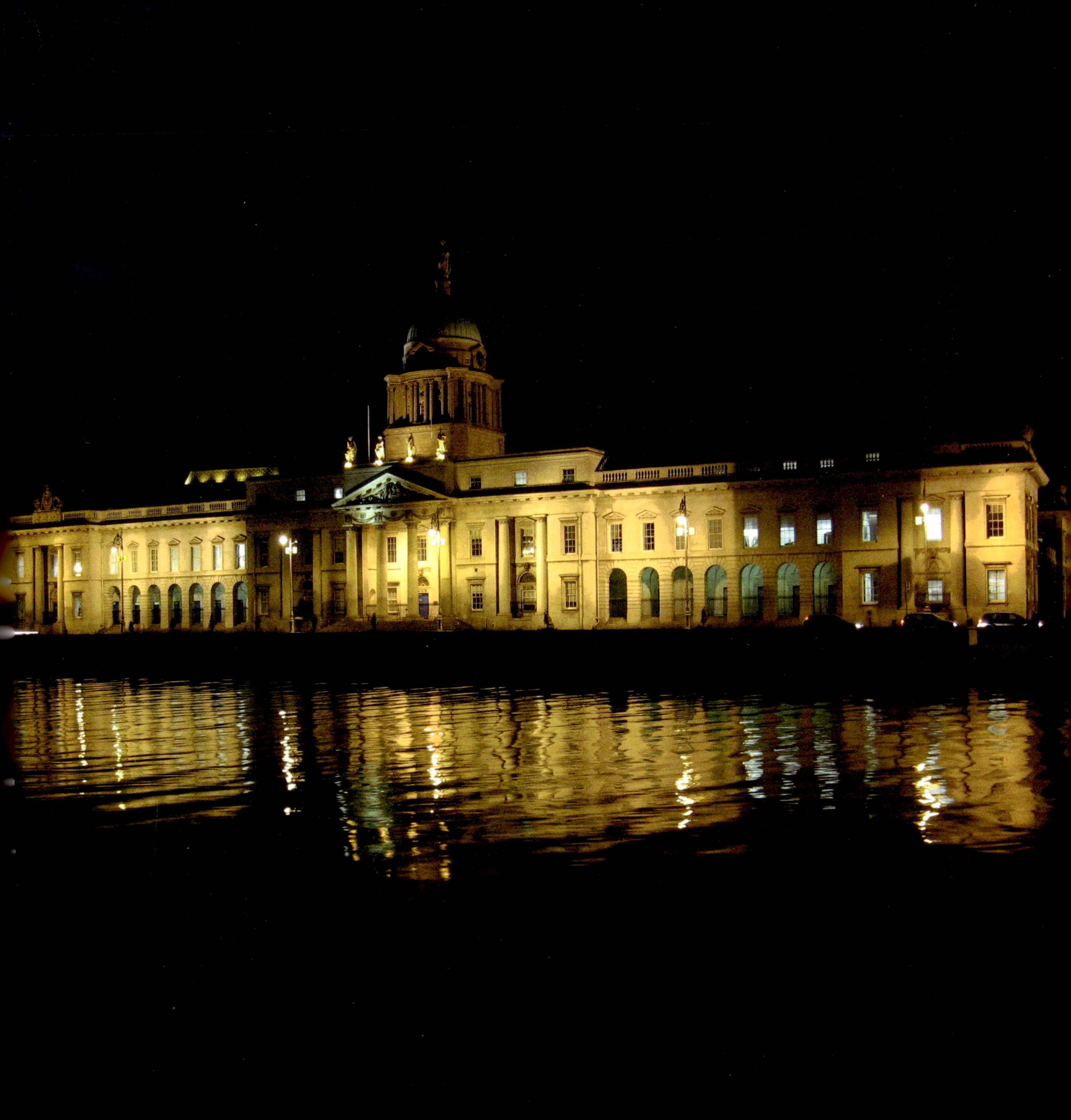

Custom House Characters

James Gandon (1743 – 1823)

In 1781, Gandon was preparing to move to St Petersburg to work for Catherine the Great when Commissioner Beresford gave him an offer he could not refuse – Dublin's Custom House. The London-born Huguenot, winner of the Royal Academy's 1768 Gold medal, had mastered neo-classical architecture under Sir William Chambers. Gandon subsequently planted his roots in Ireland, designing the Four Courts and the original Carlisle Bridge, where O'Connell Bridge stands today. He also designed many private mansions, perhaps most notably Abbeyville House for Beresford, later the home of former taoiseach Charles Haughey. Gandon lived on Mecklenburg (now Railway) Street for many years. He died in Lucan in 1823 and was buried in Drumcondra.

James Napper Tandy (1740 – 1803)

Tandy's association with the Docklands stems from his leading a mob in a short-lived protest against the construction of the Custom House in 1781. An ironmonger by trade, Tandy was a member of the Merchant's Guild and served 18 years on the City Assembly. He was a popular figure for working class Dubliners and may be seen as one of the pioneers of trade unionism. In 1791, he co-founded the Society of United Irishmen with Wolfe Tone and others. He subsequently fled to America where he remained until 1798. In that year he landed a French corvette in Donegal but fled to Hamburg where he was captured and imprisoned. Released at the personal request of Napoleon, he died in Bordeaux in 1803. Napper Tandy, incidentally, is Cockney rhyming slang for brandy.

Edward Smyth (1749 – 1812)

Smyth's career break came when he secured the post of ornament-carver for Henry Darley, chief stone-cutter at the Custom House. Assisted by sculptors Agostino Carlini, Thomas Banks, Benjamin Schrowder and others, he created the 14 beautiful riverine keystones above the windows and doors, as well as the female figures of Industry, Commerce and Plenty, and the Royal Arms at either end of the building. He also made most of the sculpture at Gandon's Four Courts. Edward and his son John Smyth were successively Masters of the Dublin Society School of Modelling and Sculpture. They lived at 36 Montgomery Street where their neighbours included John Henry Foley, the sculptor who would go on to create the Daniel O'Connell Monument on O'Connell Street and much of the Albert Memorial in London.

Sir John Rennie (1794 – 1874)

Sir John's father, John Rennie, was one of the foremost engineers of the Georgian Age. In Ireland, he built new harbours at Howth and Dun Laoghaire, as well as the Triumphal Arch by the Custom House. He also conceived the Custom House Docks but died in 1821 before they were completed. The younger John served as his principal assistant and subsequently took over the business. He completed the Custom House Docks and also designed and built Stack A (now the chq building). He is known globally as the architect of the London Bridge that was famously sold to an American entrepreneur in 1968 and rebuilt in Arizona.

Joseph Mallagh (1873 – 1959)

As a young man, engineer Joseph Mallagh worked on schemes to provide the people of Co Down with running water. From 1905 to 1915, he was Engineer to the Sligo Harbour Commissioners. Following John W Griffith's controversial retirement in 1916, Mallagh was appointed chief engineer to the Port and Docks Board, a position he held for over a quarter of a century. In this capacity, he oversaw the building of present-day Butt Bridge, the construction of several deepwater wharfs and dock warehouses, the installation of automatic fog signalling apparatus in harbour lighthouses and extensive dredging works. Under his direction, Dublin became one of the first ports to adopt the echo sounding method for the hydrographic surveys of the harbour.

Ruairi Quinn (b.1949)

Although his parents hailed from Newry, Co Down, Ruairi Quinn has made his name as a champion of Dublin's inner city. After practicing as an architect, working as a city councillor and a senator, he became a member of Dáil Éireann in June 1977. In 1982 he became Minister of State for the Environment with his headquarters in the Custom House. During his time as Minister of Finance (1994-1997) he set the ball in motion for the creation of the Dublin Docklands Development Authority. He was Leader of the Labour Party from 1997 until 2002. He is presently Labour Spokesperson on Education and Science

Custom House Quay & The Old Dock

DUBLIN KEY

Three hundred years ago, the tidal marshlands of the River Liffey rose along much of the landscape we now call the Docklands. During the early 18th century, the Ballast Office made concerted efforts to reclaim some of these lands by embanking the shores of the main river channel. One of the earliest attempts was an embankment, built between 1716 and 1725, which ran almost directly in front of where the Custom House stands today. The mound, comprising two black stone walls filled with sand, was originally known as 'Dublin Key'. It was 60ft wide at the top, and sloped from a height of 12ft along the river front to 8ft on the inside wall. When James Gandon surveyed 'Dublin Key' in the 1780s, he derided it as an inferior work, incapable of keeping the tidal waters out. He proposed that a new quay be built in front of the Custom House. Gandon's wish was Gandon's command and the Custom House Quay was effectively complete by 1792.

THE OLD DOCK

With the Custom House and its quay open for business, development of the surrounding neighbourhood began in haste. Headed up by the Hon. John Beresford, the Revenue Commissioners built the first of the three deep-water Custom House Docks along the east side of the Custom House. This was completed in 1796 and may have been designed by Gandon. It measured approximately 124m/406.8ft north to south and 60m/196.8ft east to west. A swing-bridge, which enabled people to cross the dock, was located approximately where the north entrance of the Talbot Memorial Bridge is today. The new dock was known as the Custom House Dock until the completion of George's Dock in 1821, after which it became known as 'the Old Dock'. In 1927, the long disused Old Dock was filled to make way for Memorial Road and, ultimately, forms the basis for parts of Busáras and the AIB building at the IFSC.

Far right: Completed in 1879, the original Sir Isaac Butt Bridge had an opening span which allowed ships to pass through to Eden Quay and Burgh Quay. Here we see dockers collecting coal from the quayside, loading it into their horses and carts and delivering it to the homes and businesses across the city. Right: Butt Bridge provided direct access from Custom House Quay to the new Tara Street link with the city centre.

THE TRIUMPHAL ARCH

The new Custom House Quay and its Old Dock provided useful berthage for vessels seeking to pay the Revenue Commissioners their dues at the Custom House. One of the landmark features was a triumphal arch, built in 1813 as the formal entrance to the quay, which celebrated the expected victory over Emperor Napoleon. 'Bounded by new railings and gates, this elegant arch was designed by John Rennie Senior and placed at the east end of Eden Quay'. It was later removed to the base of the ramp which led up from Amiens Street into Connolly Station. In 1988, the arch was carefully taken down and relocated to its present site beside the chq building where it has become a useful Docklands rendezvous. The reconstruction was carried out by a local team of young people, under a FÁS Community Youth Training Programme supported by CHDDA. In 2002, it was officially unveiled by the then Taoiseach Bertie Ahern and dedicated to Pat O'Shea for his service to community development.

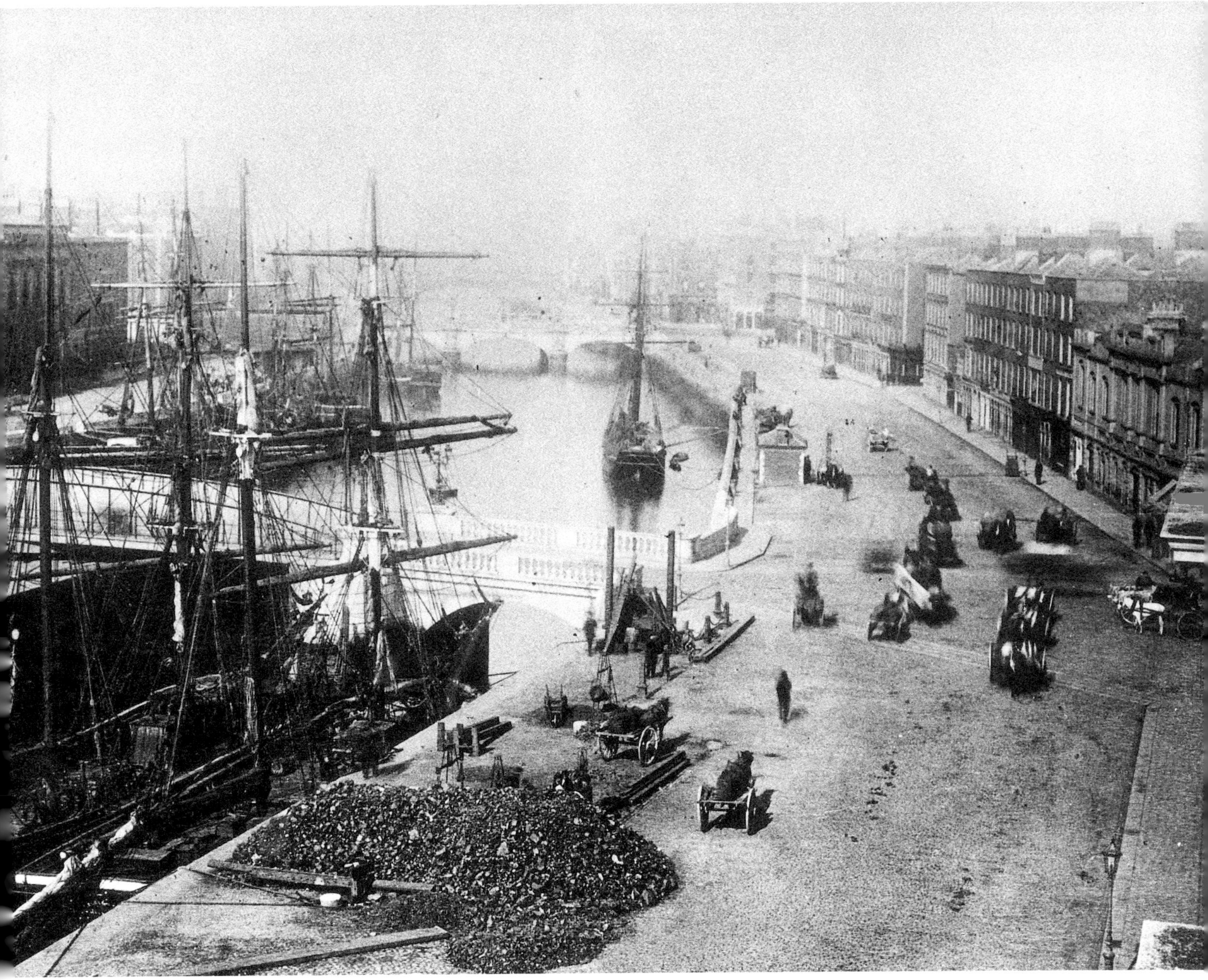

The Custom House Docks

The two main Custom House Docks were built in the early 19th century in response to the rapidly changing economic demands of the day. They were the initiative of the Duke of Richmond, Lord Lieutenant of Ireland. In 1809, he directed the Board of Customs to purchase a large plot of land east of the Custom House 'between the river and Mayor Street' for 'the new dock and for doubling the Stores'. In 1809, the total tonnage of goods and stock exported and imported from the port of Dublin was approximately 600,000 tons. Nearly a quarter of this was carried by steam vessels; the remainder being coals (which came on the collieries own sailing vessels), wines from France, bark from southern Europe and timber from the Baltic and America.

The Liffey was not suited to these new first-class steamers. They could get upstream at high tide no problem, some doubtful, others gallant. But, once the tide receded, these ponderous ships were obliged to rest on the harsh and gravelly riverbed until the waters rose again. The Richmond plan was to create deep-water docks where such ships could berth safely. However, these new docks became redundant almost as soon as they were finished. By 1830, the standard merchant ship was far too big to make it through the narrow entrance into these sheltered waters.

GEORGE'S DOCK

The completion of Eden Quay in 1814 provided a new public walkway between Custom House Quay and Carlisle Bridge (now O'Connell Bridge), connecting the Custom House to the bustling activity of Bachelor's Walk and the city centre beyond. The following year, the Scottish engineers John Rennie and John Aird collaborated on the design and construction of the two-acre George's Dock. The new dock was connected to the Liffey by a locked channel, approximately 36ft wide and 230ft long. Road access along the Quay has always been maintained, originally via a narrow swing-bridge and, since 1934, by the twinned Scherzer Bridges.

The dock was named for portly George IV, who was scheduled to formally open it in August 1821. His Majesty failed to show up having been detained by 'a social engagement' with the delectable Marchioness of Conyngham at Slane Castle. The King was oft seen 'kissing her hand with a look of most devoted submission'. In his absence, the dock was opened by Lord Castlecoote.

Above: The Outer Dock was named for the Hanoverian monarch George IV, King of the United Kingdom of Great Britain and Ireland from 1820 – 1830. This rather flattering portrait was painted by Sir Thomas Lawrence.

Today, pigeons flutter fearlessly around the granite blocks that run alongside the dock. The docksides have been completely renovated, the old cogs and pulley systems repainted, the dock waters diligently cleaned and a concrete base built as a staging area for events. In the summer of 2008, George's Dock became the location of Ireland's first 'urban beach, complete with palm trees, cabanas, beach umbrellas and a sand-castle building area. Visitors were encouraged to practice yoga and tai chi, play chess and volleyball, or kick back and watch the world roll by.

THE INNER DOCK

A second channel, also 36ft wide, leads from the north of George's Dock through to the five-acre Inner Dock, formerly the Revenue Dock. Following Rennie's death in October 1821, this much larger dock was completed three years later under the supervision of Thomas Telford, considered the foremost engineer in the British Empire. The Inner Dock is now home to a citadel of residential apartment blocks, some elevated on stilts above the water, with shimmering verandas upon which residents store bicycles, hang clothes to dry and sun themselves amid potted plants and steely deckchairs

THE STACKS & THE BOUNDARY WALL

Two huge warehouses were simultaneously built alongside the docks – the L-shaped 'New West Store' (otherwise known as Stack B, parts of which now comprise the red-brick AIB Trade Centre) and the 'New Tobacco Store' (otherwise Stack A, now known as the chq building). In the main, these stored goods liable to customs duty, specifically wines and spirits, as well as grain, timber and slates. The wine and spirits were stored in the underground vaults. The Commissioners of Revenue were somewhat alarmed by an anonymous letter in 1816 which revealed that 'individuals and small groups of both male and female' had been holding 'communication with daily watchmen and quay porters' and that stolen property was exchanging hands. An iron railing and stone parapet was consequently erected at the junction with Eden Quay while, by 1824, a soldier in redcoat and busby was standing guard at the Old Dock entrance. A high security wall was built around the whole Custom House Docks complex. Legend has it this 'Boundary Wall' was built by French prisoners. At any rate, parts of it are still in evidence today on Commons Street and Amiens Street. The downside of this wall was that it created both a physical and a psychological divide between the City and Port, to such an extent that few who board a train at Connolly Station today realise that seven acres of water-filled docks lie within a few hundred metres.

Above: The railway tracks at Connolly Station lie 24ft above the level of Amiens Street and are carried north towards the River Tolka by a rubble and brick viaduct of 75 arches. Directly below the station, these arches contained huge vaults where freight and passenger luggage was kept in storage. Some of these were deftly converted into The Vaults bar by Neil Burke Kennedy in 2002. Next page: Hogsheads of tobacco and other goods are weighed and stored in the bonded warehouses of the Custom House Docks. Stack F ran along the north side of the Inner Dock. (Photos: Dublin Port Company)

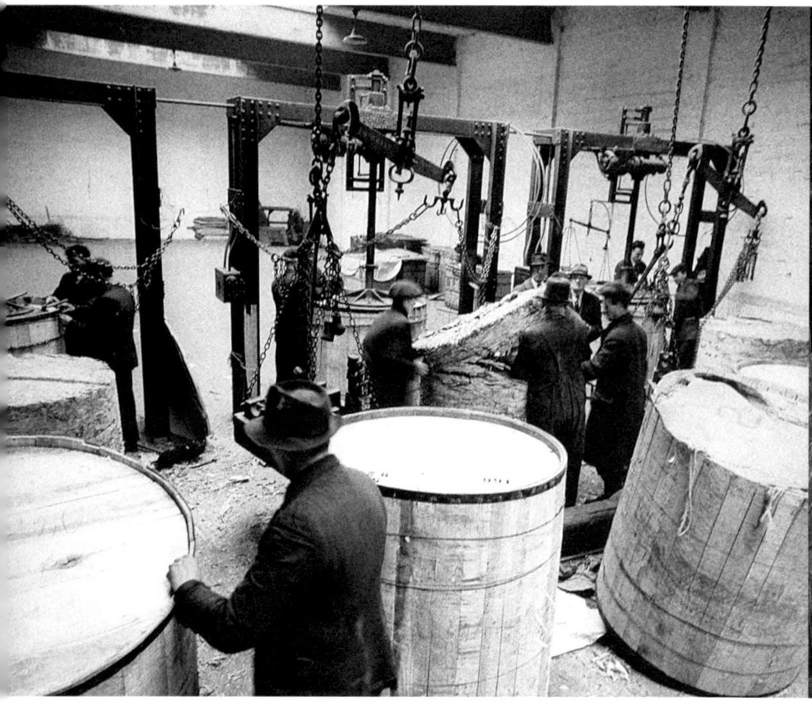

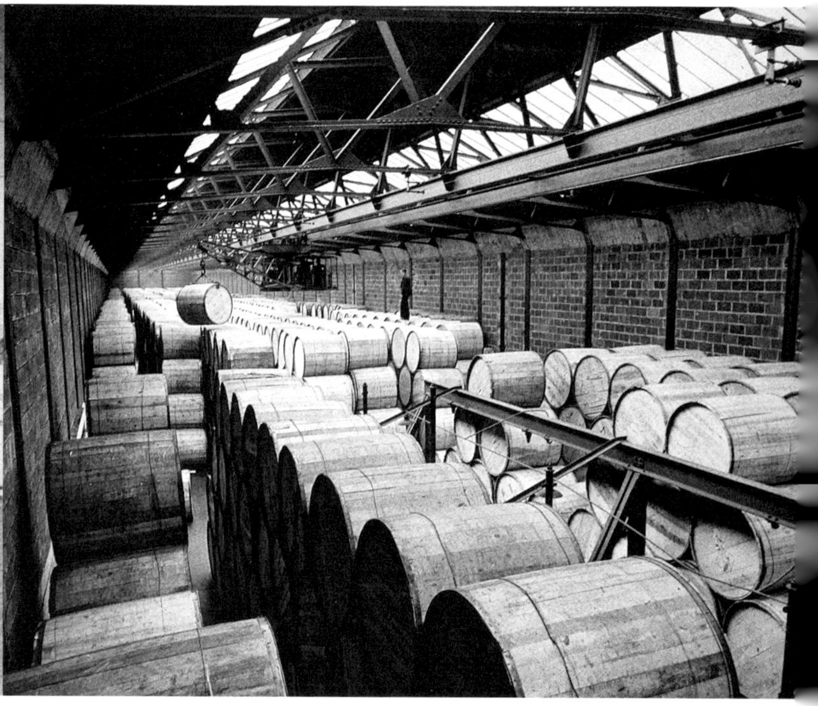

45

Jeanie Johnston

Anyone who has read Joseph O'Connor's masterpiece *'Star of the Sea'* should take a stroll along the decks of the *Jeanie Johnston*. This exceptionally handsome three-masted barque is a replica of a 19th century Irish emigrant ship, built as a Millennium Project in 2000. With its home berth at Dublin City Moorings, the *Jeanie Johnston* is already one of the landmarks of the Dublin Docklands. She is also one of the best-known sail training ships in Europe.

CANADIAN ORIGINS

The original *Jeanie Johnston* was built in 1847 on the banks of the St Lawrence River in Quebec City, Canada. Its architect was the Scottish-born shipbuilder and master craftsman John Munn. This was one of the last ships of its kind. Within a few years the world's shipbuilders, Munn included, had turned to steam. The 408-ton cargo ship was purchased in Liverpool by John Donovan & Sons of Tralee, Co Kerry. They ran a successful trade bringing emigrants from Ireland to North America, and returning with timber bound for the ports of Europe.

THE FAMINE SHIP

By 1848, famine was terrorising Ireland. On April 24th of that year, the *Jeanie Johnston* made her maiden emigrant voyage from Blennerville, Co Kerry to Quebec, with 193 emigrants on board. Over the next seven years, she made 16 voyages to North America, sailing to Quebec, Baltimore and New York, and delivering upwards of 2,500 Irish emigrants safely to the New World. The fare to Quebec on the *Jeanie Johnston* was £3.10, which represented close to half a year's wages for an Irish labourer at the time. The average length of the transatlantic journey was 47 days, or seven weeks. On one trip from Tralee to Quebec in April 1852, she carried an incredible 254 passengers. To put this in perspective, the replica ship has a day-cruise maximum capacity of 60. Generally, a whole family would share a single 6ft square berth. Those travelling alone shared with three others, often total strangers, and sometimes not even of the same sex. Quarters were cramped with berths lining both walls and a narrow table in the walkway between. Passengers lived on their own limited food supplies, provided their own utensils and cooked for themselves. Toilets were practically non-existent. Despite these arduous conditions and the long voyage, no life was ever lost on board the *Jeanie Johnston*. This remarkable feat is generally attributed to the ship's wise captain, Castletownsend-born James Attridge, and its qualified doctor, Richard Blennerhassett. There was also a fiddler or two to keep the spirits up.

THE SHIP IS SUNK

In 1855, the ship was sold to William Johnson of North Shields in England. In 1858, en route to Quebec from Hull with a cargo of timber, she became waterlogged. The crew climbed into the rigging and, after nine days clinging to the slowly-sinking ship, they were rescued by a Dutch ship, the *Sophie Elizabeth*. Even in her loss, she maintained her perfect safety record.

THE REPLICA IS BORN

As the 150th anniversary of the Famine approached in the 1990s, there was a growing demand across Ireland to know more about this 'visitation of God' that wreaked such chaos on the land. The building of the *Jeanie Johnston* replica at Blennerville was part of that process. The wooden ship was designed by Fred Walker, former Chief Naval Architect with the National Maritime Museum in Greenwich, England. The recreation project was modelled closely on that of the 17th century Dutch East India merchant ship, the *Batavia*. Work began in 1993 with in-depth research based on a Lloyd's survey of the ship from 1847. It culminated in the completion of the vessel in 2002. An international team of young people, linking Ireland North and South, the United States, Canada and other countries, built the replica under the supervision of experienced shipwrights. The ship is built with larch planks on oak frames. To comply with current international maritime regulations, some concessions to modernity had to be made. She has two Caterpillar main engines, two Caterpillar generators, and an emergency generator located above the waterline in the forward deckhouse. She is fully compliant to the highest standards of modern ocean-going passenger ships, with steel water-tight bulkheads, down-flooding valves and fire-fighting equipment.

Above: In 2003 the *Jeanie Johnston* sailed across the Atlantic from Fenit, Co Kerry, to Canada and the USA, stopping at over 20 ports along the way. She has had a busy time ever since, not least when Riverdance came to stomp upon her decks. In 2005, Captain Michael Coleman sailed her out of Waterford in the Tall Ships Race. She was purchased by the Docklands Authority that same year. She currently operates as a Class A sail training ship. But you can board her anytime, perhaps to learn more from the Famine History Museum, or maybe to head out on a six-hour day trip around Dublin Bay. (Photo: Arco Ardon)

The chq building

THE TOBACCO STORE

Latter-day Victorians referred to it as the Banquet Hall. Dockers and merchants called it Stack A or the Tobacco Store. The 21st century generations know it as the chq building, short for Custom House Quay. Whatever its name, this mighty warehouse continues to stir people to such an extent that architectural historian Christina Casey recently called it 'the single most impressive building in the Docklands'. In 1931 a well-travelled English tobacco magnate likewise declared that it was 'second to none built in America'. This industrial masterpiece forms the eastern boundary of George's Dock. It was almost certainly designed by the brilliant Scottish engineer Sir John Rennie. His father designed the pioneering cast iron tobacco warehouse known as 'Skin Floor' in the London docks, built between 1811 and 1814. The chq's original purpose was to store considerable, and valuable, cargos of tobacco, tea and spirits. Tobacco and tea were kept in separate compartments above ground. Wine and spirit casks were stored in extensive vaults below, where patrons of the Ely chq restaurant and wine bar are now seated.

AN INDUSTRIAL MASTERPIECE

At 475ft long and 157ft wide, the warehouse boasts the largest pre-20th century clear floor space in Dublin City. The influence of those graceful, early industrial days can be seen from its top-lit gabled roof and cast-iron colonnades right down to the 56 basement vaults where '4,500 pipes of wine' were once stored. The iron work was manufactured and supplied by the Butterley Foundry in Derbyshire, founded in 1791 by the canal engineers William Jessop and Benjamin Outram. An 'extensive yard for bonding timber' adjoined the premises. The opening ceremony in 1821 was greeted with 'the firing of guns and huzzaing of thousands' while a sumptuous champagne breakfast was served to special guests. This event was something of a precursor to the mighty banquet given to Crimean War veterans in 1856. (See page 50). A mezzanine floor was added to the northern, or tobacco, end in 1871. The building was reduced by 16ft as its southern end in 1884 in order to widen Custom House Quay. In 1903, John Purser Griffith, Chief Engineer of the Port and Docks Board, proposed dismantling the chq building as part of a radical scheme to modernize the Custom House Docks. Thankfully his proposal was never adopted. In 1934, the Board began work on a new tobacco store, known as Stack G, which assimilated the eastern wall of Rennie's warehouse into its structure.

MODERN TIMES

In 1987, the chq building fell within the remit of the Custom House Docks Development Authority, which arranged for the transfer of all its warehousing operations to the port estate at East Wall. CHDDA flattened the 1930s warehouse of Stack G and commissioned a comprehensive restoration of the chq building. Miscellaneous plans to convert it into an interactive science museum, a contemporary art gallery and a national folk museum did not come to fruition. Nor did Charles Haughey's vision of a museum for silver, glass and furniture. The chq building has since been much enhanced by an international team of architects, and glass and lighting consultants. In November 2007, it officially opened as a contemporary mall, just as Rennie's 'Skin Floor' did in London's Wapping 17 years earlier. Planned by Michael Collins Associates, it now offers some excellent retail therapy and dining options to the workers of the IFSC and the hordes now visiting the Docklands. The chq building was awarded the title of Best Conservation / Restoration Project at the prestigious Royal Institute of the Architects of Ireland (RIAI) Awards 2008. It was also awarded Best Conservation Project at the Irish Planning Institute's National Planning Awards 2008.

Right: The award-winning conservation of the chq building has given Sir John Rennie's Georgian warehouse a new look for the 21st century.

THE chq BUILDING

The Crimean Banquet of 1856

FERGUS FARRELL
The Crimean War Banquet was the brainchild of Fergus Farrell, a Catholic seed merchant and former deputy to Daniel O'Connell. On 2nd February 1856, Farrell was sworn in as Lord Mayor of Dublin. Eight weeks later, the Crimean War came to an end when Russia signed the Treaty of Paris, thereby opening the Danube to international trade. All wars are horrific but the Crimean death toll of 650,000 was all the worse for the fact that a staggering two-thirds of those who died succumbed to disease, primarily cholera. Perhaps Farrell remembered the appalling manner in which soldiers were treated after the Napoleonic Wars; abruptly discharged without thanks or payment. Ireland in the 1820s and 1830s was swarming with men tormented by the memories and injuries of war. At any rate, Farrell was determined the veterans of the Crimean War would not be ignored in the same manner.

IRELAND & THE CRIMEA
Ireland's role in this war is much understated. While many of the incompetent military leaders such as Raglan and Lucan had Irish connections, it was at troop level that the Irish really made an impact. It is estimated that one-third of the 111,000 men who served were Irish. Seven thousand Irishmen died in the Crimea. Many fought with Irish regiments such as the Skins (6th Inniskillings) and the Connaught Rangers while, of the 673 horsemen on the fateful Charge of the Light Brigade, 114 were Irish. Some of the 4,000 Irishmen serving in the Royal Navy were presumably cajoled into service by the moustachioed recruiting officer spotted on Sir John Rogerson's Quay in 1854. There were at least 100 Irish army surgeons. Thirty three Irish Sisters of Mercy and Sisters of Charity went out as nurses. Eight Irish priests went as chaplains; three died. Sergeant (later General Sir) Luke O'Connor from Elphin, Co Roscommon, won the first ever Victoria Cross in 1857; a further 27 Irishmen won VC's in the Crimea. The most esteemed war correspondent of the age was William H Russell (*London Times*) from Tallaght.

THE CONCEPT
On 19th August 1856, Lord Mayor Farrell began a subscription campaign for a massive banquet for 4,000 soldiers. This was not for the army officers, but rather for those common foot-soldiers who had been decorated for their actions. The campaign proved enormously popular. Within weeks, there was a budget of £3,588 to green light the banquet.

THE VENUE
In early October 1856, *The Times* announced that the organising sub-committee had secured, free of charge, the Government-owned Tobacco Stores from Stillorgan businessman Henry Scovell, tenant. Known today as the chq building, this was said to be the largest indoor premises in Dublin, capable of seating 6,000. It was fitted for gas, so cookers could operate, and Rennie's elaborate iron roof meant one less fire scare to worry about. The enclosed location within the boundary wall of the Custom House Docks was also ideal, not least because soldiers could 'muster without coming into contact with a mob of idlers who might cause inconvenience'. (*The Times*). The remarkable engineer William Dargan, the father of Irish railways, oversaw the warehouse conversion. He refused any payment and supplied timber and other materials at his own expense. The iron roof trusses were painted red, white and blue. Walls were hung with the flags of Britannia and her Turkish, French and Sardinian allies. Muskets, swords and lances were fixed to the 33 iron pillars running through the building. A bandstand was set up in the gallery, from which hung vast drapes bearing the names of the epic battles and the generals who orchestrated them. Thirty two tables ran the length of the building, each laid with plates, knives, forks and tumblers for the men. As well as the soldiers, there were tables for the dignitaries and the band. A further 1,000 non-military guests, principally subscribers, were seated in the gallery overlooking the hall. T&C Martin and Todd Burns supplied platforms, seating, tablecloths and other furnishings; other companies provided food, beer and spirits. One Dublin wine merchant, Henry Brennan, donated 8,500 quart bottles of porter and a pint of choice port wine for each guest.

Above: *The Illustrated London News* published this image of the Dublin banquet in 1856.

THE ARRIVAL

Shortly before 11:00am on the unusually bright and fine morning of 22nd October 1856, a train arrived at Kingsbridge Station. Some 1,000 red-coated soldiers disembarked; they came from the Curragh Camp, Naas, Newbridge, Carlow, Kilkenny and other military strongholds. They had been carried north free of charge by the Great Southern & Western Railway. Some 1,500 soldiers stationed in the various Dublin barracks subsequently joined them, along with 500 soldiers from other provincial depots. The combined force marched down the Liffey quays towards the Docks. The surrounding city apparently thronged with friendly Dubliners waving their hats, cheering loudly and singing louder. In case anyone got out of hand, the Lancers, Dragoons and a strong body of police were on hand. A marching band played *Cheer, boys, cheer*, as the soldiers marched from Carlisle (now O'Connell) Bridge past the Custom House, followed by the horse-drawn carriages of the Lord Mayor, the Lord Lieutenant, Lord Seaton (Commander of the Forces) and Lord Gough.

THE BANQUET

At 12:25, the band struck up *'The Roast Beef of Old England'* and the weather-beaten soldiers marched in, company by company, medals gleaming on their scarlet uniforms, and took their seats. Lord Mayor Farrell delivered Grace and the men tucked in. Supplied by Messrs Spadacini and Murphy, the food included 250 hams, 230 legs of mutton, 500 meat pies, 100 venison pasties, 100 rice puddings, 260 plum puddings, 200 turkeys, 200 geese and 250 pieces of beef. There was also 2,000 loaves of bread, three tons of potatoes, 100 capons and six ox-tongues. What extraordinary banter must have passed between those proud and bushy-whiskered soldiers as they recalled the mayhem, triumphs and sorrows of the bungle-filled campaign between mouthfuls of succulent goose and plum pudding.

THE SPEECHES

At length, four trumpeters sounded the toasts. The first was, of course, to the health of 'The Queen'. The second was to the Lord Lieutenant, the scholarly Earl of Carlisle, who delivered a stirring speech about those who had 'fought and toiled and bled… dashed along the fatal pass of Balaklava and… held the blood-red heights of Inkermann'. Lord Gough, the Tipperary-born Colonel-in-Chief of the 60th Royal Rifles, addressed his 'Brother Soldiers', declaring 'this public demonstration of a nation's gratitude' to be 'the happiest moment of a long life of military vicissitude'. (Sir) Isaac Butt, secretary to the Banquet Fund and subsequently founder of the Irish Home Rule Party, proclaimed the Crimean War as a crusade for 'liberty and civilisation', and offered 'a thousand welcomes with all the cordiality of the lush heart — to those who fought for us in far-off lands.' Proceedings came to a swift end at 4.15pm 'when the troops mustered in the Custom House yard and marched to their respective railway termini.' Whatever their thoughts of war and peace, there can be little doubt the soldiers got their rations' worth that day.

THE BANQUET FUND

Remarkably, there was a surplus of £1,100 left in Farrell's Banquet Fund at the end of it all. This was invested in British Government stock for the benefit of boys of the Royal Hibernian Military School in Phoenix Park. The school was incorporated in Dublin in 1775 and originally located on Sir John Rogerson's Quay. It subsequently moved to Clontarf and, after various amalgamations, became Mount Temple School where U2's Bono was educated. The so-called Crimean Banquet Fund was used to fund three annual awards of £15, £10 and £5 to successful students. These prizes continued to be awarded until 1924, in which year the Royal Hibernian was merged with the Duke of York's Royal Military School in Dover. Between 1924 and 1928, the income from the fund was granted to the Drummond Institution for the Daughters of Soldiers, then based in Bray, Co Wicklow. In July 1928, the High Court also granted the bulk of the RHMS property to the Drummond Institute.

The Victorian Age

CHANGING TIMES

By the 1830s, the Custom House Docks were falling into disarray. Their decline was inevitable. Like a spanking new computer in the 21st century, they dazzled everyone for a while, then drifted out of date. Many of the new ships were simply too large for the dock's narrow locks, particularly the steamers. Moreover, the locks were only operational for a three-hour period at high tide. Inevitably, the regular cross-channel services were loath to risk the potential delays of such a system.

THE BALLAST OFFICE

In 1845, responsibility for the Custom House Docks was transferred from the Commissioners to the Ballast Office. The Ballast Office commissioned John and Robert Mallet to build new entrance gates of stone and cast iron. In a bid to convert the docks into something useful, the Office opened negotiations with the Treasury in London to buy them from the Crown. In 1869, the Office officially secured ownership of the Custom House Docks and its affiliated warehouses. Plans to improve the entrance locks and the docks themselves were continually scuppered. As Harry Gilligan put it, 'the expenditure was out of proportion to the advantages'. Moreover, the forward-thinking members of the Ballast Office were focusing their attention on the possibility of new and better quays to the east, unhampered by entrance locks and capable of hosting these bigger, better, new steam ships. The North Wall Quay was duly extended and, by 1885, led all the way to the Alexandra Basin.

FERRY STEPS AND TIMBER RAILS

The warehouses of the Custom House Docks became a storage depot for cargo transported from ships berthed in the deepwater section of Dublin Port. As such, it was not necessarily a huge gesture when the Scovells offered Stack A as a venue for the Crimean War Banquet in 1856. The original 'Old Dock' fell into almost total disuse, save for its steps, used by passengers boarding William Walsh's ferry across the river; a second Walsh ferry operated from Commons Street to Creighton Street on the southside. Customs were still paid to the Harbour Master in his office but the land alongside George's Dock and the Inner Dock became coal banks and remained so until the 1970s. As for the Custom House Quay, all railings and barriers were removed in the 1830s, allowing the public free access from Eden Quay, along Custom House Quay, to the newly revamped North Wall Quay. A timber railing was constructed along the riverside in front of the Custom House.

HEITON'S & THE BLACK DIAMONDS

From the 1880s until the 1920s, the Custom House Docks and wharfs were rented from the Port and Docks Board by the wealthy Dublin coal-importing firm of Heiton's. Its coal arrived from Glasgow on a fleet of four colliers – *St Margaret*, *St Kilda*, *St Mirren* and *St Olaf*. Loading and unloading was operated by four steam cranes which, combined, were capable of discharging 2,000 tons of coal a day. In 1895, the firm's auditors registered that a mighty 158,000 tons of coal had been shipped in over the previous 12 months. A contemporary account of the colliers arriving in the docks ran thus: 'Hardly is she alongside when the fillers, shovels in hand, scramble aboard. The powerful steam cranes are throbbing and vibrating as if anxious to get to work.' By six o'clock the following morning, 160 men and 80 horses and drays were waiting to start work. Each driver crossed the weighing bridge empty and collected a docket advising them which part of the wharfage to go to in order to collect their coal. The men would then shovel the coal onto their drays and, by the time the breakfast bell sounded at 8am, they were all headed out into the city 'carrying comfort to many homes'. The steady mechanisation of the process must have unnerved some of the casual labourers queuing for work by the docks every morning. During the Lock Out, a delivery of coal from Heiton's stores at the Custom House Docks had to be accompanied by 'half a dozen mounted policemen and 12 constables'. By 1914, charismatic company director William Hewat was Chairman of the Port and Docks Board while his company was also importing coal into Spencer Dock, from 1904, and the Grand Canal Dock, from 1914. Business continued to prosper until demand for coal began to wane in the latter half of the 20th century.

Seán O'Casey Bridge

In 2006, the Seán O'Casey Bridge (*Droichead Sheán Uí Chathasaigh*) won Best Pedestrian Bridge at the prestigious International IStructE Awards run by the UK's Institute of Structural Engineers. The bridge was not simply a work of aesthetic genius. It was also one of the most useful additions to Dublin's Docklands in recent decades, enabling people to move between the Custom House Docks and Merrion Square in a matter of minutes. Following the Dublin tradition of naming the city's bridges after famous Irish citizens, the new bridge was named for the playwright Seán O'Casey (1880–1964) who lived in the East Wall area from 1897 to 1920. (See page 144). Locals quickly dubbed it the 'Bingo Bridge', uniting as it does the long-running weekly bingo games between Pearse Street on the south side and Sheriff Street on the north.

The bridge was built in 2005 as part of the Docklands Authority's regeneration programme. The winning design, selected from more than 80 national and international entries, came from Cyril O'Neill of Brian O'Halloran & Associates. The elegant swing bridge is designed to suggest a formal maritime gateway to the City. It spans approximately 100m of the Liffey, joining Sir John Rogerson's Quay in the Grand Canal Docks area to the chq building on Custom House Quay. Weighing over 320 tonnes and set on two Chinese granite piers, the pioneering bridge has two balanced 44m long cantilever arms that can swing open to allow boats pass up and down the river as far as the Talbot Memorial Bridge. The piers are founded on four piles bored over 12m into the bedrock. Aluminium decking is supported on a continuous frame of steel circular sections which, in turn, are supported by a central cradle of tapered steel sections and tension rods.

Perhaps fittingly given its proximity to the International Financial Services Centre, the bridge represents a truly European collaboration. It was built by a 12-strong team of Polish shipbuilders, sub-contracted by John Mowlem, the main contractor. The North Yorkshire firm of Qualter Hall & Company manufactured the opening section, while the balustrade was produced by canal engineers in Nottingham, the balustrade panels by French company Euroslot and the deck by Promecon in Denmark.

Above: The Seán O'Casey Bridge captured at dawn. (Photo: Monika Hinz). Far left: The bridge was opened by Seán O'Casey's daughter Shivaun and the then Taoiseach Bertie Ahern in July 2005. Left: The opening was marked by a suitably theatrical show by the CoisCéim dance company, including a 'passionate pas de deux' between long-lost lovers reunited, hinting at the benefits of this new link between the two sides of the vibrant Docklands. This was the third new bridge to be built over the Liffey in five years, following the opening of the Millennium Bridge in 2000 and the James Joyce Bridge at Blackhall Place in 2003.

Connolly Station & The Iron Horse

THE KINGSTOWN LINE

In 1834, a transport revolution erupted across Ireland when engineer William Dargan began constructing a railway track between Dublin and Kingstown (now Dún Laoghaire). On 9 October 1834, the locomotive *Hibernia* left the Westland Row terminus (now Pearse Station) and made it all the way down the 10km line to Dún Laoghaire.

BUTLER'S STATION

Railway fever swiftly enveloped Ireland. In November 1844, John MacNeill's pioneering Dublin & Drogheda Railway Company opened a train station on Amiens Street. Originally known as 'Dublin Station', the innovative Italianate building was designed by William Deane Butler. When Earl Grey laid the foundation stone in May 1844, he simultaneously knighted MacNeill on the station platform. The building comprises a symmetrical five-bay Wicklow granite façade with three towers and a large triumphal entrance arch. A central tower alerted people to the building from a considerable distance and was fitted with a clock. J & R Mallet provided the ironwork. The station's boarded and glazed roofs were altered in 1884 by William Hemingway Mills, with the addition of thin iron trusses and a central iron arcade.

VICTORIAN EVOLUTION

In 1853, the railway line was extended through to Belfast and the station was renamed Amiens Street Station after the street on which it was located. From 1876, it became the principal terminus for the Great Northern Railway. In 1891, the Loopline Bridge connected Amiens Street with Westland Row on the southside of the Liffey and onwards to Rosslare and the south east. To coincide with the new link, WH Mills built a new canopied platform and locomotive shed nearby.

EASTER CELEBRATIONS

In 1966, to mark the 50th anniversary of the Easter Rising, several train stations in Ireland were renamed after those who died during the rebellion. Amiens Street Station was renamed after James Connolly, the Socialist leader of the Citizen Army, famously executed in 1916 while strapped to a chair with a wounded leg. His statue stands beneath the Loopline Bridge facing Liberty Hall, the headquarters of the Irish Trade and General Workers' Union.

MODERN TIMES

The Dublin Area Rapid Transit (DART) was linked to the station in 1984 and the Luas in 2004. The latter connected it with Heuston Station, which serves the south and west of the country. Connolly Station remains the principal railway station for trains bound for the north and east coasts of Ireland, as well as Sligo. During the late 1990s, the seven-platform station was completely restored by Iarnród Éireann Architects, with its brickwork cleaned. They also rebuilt much of the station, including a new roof over the four terminal platforms and a shimmering new station hall with bar, shopping mall and an entrance to the International Financial Services Centre. The station is owned and operated by Coras Iompair Éireann.

THE GNR HEADQUARTERS

Located on Sheriff Street, this neat red brick and sandstone building was completed by John Lanyon in 1879, three years after the Great Northern Railway was formed. Its corner campanile echoes that of the station façade on nearby Connolly Station. Between the station and the headquarters, a handsome viaduct carries the line over two rows of 11 cast-iron columns. This was cast by Courtney, Stephens & Bailey in 1884.

Right: An MGWR train arrives into Amiens Street in the early 1950s. The loco was built by the Midland at its Broadstone works in 1909 and was probably coming from Sligo or Galway. The Great Northern Railway signal cabin is beyond the back of the train. (Photo: Charles Friel Collection).

57

Great Northern Railway

THE LINK TO BELFAST

The Great Northern Railway (Ireland) operated as an independent entity for 77 years from 1876 to 1953. It was the second largest – and by far the most enterprising – of all the Irish railway systems. Its origin stemmed from the need to link Dublin and Belfast by rail in the 1830s, a time when Ireland's population had risen to more than eight million. Dublin was still Ireland's only real city, but the industrial age was in motion and Belfast's golden age was about to commence. The Ulster Railway opened its first line from Belfast to Lisburn in 1839. The Ulster Railway reached Portadown in 1942 en route to Clones and eventually Cavan. Meanwhile, several schemes were attempting to link Dublin and Belfast, either along the coast to Drogheda or inland via Navan. The Dublin & Drogheda Railway Company line was the successful scheme and powered ahead under its brilliant engineer Sir John MacNeill.

In 1844, the company established its main terminal at Amiens Street (renamed Connolly Station in 1966) near the Custom House Docks. This was reached by crossing the North Lotts, over the Royal Canal (by a wrought-iron latticed bridge) and over Seville Place (by a 9.14m/30ft elliptic viaduct of metal girders and brick arches). The Boyne Viaduct, over which the line later travelled (and on which young Bindon Blood Stoney was Resident Engineer), is considered one of the finest engineering triumphs of its age. In May 1853, the first train crossed the Boyne Viaduct and a through-line service was finally established between Belfast and Dublin.

BOOM TIME

In 1876 – the year of the first telephone call – the four main lines operating north of Dublin were amalgamated as one and the Great Northern Railway (Ireland) was born. A 40-year boom followed as Dublin and particularly Belfast prospered in pre-war Europe. All along the line, people gathered to watch the GNR's green locomotives steaming along the tracks, pursued by its mahogany coaches. In 1891, the GNR's links extended considerably when the City of Dublin Junction Railway connected Amiens Street station with Westland Row Station (renamed Pearse Station in 1966) on the city's southside.

THE END OF THE LINE

The prosperous years of 1876-1914 paled considerably against the onslaught of partition, civil war, tariff restrictions, trade wars, the eight-hour day and the ever-evolving road transport in the decades that followed. Staff numbers were considerably depleted by the death of 87 employees in action during the Great War. A further seven were killed in the Second World War. All are recalled by name in a memorial on Platform 4 at Connolly Station. While traffic almost doubled during the Second World War, competition from road and air, falling receipts and soaring operating costs brought the company to its knees. In November 1950, the shareholders authorised the Board to close the line as soon as possible. The GNR's independence officially ended in 1953 when it was bought out by the two governments in Ireland and administered by the Great Northern Railway Board – the first 'Cross-Border Body'. Five years of shared nationalisation followed, during which much of the system was closed. In 1958, the remainder was split between the Ulster Transport Authority (later Northern Ireland Railways) and by Córas Iompair Éireann. Today, all that remains of the Great Northern is the Belfast-Dublin line, Howth to Howth Junction, Drogheda to Navan and the 'mothballed' Lisburn-Antrim line.

Right: The 5th International Railway Congress was held in the Imperial Institute, London in 1895. After the Congress, a number of foreign railway officials toured Ireland, landing at Cork and making their way, via Listowel, Ballybunnion and Limerick, to Dublin. The locomotive featured opposite was a P class 4-4-0 No 73, built by Beyer Peacock in Manchester in 1895. The loco was in the lined green livery of the Great Northern Railway. There is so much foliage on the engine that you cannot see her name, 'Primrose'. She is standing at what is now platform 4 at Connolly Station, waiting to leave. (Photo: Charles Friel Collection).

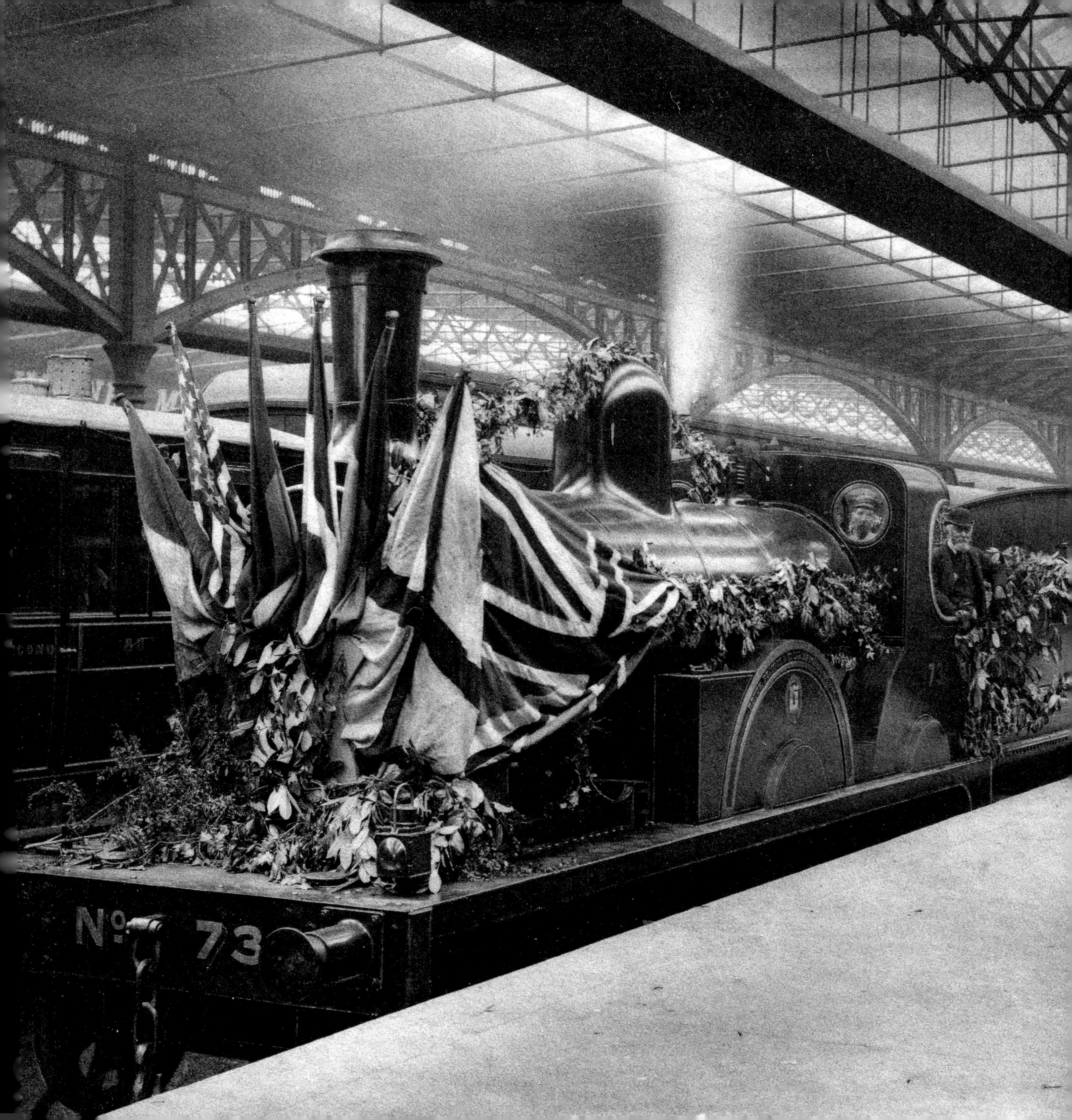
No 73

Sir Isaac Butt Bridge (1879 - 1929)

In the 18th and 19th centuries, Dublin Port kept moving eastwards as ships got bigger and berthage requirements went deeper. Almost as soon as Carlisle Bridge was opened in 1795, the city's merchants were calling for a new and better bridge even further east. By 1852, their dissatisfaction was so extreme that a New Bridge Committee was formed with the Earl of Charlemont as its chairman. The Ballast Office resisted, concentrating on the equally important measure of widening Carlisle Bridge instead. In 1876, a parliamentary act simultaneously allowed for the altering, widening and upgrading of Carlisle Bridge and the construction of a new opening bridge, operated by hydraulic machinery, to connect Beresford Place on the north to Tara Street on the south. The opening span would enable ships to continue to dock at Burgh Quay and Eden Quay. The new bridge, completed in September 1879, was designed by the Board's engineer Bindon Blood Stoney in collaboration with contractor William J. Doherty. These two men also collaborated on the rebuilding of Sir John Rogerson's Quay and the new Carlisle Bridge (now O'Connell Bridge). The Skerne Ironworks of Darlington supplied metalwork and machinery, shortly before they went bankrupt.

At the request of the Municipal Council, the new bridge was named for the late Sir Isaac Butt (1813 – May 1879), the Donegal barrister who founded the Home Rule League in 1873. Sir Isaac had a close affiliation with the Docklands from his time as Secretary to the Crimean War Veterans Banquet Fund. The bridge was also known as the Beresford Swivel Bridge on account of the rotating mechanism that allowed the bridge to open. A census taken in October 1879 showed that an average of 3,177 vehicles passed over the bridge daily, together with '6,308 pedestrians, 55 equestrians and 223 cattle'.

Right Top: Hundreds of dark-dressed men swarm across the newly opened bridge in the early 1880s. Right Bottom: The Swastika Laundry and Heiton's Coals were amongst those regularly using the bridge on the eve of the War of Independence. Far right: The present day Butt Bridge is overlooked by Liberty Hall, the 16-storey headquarters of the Services, Industrial, Professional and Technical Union of Ireland (SIPTU). (Photos: Dublin City Council)

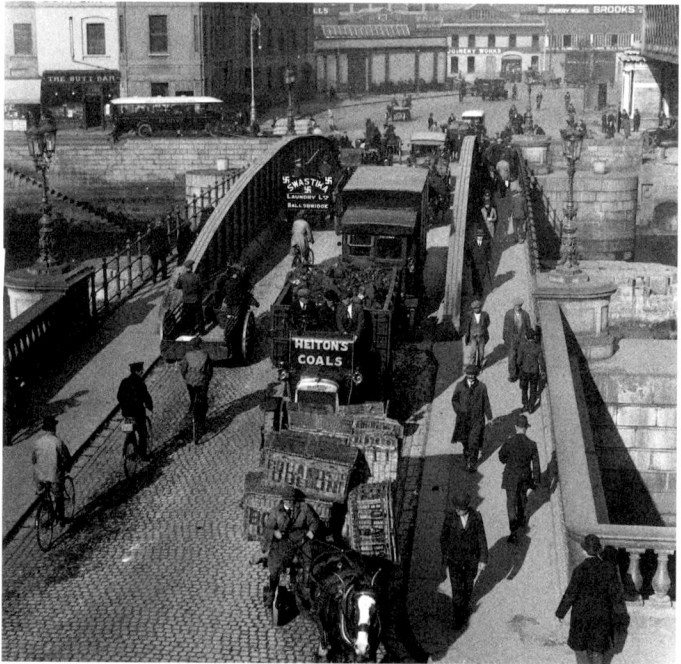

The Second Butt Bridge (1932 - Present)

Neither Eden Quay nor Burgh Quay were able to provide suitable berthage for the increasingly huge vessels coming upriver. Moreover, they had both become busy thoroughfares for public traffic making the loading and unloading of cargo a logistical nightmare. On 13th December 1888, the original Sir Isaac Butt Bridge opened for the last time. After the Loopline Railway Viaduct was completed three years later, Stoney's spans swivelled no more. The bridge came under increasing pressure from those who insisted its approach gradients were too steep and its carriageway too narrow. In 1925, the Dublin Port and Docks Board lodged a bill for the reconstruction of Butt Bridge. The bill was enacted four years later and a new bridge was designed by the Board's Chief Engineer Joseph Mallagh. He acted in consultation with Pierce Purcell (Professor of Civil Engineering at University College Dublin), with Messrs O'Callaghan and Giron as visual advisers.

The new 63ft wide three-span Butt Bridge opened to traffic in 1932, just in time for the 31st International Eucharistic Congress. The centre span, which is 110ft long, was constructed as two separate cantilevered half spans of 55ft, enabling half of the river to be kept open for barge traffic. Butt Bridge was the first bridge in Dublin to be built with reinforced concrete, courtesy of Gray's Ferro-Concrete (Ireland) Ltd. It is also believed to be the earliest recorded use of the cantilevered method of construction with reinforced concrete in Britain or Ireland.

Dublin Corporation proposed applying the name 'Congress Bridge' to this 'new and handsome bridge'. By way of compromise, the Dublin Port and Docks Board placed a plaque on the bridge acknowledging that the bridge had been re-built in the year of the 31st International Eucharistic Congress.

The Loopline Railway Bridge

In 1881, the Dublin, Wicklow and Wexford Railway Company proposed the construction of a contemporary railway viaduct across the Liffey, east of Butt Bridge. This extended the Dublin and Kingstown line from Westland Row (now Pearse Station) to Amiens Street (now Connolly Station). The link was deemed vital, particularly for conveying transatlantic passengers and mail coming from Kingstown (Dún Laoghaire) and Queenstown (Cobh). Objections were manifold and strenuous, particularly from those who realized this new bridge would 'disfigure' the City by cutting off the splendid view of the Custom House from O'Connell Bridge. Despite these protests, the bridge and viaduct went ahead and building commenced in 1888 under John Chaloner Smith, Chief Engineer to the Railway Company.

In 1939, the Labour leader James Larkin blamed the bridge on the Unionists and lambasted it as 'the foulest thing that ever disgraced the city'. For all that, the Loopline is not such a bad-looking bridge. It's rather an epic reminder of the latter days of the Industrial Age. It's simply the location that boggles and makes it such a subject of dislike.

The bridge consists of a three-span bridge of twin wrought-iron latticed girders, with a total length of 118m/387ft. It is supported on a double row of stout cast-iron piers that rise above high-water level. It carries two tracks, with the clear width of the deck between the supporting girders being 8.53m/28ft. The bridge was formerly well known for the huge advertisements that hung upon its faces, most notably for Guinness and Irish Permanent.

'A skiff, a crumpled throwaway, Elijah is coming, rode lightly down the Liffey, under Loopline bridge, shooting the rapids where water chafed around the bridge piers, sailing eastward past hulls and anchor chains, between the Customhouse old dock and George's quay'

- James Joyce, *Ulysses.*

The Famine Statues

Above: Rowan Gillepsie's haunting Famine (1997) on Custom House Quay was an act of private philanthropy by businesswoman Norma Smurfit. Designed as a memorial to the Great Famine, the site was chosen as it was from here that the first emigrant ships set sail for North America. (Photo: Stu Carroll) Left: The Loopline Bridge was completed across the Liffey in 1891 and quickly became a celebrated landmark in the annals of Dublin literature. (Photo: Luca Rocchini)

The 20th Century

REBELS & GRAIN MERCHANTS

Although the quest for deeper berthage made the Custom House Docks increasingly redundant, both Georges Dock and the Inner Dock remained active for much of the 20th century, largely due to its coal trade. A considerable blow to the locality came in May 1921 when Oscar Traynor, commander of the Dublin Brigade of the IRA, led an assault on the Custom House, destroying the historic building. Reconstruction began in 1926 and continued until 1930. In 1927, the entrance channel to the Old Dock was closed and the dock itself filled in.

Custom House Quay was gradually abandoned by all ships, except the Guinness ships. The lands and warehouses immediately east of the Custom House Docks struggled to find alternative uses. In 1914, the Merchants Warehousing Company abandoned the area when it set up its grain silos further down in the port. Slowly but surely the confident facades crumbled and the landscape decayed into one of dirty warehouses, rundown housing and half-abandoned freight yards. This was compounded by the construction of a port boundary wall and gates on East Wall Road, marking a physical as well as functional separation of Port and City. The warehousing of tobacco under bond in Stacks A and L became one of the biggest operations of the 1920s and 1930s. Wines and spirits were held in Stack C. Bailey's Irish Cream would later dominate Stack H.

FALLING DOWN

Following the bombing of North Strand by the Luftwaffe in May 1941, FW Bond, assistant chief engineer to the Port and Docks Board, built both overground and underground air-raid shelters in the grounds of the Custom House. The timber jetties either side of the entrance to George's Dock were simultaneously replaced by modern masonry quay walls.

STATE INTERVENTION

In 1941, the government established Irish Tea Importers Ltd as a purchasing agency. The Custom House warehouses were soon storing large quantities of tea chests, as well as providing services such as blending for particular merchants. In 1950, the Board sold the lands immediately north of the Inner Dock by Sheriff Street to the Department of Posts and Telegraphs, which established a new Central Sorting Office there for Dublin. Another portion of the docks was conveyed to Córas Iompair Éireann for a new central bus station, while the site of the Old Dock was transferred to Dublin Corporation to create the Memorial Road link between Amiens Street and Beresford Place.

DESERTION BY THE BALLAST OFFICE

Interest in the docks was briefly relit by an architectural competition held in 1954 to design a new central headquarters for the Dublin Port and Docks Board. This was to be sited within the Custom House Docks complex. However, the poor economic climate - combined with forceful voices urging the Board to relocate in the deep-sea area of the Port - scuppered the plan. After a short stint in Gandon House beside Busáras, the Board's new headquarters – Port Centre - was built in the old Liffey Dockyard on Alexandra Road. The area was to remain neglected and unloved until the birth of the Custom House Docks Development Authority in 1986.

Gulliver Sleeps

Above: Children gaze in wonder at a giant sand sculpture of Gulliver asleep by George's Dock. The sculpture was built by Duthain Dealbh as part of an initiative by Dublin City Council and the Docklands Authority to promote the 'Dublin: One City, One Book' campaign and celebrates Jonathan Swift's masterpiece 'Gulliver's Travels'. (Photo: Paul Sharp). Left: Smoke clouds billow out from the Custom House during the devastating fire of 1921.

1.
4.

2.

3.

5.

6.

The Guinness Barges

*'In Dublin there's a beauty that has no match,
It is brewed in St. James's, then thrown down the hatch'.*

Frank Holt *'In Praise of Guinness'*

THE FARMLEIGH BARGES

One of the more romantic images of the Liffey from times past is of the Guinness barges that once carried the black stuff from the brewery to the Docklands. They began operations during the 1870s, shortly after the Guinness brewery at St James's Gate expanded north to the River Liffey. In 1873, Guinness built Victoria Quay, named for Her Majesty. This enabled the Guinness barges, otherwise called Steam Lighters, to load and unload the wooden barrels of stout right beside the brewery gates. The first of these steam-operated barges was the *Lagan*, built in Belfast by Harland & Wolff. By the outbreak of the Great War in 1914, there were 12 barges operating on the Liffey.

In 1927, the Guinness engineers launched the *Farmleigh*, a new type of steam-driven barge, measuring 24m/80ft long and 5m/17.1ft wide, and equipped with jib cranes. It could travel at a speed of 7.5 knots while carrying up to 100 tons of cargo, or about 300 hogshead of Guinness. The *Farmleigh* was built by Vickers (Ireland) Ltd at the Liffey Dockyard. A further nine 'Farmleigh' barges were built in the same yard over the next four years and all named after places in Dublin such as *Killiney*, *Fairyhouse* and *Castleknock*.

BRING US BACK A PARROT

Each boat had a mate, an engine driver, two boatsmen and a captain. The latter was always elegantly dressed in dark blue corduroys, a shimmering peaked cap and a dark blue jersey with the word 'Guinness' etched in red on the front. During the War of Independence, all drivers and boatmen had a special pass from Dublin Castle to permit them to be outside during curfew. The barges continued to operate every day, despite the burning of the Custom House and, later, the attack on the Four Courts. By the 1930s, Guinness had become one of Ireland's primary exports. Over 5,000 people worked in the brewery and, every day, huge quantities of stout were sent by barge to the cross-channel steam ships waiting downriver. The journey from the brewery down to Custom House Quay was known as the 'Liffey mile' and took 20 minutes. An ever-blossoming legend tells how, as a barge passed beneath the Ha'Penny bridge, a young Dublin 'jackeen' yelled out 'Hey Mister, bring us back a parrot', believing the Guinness-laden barges were bound for exotic lands. She wasn't far off; some of those barrels were destined for bars in Africa and the West Indies.

THE END OF THE FLEET

At Custom House Quay, the barges unloaded the full barrels, loaded up with empty ones and returned to the brewery. With the evolution of Guinness breweries elsewhere in the world, the trade from St James's Gate calmed down. By 1938, only six of the 10 Farmleigh barges were still in operation. One of those decommissioned barges was the *Fairyhouse*, which went on to play a useful role in the evacuation of Dunkirk. After the Second World War, new stainless steel storage tanks came into vogue and the barges became redundant. The last commercial passage of a Guinness barge was by the *Castleknock*. She sailed from the Custom House with a load of empties and made her final journey back to Victoria Quay on Midsummer's Day 1961. Sadly not one of these fine vessels has survived to the present day. The Irish Ship and Barge Fabrication Company are presently seeking to recover and restore four barges scuttled off the coast of Co Antrim, namely the *Clonsilla*, *Vartry*, *Foyle* and *Killiney*. Two barges are to be refitted with steam engines burning wood-pellets, while the other two will be electrically powered.

Previous page: 1: Tea from the Behubor Tea Gardens in India is unloaded in Stack D. 2,3,4: Stack A was a warehouse for general goods. 5. Loading timber with an Arrol crane on the North Wall. 6: Grain is weighed in the loft of Stack A. (Photos: Dublin Port Company Archives)

Above: The Guinness barge 'Sandyford' makes its return voyage up the River Liffey after distibuting its cargo to the Guinness ships waiting outside the Custom House and City Quay.

Talbot Memorial Bridge

By the 1970s, Dublin City was adjusting to a new age in congestion problems. Poor old Butt Bridge was proving a nightmare for two-way traffic. The Corporation's solution was to make Butt Bridge a one-way northbound crossing and to build a brand new one-way bridge downstream of the Custom House for southbound traffic. The Talbot was the first Liffey bridge in Dublin to use pre-stressed concrete as a structural medium. The bridge's name commemorates both the Venerable Matt Talbot and all the sailors of Dublin who have died at sea. It was designed to carry four lanes of traffic, with two footpaths, giving a total width of 72ft. The bridge has three spans, with an aggregated length of 262ft, and a width of 72ft between the parapets. The maximum depth of water under the bridge is 29ft. The bridge was opened on Valentine's Day 1978 by Michael Collins, Lord Mayor of Dublin. Its peak traffic capacity is presently rated as 2,400 vehicles per hour. The greatest downside of the Talbot was that, after nearly 200 years, the Tall Ships and the much-loved blue and cream Guinness ships were no longer able to moor outside the Custom House.

The Venerable Matt Talbot

The Venerable Matt Talbot (1856–1925) was a working-class hero who became a world famous temperance campaigner in the early 20th century. As a youth he bottled Guinness and stacked whiskey in the Custom House Docks. Like many a docker, he was a formidable drinker in his spare time. In 1884, he gave up alcohol. He took to wearing a light chain around his waist as a self-reminder of his pledge to fight the demon drink. As a form of penance, he slept on bare floorboards and used a log as a pillow. Some considered him a lunatic but others, particularly those afflicted by the stigma of alcoholism, saw him as a symbol of hope. Even as he toiled in T&C Martin's timber yard off Sheriff Street, his reputation spread into Europe and North America. On the 50th anniversary of his death in 1975, Pope Paul VI declared him Venerable – the first step to sainthood. Amongst those celebrating the 75th anniversary of his death at Our Lady of Lourdes Church on Seán McDermott Street was Chief Dallas Eagle of South Dakota's Lakota tribe. He maintained that Talbot's example had helped many of his people overcome their addiction to alcohol. Talbot's statue stands today at the southern end of the bridge, notably facing away from the International Financial Services Centre.

The Liffey Swim

'Above: The Docklands Liffey Swim is an enjoyable but challenging 1.5km swim organized by the NAC Masters Swimming Club. Left: The Talbot Memorial Bridge opened in 1978. It was named in memory of the Venerable Matt Talbot and of all the sailors of Dublin who have died at sea'.

The Custom House Docks Development Authority

A REDUNDANT ASSET

The Custom House Docks Development Authority was established in 1988 and became the backbone of the entire docklands development project. It remained the foremost power in the Custom House Docks until the establishment of the Dublin Docklands Development Authority in 1997. The idea of developing the Custom House Docks began in the 1970s under the Dublin Port and Docks Board. For many years, the Board's annual reports had made for gloomy reading – an ever-declining trade, a drop in oil imports, lengthy strikes and unofficial stoppages. The Board tried to resolve labour disputes with the creation of Dublin Cargo Handling, the only authorised stevedoring company in the Port. Many long-standing tenants abandoned the area for bigger, better sites closer to the Port itself. In 1978, that sense of rejection was further heightened by the construction of the Talbot Memorial Bridge, blocking river access to the Custom House for the colourful Guinness ships. The Board was also faced with the costs of restoring the 200-year-old South Wall, extensively damaged by storms in 1982. Even the sturdy 100-Ton crane had begun to sag. The Board believed that developing the Custom House Docks could go a long way to resolving their economic troubles.

THE GREGORY DEAL

However, the government also had their eye on the docks. They reasoned that such a strategically located development could prove vital to the future of the city. In 1982, the government effectively seized control of the Docks on the back of a remarkable deal struck between the newly elected inner-city independent socialist TD, Tony Gregory, and Charles J Haughey's Fianna Fáil government. In return for Gregory's support, Haughey pledged IRL£91 million for housing and related developments in Dublin's inner city. The deal resulted in a government proposal to introduce the Urban Areas Development Bill which, inter alia, provided for the establishment of the Custom House Docks Development Authority. The Custom House Docks were to be compulsorily transferred to CHDDA for a price determined by the Minister for the Environment.

The bill was never enacted because Haughey's government fell from power just nine months later. The project would arguably have been dropped altogether were it not for the insistence of Fergus O'Brien, Minister of State at the Department of the Taoiseach (Government

Chief Whip) and a former Lord Mayor of Dublin. O'Brien persuaded Garret FitzGerald to set up a special committee to investigate the Custom House Docks potential for redevelopment. Eighteen months later, this committee gave their view that the area could indeed be revitalised if tax incentives were offered to those businesses willing to relocate in the docks.

THE BIRTH OF CHDDA

In 1986, the Fine Gael / Labour government ushered through the Urban Renewal Act, which specifically targeted the Customs House Docks as being ripe for rejuvenation. It envisaged something similar to the redevelopment of London's docklands that was then under way. Ownership of the docks was transferred to CHDDA, 118 years after ownership was vested in the Port and Docks Board. CHDDA was to have a profound effect on the future of Dublin's docklands. The Authority was formally established in November 1986 with Frank Benson as Executive Chairman and Gus MacAmhlaigh as first secretary. Their mandate was to redevelop the Custom House Docks Area, comprising seven acres of docks and 20 acres of land running east from Butt Bridge to Commons Street, north to Sheriff Street Lower, then south down Amiens Street and Memorial Road back to Custom House Quay. In 1994, CHDDA's boundary was extended to include a further 12 acres between Commons Street and Guild Street (the western edge of Spencer Dock) and incorporating the Sheriff Street flats. It also included the northern half of the River Liffey, indicative of a long overdue interest in revitalizing the river itself.

RECLAIMING THE RIVERSIDE

For most of the 20th century, transit sheds and warehouses ran all the way down Custom House Quay, the North Wall Quay and the North Wall Extension. Unless you walked deep into one of these warehouses, you simply could not see the river. Bonded goods such as wines, spirits, tobacco, grain and slates were held at the Custom House Docks. Tea and other commodities tended to be stored along the North Wall while the flour milling companies were based closer to the Alexandra Basin. The Port and Docks Board had already transferred the bulk of their warehousing operations from the Custom House Docks to the port estate at East Wall. This freed CHDDA up to clear away the more dilapidated warehouses along the Liffey and examine the potential. In time, all the warehouses, with the exception of the chq building, were felled to bring back the riverfront. Hand in hand with this was the on-going restoration of the Custom House, completed in 1991, and the evolution of the International Financial Services Centre.

Far left: The signing of the Custom House Docks Master Project Agreement in 1987, with Dan McInerney (McInerney Properties), Minister Padraig Flynn, Frank Benson (CHDDA), Mark Kavanagh (Hardwicke Ltd) and John Ritblatt (British Land Co). Former Taoiseach Charles J Haughey formally launched the International Financial Services Centre in September 1988, laying the foundation stone with developer Mark Kavanagh (middle left) and speaking on behalf of CHDDA Chairman Frank Benson (left). Next page: The IFSC was built on the site of the Old Dock and the old Custom House warehouses. The 520 or so IFSC companies presently contribute up to a sixth of Ireland's corporation tax. (Photo: Charles Howarth)

The International Financial Services Centre

HAUGHEY'S LEGACY
In the opening weeks of 1987, a revolutionary concept was being whispered in the corridors of Irish power; namely Dermot Desmond's idea of creating an International Financial Services Centre (IFSC) in Dublin. Considerable pressure was put on the incoming Fianna Fáil government to establish this new centre in either Ballsbridge or Sandyford. The then taoiseach Charles Haughey resisted, believing the Custom House Docks could be the perfect location. The area already enjoyed the financial incentive benefits of the Urban Renewal scheme. CHDDA Secretary Gus MacAmhlaigh concurred, suggesting that the IFSC could do for the northside what the Guinness family did for the southside when they relocated from Mountjoy Square to Iveagh House on Stephen's Green. Such comparisons sat well with Haughey who was rapidly seeing the potential of the IFSC to be one of the shining lights of his legacy. In March 1987, the government took the crucial decision to locate the IFSC in the 27-acre Custom House Docks.

CONSTRUCTION TIME
The CHDDA team devised a Planning Scheme, later the master plan, drawn up by Murray O'Laoire Architects. This showed the proposed location of all buildings. The tax incentives were in place. All they needed now was a developer. In September 1987, after a tendering process in which eight consortia participated, the IRL£200 million contract to develop the IFSC flagship was awarded to the Custom House Docks Development Company Ltd. The consortium comprised of Mark Kavanagh's company Hardwicke Ltd, British Land Co and McInerney Properties. Their proposal was judged to be the best overall concept although it certainly helped that British Land was backed up by a letter of credit from NAT West. McInenery subsequently withdrew and it became a 50/50 consortium between Hardwicke and British Land.

THE VALUE OF THE RIVER
The IFSC was designed by Burke-Kennedy Doyle and Benjamin Thompson & Associates. The first three blocks were built simultaneously. They were state-of-the-art, the first of their kind in Ireland, with very high specs such as 4.2m/13.7ft floor-to-floor and cutting-edge air conditioning. The West Block was completed in April 1990; the North and South Blocks the following year. These three glazed blocks swiftly became key symbols for the whole Docklands regeneration project. The government's willingness to support such a project represented a major public statement of a brave new era in Ireland's economic development. It was also arguably the first time in many decades that anybody had considered the banks of the Liffey to be an attractive place to own an office. Slowly but assuredly, the City was awakening to the real value of the river that was patiently flowing through its heart.

THREE WISE MEN
Meanwhile, in early 1988, a trio of public servants took the first of many, many flights as part of an enormous campaign to sell Dublin as an emerging financial centre. Known in governmental circles as the Three Wise Men, they were Séamus Páircéir, former Chairman of the Revenue Commissioners, Tomas O Coifaigh, former governor of the Central Bank, and the late Maurice Horgan, former second secretary at the Department of Finance. (Páircéir later succeeded Benson as Chairman of CHDDA. He was himself succeeded by Professor Dervilla M X Donnelly, former president of the Royal Dublin Society). The Three Wise Men came to an important conclusion early on. No foreign bank would come to an IFSC in Dublin unless all the Irish banks were located there. Haughey quickly met the Chairmen of both Allied Irish Bank and the Bank of Ireland and effectively ordered them to buy in. Thus, in 1988 and 1989, Ireland's two largest banks took the considerable risk of buying the first two buildings at the IFSC. In 1990, AIB established its headquarters in the West Block (now AIB International Centre), sited on the former Old Dock and the West Store. Stack B's brown-brick eastern wing was reduced in size and crowned by a glass-and-steel attic to become the AIB Trade Centre. In 1991, the Bank of Ireland moved to the North Block, renamed La Touche House after the Huguenot family who founded the bank in 1710. The South Block (now IFSC House) was subsequently purchased by financier Dermot Desmond.

THE BREAKTHROUGH

The gamble paid off. The carrot was an extremely favourable corporation tax rate of 10%. By late 1989, major international players such as Chase Manhattan, Citibank and Sumitomo Bank had come on board. Deutsche Bank and Commerzbank were the first German banks to sign up to the project. The Sorting Office on Sheriff Street and a car park for 1,000 postal workers was converted into Custom House Plaza 1 and taken by the Dutch bank ABN-AMRO. In 1991, the CHDDC consortium completed Harbour Master One, taken by the accounting firm Arthur Andersen, and Harbour Master Two, taken by the corporate law firm McCann FitzGerald. The greatest breakthrough came in 1992 when the international giant Citibank was persuaded to purchase one of the riverside buildings, which it partially financed by selling the tax incentives on to other investors. The arrival of Citibank changed everything and they couldn't build quick enough. Bankers, solicitors, accountants, insurance firms, publishers, taxation advisers – everyone wanted to be a part of it. CHDDA's remit was extended and they purchased a further 12 acres between Mayor House and Commons Street. The peak was arguably reached in 1996 when Christopher Bennett Construction Ltd paid IRL£12 million for a one-acre site, with planning permission, upon which New Century House now stands. Today, the IFSC employs over 20,000 people. Over half the world's top 50 banks and half of the top 20 insurance companies have an office somewhere in the IFSC.

Chapter Two
North Wall

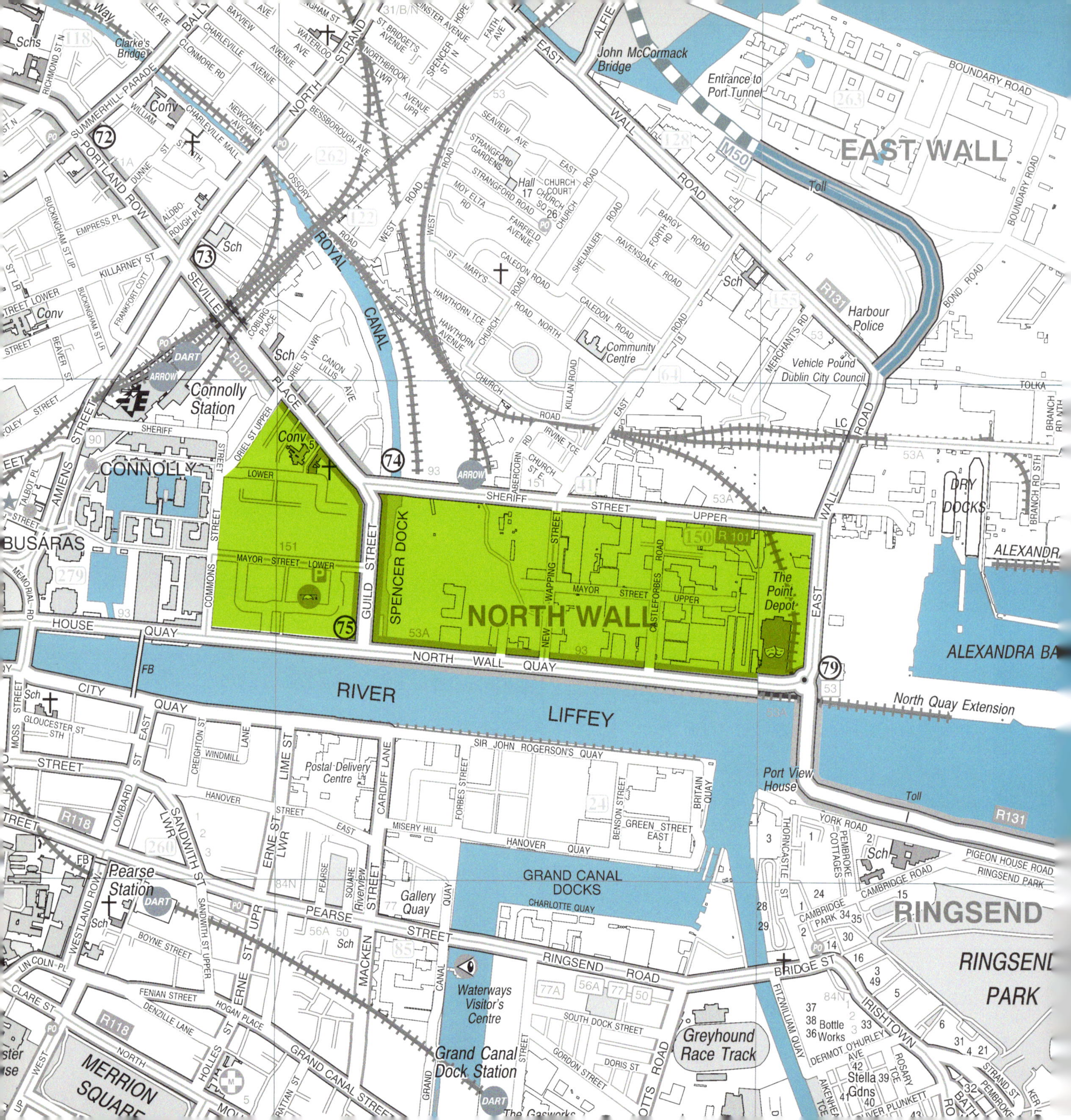
EAST WALL
NORTH WALL
RIVER
LIFFEY
RINGSEND
RINGSEND PARK
GRAND CANAL DOCKS
Connolly Station
CONNOLLY
BUSÁRAS
Pearse Station
Grand Canal Dock Station
John McCormack Bridge
Entrance to Port Tunnel
Clarke's Bridge
Harbour Police
Vehicle Pound Dublin City Council
Community Centre
The Point Depot
Postal Delivery Centre
Gallery Quay
Waterways Visitor's Centre
Greyhound Race Track
Port View House
North Quay Extension
DRY DOCKS
ALEXANDRA BA
MERRION SQUARE
ROYAL CANAL
SHERIFF STREET UPPER
MAYOR STREET LOWER
MAYOR STREET UPPER
SPENCER DOCK
GUILD STREET
NORTH WALL QUAY
SIR JOHN ROGERSON'S QUAY
CITY QUAY
HANOVER QUAY
CHARLOTTE QUAY
PEARSE STREET
RINGSEND ROAD
EAST WALL ROAD
SEVILLE PLACE
PORTLAND ROW
AMIENS STREET
NORTH STRAND
BOUNDARY ROAD
PIGEON HOUSE ROAD
BRIDGE ST
IRISHTOWN
Bottle Works
Stella Gdns
72
73
74
75
79

The North Wall is effectively a rectangle of just over 100 acres, framed between the Liffey at North Wall Quay on the south, Sheriff Street on the north, Commons Street on the west and the East Wall Road on the east. In Victorian times, this busy landscape was dominated by cross-channel ships, passenger and freight trains, and the barges that journeyed upon the Royal Canal. With the development of Alexandra Basin and other deep-sea options closer to the river mouth, North Wall went into decline. By 1916, its streets were home to some of the most impoverished families in Europe, while its pubs became the haunt of an extraordinary working class hierarchy.

Few parts of Ireland have undergone such a profound change of landscape in the past decade as North Wall. The development began in the early 1990s when the Custom House Docks Development Authority had its remit extended to cover the land between Commons Street and Guild Street where such landmarks as Clarion Quay and the National College of Ireland now stand. Meanwhile, the indefatigable businessman Harry Crosbie developed his lands around The O_2 (the former Point Theatre) into the Point Village. In conjunction with Treasury Holdings, he has also expanded his empire into Spencer Dock. By 2010, North Wall and its riverside Convention Centre, Dublin, will be intrinsically linked to the southside of the City by the Samuel Beckett Bridge. Multi-national headquarters, large public spaces, campshire walks, floating restaurants and cutting-edge bridges provide a constant buzz of human activity. Few of the 21st century's children will comprehend how, not so long ago, North Wall was the terrain of the Sheriff Street flats.

North Wall - Streetwise

Canon Lillis Avenue - Named for Canon William Lillis, a native of Co Clare and parish priest of St Laurence O'Toole Church for many years.

Castleforbes Road and Square - Named for an old manor house, built in 1729, for the family of George Forbes, Lord Mayor of Dublin in 1740. The house is presumed to have stood on the latter day site of T&C Martin's timber yard where Matt Talbot worked. The original tablet for 'Castle Forbes 1729' is set into the wall of the Lever Brothers building on Sheriff Street.

Commons Street - Named for the Commissioners, now Councillors, on the old Municipal Council of Dublin. It is said that Molly Malone lived on this street.

Excise Walk - A new pedestrian route linking North Wall Quay to Mayor Square and named for the handsome brown brick building of 'His Majesty's Excise Store' on Mayor Street.

Guild Street - Named in 1773 for the Guilds from which the Corporation of Dublin was then composed.

Mayor Street - Named in 1773 after the senior title of office in the Corporation of Dublin. Mayor Square is a 21st century creation.

Newfoundland Street - Named for the newly reclaimed lands, this originally ran between Mayor Street and Sheriff Street but was built upon in the 1930s.

New Wapping Street - Probably named after the London dock district or after Wapping Quay in Derry.

Nixon Street - Named for a family who owned property in the area, this street was built upon a spur pool of the Royal Canal Docks filled during the 1840s.

North Lotts - Nicknamed 'Newfoundland', the North Lotts were so-called after a lottery set up in 1717 by Dublin Corporation for the distribution of these newly reclaimed lands. To keep matters simple, these lots were only gifted to Corporation members.

Oriel Street - Named for the Rt Hon John Foster, created Baron Oriel in 1821, last Speaker of the Irish House of Commons and a member of the Corporation for Preserving and Improving the Port of Dublin. He was staunchly opposed to the Act of Union by which the Irish Parliament voted itself out of existence.

Phil Shanahan House - The famous Sheriff Street block of flats was named for a local publican, born in Tipperary, who was elected as a Sinn Féin member of the British House of Commons in 1918 and served as a TD in Dáil Éireann from 1919 to 1922.

Seville Place - Developed in the mid 19th century in response to the railways, the street was named for a junior title of the Earls of Aldborough. An iron works based here supplied the extensive cast-iron galleries installed along the cells of Mountjoy Prison. The film director Jim Sheridan and his writer brother Peter grew up on this street.

Sheriff Street - Named in 1773 after the second title of office in the Corporation of Dublin.

Spencer Dock - The dock where the Royal Canal cuts through Sheriff Street was opened on 15th April 1873 by Earl Spencer, Lord Lieutenant of Ireland and great-great-grandfather of Diana, Princess of Wales.

Whitworth Row - During the 1830s and 1840s, No 4 was home to William Carleton, the controversial Ulster novelist.

Right: An aerial photo of the North Wall with Commons Street running along the west-side and Spencer Dock adjoining the Royal Canal on the east. The site of the Sheriff Street flats has been converted to apartment blocks at the centre of the photo. Note also St Laurence O'Toole's church, now one of the oldest existing buildings in North Wall. (Photo: Peter Barrow)

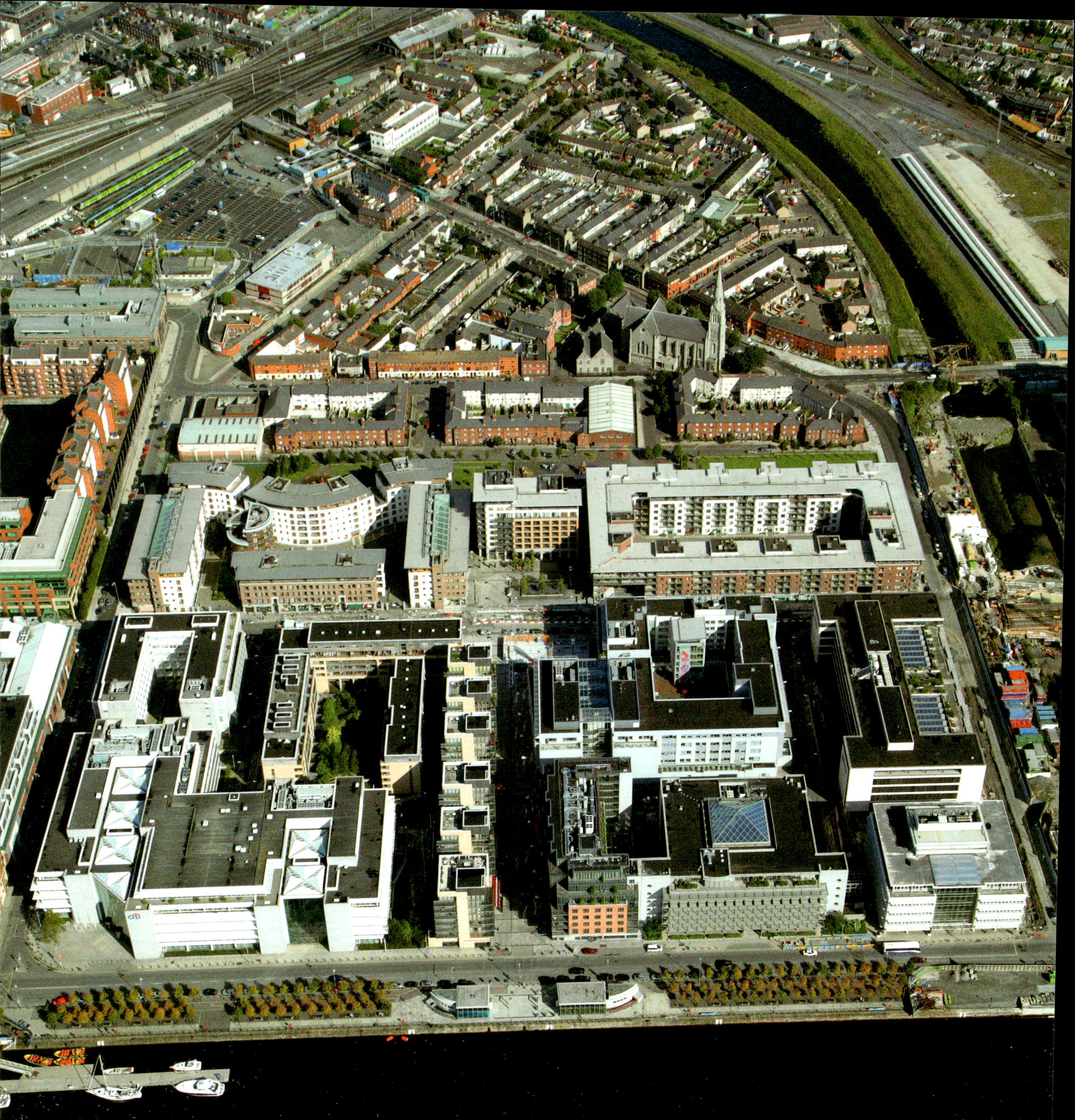

The North Lotts Project

A POTTED HISTORY

The original North Wall Quay was a roughshod sea-wall built in the early 18th century by Dublin's City Assembly. The idea was to reclaim the lands of the 'North Lotts' from the tidal Liffey and convert it into money-making allotments, or 'lotts'. The project had limited success until the construction of the Custom House in the 1790s put the area right in the heart of the City's trade quarter. During Victorian times, the wall was rebuilt and extended by the engineer, Bindon Blood Stoney. The subsequent industrial boom saw the landscape transformed into a maze of coal sheds, cattle yards, freight depots, packet stations and workers' cottages. Ironically, the river itself was largely forgotten about in the excitement. The North Wall fell into decline during the 20th century as fewer and fewer merchant ships could physically make it so far upriver. The B&I ferry to England was one of the last regular vessels to sail from the North Wall and many Irish emigrants took their last step on Irish land at this quay. The downtime halted with the establishment of the Custom House Docks Development Authority in 1986. From Commons Street to the Point Village, the entire North Wall Quay has undergone, or is presently undergoing, extensive rejuvenation. After 300 years of service, the North Wall is guaranteed a major role in the evolution of 21st century Dublin City.

FACING UP TO THE RIVER

In 1665, London was devastated by a Great Plague that killed over 100,000 people. The Earl of Ormonde, Lord Lieutenant of Ireland, knew London well. He recognised that the origins of the epidemic lay amid the untreated sewage and general waste that Londoners poured into the River Thames every day. Dublin was no better. All along the Liffey, houses backed directly onto the river to make such dumping more convenient. Ormonde ordered that not only must all new houses in Dublin face the river but that any land running immediately along the quayside should be free from obstruction to facilitate public access up and down the riverfront. Ormonde understood the necessity of space; he also bequeathed Phoenix Park to the City. Within 40 years of his directive, Dublin was the second-largest city, after London, in the fledgling British Empire.

TO TAME A RIVER

Anyone trying to enter Dublin by ship in Ormonde's time faced a rough ride. One of the worst hazards were the treacherous sandbanks at the mouth of the Liffey. These were created where the Liffey met the river Dodder on the southside and the Tolka on the northside. Untold numbers of vessels ran aground upon these unpredictable banks. In the early 18th century, the Ballast Office hatched a plan to tame the Liffey and deepen the riverbed. They built two huge restraining walls on its north and south shores. A third wall to the city's north east was constructed to put manners on the Tolka. These embankments became respectively known as the North Wall, the South Wall and the East Wall.

The point where the North Wall and the East Wall met was helpfully known as the Point, which is where the Point Village stands today. The construction of these walls greatly improved the safety of the waters within the port. It also opened up the possibility of creating new lands through reclamation. These new lands were known as the North Lotts.

MEN AT WORK

The concept of the North Lotts originated in 1682 when Dublin's City Assembly surveyed a large quadrilateral of land submerged beneath the tidal waters of the Tolka and the Liffey. The area, which they planned to reclaim from the sea, was to be divided into 152 lots. Each lot would be awarded by lottery to a trusty Assembly member or some other favoured Protestant official. However, a combination of constant tidal flooding, political uncertainty and administrative difficulties put paid to the original 'North Lotts' scheme and it was abandoned in 1686. In 1712, the North Lotts project was reborn when the Ballast Office commenced work on the North Wall. The engineers laid down 686 timber kishes, or cubical cages, made of woven willow osiers, not unlike the steel-mesh gambions used to protect coastlines today. Each kish was filled with black stones. The wall was then topped off with gravel, shingle and mud dug out of the riverbed. During the 1720s, a second wall was built to the rear of these kishes, while the East Wall along the River Tolka was simultaneously extended.

A SLOW BEGINNING

By 1717, the Assembly had divided the area into 132 lots, each portion consisting of two plots, and varying in size from 0.4 to 3.6 acres. The hope was that these would lead to residential and small-scale commercial developments similar to those successfully set in motion further upriver. The Assembly chose the lucky lot winners. In 1728, Charles Brooking's map of early Georgian Dublin showed a massive wall running from present-day Butt Bridge to about where the East Link Toll Bridge now meets the North Wall. This wall then turned northwards along present-day East Wall Road to Luke Kelly Bridge. However, this same map indicated that, despite the Assembly's best intentions, the North Wall area was 'as yet overflow'd by ye tide'. South of the Tolka, the reclaimed slob lands were divided into streets laid out in a grid-like pattern, which included Mayor St, Sheriff St, Commons St, Guild St, New Wapping St, Castle Forbes Rd (formerly Fish St), Seville Place, West Rd, Church Rd and East Rd. The Assembly named the first four of these streets after the Lord Mayor, the Sheriffs, the Guilds from which the Corporation was composed, and the Commons who elected them.

House building had still not begun in the North Lotts by the time John Rocque published his map of the city in 1756. The construction of the new Custom House from 1781 seems to have finally kick-started the first residential developments in the area, although these tended to be west of present-day Amiens Street. Many of the first houses were occupied by the artisans employed by Gandon on the Custom House project, such as the sculpting families of Smith, Schrowder and Foley who lived on Montgomery Street (now Foley Street). When work began on the Royal Canal in 1789, this brought more artisans and labourers to the area. Shops and warehouses slowly began to appear. The community gathered for merrymaking in the Curlew Tavern.

Top: Roscrea Meats was established during the Economic War with Britain in 1936. Here dockers load boneless beef into boxes for the Chicago International Packers Ltd.
Bottom: The dockers canteen opened from 7am - 5pm and served soup, sandwiches, coffee, tea, milk and lemonade. (Photos: Dublin Port Company Archives)

The Industrial Age

Top: A Morris conveyor system helps carry tiles into a North Wall warehouse.
Bottom: Stacking crates of bananas back in the days when everyone wore hats. (Photos: Dublin Port Company Archives)

THE GLASSHOUSE

Jesse Foley, father of the great Victorian sculptor John Henry Foley, arrived in the North Wall area from Winchester during the 1790s and took up work as a glassblower. In February 1787, *The Times* noted that 'a very considerable manufacture of glass has been opened upon the North Wall… in which several of the most capital workmen from Bristol have been engaged'. The business was started by 'a gentleman named Broughall, lately retired from business on a considerable fortune'. *The Times* believed it promised 'great profit' but warned that it would 'most matterially [sic] injure the English exportation of glass'. This was probably the manufacture of white flint glass, while plate glass for coaches was made and polished near the North Strand and another glass house in that vicinity exported services to Cadiz. From 1800, it is likely Broughall's factory employed a steam engine to carry out the grinding and polishing of the cast glass. The newspapers of 1787 speak of the iron mills of nearby Ballybough 'as furnishing spades, shovels and other implements of husbandry, likewise a variety of culinary utensils, equal to any theretofore imported'.

AN INDUSTRIAL LANDSCAPE

The Act of Union destroyed Dublin. Abandoned by its own Parliament, the City sank into economic decline. Development ground to a halt. In December 1810, *The Times* reported 'a dreadful fire' in the North Wall which 'wholly consumed' the Windmill and Corn Stores within five hours. The wall was again badly damaged by the great fire of 1833. Nonetheless, the area slowly emerged from the depression and, by the late 1830s, was once again a busy landscape of factories, belching chimneys and red-brick warehouses. These included 'His Majesty's Excise Stores' on Mayor Street, designed in 1821 by an unknown architect, possibly George Papworth. Now home to The Excise Bar and Restaurant, the building was used for storing spirits, kept in 16 barrel-vaulted compartments that ran down to the North Wall Quay. Another warehouse was used by the Ballast Office to hold 'sound and well-coopered casks' of rapeseed oil, seal oil and 'the best pale Spermacetl Oil' for 'use in the Irish light houses'. In 1844, John D'Alton noted that, within close proximity to the new Drogheda-Dublin railway line, there was a bottle factory, Kane's bleaching powder works and a soap boilery. The two funnels of the Dublin vitriol works on Ballybough Road dominated the skyline. But, for the most part, the North Lotts was still meadow, pasture and wasteland in the early years of Queen Victoria's reign. The 1838 Ordnance Survey map shows just seven large houses in the North Wall/East Wall area, while Sheriff Street comprised of a single terrace of five houses.

SHERIFF STREET PRISON

A prison is said to have stood on Sheriff Street during the early 18th century, built for French prisoners captured during the Napoleonic Wars. These same prisoners reputedly built the Boundary Wall surrounding the bonded warehouses of the Custom House Docks. Local historian Terry Fagan recalls meeting an old man who showed him some stables near Spencer Dock. There were iron rings in the stable walls to which, the old man said, 'they used to lock prisoners… while they waited on transportation'.

THE IRON HORSE

The residential composition of both North Wall and East Wall changed dramatically when the Dublin and Drogheda Railway (later the Great Northern Railway) arrived via an arched viaduct built over Seville Place in the 1840s. Within a few years there was a population of 4,000, mostly Catholics. The Roman Catholic Church began construction on the St Laurence O'Toole Church and Schools in 1844. The numbers were considerably swelled by the massive influx of men, women and children fleeing the Irish countryside in the wake of the devastating Famine.

AN AMAZONIAN REBEL

Revolutionary activity was never far from North Wall. In May 1848, *The Times* noted how, during the trial of Young Ireland leader John Mitchell, police were assailed on Seville Place by a mob, 'the chief leaders of which were women'. The correspondent marvelled at 'one amazon conspicuous of her daring. She hurled stones and brickbats with unerring aim at the constabulary, cursing lustily the cowardice of the men of Dublin in leaving the fighting to the women. All the efforts of the police to effect her capture were useless and she finally escaped in a crowd of combatants.'

THE CAMEL APPROACH

The original North Wall was not a magnificent work of engineering genius. James Gandon was the first of many who complained that it was in fact deceptively useless and a constant source of vexation to those who used it. The Ballast Office side-stepped the issue by continually repairing the wall and recruiting its engineer George Halpin to build the 'North Wall Basin' (known as Halpin's Pool and now part of the Alexandra Basin) to provide a deep-water berthing option for the new steamers. By the 1840s, the North Wall itself was described as a dismal swamp and had sunk from 10 to 15ft below the level of the roadway. The gap was filled with the refuse from the streets and the dredging of the river. There was scarcely a building of any kind left on it.

BOOM TIME

Between 1864 to 1869, the North Wall Quay was formidably rebuilt as a deepwater berth by Bindon Blood Stoney, Engineer-in-Chief to the Port and Docks Board. In 1873, the year the Spencer Dock opened, four of the main Irish railway companies united to form a general railway centre at the North Wall. Amongst the buildings constructed along the North Wall Quay were the Railway Hotel, the Freight Offices and the Wool Store. Meanwhile, the population continued to expand. In 1866, the Christian Brothers established a boy's school on Seville Place which, with Coburg Place, was now amongst the most upmarket addresses on the northside. When Lord Aberdeen and the Lord Mayor went on a tour of Dublin City in April 1886, they visited 'the extensive improvements being carried out in Seville Place'. Commons Street also became something of a well-to-do area, with hotels and boarding houses, while Sheriff Street thrived with greengrocers, butchers, a dairy, newsagents, a station and a post office. The 1876 Ordnance Survey Map of Dublin identifies a Vinegar & Charcoal Works on Sheriff Street. The 'Home Rule' merchant William Meagher, Lord Mayor of Dublin and MP for Meath, had his townhouse on Lower Sheriff Street in 1884.

THE MILK ROUND

Good news of a sort came to Sheriff Street with a report in 1866 from the Royal Dublin Society's milk tasters. 'We have stated that the principal object of this investigation was to determine whether the poor were worse supplied than the richer classes. It is therefore very pleasant to be enabled to state they are not – for Rathmines receives quite as bad milk as Brabazon Street or Great Britain Street, and the best of all is obtained from Sheriff Street in the heart of a decidedly poor district.'

THE FENIAN RISING

Sheriff Street was to the fore during the Fenian Rising of the 1860s, with many St Laurence O'Toole parishioners implicated. Among these were Francis Petit, a former sergeant with the 57th Regiment of Foot, who lived on Commons Street, and the informer Pierce Nagle, a church clerk in St Laurence's who later became a 'folder of newspapers' at the *Irish People* office. Nagle fared better than dockland labourer John Kenny, who was shot to death beneath the dark, damp arches of the Great Northern Railway off Seville Place in July 1882. He was killed for informing on Fenian activity in the area. A year later, a Sheriff Street tailor named Joe Poole was hanged for his murder in Richmond Prison. Poole was a member of the Invincibles but there is considerable doubt as to his guilt in Kenny's murder.

CHANGING TIMES

By the time the Protestant church of Saint Barnabas was built in 1870, North Wall and East Wall had become two very distinct communities, with the railway acting as a divisive boundary between the two. In 1873, the distinction was further defined when the Midland and Great Western Railway Company (MGWR) built the Spencer Dock, linking the Royal Canal directly to the River Liffey. In 1884, the so-called Loop Line was constructed, connecting Westland Row (Pearse Station) across the Liffey to Amiens Street (Connolly Station). With rail, canal and bridge links thriving in the neighbourhood, the riverside quay was soon studded with stores and warehouses. Many of these belonged to the highly competitive steam-packet companies. By 1890, all the land around the North Wall Quay, the Custom House Quay and Spencer Dock had been taken up by railway lines, warehouses and cattle yards. However, as the 20th century approached, North Wall was slowly evolving into one of Dublin's more impoverished inner-city landscapes. A good deal of Lower Mayor Street, from Commons Street to Guild Street, constituted tenements and stables. The tenement houses on Guild Street, Sheriff Street and Nixon Street were becoming dangerously overcrowded.

THE SISTERS OF CHARITY

Mary Aikenhead's Religious Sisters of Charity opened their pretty red-brick Convent of St Laurence O'Toole on Seville Place in November 1882. From here, the sisters visited the poor and sick, ran a primary school at East Wall, and served dinners from their large dining hall to poor men. In conjunction with the Catholic Social Service Committee, expectant mothers were also given nutritious dinners. The Sisters conducted a combined hostel for nuns and 'business girls', and a second one for girls out of employment. By Edwardian times, the Sisters were providing the celebrated 'St Anthony's penny dinners' to the poor. The Sisters continue to operate to this day and, in 2003, combined with the North Inner City Drugs Task Force to establish the Deora Project. This provides counselling for those suffering loss as a result of bereavement, suicide and addiction.

THE VANISHING RIVER

Lord Ormonde would have been very disappointed if he saw the River Liffey in the late Victorian Age. The City had once again turned its back on the river. By 1900, the waterfront along North Wall Quay comprised a long row of wall-to-wall sheds, warehouses and wharves, almost all owned by steam-packet and coal companies. All the railway companies had depots in the North Wall. As such, the place was thronged with passengers, freight and livestock. Thousands of men went to and fro on a daily basis, pushing carts, leading horses and ponies, hauling boxes, digging coal. The steel and concrete Scherzer Bridges at either end of the quay added to the industrial ambience. The Railway Hotel and the Harbour Master's garden provided the only green oases in this grimy landscape. Campion's Bar was one of a few other distractions. Indeed, walking down the North Wall Quay, you could quite easily forget that Dublin was on a river. The only way to reach the water was by walking through one of these sheds. That was the case whether you were a passenger awaiting a B&I ferry to England or a labourer unloading cargo onto a merchant ship. Knocking down that barrier and opening up the river was to be one of the first priorities of those in charge of regenerating the Custom House Docks from 1987.

100 YEARS AGO

In 1909, the 250 or so houses on Sheriff Street Lower and Upper had an appropriately diverse mix of private households, bootmakers, confectioners, vintners, grocers, coal stores, tobacconists, dressmakers, tea merchants, boarding houses, blacksmiths, warehouses and bonded stores. At its centre was St Barnabas's Church, where Séan O'Casey's mentor, the Rev Griffin, was incumbent, with T&C Martin's timber yard next door. On Upper Mayor Street, the buildings were more commercial – Haig & Haig wine and spirit merchants, the Liffey Wheel & Wagon Works and Saw Mill, the LNW Railway Building and Jonathan Potter's timber yard. Six houses were given to tenements and the remainder were occupied by two private individuals, the inspector of the LNWR and Thomas Reilly, a railway porter. Amongst the buildings on the North Wall itself were Mrs McEntee's Hotel, Prince Patrick's Hotel & Refreshment Rooms, The Old Ireland Hotel & Tavern, the Guinness shipping office, the Steam Packet Company ticket office, Ross & Walpole's iron and brass foundry, the Dublin & Glasgow Company cattleyard, the King's Excise Stores, and offices for agents of all British and Irish railway companies, as well as the Secretaries of the Irish Steamship Association and the British and Irish Steam Packet Co. The Dublin Total Abstinence Society was fighting a battle against six wine and spirit merchants. The Port and Docks Board was represented by the offices of its Engineer-in-Chief Sir John Purser Griffith and Harbourmaster Captain George Graves, RNR, as well as their patent slip, dry dock and at least nine landing sheds.

Left: Livestock were frequently exported from the North Wall. Right: Dockers gather on a cold winter morning to load the cargo ships. (Dublin Port Company Archives)

The 20th Century

FIRE ON THE NORTH WALL

In October 1910, the biggest fire of the year broke out in Archer's huge timber stores and sawmills on the North Wall. Dublin's brand new Leyland motor fire engine raced to the scene but the interior was already 'a sheet of flame shooting up in glowing showers of burning timber, illuminating the entire docklands'. The pens at the railway yard were hastily emptied of terrified cattle. The fire spread to the surrounding sheds and, were it not for the fire brigade's proximity to the water supply of the Liffey, would have engulfed some 20 cottage homes.

STRIKE AND LOCK-OUT

In 1911 Dublin's population of 305,000 registered a higher death rate than Calcutta. Twice as many deaths occurred in the city's workhouses and lunatic asylums than in the worst industrial slums of England. By 1913, one-third of Dublin's population were living in slums, with 26,000 families living in 5,000 tenements, many of which were in North Wall. The Corporation Buildings behind the Custom House were hit particularly hard. Discontent was understandably widespread amongst the working classes.

The Irish Transport and General Workers' Union (ITGWU) launched its first successful strike when carters and railway workers downed tools in 1911. In the midst of this strike, a timber merchant named TL Crowe drove down Sheriff Street with four horses. A mob surrounded him, shouting 'Blackleg!' and throwing stones and bottles. Knocked down and severely injured, Crowe pulled out a gun and fired two shots overhead to keep the crowd back. His revolver was wrenched from him and he was beaten on the head with sticks and stones. He survived to identify two of his assailants in the Northern Police Court two days later.

During the Strike and Lock-Out of 1913, workers at the Gas Company stores refused to supply T&C Martin's timber yards on Sheriff Street. Five weeks later, the Royal Irish Constabulary baton-charged a crowd of 500 strikers on Sheriff Street who had been throwing stones at 'free labourers' as they walked to work in the docks.

Another riot took place when strikers attacked police and strike-breakers walking up Commons Street. Unsurprisingly the North Wall was in the thick of the action during the War of Independence, as perhaps best exemplified by the St Laurence O'Toole GAA Club. (See page 106).

THE WORKING MAN'S HIERARCHY

For the North Wall, the middle decades of the 20th century were inevitably marred by the continuing decline of the docklands, as bigger ships tended to berth further downriver beyond the Alexandra Basin. It wasn't all bad. In 1925, the cement and plaster manufacturer Chadwicks established extensive new storage and stabling facilities on Sheriff Street in buildings leased from the Great Northern Railway. But serious decline set in with the coming of hydraulic forklifts and containerisation. Unemployment became rife, although there were still thousands of dockers operating in the area, loading and unloading the huge cargos of sugar, tea, spirits, fruit, coal, timber and machinery which arrived daily. Many joined the Merchant Navy in the 1940s. Many more emigrated to England to rebuild the cities and motorways after the war. The North Wall has particularly strong links to Birmingham as few of those who emigrated ever returned.

For those in the Port Yard who stayed behind, there was a clatter of pubs wherein the soul could at least emigrate. They drank in The Kind Lady, Jock's, Campion's Mullet's, Cleary's, McCormack's, The Blue Lion and The Railway Bar on Sheriff Street, where legendary blues singer Don Baker once worked. A strict hierarchy was always in operation, with very definite rules as to who could drink in which pub. 'Apartheid between the different trades was unbelievable', recalls engineer Niall Dardis. 'The pubs were an extension of the canteens in the Port yard - and there were 13 canteens. The electricians had one. But the electrician's assistants couldn't eat in the same canteen, so they had one of their own. The very same with the fitters and turners, the builders, the shipwrights, the motoring department … and the dockers weren't allowed into the place at all. If you crossed the boundary, you'd come home black and blue'.

CASUALS & BUTTON-MEN

Amongst the dockers themselves, there was also a fierce distinction between casual workers and 'button-men'. When dockers joined the Union, they were given buttons that identified their particular line of work - cross-channel buttons, deep-sea buttons, coal-buttons and so forth. When the stevedore, or 'ganger', was picking men on the read in the morning, the button-men were almost certainly guaranteed work. 'You, you, you and you'. After the button-men left, the ganger then decided which, if any, of the 'casuals' would be given work. Oftentimes the gangers drank tea inside and left the 'casual's standing out in rain and sleet while they made up their minds. It was all about who you knew. Moreover, if you wanted work, you had to 'look after' the ganger in the pub that night. Terry Fagan recalls being paid in Campion's by two such gangers after a day stacking beef down at the Otto Zero freezer by the Point. 'You had to buy them a whiskey with your wages. At the end of the night, they'd stack all the glasses, pour the whiskey back into the bottle and cash it in'

STATE INTERVENTION

In the 1930s, Dublin Corporation attempted to solve its housing problems by clearing the slums and building the now-demolished Sheriff Street flats. (See page 112). In 1938, the St Laurence O'Toole Boys School closed and its pupils relocated to the Christian Brother School on Seville Place, a stuccoed Modernist idiom built by Robinson and Keefe in 1936. The State made some efforts to stem the tide of despair when, in 1941, they set in motion a new central bus station beside the Custom House at Busáras. In 1950 the Department of Posts and Telegraphs purchased the lands to the north of the Custom House Docks adjoining Sheriff Street, which it developed as the new Central Sorting Office. This public sector intervention ultimately proved invaluable in preserving some form of life in these areas until the private sector finally came along to make its presence felt.

Below: Byrne's map of Dublin was made in 1819 and dedicated to Augustus Frederick FitzGerald, Duke of Leinster. (Photo: Royal Dublin Society)

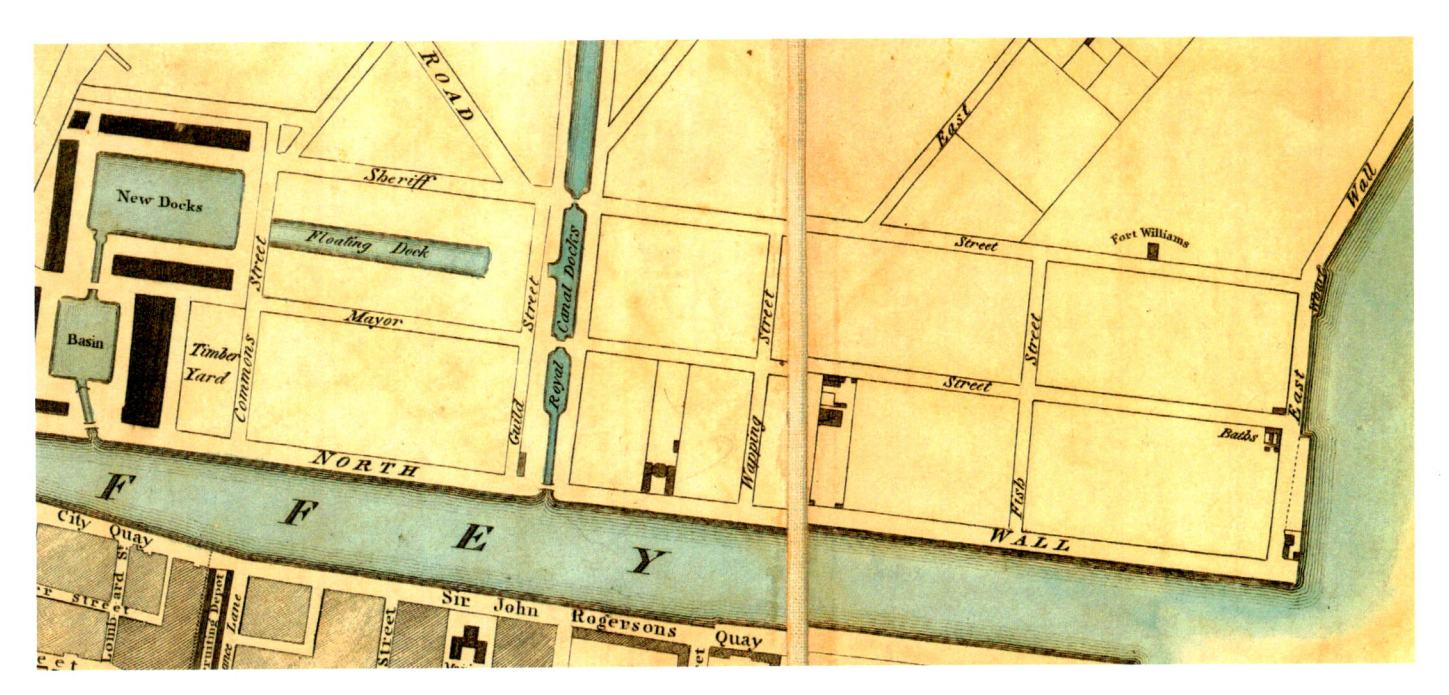

Scherzer Rolling Lift Bridges

A hundred years ago, if you mistimed yourself and arrived in your motorcar on the North Wall Quay just as the double-track drawbridge of Spencer Dock was opening, you might as well have pulled out your hip-flask and settled in for the night. The process of opening the Turner & Gibson drawbridge involved a mesmerizing but rather protracted series of events – decks on rollers slowly creaking horizontally as thin, muscley men heaved upon the mighty winches. It took a whopping 22 minutes from start to finish and that was just to let a single vessel pass in or out of the Dock, the entrance to the Royal Canal. Sir John Purser Griffith, Chief Engineer to the Dublin Port and Docks Board, decided this wait was unacceptable.

In 1912, a new system was installed – the twinned Scherzer Rolling Lift Bridges, an innovative design patented by Chicago engineer William Scherzer. This revolutionary bridge successfully debuted when it opened across the Chicago River in 1895. The North Wall structures follow the same principal. Two steel girders are rigidly connected to large steel rollers, curved like the rocking part of a rocking chair, and weighted at the rear to counterbalance the span.

To open, the bridges simply roll back on their rockers until upright like a jack-knife. The floors of the Dublin bridges were composed of 'buckled plates', an invention of Dublin-born engineer Robert Mallet, a specialist on earthquakes known in science circles as 'the father of seismology'. These plates were riveted to the floor beams and to joists fitted between the beams. Each bridge was operated by electric motors, since removed, or manually in the case of a power failure. The suspension time for traffic was dramatically cut from 22 to 4 ½ minutes for a single vessel.

These bascule bridges were such a success that, in 1932, another pair were installed by Sir William Arrol & Co of Glasgow at the entrance to George's Dock from the Liffey. These elaborate Scherzer Bridges are now landmark features along the south and north end of Spencer Dock, and at the entrance to George's Dock. The bridge at New Wapping Street has been completely refurbished and will soon be fully operational again. The bridge at George's Dock is the subject of a lighting project that illuminate its structural lines. The bridge by Sheriff Street, which operates as a lock gate between Spencer Dock and the Royal Canal, is notable for its rugged and rusty industrial complexion at time of writing.

Above: The Scherzer Rolling Lift, also known as a Rolling Bascule Bridge, was still a revolutionary technology when installed on North Wall in 1912. (Photo: Stu Carroll)

The MV Cill Airne

A FLOATING BAR AND RESTAURANT
Now berthing some 500m from the Séan O'Casey Bridge on the North Wall Quay, the *MV Cill Airne* was built in the Liffey Dockyards in 1961 and was one of the last riveted ships built in Europe. After nearly 40 years in Cork, the ship returned to Dublin in 2007 and has been splendidly renovated to house a floating bar, the inimitable White Bar, as well as two restaurants, the 'smart-casual' Quay 16 Restaurant and the Blue River Bistro Bar. This evokes the memory of *MV Arran,* an inter-island ferry from Scotland that berthed outside present-day Jury's in the 1970s and operated as a bar.

A PRESIDENTIAL ESCORT
The Cill Airne was built at the Liffey Dockyard and designed by architects Graham & Woolnough of Liverpool, a team clearly inspired by the Mersey Ferries. She and her sister ship, the *Blarna*, were commissioned by the Irish Government on 12th July 1961. Their immediate role was to meet the huge Atlantic Ocean luxury liners outside Cork Harbour and bring both mail and passengers into Cork City. The *Cill Airne*, 150ft long and 40ft wide, could accommodate up to 1,500 passengers at once – and the occasional motorcar, perhaps belonging to a wealthy American headed on a driving tour around Ireland. Amongst those carried to and from Irish shores by the ship were comic legend Stan Laurel and former US President Dwight 'Ike' Eisenhower.

RIVETING STUFF
The *Cill Airne* and the *Blarna* were amongst the very last riveted ships built in Europe. From the 1930s, riveting was rapidly replaced by electric arc welding but the incredible production of the Liberty ships during the Second World War sealed the fate of riveting forever. It seems the decision to rivet the *Cill Airne* and her sister was a political one, designed to maintain employment for the last of the riveting crews in the Liffey Dockyards.

THE SCHOOL BOAT
With the rise of the airlines in the 1970s, the luxury cruise trade succumbed and both ships became unemployed. The *Blarna* was sold to a ferry company in Quebec. The *Cill Airne*, berthed on the Custom House Quay in Cork, became a training vessel for marine engineers at the National Maritime Training College, Ringaskiddy. Here, students mastered radar, lifeboat and engine-room practices. With the necessary removal of certain life-saving devices, her capacity was cut to 500. Nonetheless, she continued to sail out on the Lee every fortnight to Cobh and back, with a band playing on her deck. It was from the *Cill Airne's* deck that the incoming Lord Mayor of Cobh traditionally celebrated the ´throwing of the dart´ every year, to represent the staking of his jurisdiction.

THE RESTORATION
In 2003, the Maritime College was relocated to a new state-of-the-art building with a mock-up engine room and ship sailing simulators, making the *Cill Airne* obsolete. The college put the vessel up for auction where she was purchased by a group of Dublin City investors. She was acquired by the Irish Ship and Barge Fabrication Company and moved to West Cork in spring 2006. She spent nine months in Hegarty's Boatyard, Skibbereen, undergoing major restoration work with a team of old-style shipwrights. The work has ensured the long-term preservation of the ship. Her engine room must be one of the few where one can hold a conversation whilst the engines are running. One commentator described her Crossley five-cylinder two-stroke engines as purring 'like a Singer sewing machine'. The *Cill Airne* is already a Docklands icon. Her sister, *Blarna*, left Cork in the mid-1960s and made her way from Bermuda to Canada, where she was recently up for sale as the *Gobelet d'Argent II*.

Above: The Cill Airne, now a floating bar and restaurant, is permanently anchored off the North Wall.

The London & North Western Railway Company

BIRTH OF THE IRISH MAIL

For many generations of Irish emigrants, the exodus from Ireland began when they boarded a Holyhead-bound ship at the North Wall. The first of these ships were the official packet ships that carried post between London and Dublin. In time this developed into a full-blown mail-coach service which, by 1819, departed London at 8pm and, favourable winds permitting, arrived in Dublin two evenings later. In August 1848, the Holyhead-Kingstown (Dún Laoghaire) paddle-steamer service began when the Chester & Holyhead Railway Company combined forces with the London & North Western Railway Company (LNWR) to launch an express railway service to London Euston. Known as the *'Irish Mail'*, this link ensured Holyhead's predominance as the main point for the transfer of mail from London. In October 1861, the LNWR transferred its main passenger terminal from Kingstown to a point just east of the Royal Canal on the North Wall Quay.

THE NORTH WALL STATION

By the 1870s, the LNWR had become the 'Premier Line' and was the largest joint stock company in the United Kingdom. In 1877, it made a concerted effort to improve its facilities in Dublin Port. A branch line was built to connect the Amiens Street (Connolly Station) network with the North Wall Quay, where the LNWR mailboats were moored. The connecting trains featured the same 'blackberry black' engines and 'purple lake' coaches as the larger locomotives operating across the Irish Sea. Between 1890 and 1907, it also constructed the North Wall Railway Station for both goods and passengers. Special 'boat trains' came from Kingsbridge (now Heuston Station) along the Liffey quays to North Wall Station and connected with the LNWR steamers.

THE FINAL CALL

The station has a somewhat poignant association with the First World War. For many who served with the British Army during that period, this was the last Dublin building they entered before boarding the troop ships and heading to the trenches. After the war, the station was converted to freight usage. It is now used by Irish Rail as a freight-handling depot and administrative offices. The glass may be gone but the elaborate Victorian canopy still sweeps over the curving section of the concourse.

EMPLOYMENT PERKS

Many young men from East Wall and North Wall areas found work on the LNWR. They often joined at the age of 14. After two years they would be made permanent and called 'juniors'. On reaching 21, they became 'traffic handlers' (labourers). Unlike other railway employees who had to buy their own uniforms, the LNWR staff were provided with free uniforms. In the early 1880s, the LNWR built a number of new houses on Mayor Street and along the east side of New Wapping Street. These houses were occupied by LNWR staff but had to be 'surrendered on retirement'. The 1901 Census shows that of the 10 family heads living on New Wapping Street, only two were born in Dublin.

The rest came from the fields of the Irish countryside and one from Scotland. It might have been tough work but for farmer's sons, working on the labouring gangs of the railways was uncomplicated, reasonably healthy and rewarding. As you fell asleep with aching back and blistered hands, at least there were shillings in your palm.

CONFLICT AND VICTORY

In the early 1900s, the Dublin Port & Docks Board raised the dues chargeable on the LNWR's ships at the North Wall. The company took this as an excuse to abandon the North Wall and return to Kingstown. All four of their mailboats were requisitioned by the Admiralty as troop ships. The *Hibernia* was sunk in 1915. In 1921, the British railway system was reorganised and the LNWR became the London, Midland & Scottish Railway Company (LMS). It continued to operate the Dún Laoghaire-Holyhead service until it was nationalised in 1948, ultimately forming the basis for Sealink. The LNWR cargo ships continued to operate from the North Wall after 1908, as they did under all its successors-in-title, including Stena Sealink. Car ferries were introduced to the Dún Laoghaire-Holyhead service in 1965 and have been sailing twice daily, when weather permits, ever since.

THE RAILWAY HOTEL

In 1883, increased traffic between the ferry and railway prompted the LNWR to purchase the Prince of Wales Hotel at the junction of New Wapping Street and the North Wall. It replaced the original building with a new ornate hotel, renamed the London and North Western Hotel. It opened in 1890 and provided much employment in the locality. The hotel was occupied by the Black and Tans during the War of Independence and was a frequent target of the IRA. It became known as the British Rail Hotel after the nationalization of the railways but ceased to be a hotel during the 1920s. It now contains offices of Irish Rail, including the architects department. Beside the hotel stands a handsome but largely derelict three-storey building known locally as the Wool Store. Constructed between 1847 and 1864, this was originally designed as a port facility but was subsequently incorporated into the North Wall Station. The ground floor was formerly used as stables by the LNWR. In the 1940s, it was referred to as the Wool Warehouse Stable.

Right: *The Irish Mail* ran from Holyhead to London Euston. It was a journey familiar to many Irish emigrants. (Derek Head) Below: The Railway Hotel stands to the right of the old Wool Store.

B & I (aka The British & Irish Steam Packet Company)

THE EARLY DAYS

The British & Irish Steam Packet Company was founded in 1836 by a group of Dublin businessmen including Francis Carleton (also a director of the City of Dublin Steam Packet Company), James Jameson (of the distillery) and Arthur Guinness (of the brewery). The company took over the business of the Dublin & London Steam Packet Company. Its first ships were wooden-paddle steamers and operated between Dublin and London, calling at Southampton and Plymouth. In 1842, their new ship, the *Duke of Cornwall*, began services from the North Wall to London, stopping at Plymouth and Falmouth.

THE MOVE TO NORTH WALL

In 1845, B&I announced it was abandoning paddle steamers in favour of propeller-driven iron ships. *The Rose* and *the Shamrock* were the first such steam ships to run the Dublin-to-London gauntlet. In 1860, the company transferred its offices from Eden Quay to 46, North Wall. By 1878, the company was also based on Sir John Rogerson's Quay. Its riverside sheds still stand on the waterfront today, beside the company's two-storey Edwardian offices. Its ships were considered amongst the best in Europe before the Great War, boasting 100 saloon-class cabins, as well as 50 state rooms, smoking rooms and bathrooms.

THE LOVELY LADIES

In 1917, B&I was one of a number of cross-channel shipping companies absorbed into the massive new UK-based Coast Lines Group. The legendary B&I link between the North Wall and Liverpool began in 1920 with *Lady Wicklow*, *Lady Louth* and *Lady Carlow* sailing the course. In 1938, the company launched two new motor ships, the *Leinster* and *Munster*, built by Harland & Wolff, which covered the Dublin to Liverpool crossing far more effectively and economically. These were far and away the most advanced cross-channel ferries in existence at that time. With the outbreak of war in 1939, the Dublin-Liverpool service was suspended. *The Munster* was transferred to the Belfast-Liverpool service and was sunk in Liverpool Bay by a mine in February 1940; all 200 passengers and 50 crew were rescued by the *Ringwall*, a coalship that belonged to

Above: The *Leinster* at sea, shortly after it joined the B&I service in 1981. Below: The *Munster* on the home straight from Holyhead in 1990. (Photos: Aiden McCabe)

the Wallace Brothers of Ringsend. The *Leinster* served as a hospital ship and survived the war intact; she later moved to the Belfast-Liverpool line and was renamed Ulster Prince. Another ship, the *Innisfallen*, was bombed and sunk in Liverpool.

DECLINE AND FALL

In 1946, B&I began rebuilding its fleet and ordered two new ships from Harland & Wolff. Slightly longer, slightly smaller, the new *Leinster* and *Munster* took up the Liverpool service in 1948. In time they were joined by the *Connacht*. However, the transport industry was in constant revolution during the 1950s; spanking new ships could quickly seem very outdated. Coast Lines hesitated with the development of the B&I Line and consequently allowed it to stagnate. In 1965, the Irish government purchased B&I from the Coast Lines Groups and appointed a new board. Two years later they made the controversial decision to replace the passenger ships with roll on-roll off (ro-ro) car ferries. However, the increased availability and the massive reduction in the cost of flights were gradually removing the passenger ferry's domination of the travel industry.

END OF THE LINE

By the mid 1980s, the B&I Line was struggling to stay afloat. An attempt to depose Sealink from the Holyhead monopoly failed. The Cork service was closed and *the Munster* sold. Losses kept mounting. Officers went on strike. The Liverpool service was closed and the *Connacht* sold. In 1990, the government privatised the company and sold it to the Irish Continental Group, trading as Irish Ferries. Today, Irish Ferries runs two ships between Dublin Ferryport and Holyhead – the *Jonathan Swift* fast ferry (1 hour, 49 minutes) and the company's flagship, the *Ulysses*. The latter was the world's largest car ferry at its construction in 2001.

With a wack-fiddle-day
Paddy gonna go on a holiday
Leavin' on a B & I Ferry
Tomorrow
Ain't gonna be no sorrow
Cos I'm leavin tomorrow

From 'B & I Ferry', written by Shane MacGowan

Above: Strikers gather outside the B&I steamer sheds on Sir John Rogerson's Quay during the 1913 Lock Out. Built in 1909, these sheds were designed for holding cargo and passenger luggage. (Photos: Dublin Port Company Archives)

The 100-Ton Crane / North Wall Extension

THE 100-TON CRANE (1905 – 1985)

In 1901, Sir John Purser Griffith, 'Engineer in Chief' of Dublin Port, visited his friend Johannes Dalmann, Chief Engineer of Hamburg Port. Dalmann introduced Griffith to the new concept of electricity-driven cranes sweeping into the industrial belt of Kaiser Wilhelm II's increasingly powerful Fatherland. Griffith sold the idea to his employers, reminding them that the new Corporation electricity depot at the Pigeon House was about to come on-stream. The Port and Docks Board gave him the nod and soon the Munich-based MAN AG engineering company was manufacturing Ireland's first electric crane. Its motors were designed by Siemens Brothers of London. The 100-Ton Crane stood on the North Wall Quay Extension. When it was erected in 1904, the foreman was so confident in his men's ability that he stood directly beneath it when the first 100-ton load was lifted. The crane quickly became a major landmark to such an extent that, when the Great War finally ended, the highest flag in Dublin hung from its beams. For 81 years, it stood and worked, day in, day out, loading and unloading. It was a long way up the spiral staircase to the top of the crane. Niall Dardis, who worked in the engineer's office for many decades, said you'd be 'pucked' by the time you got there. 'The smell in it was desperate', he recalled. 'Pigeons would roost in it and make their mess and there was always broken eggs'. One of its last jobs was the unloading of the Dart carriages in the early 1980s. By then it had been de-rated to 50 tons as the foundation bolts holding it had started to weaken. In 1986 the crane was decommissioned and, some time later, demolished.

THE NORTH WALL EXTENSION

Between 1871 and 1885, Bindon Blood Stoney oversaw the construction of the North Wall Extension running towards the Poolbeg Lighthouse. This 700m/2296ft-long, deep-water quay brought Stoney considerable international attention on account of his pioneering and cost-effective technique of building the wall with pre-cast concrete blocks. Each block weighed an unprecedented 360 tons and was made from Portland cement and gravel from the riverbed. These huge blocks were lifted across the water by an enormous iron floating crane, or shears, specially invented by Stoney. Each block was then dropped into a position specially prepared by men working from the celebrated diving bell, also designed by Stoney.

Above: The electric 100 Ton Crane was built in Germany and began operating in 1905.
Left: Dockers at work carting fruit into transit sheds along the North Wall. (Photos: Aiden McCabe)

St Laurence O'Toole Pipe Band

The year 2008 was a golden one for the St Laurence O'Toole Pipe Band, with victories in the British, Scottish, All-Ireland and Mid-Ulster Pipe Band Championships, and second place in the European and Cowal Championships. The band was also crowned Champions Supreme for 2008 – the first non-UK band to take the title and the first new name on the trophy since 1976.

Although presently based in Tallaght, the Pipe Band's origins are firmly rooted in the Docklands. Its history began in 1910 with a meeting of the St. Laurence O'Toole Gaelic Athletic Association Club held at the Christian Brother School in Seville Place. Amongst those in attendance were the future Easter 1916 martyrs Thomas Clarke (President of the band), Pádraig Pearse and Seán McDermott, as well as Sinn Féin founder Arthur Griffith, future Irish President Douglas Hyde and the playwright Seán O'Casey. The club decided to form a Pipe Band with O'Casey as first Secretary and future Senator Michael Colgan as the first Pipe Major.

O'Casey raised a good deal of money for the club through plays staged by the St Laurence O'Toole Dramatic Society. By the time the General Strike was called in 1913, the band were sufficiently well established to lead a contingent of workers on a protest rally to the Irish Trade Union headquarters at Liberty Hall. They were set upon by mounted police at Lombard Street, who wounded some members and smashed their instruments. The band headquarters on Seville Place were inevitably and repeatedly attacked by the British military during the War of Independence. They played at the funerals of many nationalist leaders, including Thomas Ashe, O'Donovan Rossa, Arthur Griffith and Michael Collins.

The band had ceased to have any political affiliations by the time they became the first band to be broadcast on the newly formed Radio Éireann in the 1930s. Their performance at the Cowal Games in Scotland in 1925 was one of the earliest broadcast in Scotland. St. Laurence O'Toole's were also the first Irish pipe band to visit England and America.

The Halpins - Father & Son

Perhaps the most dominant partnership operating in the Docklands during the first half of the 19th century was the engineering father-and-son team of George Halpin (1775 – 1854) and George Halpin Junior (1804 – 1869). The elder George was certainly one of the most competent civil engineers Ireland has ever produced. He was an administrator of exceptional ability, praised in equal measure for the extraordinary number of works he carried out and the intense perfectionism applied in each case. We do not yet know where he was born or who his parents were. George Halpin was a trained mason, a builder by trade, and never attained any academic engineering qualifications. His lucky break came in 1800 when, following the death of Francis Tunstall, Dublin Corporation sought a new Inspector of the Corporation for Preserving and Improving the Port of Dublin (known as the Ballast Office). George was just 25 years old when he got the job. His role was to oversee the design, construction and maintenance of all civil and mechanical works within Dublin Port, from Sutton on the north side of Dublin Bay to Bullock Harbour on the south.

During his 54 years of service, George Halpin built up a truly outstanding portfolio. One of his greatest achievements was to completely rebuild the walls of the Liffey on both sides of the river from Rory O'More Bridge to the Custom House. He also raised that better-built part of the South Wall east of the Half-Moon Battery to its present height. As Inspector of Lighthouses, he oversaw the construction of at least 53 of the 72 lighthouses operating in Ireland by 1867'.

In 1830, the Ballast Office officially appointed George's son and namesake, George Halpin Junior, to be his assistant Inspector of Works and assistant Inspector of Lighthouses. Between 1834 and 1840, the younger George was greatly involved in deepening the channels and building new quay walls east of the Custom House.

The workload was intense. In July 1854, George Halpin Senior collapsed and died while carrying out a lighthouse inspection. His son duly succeeded as Chief Engineer to the Ballast Office but he too was already dogged by ill-health. This was probably due to the stresses of his job, the travel and long absences involved in going from one damp lighthouse to the next. The Ballast Office relieved him of his duties at the Port, passing them over to his assistant, Bindon Blood Stoney.

A rift soon emerged between Halpin and Stoney. While Halpin was away from Dublin on lighthouse duties, his ambitious assistant submitted a proposal to the Board advocating the extension of the North Wall Quay by using 350-ton super-blocks, to be put in position by means of a special floating crane and diving bell. Halpin was furious that Stoney had gone to the Office without first consulting him. He also argued that the size of the proposed blocks was unfeasible. Stoney begged to differ, pointing out that blocks of similar size had been successfully used in London Port for many years. The Board were eager to act on Stoney's cost-effective proposals but did not wish to offend Halpin.

As it happened, Halpin saved their embarrassment when he retired in March 1862. Stoney was appointed the new Inspector of Works and, in 1868, became the first Engineer-in-Chief of the newly constituted Dublin Port and Docks Board. George Halpin Junior died in Dublin in 1869.

Below: Work on the handsome Poolbeg lighthouse commenced under George Halpin Junior and was completed in 1869, a year after his death. (Photo: John Wallace). Far left: The St Laurence O'Toole Pipe Band was founded in 1910 with playwright Seán O'Casey as its first secretary. (Photo: Mervyn Herron)

Bindon Blood Stoney (1828 – 1909)

Walking the southside Docklands today, many newcomers find themselves looking twice at the name of a street called Blood Stoney Road. It all sounds rather grim. However, the road is in fact dedicated to one of the most remarkable civil engineers to emerge in Ireland during the late 19th century. Bindon Blood Stoney, LLD, FRS, EC, was chief engineer to the Port and Docks Board for nearly 40 years from 1859 to 1898. His constant resourcefulness has led one recent scholar to christen the impressively bearded engineer 'the father of Irish concrete'.

In his younger years, Bindon Blood Stoney was first mathematical assistant to the 3rd Earl of Rosse at the Parsonstown Observatory in Birr. His astronomical observations included the most accurate delineations of nebulae then known, including a remarkably accurate sketch of the spiral character of the great nebula in Andromeda. In 1852 he went to Spain to work as an engineer on the railways construction. He returned to Ireland to help build the Boyne Railway Viaduct which, when completed in 1857, boasted the longest span in the world. In 1856, Stoney was appointed Assistant Engineer to George Halpin, Jnr, at the Ballast Office. By 1859, with Halpin dogged by ill-health, 31-year-old Stoney was acting as executive engineer. He succeeded Halpin as Inspector of Works in 1862.

In 1868, he became Engineer-in-Chief of the newly constituted Dublin Port and Docks Board. In this capacity, he greatly improved the channel between Dublin Bay and the City with a specially designed dredging plant. He rebuilt nearly 7,000ft of quay walls along both north and south banks of the River Liffey, replacing the tidal berths with deepwater berths for overseas vessels. He built O'Connell Bridge, as well as the North Wall Extension and the 70-acre Alexandra Basin. For both the Extension and Basin, he used the pioneering technique of pre-cast concrete blocks, lifted across the water by an enormous iron floating crane, or shears, specially invented by Stoney. The landing ground for each block was prepared by men working within a huge diving bell, also designed by Stoney, now located on Sir John Rogerson's Quay (See page 180). He later employed the same strategy at the Poolbeg lighthouse, using the shears to deposit large concrete rubble blocks around its base and so give it added protection against winter storms.

As Engineer-in-Chief, it was Stoney's job to look after and improve everything the Halpins had either built or maintained. From his office on the North Wall, he pored over charts and drawings, examined tenders and specifications, considered the implications of 'three screw iron hopper barges' and 'double steam dredgers', arranged for the installation of fog sirens and bells for lighthouses and kept a very close eye on the river walls and the Liffey bridges. When the Prince and Princess of Wales came to formally open the Alexandra Basin in 1885, it was widely rumoured Stoney was in for a knighthood but nothing came of it. He retired in 1898 and died at his Elgin Road residence on 5th May 1909.

Sir John Purser Griffith (1848 – 1938)

Sir John was born in 1848 at Holyhead, Wales, where his father was a Congregational minister with the Moravian church. He owed his second given name to a longstanding friendship between his father and John Tertius Purser, owner of Rathmines Castle. Purser's great-grandfather John (Primus) and father John (Secundus) both worked as senior brewers with Guinness in Dublin and became partners in 1820. In the 1860s, Sir John went to stay with the Pursers in Dublin and entered Trinity College, where he took his License in Civil Engineering in 1868. Three years later, he married Tertius Purser's daughter, the marvellously named Nina Benigna Fridlezius Purser (1837–1912). John might have expected a reasonable dowry from Tertius Purser. However, Tertius was a religious man and, when Sunday drinking was introduced to pubs in 1882, he retired from the brewery and emigrated, barrel money in hand, to San Francisco. Nina inherited Rathmines Castle when her brothers – both unmarried university professors – predeceased her.

After Trinity, John served under Bindon Blood Stoney, the Engineer in Chief of the Dublin Port and Docks, and was at his side throughout the successful North Wall Extension. When Stoney retired due to ill health in 1898, Griffith inevitably succeeded as Engineer-in-Chief, retaining the post for 15 years. His achievement at Dublin Port included the deepening of the approaches to the quays, many of which were rebuilt. In 1903 and 1907, he proposed improving the Custom House Docks by the demolition of 'the Queen's Timber Yard, Stack A, Georges Dock outer, Stack C and the old dock', which he maintained were 'obsolete and unsuited to the present-day requirements of the port'. Fortunately the project did not go ahead. In 1913, he retired and was succeeded by his son, John William Griffith (1875 – 1936).

In the Coronation Honours of June 1911, he received a knighthood from George V for his valuable services to the Port and Docks Board, and to the Royal Commission on Canals. However, Sir John was an outspoken critic of the Board's financial policies, in particular their penchant for cutting staff to save money. In July 1916, he resigned from the Board and, the following day, his son tendered his resignation as Engineer in Chief. The younger John was succeeded by Joseph H Mallagh.

Following retirement, Sir John worked in private practice as one of the Empire's foremost Consulting Engineers. He was perhaps best known for kick-starting the Irish peat industry in the 1920s. He was also a considerable influence in the creation of the Poulaphouca Reservoir, which gave Ireland a second hydroelectric station and provided a major water supply for South Dublin. In the 1930s, Sir John and his late wife's cousin, Sarah Purser, endowed the Purser Griffith Travelling Scholarship and the Purser Griffith Prize to the two best-performing students in European Art History at University College Dublin. The veteran engineer died at Rathmines Castle in Dublin on 21st October 1938.

St. Laurence O'Toole's (Roman Catholic) Church

ARCHBISHOP LAURENCE O'TOOLE

Saint Laurence O'Toole was born near Castledermot, Co Kildare, in 1128. As a young boy he was taken hostage by the MacMurroughs and imprisoned in a herdsman's hut with just enough food to survive. After his release, he entered the church, becoming Abbot of Glendalough and then, aged 32, Archbishop of Dublin, the first native-born Irishman ever to fill the See. His elevation marked the end of Scandinavian domination in Dublin. As Archbishop he made a considerable impact on improving the lot of the poor, paying for certain people to holiday in the fresher climates of England.

Laurence was centre stage for the Anglo-Norman invasion of 1169 as his sister was married to Dermot MacMurrough, the villain of Irish history blamed for inviting the Normans to Ireland. During the subsequent peace negotiations, Laurence was the foremost ambassador for Irish interests. His efforts took their toll and he died in 1180 on the coast of Normandy following a meeting with King Henry II.

He was buried in the Augustinian Abbey at Eu where his shrine still survives in the parish church. He was canonized just 45 years after his death. In 1914, a small bone from his hand was brought from Eu to Dublin and the relic was placed in a shrine in the St Laurence O'Toole Church on Sheriff Street.

CHARLES KENNEDY AND THE FOUNDATION STONE

The arrival of the Dublin & Drogheda Railway (later the Great Northern Railway) in the early 1840s created huge employment opportunities in the North Wall. By 1843, the population of the North Dock Ward was estimated at nearly 4,000, mostly Catholics. Daniel Murray, the Catholic Archbishop of Dublin and co-founder of St Vincent's Hospital, insisted that such a large population should have a church. A generous benefactor, Charles Kennedy gifted the church a triangular plot, measuring 20,000sq ft, on the corner of Seville Place and Sheriff Street.

At the time, Church Road came to a point just opposite Kennedy's land. However, with the expansion of the railways and canals, the southern end of Church Road was cut off from Seville Place and its community vanished into East Wall. Kennedy, whose coffin lies in St Laurence's vault today, also provided donations amounting to £1,000 (£68,450 today's value). This ignited a major fund-raising drive. The architectural contract was awarded to Joseph B Keane, who conceived a spacious church of dressed limestone built in the Gothic style. The first stone was laid on 13th June 1844. In 1847, the first stones of the St Laurence O'Toole schools were laid just behind the church.

OPEN FOR BUSINESS

The opening ceremony of the landmark Catholic Church took place on 24th June 1850 and was attended by 13 bishops, including the new Primate, Dr Paul Cullen. The clergy of the diocese donated the altar, made of Carrara marble from Italy. In October 1853, the district of Seville Place was declared a separate parish. The first parish priest and school manager was Father Michael Farrington PP. One of the Church's regular parishioners was the revered ascetic Matt Talbot, who worked as a labourer in Messrs T&C Martin's timber yards just next door to the church. He often came to morning Mass direct from his job in the creosote yard, the tar from the sleepers still shimmering on his clothes. Amongst other parishoners was Church Road resident Patrick Byrne, a Kildare man who lived at No 10. In 1903, Patrick married Isabella Carrick in this same church. Upon the outbreak of the Great War, he joined the 6th Battalion of the Royal Dublin Fusiliers and died at Gallipoli aged 43.

UNION OF PARISHES

In 1941 the East Wall & North Strand Parish was formed from part of St Laurence O'Toole's. This included the flock of St Joseph's Church in East Wall, built in 1919 and rebuilt in 1956. The church still opens for morning and evening services throughout the week.

Above: A herd of cattle make their way down Sheriff Street from the Prussia Street Cattle Market to the North Wall where they are to be shipped to England. (Photo: Paddy Curtis Collection).

St Laurence O'Toole's GAA Club

The St Laurence O'Toole GAA club was founded on Seville Place in 1888 and, associated with the Gaelic League from earliest times, became one of the most iconic clubs in the city. During the Easter Rebellion of 1916, over 70 members of the O'Toole club took their stand among the city garrisons. Tom Clarke, President of the St Laurence O'Toole Pipers, was executed after the Rising, as was Seán MacDermott, a non-playing member of the O'Toole club. Other club members who took part included Liam O'Briain, Professor of Romance Languages at UCG; Citizen Army Sergeant, Frank Robbins, who later became Chairman of the Dublin Port and Docks Board; and Tom Ennis, who was later a Free State Army General.

The 1920s was the football club's golden age, winning two All-Ireland and five Leinster titles. Between 1918 and 1931, the club won the Dublin Senior Club Football Championship 11 times. The various McDonnells, Synotts and Kavanaghs who played for the club have become part of Dublin folklore. Nine of the Dublin footballers playing at Croke Park during the infamous Bloody Sunday massacre were from O'Toole's club. The fleeing Tipperary players were taken to the streets of Seville Place and hidden in the houses of O'Toole's players. Amongst these were the McDonnell brothers, who were apparently the receiving point for weapons smuggled in at the North Wall from London and Glasgow. After the match, Johnny McDonnell had to quickly dispose of a kitbag of revolvers and other weapons in his house.

Johnny's brother Paddy co-founded the St Laurence O'Toole Drama Society in 1917 with playwright Seán O'Casey, also present in Croke Park that day. It was with this Society that Peter and Jim Sheridan would experience their first taste of the thespian life, performing O'Casey's *'Shadow of a Gunman'*.

The club's last football victory was in 1938. In 1969, O'Toole's won their first senior hurling championship. They have won seven more since, most recently in 2002. In recent, times O'Toole's has shifted its operation to the Malahide Road.

Below left: Continuing the tradition of the St Laurence O'Toole GAA Club, the Docklands Authority runs the Festival of GAA for local children every summer. Below: Irish soccer international and Sunderland Chairman Niall Quinn is amongst those on hand to give the children coaching lessons.

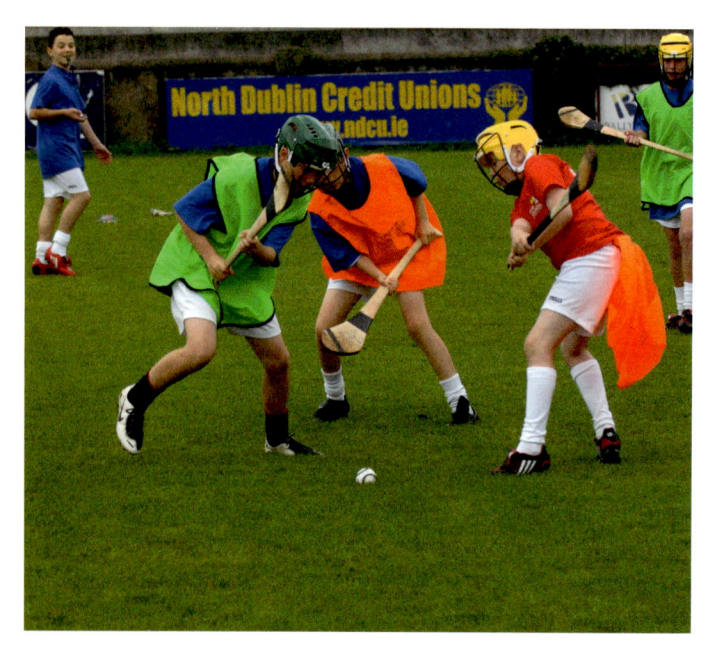

The National College of Ireland

One of the greatest boosts for the northside was the establishment of the National College of Ireland on Mayor Square. The success of this project can be attributed to the formidable Joyce O'Connor, President of the NCI from 1990 to 2007. In 1997, she approached Lar Bradshaw, chairman of the newly-established Dublin Docklands Development Authority, with a bold plan to create a 'campus without walls'. Its specific aim was to extend 3rd level education to people from every type of socio-economic background. Bradshaw was instantly sold on the idea because, money aside, the core of O'Connor's plan was fundamentally a perfect fit with the Authority's ideals for revolutionizing the educational opportunities within the Docklands. To locate the National College of Ireland within the Docklands would go a long way to injecting a renewed sense of soul into the area. Following considerable and sometimes-heated debate, the Authority endorsed O'Connor's radical plan in October 1998 and began a programme of fund-raising to secure tax breaks and help build the new college.

The NCI was not strictly a new college. It was a relocation and rebranding of an older college in Sandford Road, Ranelagh, originally founded by Jesuits. This had been a 'workers college', offering education to employees, developing leadership and increasing awareness of social rights. By 1966, nearly 1,300 students from union and management backgrounds were learning together at the National College of Industrial Relations.

Sited on two acres of former warehouse space, the new NCI comprises a 50,000 ft sq, 5-story, state of the art campus, complete with modern lecture halls, a hi-tech library, a gym, a canteen and 53 residential apartments. It officially opened on 9th Sept 2002, the first day of the new academic year, when Professor O'Connor and businessman Denis O'Brien led the students into the college. That same year, Atlantic Properties awarded the college €7.6 million to develop and enlarge the new campus. There are now 5,000 full and part-time students and over 130 full-time and 220 part-time staff. The current President, Dr. Paul Mooney, is the first former student to lead the college.

Right: The first third level college in the Dublin Docklands was opened by former Taoiseach Bertie Ahern, with Professor Joyce O'Connor, in 2000.

St. Laurence O'Toole's Girls School

THE NEW SCHOOL

Work was already under way on the new Gothic-style Roman Catholic Church on Sheriff Street when the first stones of the St Laurence O'Toole schools were laid directly behind it on 18th April 1847. Completed in November 1848, the new buildings comprised a pair of steeply gabled two-storey girls' and boys' schoolhouses. Between them was a simple gabled block, designated a temporary chapel, where Mass was celebrated once a day and twice on Sundays until the church was completed. In 1848, there were over 350 both boys and girls at the school. In 1938, the boys were relocated to the new Christian Brothers School on nearby Seville Place. Substantially renovated in 1984, a completely new building is now pending. The school is known throughout Dublin's sporting world as the home of the 'Larrier Girls'. There are now approximately 120 girls on the roll, from second class to sixth, most with strong family links to the school that run back several generations.

THE LARRIER GIRLS

While Irish dancing, drama and music have long been hallmarks of St Laurence's, it is a combination of soccer and GAA that has brought the school most press in the past decade. When new teacher Aodhán Ó Ríordáin arrived at the school in 2000, he came with the conviction that through sport a community can master self-respect and find a common identity. He duly organised the girls into Gaelic football and soccer teams, the first in the school's long history. The unofficial school motto became: Have pride, play for your family, your school, your area.

Eight years later, Ó Ríordáin is school principal and the green and white Larrier Girls are amongst the most feared opponents in the school system. Since 2001, they have won three Cumann na mBunscol football titles and four FAI Dublin Schools' soccer titles. Two former pupils are on the Republic of Ireland's international Ladies soccer team

– Michelle Kane and Olivia O'Toole (the Irish captain and the team's all-time highest scorer with 53 goals). Supported by the likes of John Giles and Niall Quinn, O'Toole now coaches the children of Sheriff Street in the art of soccer. In 2008, the Junior Inner-City Cup, founded in 2002, was re-named the Olivia O'Toole Cup in her honour. The Larriers duly won the inaugural competition. The local soccer club, Sheriff YV, provide transport for all games. Dublin GAA manager Paul Caffrey is also on hand to promote Gaelic football and many parents are now involved in coaching. The importance of this new sense of self-esteem cannot be overstated. It is contagious; parents absorb their children's success and ripple with pride. Ó Ríordáin, who is on the Docklands Council, became school principal in 2008. He founded the Right to Read Campaign and was elected to Dublin City Council in 2004, served as Deputy Lord Mayor of Dublin in 2006 and is the Labour Party's candidate for the Clontarf Electoral Ward in 2009.

DOCKLANDS SUPPORT

The Docklands Authority has been active in supporting the school for 10 years, gifting each class a substantial library. Since 2002, they have sponsored French lessons in all classes in the school, culminating in the fifth class visiting Eu in Normandy for three days. During this trip, they visit St Laurence O'Toole's crypt and attend the local school with French students. The Docklands Authority also sponsors Words Week, where the pupils hear talks and readings by Peter Sheridan, Frank McNally, Roddy Doyle, Terry Fagan, Patricia O'Reilly and local politicians.

Below: The Larrier girls with coach Aodhán Ó Ríordáin. Their anthem is: 'We come from Sheriff Street, We're strong and proud, And we sing very loud'. Left: First communion at St Laurence O'Toole's Church in 1962. (Photo: Paddy Curtis Collection).

Luke Kelly (1940 - 1984)

In July 1914, Erskine and Mary Childers sailed the *Asgard* into Howth with a cargo of German guns for Irish Volunteers. The King's Own Scottish Borderers were called in to intercept the weapons. As they returned from a modestly successful arms seizure, an angry crowd of civilians followed the troop up the Liffey, pelting them with insults and stones. A series of unfortunate events ensued which concluded when 21 soldiers discharged their weapons into the crowd at Bachelor's Walk. Three people died and a further 38 were wounded. Among those 38 injured was a young boy called Luke Kelly. His son, also Luke, was one of the founding members of The Dubliners.

Indeed, when it comes to gravelly-voiced balladeers that can silence a thousand mouths with a solitary rasp, few could hold a match to Luke Kelly. He was born on Sheriff Street in 1940, at a time when the 'flats' were fully under construction. By then his father was working in Jacobs Biscuit Factory, where he worked all his life. Young Luke attended the Laurence O'Toole School where he achieved fine grades in most subjects. In 1953, the Kelly's flat was destroyed in a fire and Dublin Corporation shifted the family out to Whitehall. For a while Luke continued to attend O'Toole's, taking a bus in every day, but he quit aged 13 to ride a messenger boy's bicycle. A year later he started work in Jacobs alongside his father, his mother and the rest of the family. Always restless, he subsequently found casual work as a docker, a builder, a drain-digger and a furniture remover. In 1957, like so many of his generation, the 17-year-old redhead took a ship from North Wall to England.

He worked as a builder in Wolverhampton until he was sacked after asking for a raise. He later sold vacuum cleaners in Newcastle, although 'the town was no cleaner for all the vacuum cleaners I sold'. It was during his time in Newcastle, circa 1960, that he walked into his first ever folk club and was bitten by the bug. He perfected the banjo (which he'd been playing since he was 5) and started memorising songs. With Ewan MacColl at the helm, the folk revival was under way all across Britain and Ireland. By the early 1960s, his network was rapidly expanding as he attended *Fleadh Cheoil*s in Ireland, folk clubs in Leeds and Birmingham, Irish pubs and Communist halls in London and Glasgow.

Returning to Dublin in 1962, he began singing in O'Donoghue's Pub on Merrion Row with, among others, Ronnie Drew and Barney McKenna. In 1964, Luke made his way, via the Ronnie Drew Ballad Group, into a new band called The Dubliners. The following year, the bearded balladeer married Deirdre O'Connell, founder of the Focus Theatre. The Dubliners became a huge sensation both sides of the Atlantic. For many, the greatest songs produced during those years were Luke's haunting interpretations of '*Raglan Road*' and '*Scorn Not His Simplicity*'. His father's memories of the Bachelor's Walk Massacre must have echoed through his mind to sing with such staggering conviction.

A heavy drinker all his life, Luke collapsed on stage during a concert in the Cork Opera House in 1980. This was the first indication of the brain tumor that ultimately carried him away on 30th January 1984 at the age of 44. His legacy is recalled in the name of the bridge across the River Tolka at Ballybough. A bronze memorial is also to be installed to his memory.

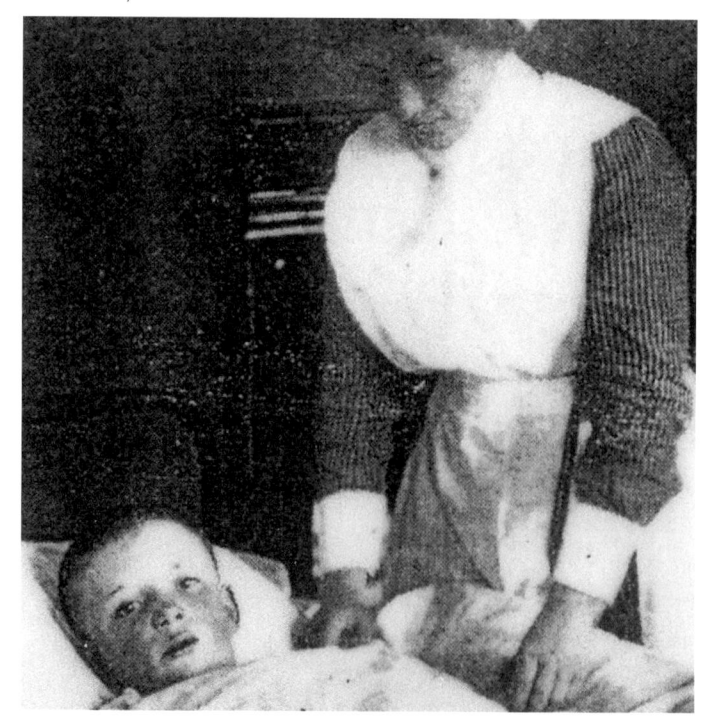

Left: Luke Kelly's father lies in his hospital bed after being shot by British soldiers on Bachelor's Walk in 1914. (Photo: Terry Fagan Collection) Above: Born on Sheriff Street, Luke Kelly epitomized the working class Irishman for a generation defined by emigration and hard-drinking. (Photo: The Dubliners Collection)

The Sheriff Street Flats

THE CORPORATION FLATS
In the 1930s, Dublin Corporation attempted to solve its housing problems by clearing the slums and building flat complexes, or tower blocks. Amongst the most famous of these were the now-demolished Sheriff Street flats, built between 1930 and 1952, which housed large numbers of dockers, stevedores and cattle drovers' families. A total of 445 flats were built in 18 four-storey flat blocks. Each tower had a name such as St Laurence's Mansions, St Bridget's Gardens and Phil Shanahan House. The latter was named after a local publican whose pub was a respected Republican headquarter during the War of Independence. Each flat typically consisted of either two- or three-bedroom units. Around the flats, the landscape was replete with the brick walls and asbestos roofs of warehouses. Residents tended to suffer from high levels of unemployment and education standards were consistently low.

THE COWS ARE COMING!
On Wednesday mornings, the cattle herds came clattering down to board the boats for England. The Sheriff Street children would religiously assemble to prod them along the final distance and maybe make a few pennies. Occasionally a cow broke loose and escaped into a church or home. Two Gardaí were interviewing a resident of the Sheriff Street flats about a missing cow when they heard a definitive 'moo' from within. 'Ah no, that's me guard dog', said the fellow confidently.

THE STUFF OF LEGENDS
In his award-winning documentary 'Alive Alive O! A Requiem for Dublin', film-maker Sé Merry Doyle included footage of a fresh-faced U2 playing a gig on Sheriff Street in 1982. The film director Jim Sheridan who grew up beside St Laurence's Church did not forget the landscape of his childhood. Sheriff Street features in both 'In The Name of The Father' (1993) and 'The Boxer' (1997).

THE DEMOLITION OF THE FLATS
With the incorporation of the Sheriff Street flats into CHDDA's designated zone in 1987, the area entered a new age. A decision was taken to knock the flats, 385 of which were still occupied at the time. Over 1,000 residents were duly re-housed by Dublin Corporation under the watchful eye of the Sheriff Street Committee. The de-tenanting of the Sheriff Street flats was completed in 1996 and, the following year, Chesterbridge Developments acquired the 5.7acre site. On 24th and 25th February 1998 the flats were demolished, an event recalled by Peter Sheridan in his 2003 novel, *Big Fat Love*. Chesterbridge duly developed the flats into a series of blocks, comprising 600 apartments laid out around courtyards, and present-day Mayor Square, making it one of the most profitable residential and retail developments in Dublin. Architect Anthony Reddy Associates won an RIAI Silver Award fo the project.

STAGE AND SCREEN
Throughout the downtimes of the 20th century, the Sheriff Street community somehow managed to retain an element of self-respect. Inspired by the success of local boys Jim and Peter Sheridan, a theatrical bent has never been far away, not least with the celebrated Balcony Belles drama group in the 1990s. One of the areas best known sons is Boyzone star Stephen Gately, the second of five children raised between Sheriff Street and Seville Place. The actor Liam Cunningham, who portrayed Dan the train driver in *The Wind that Shakes the Barley*, is the son of a North Wall docker and grew up in St Laurence's Mansions. Other local heroes include Luke Kelly and Séan O'Casey, both dealt with separately in these pages.

Right: Although set in Belfast, 'The Boxer' was almost exclusively shot in the run-down docklands. With watchtowers, roadblocks and republican graffiti, the flats were transformed into a part of Belfast at the height of the Troubles. The flat complex where Daniel Day-Lewis's character lives was earmarked for demolition but this was postponed until filming was completed. This photo was taken during the filming and shows St Laurence O'Toole's Church rising in the distance. (Photo: Stu Carroll).

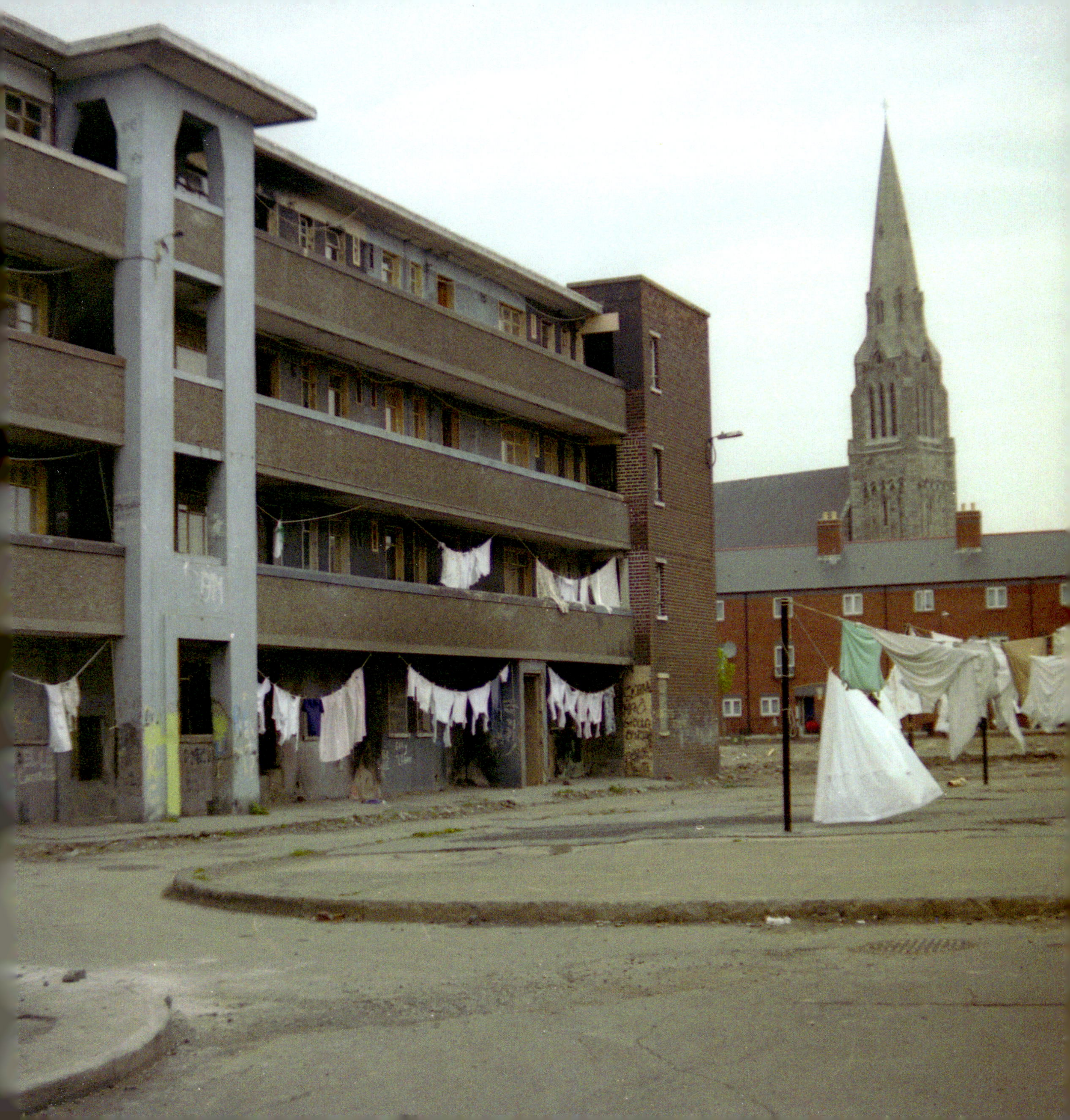

Spencer Dock & The Royal Canal

THE EARLY YEARS

In 1789, as France tumbled into revolution, the most enterprising Irish Parliament of the century authorised the construction of the Royal Canal. By 1803, the Royal Canal had carved its way through the misty slobs and early street grid of Dublin's Docklands, connecting with the River Liffey (and the Irish Sea beyond) through lock-gates at North Wall Quay. Two berthing pools and a spur pool, known as the Royal Canal Docks, ran between the Quay and Sheriff Street, divided by present-day Mayor Street. By the 1840s, these were capable of admitting ships of 150 tons. Sometime before 1850, the spur pool was filled in to become the site of Nixon Street and the now-vanished Newfoundland Street.

MIDLAND & GREAT WESTERN RAILWAY COMPANY

In 1807 a regular passage boat service began operating along the Royal Canal from Dublin through Enfield and Maynooth to Mullingar. Ten years later, the inland waterway celebrated its breakthrough connection with the River Shannon at Cloondara, Co Longford. In 1845 the Midland & Great Western Railway Company (MGWR) purchased the Royal Canal Company with the intention of draining the canal and running a railway along its bed. It later changed tack, building the railway line that famously ran alongside the canal for much of its Dublin to Mullingar leg.

THE NEW DOCK

Spencer Dock was designed to accommodate the MGWR coal ships, which were importing British coal into Ireland. The original Royal Canal Docks were too small to accommodate these huge coal ships and the company was losing ground to the Grand Canal Docks on the south. Thus the new dock was planned and built, affording 3,000sq ft of quayage and connected to an outer dock by 'an ingenious hydraulic bridge'. A secondary railway linked the dock to MGWR's terminus at Broadstone by Constitution Hill.

THE BAPTISM

On the beautiful afternoon of 15th April 1873, (Sir) Ralph Cusack, Chairman of the MGWR, opened the new dock and formally named it Spencer after the Lord Lieutenant, Earl Spencer, great-great grandfather of Diana, Princess of Wales. As the Earl entered the new dock on board the Royal yacht Hawk, steamships let off their fog horns and there was a flourish of trumpets. The Coldstream Guards, clad in bright scarlet, stood along the riverfront and a military band played at the Guild Street entrance. Flags and inscriptions floated from windows while, all along the river, ships were decked in brilliant bunting. The Times reported that 'numbers of the most daring and persevering class [had] clambered to the roofs of the stores and clung to the rigging of the ships in the river and other prominent but perilous positions'. At dinner that night, the Earl repaid Cusack with a knighthood.

THE DECLINE

By 1900, all the land around the North Wall Quay, the Custom House and Spencer Docks had been taken up by railway lines, warehouses, cattle yards and coal sheds. However, with the railways in the ascendance, the Royal Canal and its docks went into decline. Average annual tonnage fell from 30,000 tons in the 1880s to less than 10,000 tons in the 1920s. As the railways too came under pressure, so Spencer Dock became increasingly irrelevant. In 1938, ownership of the Royal Canal passed to the Great Southern Railway, which enjoyed a brief boom during the Second World War. In 1944, the Royal Canal was purchased by Córas Iompair Éireann (CIÉ). In 1955, Douglas Heard's Hark became the last officially recorded boat to pass through the Royal Canal, which closed to navigation in 1961. The original Spencer Dock Sea Lock fell into disrepair.

A NEW AGE

In 1986, most of the Canal was acquired by the Office of Public Works. At the time, the land around Spencer Dock still comprised of abandoned freight yards and crumbling warehouses owned by CIÉ. In 2003, permission was granted to the Spencer Dock Development Company (SDCC) to construct the Convention Centre, Dublin, and also for a commercial and residential development on part of the 51 acre Spencer Dock site. SDCC is a joint venture between Treasury Holdings, CIÉ and Harry Crosbie.

Above: In 1904, Heiton's merchants rented the Spencer Dock Wharf as a base into which their coal supplies could be imported. (Photos: Dublin Port Company Archives)

The first phase – over 500 apartments – sold out over a single weekend. Over Easter 2007, PricewaterhouseCoopers relocated some 2,000 staff from their other Dublin offices to a brand new, carbon-neutral headquarters at One Spencer Dock. This was the largest move ever over a single weekend in the history of Ireland. It was followed shortly afterwards by Belgian bank Fortis, whose headquarters were designed by Michael Collins Associates. The Central Bank has plans to move part of its operations to the seven-storey West Block beside the Convention Centre, Dublin, and is expected to be joined by other leading financial institutions.

THE FUTURE

The completed Spencer Dock development will include over 3,000 apartments, offices and shops, and will be linked to the IFSC by the new Luas Bridge. Also within this umbrella are the Convention Centre, Dublin and the Royal Canal Linear Park, while the new Calatrava-designed Samuel Beckett Bridge across the Liffey will provide a stunning gateway to the scheme. Spencer Dock promises to be one of the most dynamic and exciting areas of 21st century Dublin, with the Samuel Beckett Bridge and the Convention Centre, Dublin at its riverside entrance, and incorporating such landmarks as the Luas Bridge and the Royal Canal Linear Park.

THE COURTYARDS

In 2008, four courtyards in the Spencer Dock scheme won an award for "Outstanding Achievements in Landscaping and Design" from ALCI (Association of Landscape Contractors of Ireland). The courtyards, by English company Hyland Edgar Driver in conjunction with Malahide-based Peter O'Brien and Sons, are based around the idea of a journey from the country to the city, a reference to the Royal Canal's long trek across the Irish countryside.

RESTORATION OF THE SEA LOCKS

In 2008, a 250-ton crane installed a new pair of outer tidal lock gates at the Spencer Dock Sea Lock, which should dramatically reduce the risk of tidal flooding along the canal's banks between the River Liffey and Newcomen Lock. Inner lock gates will soon be installed and repairs are being made to the historic lock walls. Preparations are also under way for the diversion of the water, electrical and communication services that presently restrict vessel access from the River Liffey through to the Royal Canal. Once the restoration is complete, vessels will be able to safely navigate from Spencer Dock through to the River Liffey for the first time since its closure in 1961.

The Royal Canal Linear Park

The Royal Canal Linear Park is an on-going project based on a winning design by Paris-based French landscape and urban design company Agence Ter. The 15-acre (6-ha) public green will eventually run from the Liffey, beside the new Convention Centre, Dublin, northwards for 1.4km to North Strand Road. Blurring the distinction between canal and bank, the design includes floating gardens on pontoons, semi-transparent pavilions, cafes, playgrounds, cycling paths and sports pitches. Trees will be native species, such as oak and white willow, while flower beds will be mostly planted with exotic plants. Lighting designer Yves Adrien, of Coup d'Eclat, will work with the plant colours in his scheme, offering red glows against crimson blooms and such like.

The park will work neatly alongside the new Luas canal bridge designed by Future Systems. The project will also open up the Royal Canal as a public amenity, encouraging use of the inland waterways between the River Liffey and the River Shannon for boating, walking and fishing.

Far left: The Convention Centre, Dublin, during construction in autumn 2008. Below: The first phase of the Linear Park on the Royal Canal aims to provide Docklands residents with a large public green. Below right: By 2010, anyone approaching Dublin by river will be greeted by the ambient lights of the Convention Centre, Dublin and the Samuel Beckett Bridge.

The Convention Centre, Dublin

The innovative glass-fronted Convention Centre, Dublin is scheduled to open in September 2010. It overlooks the Liffey at Spencer Dock and contains a 2,000-seat auditorium, two 450-seat multimedia halls, exhibition spaces, conference and banqueting halls, meeting rooms, and lecture rooms. The glass atrium provides panoramic views of the River Liffey, Dublin city centre and the Wicklow mountains. Dublin has been selected as European City of Science 2012, and the Convention Centre, Dublin is scheduled to host the 8,000-delegate Euroscience forum in July 2012.

The Centre's Pritzker Prize-winning Irish-American architect Kevin Roche was one of the bright young things who worked on Busáras in the 1950s. His subsequent portfolio includes the TWA Terminal at JFK Airport, the Oakland Museum of California and New York's Metropolitan Museum of Art.

The Convention Centre, Dublin is located on the site of two North Wall stalwarts – Campion's Bar, a once-celebrated Victorian pub, and Kilmartin's Turf Accountants.

New Luas Bridge at Spencer Dock

One of the most exciting aspects of Spencer Dock is the new Luas Bridge – a curvy 131 ft-long span located within the Royal Canal Linear Park, jointly funded by the Docklands Authority and the Rail Procurement Agency. Designed by Future Systems, this bridge will carry automobiles, pedestrians and the new Luas line. The bridge features a 62ft to 95ft-wide, shallow deck – just 2ft thick – supported at its centre by two piers. The €4.5 million bridge has been likened to a manta ray, although this wasn't actually the inspiration behind the design. From west to east, the main deck slopes up like a fin, rising by some 6ft along its length. The centre points of the bridge's north and south sides bow out some 16ft to form cantilevered decks over the water, offering views up and down the canal. These viewing spots are also devised as useful meeting places for people. At night, the bridges' white concrete-clad underside will be illuminated by vibrant coloured lights bringing it into step with the lights of the Royal Canal Linear Park.

North Wall Today

The North Wall Quay today presents a waterfront that no one who left Ireland in past decades could begin to recognise. Where once there were dusty warehouses, four-masted ships and rusty cranes, the waterfront is now a skyline of contemporary, glazed, low-rise offices running all the way from the chq building to the Point Village. Until the 1960s, the most familiar sight on the quays on a Wednesday morning were the droves of cattle coming down from the Prussia Street market to board the boats at North Wall. Now the droves are the smart-dressed folk working in the new buildings that run along the waterfront – A & L Goodbody, Citigroup, Commerzbank, AIG Insurance and, come 2010, the Convention Centre, Dublin.

The Quay has been entirely opened to the public while a campshire walkway runs right along the water's edge all the way to the Point Village. The Luas extension to the Point is now well under way and will include stops at George's Dock, Mayor Square, Spencer Dock and the Point Village. The *Cill Airne*, Dublin's first floating bar and restaurant, has been moored outside PricewaterhouseCoopers since 2007. Over the June bank holiday weekend, the *Cill Airne* is joined by dozens of other ships as the river erupts with the Docklands Maritime Festival, which embraces the Liffey as something Dubliners can and should treat with pride and affection.

The North Wall's renaissance effectively began in 1998 with the second phase of the International Financial Services Centre. The Sheriff Street flats were knocked down and the site now contains Mayor Square and the National College of Ireland, as well as several multinational company headquarters, hotels, restaurants and numerous apartments and studios. This brand new district is actually based on the original street grid devised by the 18th century North Lotts project. The only alteration to that ambitious Georgian design has been the creation of Excise Walk, a pedestrian route linking the North Wall Quay to Mayor Square.

Amongst the more imaginative new builds are the seven-storey, yellow-brick and timber apartment towers of Clarion Quay, built by Urban Projects, winner of the 2004 Silver Medal for Housing by the Royal Institute of the Architects of Ireland. Seven of the 190 apartments are managed as affordable rental housing by the Cluid housing association, demonstrating the potential for integrated, well-managed, mixed-tenure housing. The Spencer Dock and Point Village redevelopments are also fully under way. (See page 120).

As North Wall prospers, perhaps the most vital development has been the links across the river with the southside – over the Séan O'Casey Bridge and the landmark Calatrava-designed Samuel Beckett Bridge, scheduled to open in 2010. The importance of these connections between the north and south docks cannot be overstated, putting the Liffey right back at the heart of the city. The evolution of the North Wall would not have been possible without the cooperation and support of local community groups such as the Dublin Inner Cities Partnership, the North Centre City Community Action Project, FETAC and FAS. The Docklands Authority have shown a keen determination to boost the artistic spirit of the area by hosting such events as the Maritime Festival, and commissioning such works as Martin Richman's sequinned facade for the new AGI gas building along the quay.

The next phase in the evolution of the North Lotts is now underway. A revised planning scheme comprises several creative proposals for the campshires and the River Liffey, designed to improve the urban structure with a high-quality, high-density, mixed-use development. This will include several new civic attractions and enhanced amenities, some possibly projecting beyond the quay walls into the river itself. This includes an innovative cluster of tall buildings unlike anything seen in Dublin before. The area is served by the Docklands Railway Station on Sheriff Street. By 2015, the Spencer Dock Station will connect to the DART network at Pearse Station via the 5.2km DART Interconnector tunnel, as well as with the extended Luas red-line at Heuston Station. Iarnród Éireann's proposed underground rail link will actually pass under the Docklands by Spencer Dock, then run beneath the River Liffey before curving westwards beneath Pearse Station towards Heuston Station.

The O₂

EARRLY ORIGINS

Fommrerly known as the Point Depot, The O₂ started life as a very big cast-iron warehouse. It was built in 1878 by the Great Southern and Western Railway Company as a riverside goods depot. Its location beside the point at which the East Wall and North Wall met provided its useful name. During the 1940s and 1950s, its particular forté was the maintenance, service and storage of vehicles. By the 1980s, the building was abandoned and facing collapse. In 1988, local businessman Harry Crosbie purchased the 15-acre site, depot included, from CIÉ for £750,000 (€952,500). Crosbie recruited Shay Cleary Architects to convert the building into a multi-purpose concert, exhibition and conference centre. While the premises were being fitted out with balconies, offices and backstage facilities, a band called U2 recorded part of their *Rattle and Hum* album in the building. They later gave their seal of approval to the completed venue when they played four nights here at the end of their Lovetown Tour in 1989.

THE POINT THEATRE

In 1988, the Point Theatre opened with a concert by San Francisco rockers, Huey Lewis and the News. By the early 1990s, the Point was firmly established as the number one music venue in Dublin for those seeking a big crowd. It hosted the Eurovision Song Contest in 1994, 1995, and 1997, and is thus far the only venue to have hosted the final three times. During an interval in the 1994 Contest, the debut performance of Riverdance sent ripples up spines across the world and a phenomenon was born.

The 1999 MTV Europe Music Awards was also held at the Point while the impressive litany of bands to perform here spans the generations from Bowie to Beyoncé, with Westlife notching up a record 12 concerts. It also served as an ice rink, a conference hall, an exhibition centre, a wrestling ring, a theatre, an opera house and a three-ring circus. The final event to take place in the Point before refurbishment was the European Super-Bantamweight Championship of August 2007 in which Spanish challenger Kiko 'La Sensacion' Martinez floored Irish boxer Bernard Dunne within the first minute.

THE O₂

By the summer of 2007, Crosbie had formed a partnership with Live Nation, a major events company based in Beverly Hills, California. They closed the Point down, pumped €80 million into refurbishing the building and reopened it as a 21st century amphitheatre in 2008. The building was carried out by Walls Construction who, as it happens, were the contractors who transformed the Point Depot into the Point Theatre 20 years ago. The new name is a nod to corporate sponsors Telefónica Europe plc, the European telecommunications giant better known by the brand name of O₂. They also sponsor the multi-award winning O₂ in London and the new O₂ Arena in Berlin.

STANDING OR SITTING, SIR?

The old Victorian warehouse is still very much in evidence at The O₂, yet its bricks and pillars have been shuffled about to create a considerably more spacious ambience. This cutting edge new arena has a capacity of over 14,000 standing. In fact, performers have the option to request whether their audience should be seated or standing. The owners expect The O₂ to be in use for around 150 nights each year - with a projected audience figure of two million a year. As the premiere music venue in Dublin, we can expect The O₂ to draw a large number of major acts deep into the docklands.

THE POINT VILLAGE

Hand-in-hand with the opening of The O₂ is the creation of Harry Crosbie's €850 million Point Village. This new city quarter is scheduled to include the 100m high 'Watchtower', with circa 150 apartments, 500 m² of office space and a rooftop bar. Elsewhere in the Village, there will be a 23,000 m² shopping centre, a 250-room 4-star hotel, 13,000 m² of offices, a 3-storey underground car park with capacity for 1,000 vehicles, a smaller 2000-seater theatre and a 12-screen cinema. There are also plans for an additional cultural facility to attract visitors to the area. The Point Village will be connected to the city centre by an extension of the Luas light rail extension into the heart of the village.

Above: The O$_2$ incorporates the former Point Depot at the juncture, or 'point', where the North Wall and East Wall meet. (Photo: Donal Murphy).

Chapter Three
East Wall

EAST WALL
NORTH WALL
RIVER
LIFFEY
RINGSEND
RINGSEND PARK
ALEXANDRA BASIN
ALEXANDRA QUAY
GRAND CANAL DOCKS
CONNOLLY
Connolly Station
Pearse Station
ROYAL CANAL
Annesley Bridge
John McCormack Bridge
Clarke's Bridge
Entrance to Port Tunnel
Toll
Harbour Police
Vehicle Pound Dublin City Council
Community Centre
The Point Depot
DRY DOCKS
North Quay Extension
Port View House
Postal Delivery Centre
Gallery Quay
Waterways Visitor's
EAST WALL ROAD
NORTH STRAND ROAD
SHERIFF STREET UPPER
SHERIFF STREET LOWER
NORTH WALL QUAY
SIR JOHN ROGERSON'S QUAY
SPENCER DOCK
GUILD STREET
MAYOR STREET LOWER
MAYOR STREET UPPER
SEVILLE PLACE
CHURCH ROAD
CALEDON ROAD
TOLKA QUAY ROAD
ALEXANDRA ROAD
BOUNDARY ROAD
BOND ROAD
PEARSE STREET
RINGSEND ROAD
HANOVER QUAY
YORK ROAD
PIGEON HOUSE ROAD
BRIDGE ST
ALFIE BYRNE ROAD
BALLYBOUGH ROAD
AMIENS ST
M50
R131
R101
Sch
Hall
PO
DART
ARROW
LC
FB
72
73
74
75
79

East Wall, they say, is something of an independent republic. Three hundred years ago, the area comprised of nothing but mud flats, almost entirely submerged beneath the tidal waters of the River Tolka and Dublin Bay. The only hint of anything older was an iron knife, possibly Viking or medieval, unearthed during excavations on Church Road in the 1950s. In 1710, the Ballast Office began construction of the North Wall to contain the Liffey and reclaim the North Lotts. By 1728, the City's engineers had constructed the first sections of a massive enclosing wall – the East Wall – that effectively created the lands on which the residential precinct of the East Wall now stands. Since Victorian times, the area has been bordered by the North Wall, the East Wall Road, the River Tolka, the Royal Canal and a broad sweep of cast-iron railway tracks. For the 1,700 or so households in East Wall, this has created an extraordinary sense of unity. The earliest residents were invariably working class migrants from the countryside. Coal and the railways counted the greatest number of employees. With the decline of such industries, East Wall entered the doldrums, although there was still a strong and defiant spirit in the air. Local hero Seán O'Casey captured the essence of this in many of his plays. There was always someone to maintain pride in the community – 'The Building Parson', the women who rebuilt St Joseph's Church, the organizers of the East Wall Festival, the architects of the new Seán O'Casey Community Centre. In the late 20th century, B&I, Wiggins Teape, Rathborne Candles and Lego were among those who provided employment. Today, the Docklands Innovation Park and the late Dermot Pierce's East Point Business Park bring thousands of multi-national workers to the area daily. The buildings around East Wall may keep getting higher but the community within are determined and feisty enough to retain their independence.

East Wall - Streetwise

Abercorn Road - Named for James Hamilton, 1st Duke of Abercorn, Lord Lieutenant of Ireland from 1866–1868 and 1874–1876. He was Grand Master of the Freemasons of Ireland from 1874 until his death.

Alfie Byrne Road - Named after the popular Irish nationalist politician, known variously as the 'Children's Lord Mayor' and the 'Shaking Hand of Dublin'.

Annesley Bridge - Originally built in 1797 and named after the Hon Richard Annesley, Commissioner of both the Irish Excise and Customs, and director of the Royal Canal Company. His wife was a sister of Commissioner Beresford. He succeeded his brother as 2nd Earl Annesley in 1802. The present bridge dates to 1926.

Bargy Road - Several roads in East Wall were named for the 150th anniversary of the 1798 rebellion in Co Wexford. This road is named after the barony of Bargy in Wexford. Other Wexford baronies in the East Wall are recalled by Shelmalier Road and Forth Road, while Killan Road and Boolavogue Road are named after revolutionary hotspots in Wexford.

Caledon Road - Possibly named by former residents of Caledon, Co Armagh, who moved to East Wall to work with the Great Northern Railway.

Church Road - One of the three main arteries of East Wall, dating to the mid 18th century, Church Road once linked with Seville Place in North Wall. It appears to have been named for a church that was planned but never built. An air-raid bunker off Church Road is said to have been connected by a tunnel to O'Connell Street but was filled in a few years ago.

Coburg Place - Built in 1817 and named for the capital of the Duchy of Saxe-Coburg and Gotha in Bavaria into which the luckless Princess Charlotte, only child of George IV, was married in 1816. Queen Victoria's husband and mother both descended from this same family.

East Road - One of the three main arteries of the East Wall, dating to the mid 18th century.

East Wall Road - Named for the first enclosing wall built in the early 18th century to reclaim the mud flats of the North Strand upon which East Wall stands. The older generation know this as Wharf Road after a bather's slip constructed in the 18th century, now under reclaimed land.

Fairfield Avenue - Named for the Fairfield Shipyard in Glasgow. The original buildings, still called the Scotch Blocks, were built for Glaswegian workers who came to work in Dublin during the early 19th century.

Five Lamps - Named for an ornamental lamp-lit drinking fountain built in memory of Galway-born General Henry Hall, CB, of the Indian Army.

Forth Road - Probably named after the barony in Wexford, although a Miss Forth owned land here prior to 1815.

Hawthorn Terrace - In the 1880s, Hawthorn Terrace was populated by ships captains, bottle blowers and mechanics employed in nearby factories. Amongst these was the family of young Seán O'Casey.

John McCormack Bridge - Situated on the Alfie Byrne Road, this twin-spanned concrete structure crosses the River Tolka right at the point where it enters Dublin Bay near East Wall Road. It was named after the great Irish tenor on the occasion of his centenary in 1984.

Johnny Cullen's Hill - Named for Cullen's dairy, which stood at the foot of the hill.

Luke Kelly Bridge - At Tony Gregory's suggestion, the Ballybough Bridge was renamed after the legendary founding member of The Dubliners.

Malachi Place - Probably named for High King Malachy II, elder brother of Brian Boru. The 19th century poet Thomas Caulfield Irwin lived here.

Merchant's Road - Built by the Merchants' Warehousing Company for its workers. During the 1913 Lock-Out, the company evicted 60 striking residents and used the buildings to house imported labour.

Moy Elta Road - Moy Elta, meaning the 'Plain of the Herds', was the burial place of Partholón, who traditionally led his people into Ireland after the Great Flood. The name may be a play on *Sheanmháigh Ealta Eadair*, referring to extensive sloblands off the coast of Dublin.

Newcomen Avenue - Named for controversial banker Sir William Gleadowe Newcomen, one of the directors of the Royal Canal Company in 1791 and former owner of Carriglass Manor in Co Longford.

North Strand Road - This road marks part of the original coastline that ran from close to the Abbey Theatre, up Amiens Street and Ballybough Road, to the Luke Kelly Bridge and onwards to Fairview. The road was created after the Ballast Office built the North Wall in the early 1700s.

Ossory Road - Possibly named for the diocese of Ossory, of which Commissioner Beresford's brother became Bishop in 1789. It is now home to the Crosbie's Yard apartments, designed by Scott Tallon Walker.

Ravensdale Road - Named for a town on the Cooley Peninsula in Co Louth.

Russell Avenue - Formerly known as the Bull Ring, the avenue features on the 1911 Census and includes a small row of artisan cottages. These houses were built by Dublin Corporation in the 1930s.

Seaview Avenue - Named for its fine view of the Irish Sea before the land was reclaimed.

Stoney Road - Named for Dr Bindon Blood Stoney, Engineer-in-Chief to the Port and Docks Board, who lived in Fir House on Church Road.

Strangford Road - Originally destined to be called 'Utility Road', this was possibly named by workers of the Great Northern Railway after their homeland on Strangford Lough in Co Down. The houses at St Barnabas Gardens and Strangford Gardens were built by the celebrated 'Building Parson', Rev DH Hall.

Teeling Way - Named for the late Joe Teeling, founder of the Amateur Sports Karate Organization and the East Wall Water Sports Club at East Point Bridge. He was also one of the key players in the construction of the *Dyflin*, a replica Viking long ship.

The Smoothing Iron - Named for a large granite stone at the 'slip' on East Wall (Wharf) Road, once used for berthing ferries to Clontarf Island. It was also a popular diving board in the early 20th century.

West Road - One of the three main arteries of the East Wall, dating to the mid 18th century.

The Creation Of A Community

RIDERS OF THE IRON HORSE

The original East Wall community had a distinctly nautical bent, focused upon Dublin Port, which lay directly to its east, and the Royal Canal, which cut its way through the roads in the 1790s. The arrival of the railways in the 1840s brought hundreds, if not thousands, of new residents to the community. Skilled and unskilled, Catholic and Protestant, rural and urban, the East Wall was soon swarming with men, women and children from all across the British Isles.

Huge numbers arrived from the Irish countryside, fleeing the desolation of the famine, driven by the urge to survive. Many from Ulster found work as engine drivers and railway men with the Great Northern Railway, with whom the playwright Seán O'Casey would later work. A mostly Protestant influx from England, Scotland and Wales were employed by the London & North Western Railway on the North Wall. Still more were to be found working as mechanics and shipbuilders or queuing up along the docks of the Liffey, awaiting the nod of the stevedore.

St Barnabas Church was built for the Protestant 'swaddlers' in 1870. The Catholics attended St Laurence O'Toole's Church on Sheriff Street, opened in 1850, until St Joseph's Church (known as 'The Little Tin Church') was erected on Church Road in the early 1900s.

DIVIDED BY THE TRACKS

While the railway provided considerable employment for the East Wall community, the great swathe of train tracks laid in the 1840s served to isolate them from the rest of the City. These tracks severed the main arteries of Church Road, East Road and West Road from the Sheriff Street neighbourhood. Now known as an East Wall stronghold, Church Road originally culminated opposite St Laurence O'Toole's Church in North Wall. As the railways and canals expanded, the southern end of Church Road was cut off from Seville Place. Adding to the sense of claustrophobia, the construction of the Great Northern Railway embankment removed North Strand's once uninterrupted view of Dublin Bay.

SCOUNDRELS AND HORSEMEN

For many decades there was no bus service between the city and East Wall but one enterprising soul ran a private shuttle service to Amiens Street. He could not be relied on though as once 'he had enough made, he'd go off into the Wharf Tavern and have a few pints'. More villainous intents were behind Conker Barry, famed for stealing clothes off the lines and pawning them, and Josh Bollans, the headless horseman who lost all his money in an ill-advised flutter and was hung on West Road.

Above: The new Seán O'Casey Community Centre dominates the East Wall skyline. In the foreground, a man walks up Johnny Cullen's Hill towards Sheriff Street. In the distance, a commuter train makes its way from Connolly Station to Fairview. (Photo: Michael Moran). Left: Constructed in the 1840s, this broad swathe of railway tracks meant the East Wall residents became isolated from their fellow Docklanders. (Photo: Paddy Curtis Collection).

The 20th Century

THE RUNNER-IN'S

Many East Wallers lived in cottages built and owned by the companies who employed them. Men worked hard and drank harder, while the women raised large families and scrubbed the home floorboards spotless every morning. But if life was difficult, the people were generally robust and jaunty. Music was a ritual and sport an institution. Otherwise the streetscape remained largely unchanged until the Rev DH Hall began building new semi-detached houses in the area after the First World War. By then most of the community were working-class Catholics, although Canon Hall was careful to ensure his houses were built on an ecumenical basis. In the 1930s, Dublin Corporation followed suit and deliberately established a residential area in the East Wall, starting at Russell Avenue. The area was still considered part of the countryside at this time. Many of the new Corporation houses were occupied by former tenement dwellers from Pearse Street. The newcomers were known as Runner-ins. In the 1920s and 1930s, East Wall children were either educated at St Laurence O'Toole's School in North Wall or at the Wharf School on the East Wall Road. In 1939, East Wall got its own school when St Joseph's National School opened on St Mary's Road.

THE BIG SQUEEZE

As the 20th century wore on, dwindling employment opportunities and the physical barriers of the ever-busy East Wall Road and East Road amplified the sense of isolation that had been inherent since the laying of the railway tracks in Victorian times. For the whole community – indigenous East Wallers and Runner-ins alike – the big squeeze was never far away. Up until the 1960s, the view from East Wall Road took in Dublin Bay spreading out to Fairview and Clontarf. Then the road was developed by portside businesses and the view vanished. The local Protestant community must have felt particularly glum when St Barnabas's Church was demolished and replaced by a carwash.

Nonetheless, during the 1960s and 1970s, East Wall was still pulsating with the noise of flour mills, printing works, timber yards, granaries, coal yards, warehouses, dockyards and railways. The biggest employer was the British & Irish Steam Packet Company, commonly known as B&I. Fiat had a car assembly plant where Merchants Court is now, while Rathborne Candles, Fry Cadbury (later Wiggins Teape), Lego, Tonge and Taggart, Cahill's Printers and Collen Brothers Construction also had a significant local presence.

The School Boy Strike of 1911

On 5th September 1911, 30 boys marched out of Bigyn council school in Llanelli in south west Wales to protest over the caning of one of their peers. Within days, pupils in more than 60 towns throughout Britain had taken to the streets to express their grievances. The first pupils in Ireland to go on strike were from the Wharf National School in East Wall. On 13th September, the Wharf's teachers arrived to find ominous words written in chalk upon the school door: 'Strike, boys, strike for Free Books and shorter hours and to get home daily at 12:30 for Lunch'.

The revolution was plotted at secret meetings held in fields by night. On the first morning of the strike, the knickerbocker-clad, cap-wearing schoolboys formed themselves into a line four deep, close to the school, and dug in their heels. Any boy who attempted to go to school was turned back by the pickets. When the School Attendance Officer approached, he was loudly booed. When some parents tried to intervene, they too were driven back. Generally it was a peaceful affair, although blacklegs were pelted with cabbage stalks and, on occasion, stones.

The next day, the strike continued – and the next, and the next. The boys' grievances were perfectly reasonable. Such schools were often filthy and many children became ill because of the long hours they were obliged to spend there. Books were also so expensive that they cost a hard-working man a full weeks wages to buy just one copy. It seems the strike petered out after a week without any of the demands being met. But one can only imagine the sense of purpose it gave to a class of teenage boys on the eve of the War of Independence.

Left: Cloth-capped East Wall men, presumably employed by the same company. Below: The Wharf National School on East Wall Road. (Photos: Paddy Curtis Collection).

Sporting Times

HANDBALL KINGS

As early as 1904, the four young Grace brothers of Caledon Road were to be found playing handball against the side-wall of Brennan's shop on Church Road. A later icon of this sport was Séamus O'Hanlon of Church Road, who went on to found the Irish Amateur Handball Association. The St Laurence O'Toole GAA Club had a massive following.

THE BOXER

East Wall boxer Christy Rafter (b. 1937) served with the US Army and represented Ireland's boxing team in the men's bantamweight at the 1964 Tokyo Olympics. He had won the play-off bout for the 1960 Olympics but was somewhat controversially not selected.

THE FOOTBALL CLUBS

Despite the pre-eminence of the GAA, there were two local soccer clubs, Strandville and St Barnabas, who played in Fairview Park. These would later inspire the rivalry plot in O'Casey's *The Silver Tassie*. East Wall United Football Club (now East Wall Wharf United) was founded in 1949/1950 and became one of the most successful junior clubs in Ireland. At the same time, Father Larry Redmond, the young curate at St Joseph's, combined forces with an East Waller called Hubert Fuller and the bus drivers and conductors of CIÉ (from the men's section of the Legion of Mary). They began 'The Famous Streets Soccer League', canvassing the streets of East Wall and North Strand for sprightly young lads who'd play ball. Teams were assembled and matches played at Fairview Park. At these matches, the crowds were entertained by the St Joseph's Boys Club Band, also established by Father Redmond, aided by Sergeant O'Rourke of the Army School of Music. In 1959 three East Wallers lined up to represent the Irish international team against Czechoslovakia. Noel Peyton, Dick Whittaker and Liam Tuohy. It wasn't the best of games for Ireland. The Czechs hammered them 4-0.

Opposite: St Joseph's of East Wall, where former Republic of Ireland manager Liam Tuohy was educated, has had a strong football tradition since the 1920s.

EAST WALL STRIKERS

Alex Stevenson (1912 – 1985) - One of just three Irish footballers to have played for Rangers, Alex was the only one to have simultaneously played for Rangers and the FAI XI. In 1934 he signed for Everton. He remains one of Everton's all-time top goalscorers. As a young man he played with the Dolphins, whose East Wall grounds became the site of the current St Joseph's Church. He subsequently coached the national football team.

Christopher "Kit" Lawlor (1922 –2004) – The East Waller began his League of Ireland career playing with Shamrock Rovers. During the 1950s, he played five seasons with Doncaster Rovers, scoring 46 goals in 128 appearances. In 1957, he was part of the Drumcondra side who scored a shock victory against the Shamrock Rovers in the Cup final. He won three caps for Ireland. His son Mick Lawlor won four caps for Ireland in the 1970s and is now kit manager for Ireland.

Paddy Waters (d. 2004) – The Irish international made 117 senior appearances for Bohemians, most memorably when they won the Inter City Cup in 1945. He finished his career at Carlisle United under the management of the legendary Bill Shankly.

Noel Peyton (born 1935) - Peyton's tally included six caps for Ireland, five League of Ireland caps and one B international. He transferred from Shamrock Rovers to Leeds United in 1958 where he scored 20 goals in 117 games in over five years. His brother Willie played for St Patrick's Athletic FC.

Liam Tuohy - As well as being a milkman, Tuohy won eight caps for Ireland and was sometime manager of both the national team and Shamrock Rovers.

Dick Whittaker (1934 – 1998) - Ireland's international right back played 48 times for Chelsea in the 1950s.

'Short trousers in the winter, your schoolbag on your back
Walking home from Larriers along the railway track
Or hanging 'round the slaughter-house to chase the sheep that strayed
Or down to Fairview Park to play football all the day
All the day, down by Bargy, whistling all the way'

East Wall All The Day, Paul O'Brien

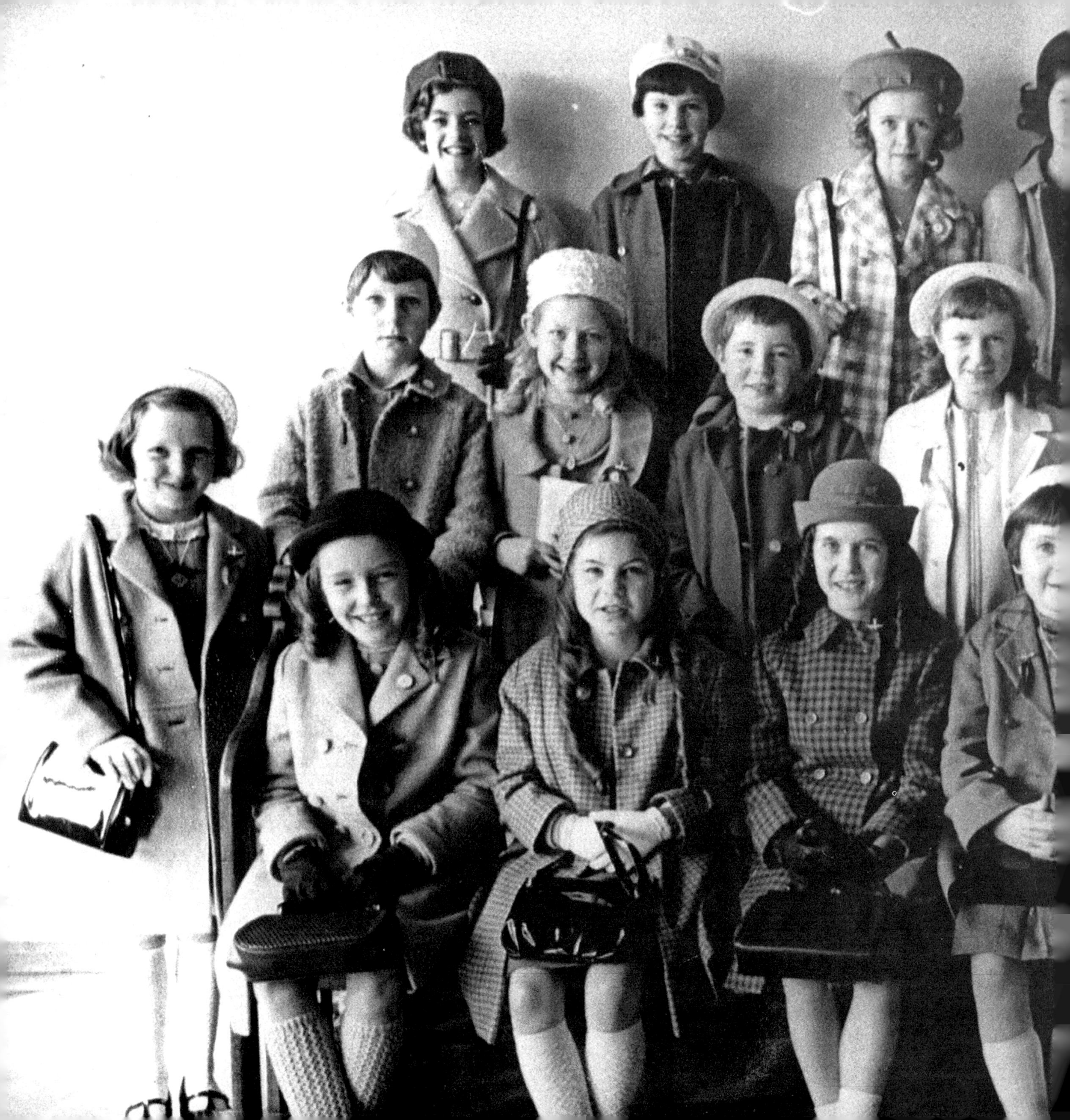

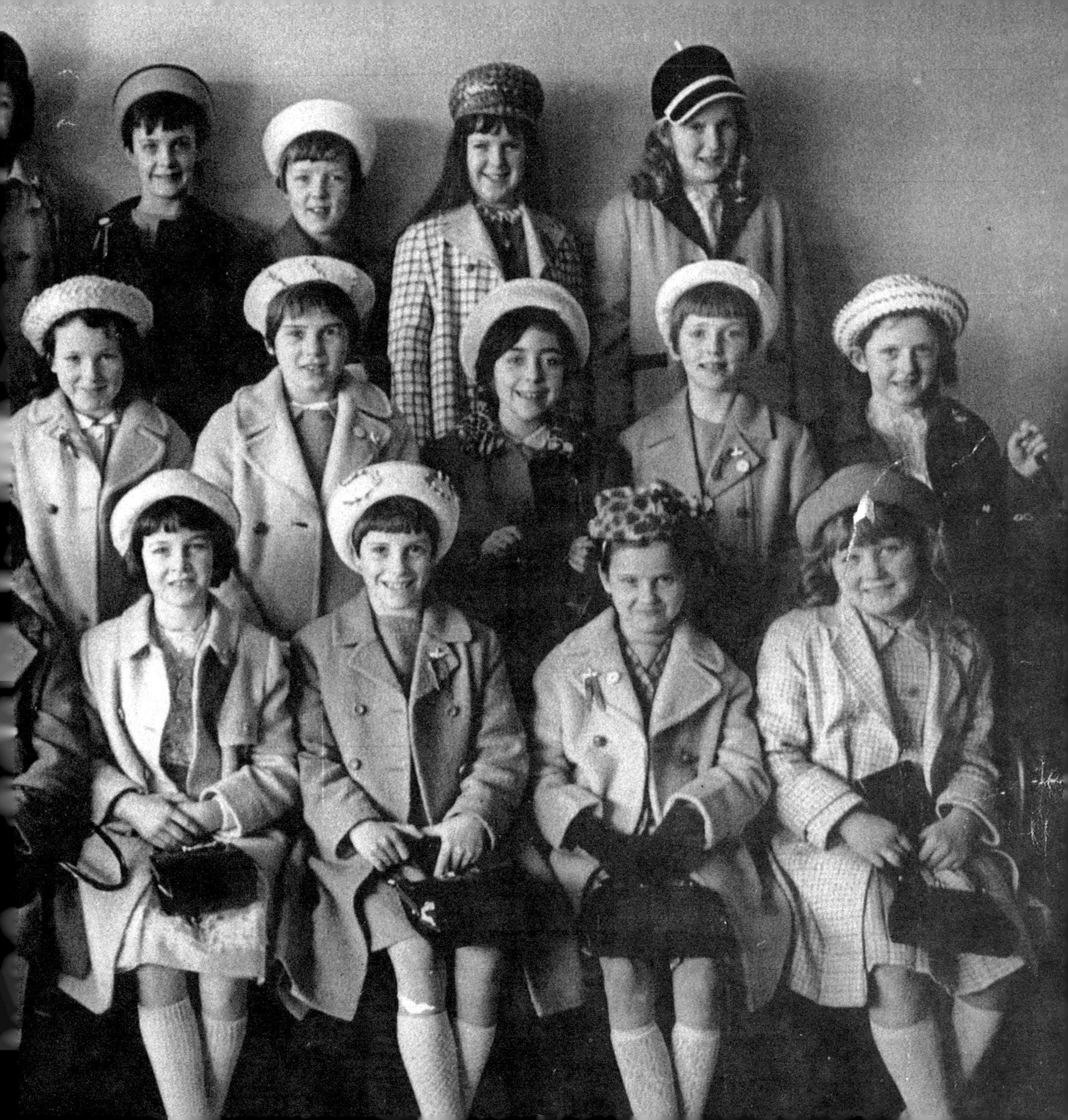

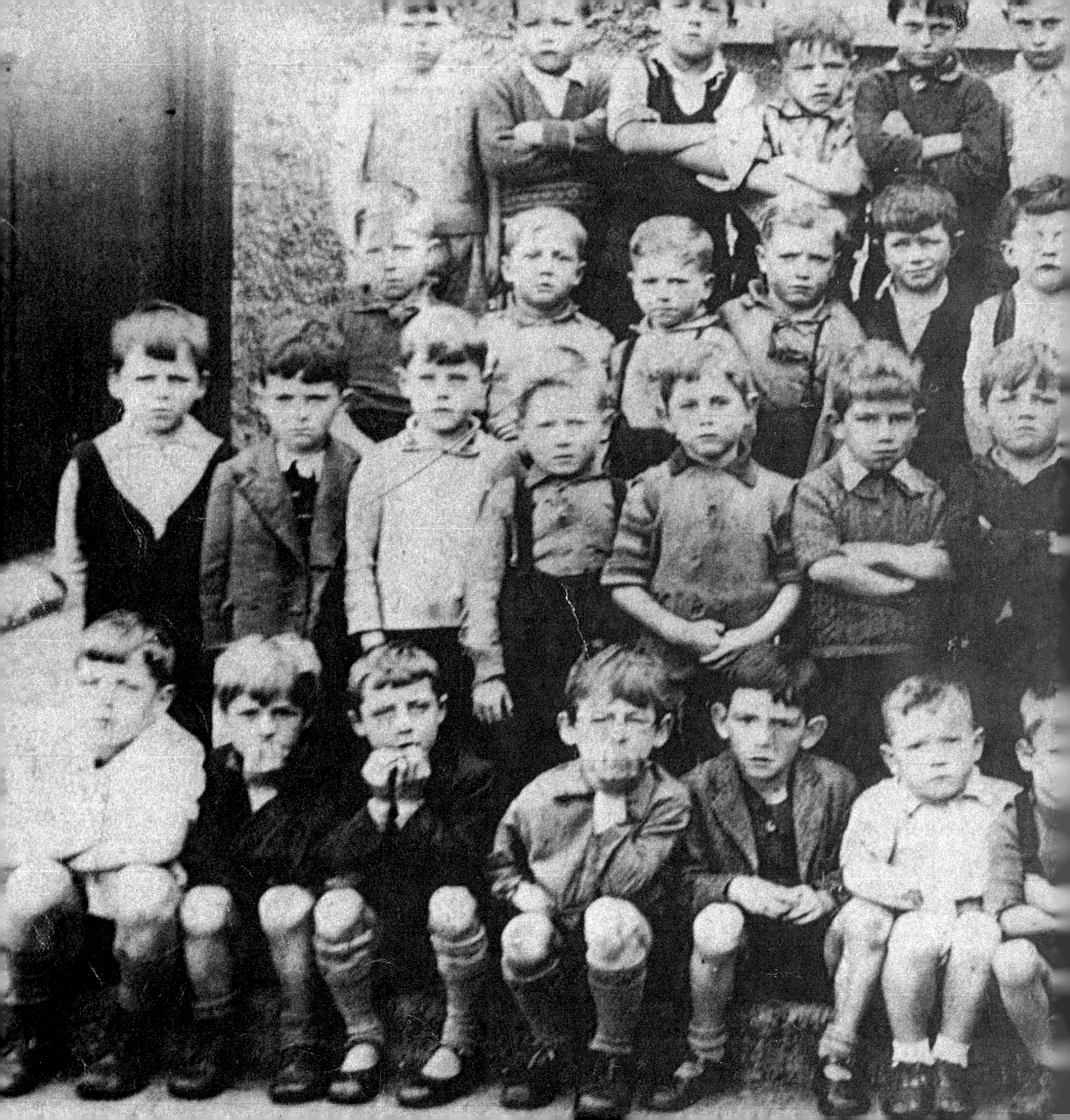

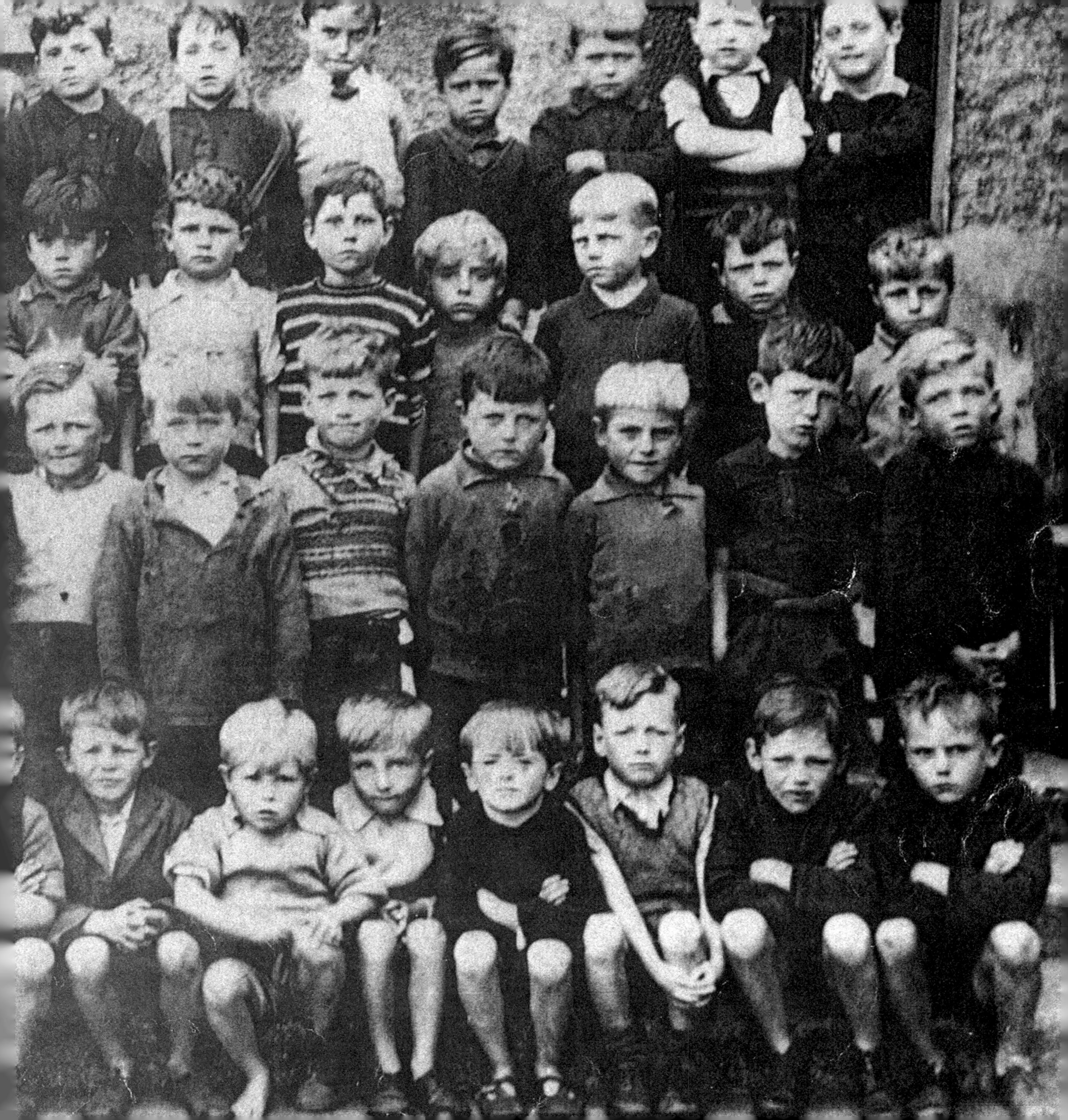

Splendid Isolation

BYZANTINE EFFORTS

Perhaps the isolation was not all bad. It certainly gave East Wallers a common bond, cemented in the clubs, churches and pubs such as The Wharf, Cusack's and Graingers. From the flood-drenched 1950s through to the festive 1970s, the community engineered a fresh identity that permeated the roads of East Wall. The catalyst for this new age was the sale of St Joseph's Church in the 1940s; it had become a furniture factory by the 1970s. Two local women, Mary Desmond and Clare Carberry, responded to the sale by launching a church building fund. The fund was so successful that the brand new Byzantine-style St Joseph's Church was up and running by 1955. East Wallers had awoken to the fact that, if they wanted to ensure their community's survival, it was up to the community to generate the means to do so.

KARATE CHOPS & VIKING SHIPS

East Wall erupted with clubs and organizations, catering for everything from swimming and karate to the Wharf Tavern Social Club and the St Mary's Youth Club on Strangford Road. Both St Joseph's Indoor Bowling Club and the East Wall Scouts were formed in 1972; the Wharf Sailing Club was revived in 1975; and the Ladies Leisure Club in 1976. In Dublin's Millennium year of 1988, a team of East Wall volunteers built *the Dyflin*, a full-size, 75ft long replica of a Viking Gokstad ship excavated in Norway in 1882. The East Wall Youth Club is vibrantly active all year, encouraging everything from soccer and dance to circus acts and graffiti lessons. The East Wall Residents Association has been continuously active since the 1960s, while the Nascadh Community Development Project is constantly seeking to bridge the generation gap between old and young.

THE EAST WALL FESTIVAL

This sense of pride propelled the organizers of the East Wall & North Strand Festival, which ran from 1975 to 1978. The event was born out of the tragic drowning of Johnny Hogan who, at 18 years of age, was treasurer of the Mini Olympics Committee and a promising Youth Leader with St Mary's Youth Club. Jim Quigley, Chairman of the East Wall Residents Association, gathered all the clubs and organisations in the area together to plot ways of helping the Hogan family. From this voluntary gathering came the organising committee of the festival.

The Festival of June 1976 was specifically designed to halt plans to run a motorway through East Wall. Alderman Kevin Byrne urged the residents to display 'bunting and flags from every house in every road and street' to show the world they were a living community with traditions and pride. It worked. The Festival comprised a parade from Russell Avenue Playground up Church Road and then up and down the roads of East Wall, concluding on St Mary's Road. President Cearbhall Ó Dálaigh was amongst the first visitors.

One highlight was the Soap Box Derby, a trolley race down the hump-back bridge (known as 'Johnny Cullen's Hill') that separates East Wall from North Wall. Youngsters would line up trolleys made from old wooden pallets with steel bearing wheels. They would clatter downhill at high speed while their mothers were busy fixing bunting from the bedroom windows to the garden railing. Other events included a talent show, a ladies dance, a basketball tournament, a karate match, GAA and soccer matches, sack races, pram races, a fancy-dress contest for children, darts and debates, raffles and quizzes, and concerts by the likes of Chips and Sandie Jones. Some of the main shows took place in the North Strand Cinema, subsequently converted into a bowling alley and now an apartment block.

There have been revivals of the Festival in more recent times, but they have yet to reach the heights set in the 1970s. That said, the Festival gave East Wall an excellent taste for the aesthetic. Indeed, among those early participants was East Wall sculptor John Behan, RHA, celebrated for his bull sculptures, and Joe Moran, whose bronze and wooden sculpture *The Door* was unveiled at the Library Plaza in Ringsend in March 2008. Alderman Kevin Byrne is himself a poet and writer of repute, and co-founded the Saor-Ollscoil na hÉireann (Free University of Ireland) in 1986.

Above: Sunrise over East Wall with the Poolbeg chimneys on the distance. (Photo: Barry Keogh) Previous pages: The elegantly dressed girls of the East Wall girls school contrast with the bare-foot, sockless and somewhat raggedy pupils of the Wharf Boys School. (Photos: Paddy Curtis Collection). Next page: The East Wall Festival was one of the liveliest events in the Dublin calendar during the 1970s. (Courtesy: Joe Mooney)

EAST WALL FESTIVAL
JUNE 8th
to
JUNE 15th
1975
price 10p

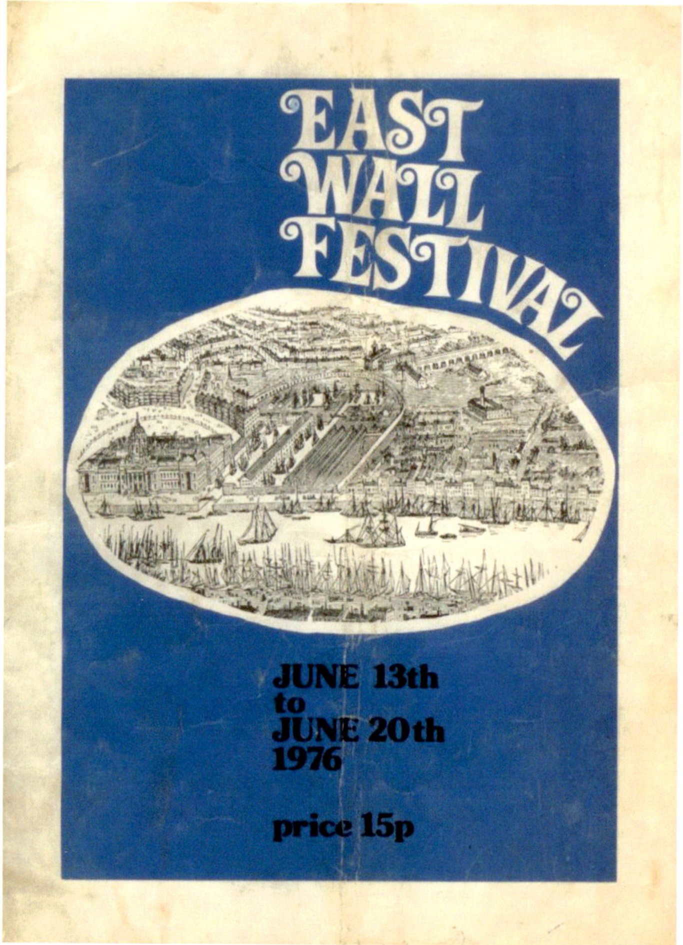
EAST WALL FESTIVAL
JUNE 13th
to
JUNE 20th
1976
price 15p

EAST WALL & NORTH STRAND FESTIVAL '77
June 19th to June 26th   Price 15p

EAST WALL & NORTH STRAND FESTIVAL '78
FESTIVAL WEEK June 25th - July 2nd
Festival Queen Bernadette Payne
Price 20p

Rathborne Candles

IRELAND'S OLDEST COMPANY
In 1488, four years before Columbus reached America, an English candlemaker called Joseph Rathborne arrived in the old city of Dublin and established his business on Wynetavern Street by Christchurch Cathedral. Born in Chester, Rathborne had been obliged to relocate when that town's River Dee unexpectedly silted up, destroying his trade links with Ireland, Scotland and the ports of Europe. Today, Rathborne Candles is Ireland's oldest company and the world's oldest candlemaker. For most of the 20th century, the company was headquartered on the East Wall Road.

THE MOVE TO EAST WALL
Before the days of electricity and paraffin lamps, Rathborne's handmade wax candles lit everything from the streets of Dublin to the lighthouses along the coast. The Candlelight Law of 1616 decreed that every fifth home should display a light for passers-by. Four years later, Joseph Rathborne's great-grandson relocated to bigger and better premises north of the river at St Mary's Abbey. In the 1860s, company boss John G Rathborne purchased a site in Dublin's North Lotts. He subsequently constructed an extensive storage facility on the East Wall Road. The building was called the Dublin Petroleum Stores and would later become the Rathborne headquarters.

FLICKERING TIMES
The last member of the Rathborne dynasty to run the factory was Henry Burnley Rathborne. In 1914, he sold the factory to John Barrington & Sons of Parnell Street, a subsidiary of Lever Bros, now Unilever. In 1923, the company was sold to a consortium of oil companies, Shell & BP Ltd, now Irish Shell. The firm re-located to the Merchant's Yard site on the East Wall Road, where a new factory was completed in March 1925. Seven years later, the company made sure it had the very latest equipment to meet the immense demands of a once-divided nation praying together at the 31st International Eucharistic Congress in 1932. However the company went into decline during the war years and, by 1945, consisted of just 12 office staff and eight factory workers.

HIGH EXPLOSIVES
Despite the recession of the 1950s and the risk of rural electrification making candles irrelevant, the company expanded with the enigmatic Eimar 'High Explosive' McCormick (1918–2003) at the helm. By the early 1960s, there were 125 people employed at the East Wall Road factory, making household, church and festive candles. McCormick travelled extensively throughout Europe, the US and Canada, building up invaluable contacts with the Irish diaspora and foreign clients. This enabled Rathborne to expand during the more optimistic 1960s, when novelty candles shaped as rugby balls and Irish coffees became increasingly popular. In 1966, Rathborne acquired the respected Lalor Church Candles of Ormond Quay, establishing both companies at East Wall Road. Irish Shell took full control of the business in 1984. One of the last jobs of the East Wall candlemakers was the manufacture of the Millennium candles given by the government to 1.5 million households in 1999. By the time the company moved to new premises in Blanchardstown in 2002, it was selling approximately 10 million candles a year. Nearly half of these were sold to churches around the country in the form of shrine and votive tealights, Paschal candles, altar candles, and Advent, Easter and Candlemas Day candles. Like all Irish candle manufacturers, the company has come under serious pricing pressure with imports from lower-cost manufacturers in Eastern Europe and parts of Asia.

CANDLE TIPS
1) If you have room, keep them in a fridge. Wax contracts when it gets cold, so the colder they're kept, the longer they'll last.
2) You can tell a handmade candle by looking at the bottom; it should have rings, one for each time it was dipped, just like the rings of a tree.

Right: The white-washed enclave of Cody's Cottages on Ossory Road has since disappeared. (Photo: Paddy Curtis Collection).

Cody's Cottages
Ossory Rd

Seán O'Casey (1880 – 1964)

'The great art of the theatre is to suggest, not to tell openly; to dilate the mind by symbols, not by actual things; to express in Lear a world's sorrow, and in Hamlet the grief of humanity' – Seán O'Casey.

A GOOD NAME

When the Docklands Authority announced a competition to name the new pedestrian bridge across the Liffey in 2005, the community of East Wall successfully proposed the name of Seán O'Casey. Seán O'Casey was not just a Dublin playwright and author. He was a child of the Docklands, bred in the East Wall. In his 20s, he worked for the Great Northern Railway. At 31, he co-founded the St Laurence O'Toole Pipe Band. Two years later he was appointed first secretary of the Irish Citizen Army, although he stepped down when words of rebellion whispered on the breeze. In later life, he highlighted the plight of working-class Dubliners in a series of highly acclaimed plays, novels and memoirs.

THE MOVE TO EAST WALL

Seán O'Casey was born on 85 Dorset Street on 30th March 1880, the youngest of seven children in a lower-middle-class Protestant family. His father, Michael Casey, was a part-time teacher and secretary to the Irish Church Missions, a proselytizing body established to convert Roman Catholics to the Church of Ireland. His mother, Susan Archer, was the daughter of a prosperous auctioneer. Seán was christened 'John Casey' at John the Baptist Church in Clontarf. From an early age he was plagued by chronic trachoma, a common eye disease in poorer parts of Dublin. O'Casey's father died of a spinal injury when the author was only six years old. Low on money, Susan Casey moved her family to the Parish of Saint Barnabas in the East Wall, an unequivocally working-class area between the Great Northern Railway and the Docklands. She took a house on Hawthorn Terrace, between Church Road and West Road. This was the landscape that permeated her son's writings, a grimy industrial world on the slide.

ST BARNABAS SCHOOL

Due to his family's reduced circumstances and his own lousy vision, O'Casey received little formal schooling. He was one of 60 Protestant boys at St Barnabas Boys' School on Upper Sheriff Street. The hard times he endured under tyrannical headmaster John Hogan were vividly recalled in *I Knock at the Door*. One benefit was that O'Casey later made the enlightened concept of child-centred education one of his keynote battle cries, and was to prove a fine father to his own three children. With the aid of his elder sister Bella, a teacher, Seán mastered Shakespeare and other classics. He found a father figure in the Rev EM Griffin, Rector of St Barnabas, who encouraged him to learn how to read. In later life, O'Casey dedicated one of his autobiographies to Griffin.

THEATRICAL ORIGINS

By the age of 14, he had also begun taking on various odd jobs, moderately paid clerical positions and manual labour with Eason's bookshop. In 1894, his brother Tom returned from army service and found work as a railway shunter in the North Wall Goods Stores. The family then relocated to 4 Abercorn Road (now No 18) in the East Wall, where Seán and his older brother Archie staged performances of plays by Dion Boucicault and Shakespeare. Seán also got a small part in Boucicault's *The Shaughraun* in the Mechanics' Theatre, which stood on what was to be the site of the Abbey Theatre.

PIPES AND LOCK OUTS

In 1903, Seán went to work with a pick and shovel at the Great Northern Railway on Amiens Street. That same year, he joined the Gaelic League and the Gaelic Athletic Association, and began to use the Gaelic form of his name by which he is known today, Seán O'Casey. He learned the Irish language and the Irish pipes, and founded the St Laurence O'Toole Pipe Band. He joined the Irish Republican Brotherhood and became involved in Jim Larkin's Irish Transport and General Workers' Union. In 1913, he supported the union cause during the five-month Dublin Lock-Out, publishing newspaper articles and devoting time as an organizational and secretarial volunteer. Meanwhile, his heavy-drinking brother Mick spent 14 months in jail for assaulting an army sergeant who dared call him 'a good-for-nothing Irish bastard'. Long after Seán left Dublin, Mick, a talented artist and sociable wastrel, remained a familiar sight in the streets and pubs of the North Wall area: 'a comic little figure in a cap and muffler, with a strutting gait and a walking stick which he carried like a field marshal's baton'. Mick's arrest influenced the author's political stance and, during the same year, he helped to form, and became the first secretary for, the Irish Citizen Army – a militant branch of the Irish trade-union movement. He helped draw up its first socialist-inspired constitution but left a year later when James Connolly's leadership turned the ICA toward a more radical nationalism.

THE PLAYWRIGHT

In the late 1910s, O'Casey began writing his first plays, several of which were rejected. His first full-length play, *The Shadow of a Gunman*, was performed at the renowned Abbey Theatre in 1923. The play became very popular, establishing O'Casey as a true working-class hero. The following spring the Abbey produced O'Casey's *Juno and the Paycock* and, in 1926, came his anti-war epic *The Plough and the Stars*, arguably O'Casey's most popular play. These first three plays all depicted the harsh physical and political realities of life in the East Wall tenements of Dublin.

In 1927 he married Irish actress Eileen Carey Reynolds. The couple settled in England, where O'Casey wrote *The Silver Tassie*, an experimental play examining the effect the Great War had on Irish society. WB Yeats rejected the play on behalf of the Abbey Theatre. O'Casey had it produced in London, where it was a critical success but a popular failure. During the 1930s, O'Casey produced little drama, focusing instead on criticism, short stories and his memoirs. His first autobiography, *I Knock at the Door*, was published in 1939 and was followed by five more volumes during the 1940s and early 1950s. In 1943, he completed his most autobiographical work, *Red Roses for Me*, while 1949 gave rise to the beautiful *Cock-a-Doodle Dandy*. Seán O'Casey died aged 84 on 18th September 1964, in Torquay, England.

The Seán O'Casey Community Centre

The memory of Seán O'Casey is also recalled in the Seán O'Casey Community Centre in the East Wall. Commissioned by the Docklands Authority and Dublin City Council, the new centre opened in 2008. While it caters to the entire community, its facilities are particularly geared to senior citizens and pre-school children. There is a theatre, gym, games room, pottery room, gardens and café. The solid block building is distinguished by circular port holes that punctuate its façade. Three sizes of window provide for standing, sitting and full height views out to the street and the wider city. These windows also act as communication devices at a larger scale, representing a community landmark visible from the elevated train lines to the north, the sea to the east and the river to the south.

Below: The Seán O'Casey Centre was designed by O'Donnell + Tuomey. (Photo: Michael Moran). Right: St Barnabas Church was an icon of East Wall for 100 years before its demolition in 1969. (Photo: Paddy Curtis Collection).

St Barnabas Church

THE REDOUBTABLE GRAINGER

The parish of St Barnabas was established in 1866 and named for St Paul's Jewish companion, St Barnabas, stoned to death in Cyprus in 61AD. The first parson appointed to the parish was the charismatic Rev J Grainger from the parish of St Thomas. His brief was to look after the Protestant families of English and Welsh men employed by the London & North Western Railway (LNWR) at the company's facilities on the North Wall Quay and on the trains and steamers operating, via Holyhead and Liverpool, between Dublin and London. By holding services in private houses in the area – primarily at 7 Seaview Terrace and on Albert Avenue – he managed to increase his congregation in three years from 800 to 2,000.

THE NEW CHURCH

Among Grainger's early fans was a Miss Shannon of Rathmines. In her will, this wealthy lady left sufficient money for the founding of three churches for needy people. St Barnabas was one of the lucky recipients and, by 1869, the Rev Grainger was addressing his parish from the pulpit of a brand new £4,000 Gothic church, designed by Alfred Jones of Molesworth St, who also designed the Davenport Hotel. It was built on a site donated by solicitor Charles Gaussen. Jones also oversaw the construction of the adjoining St Barnabas School, paid for with a £400 donation by J Ball Esq. On account of the large number of dockers, the church became known as the Mariner's Church. Those awaiting the boat and staying at the redbrick Railway Hotel on the North Wall Quay were often to be found on bended knee within, praying for safe passage across the Irish Sea.

DAUNT, FLETCHER AND GRIFFIN

Grainger was transferred to Co Antrim before the church was finished and his place was filled by the Rev William Daunt. In 1872, Daunt was replaced by the Rev Harry Fletcher, who lasted 27 years and improved the church considerably with money donated by the LNWR. In 1899, Fletcher was obliged to leave the parish because of opposition to his high-church principles.

Into the pulpit stepped the Rev EM Griffin, a kindly bearded parson who, clad in black, always sported a green scarf and carried a walking stick. He steered the church through the Lock-Out, the Easter Rising and the First World War, during which 12 of the 27 parishioners serving on the Front were killed.

As a young man, Seán O'Casey sang his hymns in Irish here before heading off to hurl in the Phoenix Park. O'Casey was extremely fond of Griffin. His play *Red Roses for Me* is centred upon a church called 'Saint Burnupus'. The liberal Protestant clergyman, the Rev Clinton, is clearly based upon Griffin. Indeed, O'Casey not only dedicated the second volume of his autobiography to Griffin but, in 1946, published *The Biography of Rev E M Griffin, Who By Refusing to Be Either an Orangeman Or Freemason, Kept the Door to the Church Open for All to Enter*.

HALL AND SHORTT

The Rev DH Hall, aka the Building Parson, succeeded Griffin in 1918 and held tenure until 1929. (See page 148). His successor, Canon Shortt, remained Rector until the parish closed in 1965. The church had fallen into considerable disrepair after the Second World War. Film director Jim Sheridan recalls attending one of many fundraisers at a time when pigeons were flying through a large hole in the roof. The remaining church members were integrated into the United Parish of Drumcondra, North Strand and St Barnabas. The shell of the church remained for four years and was finally demolished in 1969, exactly 100 years after its foundation.

The Building Parson

THE STATE OF THE PARISH

In 1918, an energetic young Protestant clergyman called David Henry Hall arrived at St Barnabas Church to commence what would become an 11-year stint in the community. Upon his arrival, Hall walked the length and breadth of his parish. A heavily industrialized landscape, bounded by railways, canals and docks, this was amongst the poorest areas not just in Dublin but in all of Europe. The death rate in the parish was 46 per 1,000, nearly triple the city's average. Housing conditions were particularly wretched. An extreme instance was 10 Commons Street where Canon Hall found 84 children living under one roof. Ironically, these houses were frequently surrounded by large wastelands and derelict warehouses.

THE CANON'S REMEDY

Canon Hall's solution was practical and obvious. To reduce overcrowding, they needed to build more houses. When Canon Hall took this notion, it ran in the face of all advice from his contemporaries. Much of Europe still lay in ruins after five years of warfare. With Ireland on the cusp of another period of internal war, the political climate was considered far too precarious to risk investing in housing. The whole building trade was greatly unsettled. There were chronic shortages of both labour and materials. But Canon Hall was a persuasive soul. He understood the situation and believed urgency was required. If he was to sustain life in his parish, he had no option but to build. As he sermonized one Sunday, new houses would not only 'render happy the lives of many existing under conditions too awful to be described', but they would also create local employment.

IRELAND'S FIRST PUBLIC UTILITY SOCIETY

In the autumn of 1919, Canon Hall acquired a site of 3 ½ acres (c. 1.4ha) in his parish at a cost of £700 freehold. In January 1920, he established the St Barnabas Public Utility Society, the first operative public utility society in Ireland. He raised £1,000 from his parishioners, giving a particular nod to '67 gallant ladies [who] invested in the scheme', and secured a considerable grant from the British Government. On June 24th 1921, Lord Mayor Laurence O'Neill laid the namestone for St Barnabas Gardens, a short cul-de-sac of 10 semi-detached houses built on a one-acre site. They were designed and 'economically planned' by Messrs Batchelor and Hicks, who consulted a number of local women regarding how each house could work most smoothly. The inclusion of women in the planning process was particularly unique and radical. Each house included a bath and 'other necessary conveniences' with a small garden. By 1926, Hall's society had built over 170 new houses in East Wall. Bankrupt and directionless, Dublin Corporation only managed to build 162 dwellings during the same period.

AN ECUMENICAL VICTORY

The houses were owned by the society but there was a form of tenant purchase which ensured these artisans could become full owners in due course. One of the remarkable aspects of the St Barnabas scheme, particularly given the troubled political situation, was the ecumenical ambience. Hall may have been a Protestant but all denominations were present among the shareholders and tenants. Of the first 36 families who occupied the houses, 15 were Protestant and 21 Roman Catholic. In terms of resolving overcrowding, the new builds did not have all that much impact. In order to pay back monies owed, the society was obliged to charge relatively high rents, meaning the first wave of tenants tended to be from the 'most useful and intelligent section of the working classes'. Indeed, five of the houses went to former officers of the Royal Irish Constabulary.

A GENUINE UNSUNG HERO

In 1929, Hall was transferred from St Barnabas to Glenageary, where he remained until his sudden death on 27th February 1940. The final houses of the St Barnabas Scheme were bought out in the 1960s and Hall's Society was formally wound up. Canon Hall is now considered one of the key figures in Irish housing reform, establishing the idea of public utility societies as agents in housing provision.

Local Heroes

JOCKEYS, DONKEYS AND BILLY CANS

Harrison's Bakery, Johnny Cullen's Dairy and the Hibernian Dairy were landmarks of Church Road in the 1930s. One of Johnny Cullen's milkmen was a young boy called Séamus 'Tich' Tyrrell. With Johnny's encouragement, Tich approached Brackenstown trainer Paddy Usher and said he wanted to be a jockey. Usher gave him the job and, by the 1940s, Tich was Ireland's top jockey. Tich would have been familiar with Jerusalem and Bethlehem, two donkeys who lived in the front garden of the Maher's house on the Forth Road in the 1940s. When Bethlehem died during a particularly hard winter, the family took Jerusalem into the house and stabled him in the sitting room.

Another of Tich's contemporaries was Fluther Good, immortalized by O'Casey in *The Plough & the Stars* as the wise soul who noted that 'the world is in a state of chassis'. Fluther was employed to build jumps out of hay for the young horses.

In 1923, Sergeant Murphy a 13 year old gelding trained locally by Mr Nugent, won the Aintree Grand National. The horse was paraded through East Wall after its victory. When food became scarce after the Second World War, Mr Nugent slaughtered his herd of cattle to provide a week's supply of meat to East Wall. Charitable souls were never far away with gallant nurses and robust midwives always on the prowl. Sister Vincent ran a food centre on Church Road where children would gather with billy-cans that she would fill with potatoes, stew and rice – with a 'penn'orth of custard' to flavour the rice.

SONGSMITHS AND STRUMPETS

One present-day character is songwriter Paul O'Brien whose *Songs From The North Lotts* provides a charming, humorous and often poignant collection, including *The 100-Ton Crane* and *The Church Road 1970*. Television audiences will be familiar with local hero Vinnie McCabe, who played Pat Bannister in the RTE dramatization of *'Strumpet City'* and is currently starring as Seamus McAleer in *'Fair City'*. Another well-known East Wall citizen is Rúaidhrí Conroy who played young Tito in *'Into the West'* and subsequently won the Theatre World Award in 1998 for his star turn in Martin McDonagh's play *'The Cripple of Inishmaan'*.

Wiggins Teape

CHOCOLATE, CIGARETTES & WIGGINS TEAPE

One of the last great landmarks in the East Wall was the Wiggins Teape building. Built in 1931 for the Gallaher tobacco group, this was one of several such factories constructed at this time due to the operation of protective tariffs on tobacco. Here they manufactured cigarettes, pipe tobacco and hand-rolling tobacco. The architect was John Stevenson (1890-1950) of Samuel Stevenson & Sons, Belfast, President of the Royal Society of Ulster Architects from 1939 to 1943. Stevenson's classical bent was evident in the skilful massing, composition and detail of the façade, which was one of the earliest known uses of reconstituted stone in Dublin. The building was originally named Virginia House as a nod to the state from which Gallaher's acquired their tobacco. In the late 1930s, ownership was transferred to Fry Cadbury, who renamed it Alexandra House. The building was acquired by the paper manufacturers Wiggins Teape in 1965 and renamed Gateway House.

THE BIG TUMBLE

In 2000, Dublin Corporation gave the Collen Group the go-ahead to redevelop the Wiggins Teape site for offices. The planning permission effectively authorised the demolition of the building, with the exception of part of the central portico. Local artist James Hanley successfully appealed the decision. An Bord Pleanála agreed that the factory was of architectural and historical significance and should be retained. Just three days after An Bord Pleanála's ruling, bulldozers slipped into the East Wall and bulldozed the neo-classical beauty. *The Irish Times* described the demolition as 'disgraceful'. The Independent TD Tony Gregory called it 'an act of despicable vandalism'. The Collen Group maintained they were within their rights as the building was unlisted and dangerous.

Modern Times

THE EAST WALL VILLAGE

Under the direction of the Docklands Authority and Dublin City Council, East Wall has witnessed further regeneration in recent years. Dermot Pierce's East Point Business Park north of the Tolka may have provided an inspiration but it was the community itself that took the lead. The local population numbers about 3,800, with a higher-than-average number over the age of 65. Most of those who work are employed in manufacturing, transport and commerce. Work is under way on more than 400 new houses and apartments along the East Road, as well as a large underground car park. The hook-shaped Church Road is being developed as the centre of a new 'East Wall Village', with St Joseph's Church as the spiritual, communal and practical focal point. The playground at Russell Avenue East, recently upgraded, provides an additional focal point, as does the new Seán O'Casey Community Centre.

DOCKLANDS INNOVATION PARK

The old T&C Martin's timber yard on the East Wall Road has been converted into the Docklands Innovation Park, headquarters of Ireland's only special-interest radio station, Dublin City FM (formerly Anna Livia). The station broadcasts on 103.2FM seven days a week from 07:00 to 02:00. Among the programmes that the station produces and broadcasts is 'Sound School' in which secondary schools from the Docklands present their own show over the course of the school year. The Innovation Park is also home to the After-School Study Programme offices, helping local students prepare for the junior and leaving certificate exams.

SEÁN O'CASEY PARK

Located on Church Road, the small pocket park was officially opened by Bertie Ahern on 12th February 2007. The transformation of this hitherto unattractive wasteland was a collaborative effort between the East Wall Community Council, Dublin City Council, CIÉ and the Docklands Authority. Under the direction of Hugh McKenna, over 40 tons of material and topsoil were removed to make way for a plantation covered in dark green Heliz Hibernica ivy and 10 semi-mature silver birch trees. The black stone wall was also rebuilt and new gates installed.

East Point Business Park

ACQUISITION OF A LANDFILL SITE

Situated at the City-side entrance to the Port Tunnel, the East Point Business Park was the brainchild of the late property developer Dermot Pierce, FRICS, (1947 – 1999). This profoundly energetic butcher's son from Clontarf was a chartered surveyor by profession. He came to prominence in the 1980s when he masterminded the conversion of part of Dublin's dilapidated Earlsfort Terrace into the avenue of glazed contrasts that presently lights and reflects the National Concert Hall opposite. By 1990, Pierce had acquired a landfill site of 27 acres for IRL£3.75 million (€4.76 million) opposite the Clontarf seafront on the northern shoulder of Dublin Port. The site formed part of lands reclaimed in the 1960s from the tidal backwater by Dublin Port. Surrounded by oil storage tanks, container shipping berths and rusting cranes, it was accessed by a short concrete bridge over the Tolka estuary from the Alfie Byrne Road on the mainland.

THE GREEN LIGHT

Pierce was convinced this landfill could be converted into a light industrial park where thousands might work. He set up a hut on site and invited Harry E McKillop from Ballycastle, Co Antrim and Dallas, and his colleague, Isaac Manning, architect of a 17,000-acre industrial office park in Dallas, to survey the scene. Pierce gave them the full pitch and worked out the sums on a packet of 20 Major cigarettes. As Chief Executive of Earlsfort Centre Developments, he subsequently orchestrated the entire operation, abetted by a band of disciples. As costs soared, budgets vanished and his high-risk visions exploded, many would-be investors understandably paled. Legend has it that, while walking some senior bank officials around the site trying to convince them of its potential, Pierce suddenly stopped and said: 'It's a pile of shite, isn't it?' The remark brought considerable release and laughter to an otherwise tense situation. In the end, Anglo Irish Bank stepped up to the mark.

HITTING THE JACKPOT

The vast bulk of the park's first 23 buildings were designed by Brian Roe of Scott Tallon Walker and built by Ged Pierse Contracting (no relation of Dermot). The landscaping by Charles Funke Associates has received several major awards, both for the original planting and for the on-going maintenance. A further nine buildings have since been completed on an 11-acre extension made available by Dublin Port. In 1995, the first 64,000sq ft building was bought by four investors for £7.25 million (€9.2 million) and pre-let to ACT Kindle, the financial services software company founded by Kieran Nagle. The company proved a valuable launch customer and was subsequently joined by Oracle, Lufthanasa, Sun Microsytems, Cisco, Quintiles, AOL and Bertlesmann. Before long there was a constant stream of inward investment projects coming straight from the airport. Today, the industrial park also hosts offices for Google, Yahoo and, since August 2008, the headquarters of Enterprise Ireland.

SOMETHING FROM NOTHING

By the time of his premature death in June 1999, Pierce's dream was a reality, albeit a campus driven by hi-tech software, telemarketing, and research and design, rather than the light industrial park he had originally envisaged. He had achieved the remarkable, creating something from nothing. One-and-a-half million square feet of waterside, tree-lined, air-conditioned offices bring together more than 6,000 multinational workers who, between them, form one of the most dynamic corner stones of the modern Irish economy.

Left: The East Link Toll Bridge is presently the most easterly of the River Liffey crossings. Built by entrepreneurial Dublin businessman Tom Roche, it provides a link from the East Wall Road to Ringsend for both pedestrians and vehicles. (Photo: William Murphy)

Chapter Four
Westland Row & The South Quays

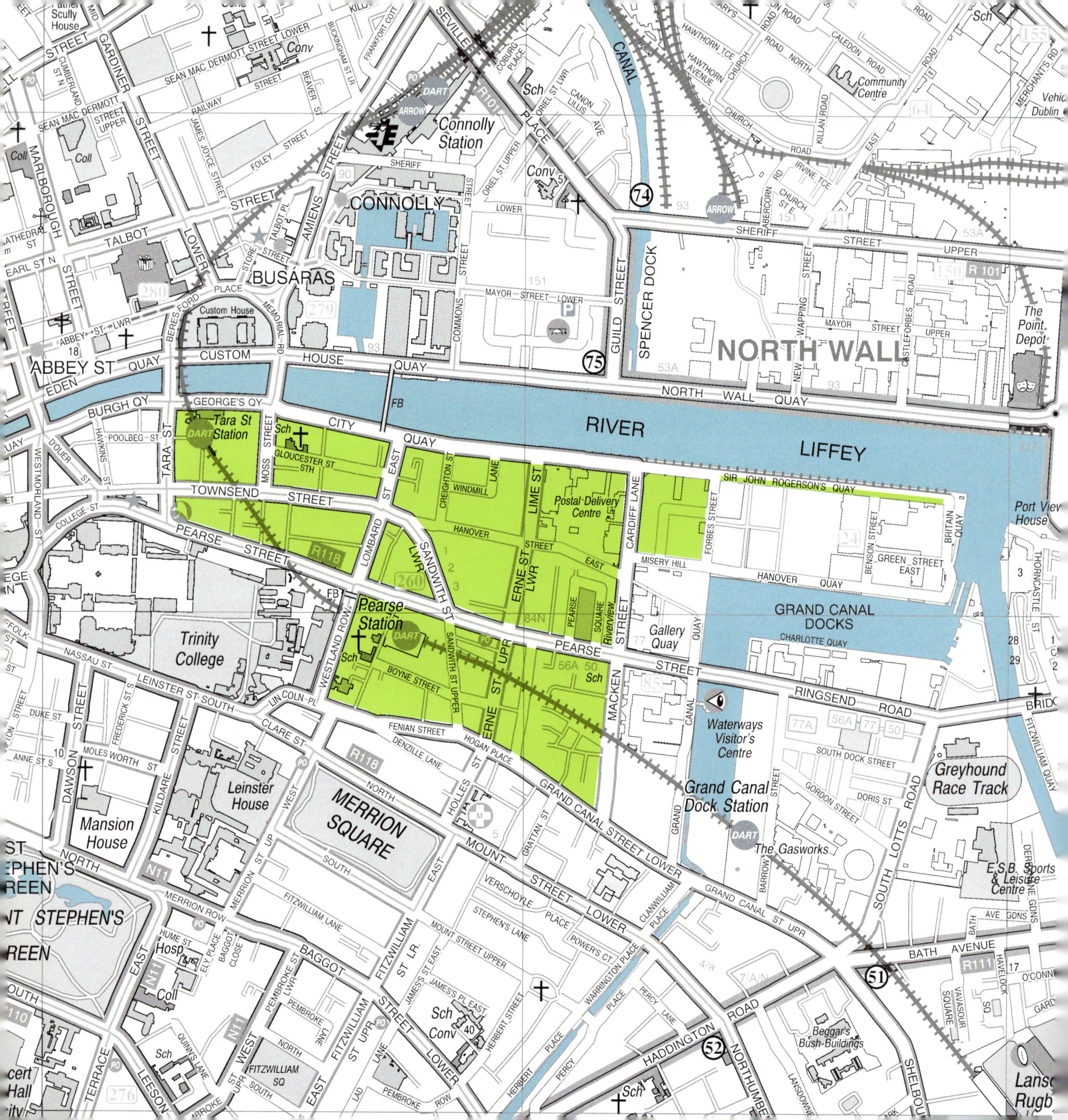

Connolly Station
CONNOLLY
BUSÁRAS
Custom House
ABBEY ST
CUSTOM HOUSE QUAY
NORTH WALL
NORTH WALL QUAY
RIVER LIFFEY
CITY QUAY
GEORGE'S QY
BURGH QY
EDEN QUAY
Tara St Station
TOWNSEND STREET
PEARSE STREET
Pearse Station
Trinity College
Postal Delivery Centre
SIR JOHN ROGERSON'S QUAY
HANOVER QUAY
GRAND CANAL DOCKS
CHARLOTTE QUAY
Gallery Quay
Waterways Visitor's Centre
Grand Canal Dock Station
The Gasworks
RINGSEND ROAD
Greyhound Race Track
E.S.B. Sports & Leisure Centre
MERRION SQUARE
Leinster House
Mansion House
ST STEPHEN'S GREEN
Port View House
The Point Depot
SPENCER DOCK
CANAL
SHERIFF STREET UPPER
MAYOR STREET LOWER
Community Centre
Beggar's Bush-Buildings
HADDINGTON ROAD
BATH AVENUE
MOUNT STREET LOWER
GRAND CANAL STREET LOWER
FITZWILLIAM SQ
SOUTH LOTTS ROAD

When Trinity College was founded in 1592, the landscape directly to its north comprised of a marshy swamp with an old hospice from which pilgrims set forth to Santiago de Compostella. In the following century, the first steps were taken to control the river and reclaim the land. By 1715, the Protestant Ascendancy were securely in power and the Dublin merchants began walling both sides of the river. John Mercer died before he could complete his dreams along City Quay but Sir John Rogerson's Quay was to have a profound effect on the shaping of the city, enabling the creation of the South Lotts. The evolution was slow but by the mid-19th century, the South Quays were teeming with industry. In Victorian times, the railways and tenement houses arrived practically hand-in-hand as the lands around the Grand Canal Docks developed into a hive of chemical factories and coal-yards. Bindon Blood Stoney's diving bell, used to rebuild the quay walls in the 1880s, stands today on Sir John Rogerson's Quay. Among the influential souls associated with the area were Daniel O'Connell, Oscar Wilde, Padraig Pearse and the Italian fish and chips guru Giuseppe Cervi. Activity along the quays continued a-pace through the 20th century but inevitably began to wane with the advent of containerisation and deeper berthing options in Dublin Port. When the Guinness ships ceased mooring along City Quay in 1993, it was truly the end of an era. However, four years later, the arrival of the Dublin Docklands Development Authority on Sir John Rogerson's Quay set in motion a new epoch, which has already had a profound and extremely positive impact on the surrounding inner city. The ongoing refurbishment of the campshires has been further boosted by two new bridges, named for Seán O'Casey and Samuel Beckett. For the hundreds of thousands who stroll through Dublin city centre every day, this new riverside quarter commands attention.

Westland Row & The South Quays - Streetwise

Boyne Street - Named for the battlefield on which William of Orange secured victory for the Protestant establishment. During the 1920s, Dublin Corporation built a number of houses here alongside stables used by coal-carrying dray horses.

Cardiff Lane - Named for Matthew Cardiff, or Kerdiff, a shipbuilder of Manx origin who moved his shipyard here from City Quay in 1786. His foreman was John Hammond, a friend of the Emmets and Sarah Curran, who in 1797 abandoned shipbuilding to become a harpsichord maker. Cardiff's yard later became Sheridan's coal yard and is now the site of the Maldron Hotel and the ESRI.

City Quay - See page 158.

Clarence Place - Named for the Duke of Clarence, later William IV, King of Great Britain and Ireland from 1830 to 1837.

Creighton Street - Named for the family of Abraham Creighton (Crichton), 1st Baron Erne of Crom Castle. His wife Elizabeth was granddaughter and heiress of Sir John Rogerson.

Cumberland Street - Built in 1773 and named for the 2nd Duke of Cumberland, younger son of George II. He was known as 'The Butcher' for his violent suppression of Jacobite rebels after the battle of Culloden Moor in 1746.

Denzille Lane - Named for the family of John Holles, 1st Earl of Clare. One of his daughters married Charles I's notorious henchman, 'Black Tom' Wentworth, while another married the 2nd Viscount Fitzwilliam.

Erne Street Upper & Lower - Named for Abraham Crichton, 1st Baron Erne of Crom Castle, Co Fermanagh, who married the Rogerson heiress.

Fenian Street - Formerly Denzille Street and renamed Fenian Street after the Fenian leaders who operated from here in the 1850s. The art deco Archer's Garage, illegally demolished in 1999, was the first building in Ireland to be made of reinforced concrete and fitted with fluorescent lighting.

George's Quay - Formerly Mercer's Dock, this was rebuilt as a quay in about 1714 and named for the new King George I. The shimmering glazed and copper-crowned pyramid of George's Quay Plaza (2003) and the Ulster Bank headquarters (2000) form a landmark known by wags as Canary Dwarf.

Gloucester Street - Located to the rear of City Quay Church, this was known as Martin's Lane in the 1720s but renamed in 1756 for the Duke of Gloucester, brother of George III and Chancellor of Trinity College from 1771 to 1805.

Great Brunswick Street - The former name for Pearse Street commemorated the German Duchy of Brunswick, owned by the Electors of Hanover, from where George IV's Queen Caroline came.

Hanover Street East - A number of warehouses in the area date to the 1890s and may be associated with the short-lived Dublin City Distillery, capable of producing 1,500,000 gallons of whiskey per year. The distillery operated from 1890 to 1905.

Hogan Place - Formerly Wentworth Place, this was renamed for John Hogan (1800–1858), the Waterford-born sculptor and nationalist who lived here for the last nine years of his life. Among his best-known works is the *Farrell Memorial* in St Andrew's Church, Westland Row.

Lazar Hill - See page 160.

Lime Street - In the 18th century, daubing a ship's planks with burnt lime powder was the preferred method for disinfecting wooden ships. Many of the quicklime stores were based here on this street.

Lombard Street - Originally comprised of shipyards that ran all the way down to City Quay this was named in about 1794 for property developer James FitzGerald Lombard. In 1858, the Irish Republican Brotherhood held its first meeting at 16 Lombard Street, home of Peter Langan, lathe-maker and timber merchant.

Macken Street - The street was originally Great Clarence Street, named for William IV, the Sailor King, and immediate predecessor to his niece Queen Victoria. In 1923, Dublin Corporation renamed the street for Peader Macken, an ardent Gaelic revivalist and Labour alderman for the South Dock Ward. He attended the meeting at which the Easter Rising was planned but was killed in the fighting at Boland's Mills.

Martin's Terrace - Named for Sir Richard Martin's timber yard which lay behind the wall on the site now occupied by An Post's Dublin 2 Delivery Office. Sir Richard, an affluent ship-owner, was Chairman of the Port Authority from 1899 until his death in 1901.

Misery Hill - In medieval times, this was the last refuge for pilgrims and lepers bound for Saint Iago de Compostella who could not afford to stay in the hospice at Lazar Hill. It apparently derives its name from an age when the corpses of those executed at Gallows Hill near Upper Baggot Street were carted here and strung up to rot as a warning to other would be troublemakers.

Moss Street - Formerly called Moss Lane, this was probably a corruption of 'Mercer's Lane', though some claim it was named for Dr Bartholomew Mosse, the pioneering surgeon who established the world's first purpose-built maternity hospital at the Rotunda. The City Arts Centre on the riverfront was formerly Eckford's Ships' Chandlers Emporium, selling 'everything from copper nails to ships' anchors'.

Pearse Square - Formerly Queen's Square, this enclosed, fully serviced development was laid out in the 1830s and named for the new Queen Victoria, crowned in 1837. Many of its early residents were actors associated with the Queen's Royal Theatre on Pearse Street.

Pearse Street - Originally known as Great Brunswick Street, this is one of the longest streets in Dublin. It was renamed in December 1921 for the Easter 1916 heroes, Padraig and Willie Pearse.

Sandwith Street - Named for Quaker businessman Joseph Sandwith, one of the Commissioners of the Ballast Office who set up the Port and Docks Board. This street was the Liffey shoreline 400 years ago. To this day, certain premises have to pump water out of their basements at spring and neap tides.

Shaw Street - Named for Sir Robert Shaw of Bushy Park, Tory MP for Dublin from 1804 to 1826.

Sir John Rogerson's Quay - Named for a former Lord Mayor of Dublin who privately funded the construction of the original wall on which the quay now stands.

Tara Street - Named for the ancient Royal capital of Ireland at the Hill of Tara, Co Meath. The present street dates to 1885 and was rebuilt as an extension of Butt Bridge, comprising the former alleys, Stocking Lane and Shoe Lane. The multi-storey Fireworks Nightclub occupies the central fire station built here in Edwardian times.

Townsend Street - See page 158.

Westland Row - See page 158.

Windmill Lane - Named for a windmill recorded here in 1823. The stump of the windmill remained until the 1960s. A former Bovril factory was converted into the prestigious Windmill Lane Recording Studios, now owned by Spice Girls and David Gray producers Biffco.

City Quay & Townsend Street

CITY QUAY

In 1712, shortly before George I brought the House of Hanover to power in the United Kingdom, a parcel of marshland just north of Trinity College came under the ownership of John Mercer. In 1713, Mercer began work on a river wall to tame the marsh in an area now bordered by Townsend Street and Poolbeg Street. However, ill-health put paid to his ambitions and he died in 1718. The City took over the construction of the wall, completed by 1720 and named City Quay.

TOWNSEND STREET

In the 19th century, a 'Townsender' was the name of a miser who retired to a remote place to count his wealth. This referred to the fact that this street, formerly known as Lazar's Hill, was a low, muddy and rambling coastline at the 'end of the town' running down through meadows to low crumbing cliffs. Despite the coincidence, the street was most likely named after Field Marshal Viscount George Townsend, Lord Lieutenant of Ireland from 1767–1772. The first of the Magdalene Laundries (aka 'rescue homes for fallen women') was opened here in 1798 by Mrs Brigid Bourke and Patrick Quarterman. Five years later, two of Robert Emmet's accomplices were hanged on the street. The famous heavyweight boxer Dan Donnelly was born in Townsend Street in 1788 while No 6 was home to the first coffee palace in Ireland, run by the Dublin Total Abstinence Society. Founded in 1909, the Irish Transport & General Workers Union had its humble beginnings in a tenement in Townsend Street where it assets were 'a couple of chairs, a table, two empty bottles and a candle'.

Right: George's Quay, City Quay and Sir John Rogerson's Quay run along the southside of the River Liffey to the point where it meets the River Dodder and the Grand Canal Docks towards the top right of the photo. The parish of Westland Row comprises much of the city beyond the Trinity College playing fields in the bottom right of the photo. (Photo: Peter Barrow)

Westland Row

In the 17th century, the newly reclaimed lands around the Pearse Street - Westland Row intersection comprised a 5-acre brickfield owned by John Hansard of Lazar's Hill. In 1710, the brickfield was purchased by William Westland of Cow Lane who was buried in St Audeon's in 1730. Westland Row was completed by his son in 1772. Daniel O'Connell lived here from 1802 until his move to Merrion Square in 1809. Twenty years later, he secured Emancipation for Ireland's Catholics. In 1832, work began on St Andrew's, the first Catholic Church in Ireland to be built on a main street since penal times. Not surprisingly, O'Connell was its chief parishioner. Many babies born in the Holles Street Maternity Hospital were baptised here including the Pearse brothers, Kevin Barry, Brendan Behan and Hugh Leonard. In 1844, the Christian Brothers established their school at the back of the church. Its past pupils include the Pearse brothers and Philip Monahan, Ireland's first Local Authority Manager. In 1854, Oscar Wilde was born at No 21. In 1871 the Royal Irish Academy of Music moved to No 36 Westland Row, acquiring the two neighbouring houses of Nos 37 and 38 in 1911. The Westland Row Railway Station was completed in 1884, greatly increasing the footfall in the surrounding area. In the 1940s, proximity to this station led the Catholic Social Welfare Bureau to establish their main Emigration Centre for those leaving Ireland at No 18.

Every Sunday there's a throng
Of pretty girls, who trot along
In a pious, breathless state
(They are nearly always late)
To the Chapel, where they pray
For the sins of Saturday.

From 'Westland Row' by James Stephens.

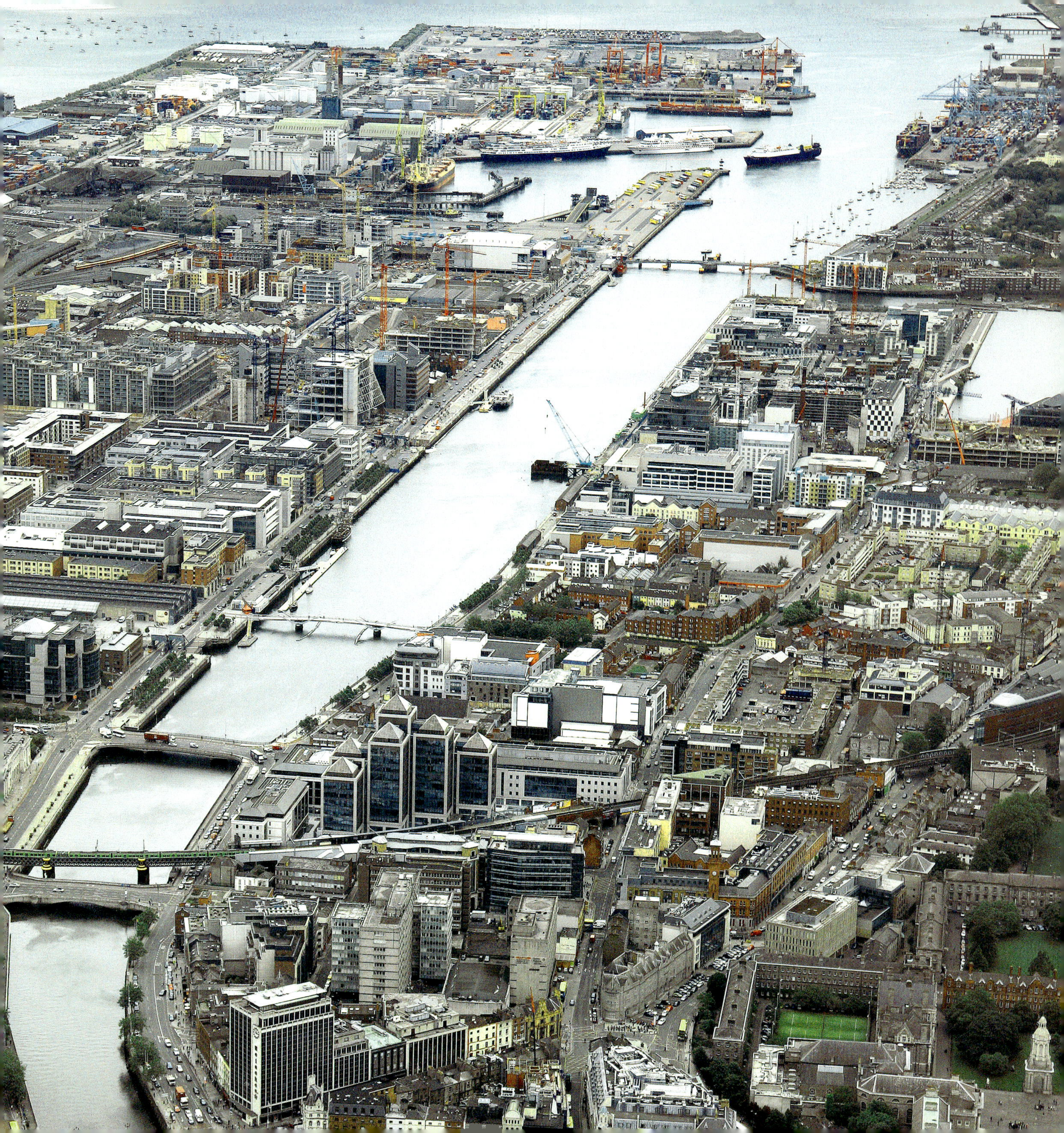

The Hospital On Lazar's Hill

In 1216, Henry Blund, Archbishop of Dublin, founded the Hospital of Saint James, a hostel for pilgrims and the poor of Dublin, on present day Townsend Street, then known as Lazar's Hill or Lazy Hill. It stood roughly where Pearse Street Garda Station stands today, right beside the All Hallows Monastery which later became Trinity College. Indeed, this was almost precisely where the first Danish long-ships are said to have landed, an event commemorated by the memorial long stone, or Steyne, created by Cliodhna Cussen.

The Hospital was named for the apostle Saint James the Great, also known as Saint Iago, whose remains are said to lie beneath the Cathedral of Santiago de Compostella in Galicia in North West Spain. Known as The Way of St James, Santiago was one of the most important Christian pilgrimage destinations of medieval times. Before the River Liffey was contained, the tidal waters came right up to Townsend Street and College Green. Pilgrim ships destined for Santiago apparently berthed alongside this Hospital, then sailed directly to the coast of Galicia and anchored at Ferrol or A Coruña, from where the pilgrims made their way to Santiago overland.

By the mid 13th century, some of these ships were carrying lepers desperate for a miraculous cure. Leprosy has been tormenting mankind since at least 600BC when the Hindu author of *Atharva-veda* suggested some ritualistic cures for the condition. In the 11th century, the crusading warriors of the Middle East found their makeshift hospitals overrun with persons afflicted with leprous skin conditions. The Order of St. Lazarus of Jerusalem was duly founded with the specific purpose of establishing leper hospitals. The first recorded leprosarium was built in Harbledown near Canterbury in 1084. By the early 13th century, there were some 19,000 such hospices across Europe.

The Hospital of Saint James seems to have evolved into a leper hospice within a short time. Run along strict Augustinian principles, it was a well-run retreat, providing a good diet, clothing and sanitation. Not all lepers could afford such luxury. A rather more downtrodden colony is said to have existed further east on Misery Hill. Lepers lived in these monastic-type establishments not simply for the good of their health, but also as a form of perpetual quarantine. The only acceptable way to check out of a leper hospice was to perish.

Another word for these quarantine stations was 'Lazaretto' and it is from this that Townsend Street took its former name of Lazar Hill, sometimes corrupted to 'Lazy Hill'. Bound by marshy slobs to the north and meadows and orchards to the south, this gentle slope was the only route between Dublin and Ringsend. The use of the word 'Lazaretto' has rather morbid connotations, linked to Jesus Christ's good friend Saint Lazarus. Roman Catholic tradition holds that Saint Lazarus, who Jesus raised from the dead, was a leper. In the dark, superstitious and utterly frightful Medieval Age, it was widely believed that lepers were simply going through Purgatory on Earth. Thus their suffering was considered more holy than the ordinary person's. The medical opinion of the day held that leprosy was contagious, contracted by eating raw meat and that whiskey was the best medicine. For most people, lepers simply existed in a place somewhere between life and death. They were still alive, but their reality was something rather more ethereal. This perhaps explains why everyone went silent and fled inside whenever the 'unclean' were passing up Lazar's Hill, one man tolling a bell and another carrying a 40-foot white pole to keep everyone at a safe distance. Hence the expression: 'I wouldn't touch him with a 40-foot pole'. It was not until the introduction of multidrug therapy (MDT) in the early 1980s that leprosy was properly diagnosed. In 2008, the World Health Organization registered 212, 000 people who were disabled because of leprosy.

BRIAN: Who cured you?
EX-LEPER: Jesus did, sir. I was hopping along, minding my own business. All of a sudden, up he comes. Cures me. One minute I'm a leper with a trade, next minute my livelihood's gone. Not so much as a by your leave. 'You're cured mate.' Bloody do-gooder.
   From Monty Python's *'The Life of Brian'*.

Pearse Railway Station

In 1834, Dubliners became the first people in Ireland to have a public railway with the opening of the line south along the coast to Kingstown (Dún Laoghaire). By 1855, the city had rail connections with the south and west of the country, as well as Belfast. At this time, a number of independent and competing companies operated the railway service. Each sought to ensure their passengers enjoyed as comfortable and convenient a journey as possible. Completed in 1884, Pearse Station (then known as Westland Row Station) was the original terminus for the Dublin and Kingstown Railway before the Loopline Bridge was built across the Liffey, connecting it with Connolly Station (then known as Amiens Street Station). As well as handling all the freight and passengers, the station had to be able to cope with the arrival and departure of several trains at once.

The barrel-vaulted building was designed not so much as a railway station but as a train shed in which trains might be given some form of protection from the elements. It also enabled passengers to board and alight in comfort. The large curved roof was based on an early Victorian design which Dublin iron founder Richard Turner created for the Lime Street station in Liverpool. Its principals and arched girders were made in Chepstow. The Dublin foundry of Courtney, Stephens and Bailey supplied the remaining ironwork.

After the connection to Amiens Street was established in 1891, the north-west end of the station was modified to make room for the new trains. An innovative street-facing façade was also built, consisting of wrought-iron pillars inserted between the existing masonry abutments, with decorative cast-iron panels to match the ornamentation of the new bridge spanning Westland Row. Pearse Station doubled as Limerick train station in Alan Parker's film adaptation of 'Angela's Ashes'.

Below: *The Linesman* on City Quay by Dony MacManus.

City Quay – A Potted History

THE SOUTH QUAYS

City Quay runs from the Talbot Memorial Bridge past Seán O'Casey Bridge to the Samuel Beckett Bridge by Sir John Rogerson's Quay. Together with George's Quay, these became known as the 'South Quays' and swiftly developed into one of the busiest shipping areas in Ireland in the 19th century. In 1846, the *Illustrated London News* produced a panorama of the Liffey which showed the South Quays to be utterly crammed with shipping. However, the accompanying text observed that business had waned considerably since the start of the century. The author placed the blame squarely on the Act of Union for making Dublin a 'deposed capital' and hampering 'all further progress' of the port's trade'. Fifty years ago, the South Quays was still a frenetic waterfront, teeming with schooners, trawlers, ships, Brixham smacks, cranes, horses and humanity. In the mornings, thousands of cloth-capped dockers gathered along the quayside on the off-chance that they would be selected for a days' work. Their job could be loading or unloading anything from Brillo Pads to Chrysler cars. At this time, City Quay was home to the 'free berths' used by Clyde Shipping, Bristol Steam and the Bridgewater schooners who unloaded their cargo of earthenware and bricks. One man threw each brick onshore; two men caught them on the quayside. In 1897, Tedcastles combined with John McCormick to form Tedcastle & McCormick. Their slack 'nuts' proved a huge hit across the country, heating houses and driving steam lorries from Limerick to Letterkenny. The Tedcastle steamers berthed along City Quay and Sir John Rogerson's Quay. Many of its Republican-minded crew ran guns between 1916 and 1922. When Michael Collins secured de Valera's escape from Lincoln Gaol in 1919, it was a Tedcastle coalship that escorted him back to Ireland.

THE SEAMAN'S CHURCH

The Church of the Immaculate Heart of Mary on City Quay was built in 1861 to a design by John Bourke and JL Robinson. Specifically aimed at seamen, it serves the small Parish of City Quay, which runs along the quays from Tara Street to Macken Street. Originally built to serve as a chapel of ease to St Andrews Church on Westland Row, it became a parish of its own right in 1908. In 1998 its diocesan priests handed the parish over to the Divine Word Missionaries (SVD) who now work alongside 'The Poor Servants of the Mother of God's Sisters'.

GOOD STOUT AND IRON STRUMPETS

From the 1920s onwards, City Quay became synonymous with the Guinness ships and barges that moored here. (See page 68 & 165). Heiton's had their offices and an iron and steel warehouse next to The Happy Brig pub. On summer evenings, the local women gathered along the quayside, clad in starched white aprons, to chatter about days gone by. One of the most visually stimulating aspects of the 20th century was the coming and going of the B+I passenger ferries. The B&I Line had a major depot in the Edwardian redbrick warehouse that stands beside the Ivory Building on City Quay. The sheds alongside which the Liverpool-bound steamers anchored are still there today. So too is the warehouse, with its elegant railing, later leased to the New York merchant firm of Raimey, traders of coffee, tea, sugar, wheat, rubber and silk. Further east along the riverfront, the coal and timber yards ran as far as the Grand Canal Docks. On Windmill Lane, to the rear, was the Tonge & Taggart ironworks where the men stoked red-hot furnaces and moulded buckets, pipes and manhole covers, like Morgan's Foundry where Fitz and the boys worked in *'Strumpet City'*.

ST MARK'S (CHURCH OF IRELAND), PEARSE STREET

Better known today as the Family Worship Centre, the origins of St Mark go back to 1707 when the parish of St Mark was separated from that of St Andrew. Construction on this modest church commenced in 1729 but it was not roofed until 1752. Oscar Wilde was baptized here while among those buried in the grounds are Charles Spalding and Ebenezer Watson, the Scotsmen who drowned while experimenting with their Diving Bell in the Bay in 1783.

Sculpture & Chip Shops

A SCULPTED STROLL

Today, tourists, couriers, labourers and smart-dressed office workers hurry to and fro along the quayside, slaloming between bicyclists and handsome yellow lime trees. The Irish Merchant Seamen's National Memorial by Lombard Street commemorates those lost at sea during World War Two. Nearby is a statue of the *Venerable Matt Talbot,* with his back pointedly turned to the IFSC. Commissioned by the Docklands Authority in 2000, *The Linesman* by Dony MacManus is an enchanting bronze of a docker hauling on a rope along the City Quay campshire. An Bord Pleanála has granted permission for a new work to stand where Lombard Street meets City Quay. The proposed ethereal giant is a 46m (151ft)-high black steel lattice sculpture of a male figure by Turner Prize-winning artist Antony Gormley. 'I'm trying to make something that is unequivocally of its time', explained the sculptor. 'That is, in terms of tools, and techniques, and even in the idea of a virtual being, we're pushing at the limits of what's possible'.

IRELAND'S FIRST FISH & CHIP SHOP

In the early 1880s, Giuseppe Cervi disembarked from an American-bound ship at Cobh and walked to Dublin. The young Italian worked as a labourer until he saved enough money to buy a hand-cart and a coal-fired cooker. He began selling chips to hungry Dubliners as they piled out of pubs. By 1900 Giuseppe and his wife Palma had a fish and chip shop on Great Brunswick Street, now Pearse Street. Palma's English was so poor that she would simply point to the fish and chips, saying 'uno di questo, uno di quello?', meaning 'one of this and one of the other'. This eventually passed into Dublin parlance as 'a one and a one'. Giuseppe's grandson Joe was subsequently manager of the Rabbitte family's wholesale and retail Italian food business, now based at Little Italy on North King Street.

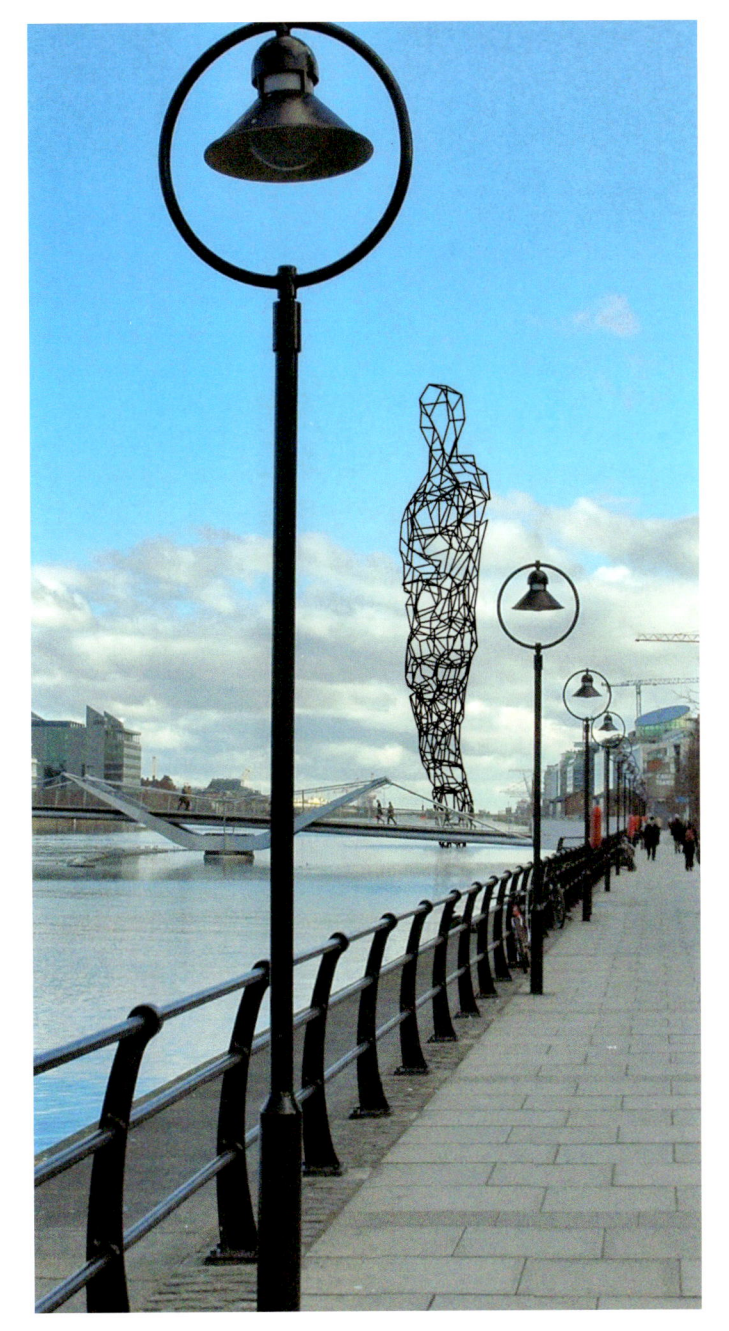

Right: A simulated image of Antony Gormley's proposed sculpture for the Liffey.

The Brothers Pearse

During the 1850s, there was a terrific revival in church building across Ireland by the Catholic Church. In the 1860s, English stone-mason James Pearse moved to Dublin from Birmingham to work on Pugin's marvellous new Church of SS Augustine and John on Thomas Street. In 1870, James set up his monumental sculpture works at 27 Great Brunswick Street, subsequently named Pearse Street after his two sons. Somewhat ironically, the late Georgian house stood just two doors up from the British Army Recruiting Office.

In 1877, James Pearse married Margaret Brady, mother of his two sons Padraig (1879-1916) and Willie (1881-1916). The bothers were born in No 27 and educated locally in Wentworth Place (now Hogan Place) and at the Christian Brothers School on Westland Row. The pensive Padraig was an early adherent to the Gaelic League and, at the age of 23, became editor of the League's newspaper, *An Claidheamh Soluis* ('The Sword of Light'). In 1908 he set up Scoil Éanna (St Enda's School) in Ranelagh, where pupils were taught in both Irish and English. In 1910, the school was relocated to Hermitage in Rathfarnham.

When James Pearse died in 1900, Willie took over the Great Brunswick Street studio, subsequently known as 'Pearse & Sons'. At its peak, this was the largest monumental sculpture firm in Ireland, employing up to 86 workers. The firm produced many altarpieces, monuments and ornamental features of considerable beauty. Willie himself studied sculpture at the Metropolitan School of Art in Dublin under Oliver Sheppard. Among his best-known works is the rather prophetic '*Mater Dolorosa*' at St Andrew's Church in Westland Row. He was also employed as deputy headmaster to his brother at Scoil Éanna, looking after art, drawing and theatre.

By 1913 the fervently Catholic Padraig was one of the key players in the Irish Volunteers. In December 1914, Padraig was sworn into the secret Irish Republican Brotherhood and co-opted onto the Supreme Council. He was among those who planned the 1916 Easter Rising. The Brothers Pearse were at the head of the Irish Volunteers when they stormed the General Post Office. From its steps, 36-year-old Padraig Pearse read the Proclamation of Independence. Six days later, Padraig issued the order to surrender. Padraig was executed by firing squad at Arbour Hill Barracks on the morning of 3rd May 1916. Willie was executed exactly 24 hours later.

In 1996, No 27 was close to collapse when acquired by the Ireland Institute, a body designed to promote the international ideals of republicanism, but with no links to political parties. The artist Robert Ballagh is its president. The building was sensitively restored and, in 2000, it discreetly reopened as the Ireland Institute's official headquarters. In 2008, a space to the rear of No 27 was converted into the 75-seat Pearse Centre. This is designed for theatre, lectures and political debate and hosted the Desmond Greaves Summer School in 2008.

Lord, thou art hard on mothers;
We suffer in their coming and their going;
And tho' I grudge them not, I weary, weary
Of the long sorrow - And yet I have my joy;
My sons were faithful, and they fought

From '*Mother*', written by Padraig Pearse to his mother the day before his execution.

Below: No 27 Pearse Street where Padraig and Willie spent their childhood. Right: Loading kegs of Guinness onto the ships waiting along City Quay.' (Photos: Guinness Archives)

The Guinness Ships

The first record of Guinness being exported out of Ireland dates to 1769, when 6½ barrels were shipped to England. The brewery expanded its links to the Isle of Man in 1810, Lisbon in 1811, Bristol in 1819 and the Channel Islands in 1822. By 1840, you could drink the black stuff in Trinidad, Sierra Leone, Barbados and New York. In 1873, the company built Victoria Quay alongside the brewery from which the legendary Guinness steam barges carried the barrels downriver until the advent of transportable tanks in the 1950s. (See page 68).

Up until 1913, all Guinness was exported by regular shipping companies. In December 1913, the company purchased its first vessel, the ss *W.M. Barkley*. For the next eighty years, the Guinness ships were to be a familiar sight to all who worked in the Dublin Docklands. *W. M. Barkley* was torpedoed and sunk near the Kish Lighthouse in 1917.

By 1930, the export trade to London was such that a new ship, the ss *Guinness* was built, tailormade to carry 3,000 hogsheads. Between 1952 and 1962, three new Guinness motorships were launched, each one named for members of the Guinness family – *Lady Grania*, *Lady Gwendolen* and *Lady Patricia*. The latter was converted into the world's first bulk beer tanker, capable of carrying 1.64 million pints. In 1976, *Lady Patricia* was joined by *Miranda Guinness*, the first purpose-built beer tanker, named for the Countess of Iveagh. The beer now came direct from the Brewery to City Quay on stainless steel 'Silver Bullet' road tankers. Each tanker carried 130 barrels which were then discharged into the ships tanks - *Miranda Guinness* had 15 such tanks. The two ships sailed from City Quay across the Irish Sea to Runcorn and Garston, where the beer was again discharged into road tankers before its final journey to the pubs of England, Scotland and Wales.

In 1987 management of the Guinness fleet passed to the Irish Marine Services Ltd. However, as Guinness opened breweries all over the world, so the relevance of the ships declined and, in 1993, the company discontinued its tanker operation. Stout was henceforth pumped into tanker containers and carried on ordinary ships. *Miranda Guinness* was renamed *Maigue* and demolished at Bramley Moore Dock, Liverpool, in 1993. *Lady Patricia* was renamed *Maine* and broken up in a Manchester dry dock the following year.

Asgard II

On September 11th 2008, many were stunned to hear that the *Asgard II* had sunk in the Bay of Biscay. The sail-training vessel was a regular visitor to the Dublin Docklands. Owned by the Ministry of Defence and managed by Coiste an Asgard, the ship was built to absolute perfection in Arklow, Co Wicklow. Completed in 1981, its architect was the late Jack Tyrrell, a consummate craftsman who hand picked every single plank of oak. The design was based on that used by Brigantine pirates in the 17th century and was operated by muscle and wind. Frank Traynor, skipper for eight years, reckoned she was one of the fastest, safest and sturdiest ships ever built. She was heading to a maritime festival in La Rochelle when she sank. The crew and the trainees were picked up by the French Coast Guard and taken to the Island of Belle-Ile. At time of print, the vessel has been located on the seabed and appears to be upright and largely intact. Further investigations are underway but it is widely hoped that the priceless ship may yet be salvaged.

The *Asgard II* was named for *Asgard*, a gaff rigged Ketch designed and built by Colin Archer of Larvik, Norway, in 1905. The name 'Asgard' is an old Norse word meaning 'Home of the Gods'. The original two-master was destined for considerable fame when Dr. and Mrs. Hamilton Osgood of Boston presented it to their daughter Mary on the occasion of her marriage. Her husband was the writer Erskine Childers, subsequently one of the most controversial figures of the Irish War of Independence. In July 1914 Erskine, Mary and four others sailed *Asgard* to the North Sea to collect a cargo of German guns for the Irish Volunteers. The cargo landed at Howth on 26 July 1914, just two days before the outbreak of the Great War. *Asgard* was sold in 1926 and passed through several hands before being purchased by the Irish Government in 1961. She was transferred to Kilmainham Jail Historical Museum in 1979 for exhibition to the public, and is now owned by the developer Harry Crosbie. In 1973, Erskine and Mary Childers's eldest son Erskine became the fourth President of Ireland.

The Gilbert Library

Commissioned by Dublin Corporation and built between 1907 and 1909, the purpose-built classical library on Pearse Street was funded by one of the earliest philanthropic grants from Scottish-born steel magnate Andrew Carnegie. Designed by Charles J. McCarthy, City Architect, the Georgian Revival building features a façade of Mount Charles sandstone, dressed with Ballinasloe limestone. The building was sensitively remodelled by Bernard Grimes in 2002 with a new four storey range to the rear and now also contains the Dublin City Archive. This excellent library was named for John T. Gilbert (1829-1898), author of the influential three volume 'History of the City of Dublin', published from 1857-59. Another of his great achievements was the establishment of the Public Records Office in the Four Courts. His valuable library of 17th and 18th century books and manuscripts relating to Dublin and Ireland was purchased by Dublin Corporation after his death. Held by the Pearse Street library, it is known today as the Gilbert Collection. Other collections held by the library include the medieval City Charters and City Assembly Rolls; the archives of the 18th century Wide Streets Commission; the archives of the Mansion House Fund, and the papers of notable theatrical figures Jimmy O'Dea and Mícheál Mac Liammóir. Discreetly on display in the library is the head of Admiral Nelson, salvaged when Nelson's Column was blown up in 1966.

Queen's Royal Theatre

"Children in arms cost one guinea. The public are advised that there are police in attendance. Bicycles are stored free. Gentlemen in bare feet are not admitted." These, according to the last assistant manager of the Queen's Royal Theatre on Pearse Street, were the quaint words emblazoned upon an old promotional poster from the 1950s. Known simply as the Queen's, the theatre was built in 1844 on the site of the former Adelphi Theatre. During the 1930s and 1940s, this was the home of the Happy Gang, a troupe of comics, singers and musicians who specialised in farce and pantomime. These were the vaudeville days when everyone tended to sing-a-long to *'Jake the Peg, diddle-iddle-iddle-dum'* and so forth. Gang members included Danny Cummins, Cecil Nash and Rose Tynan. In 1935, Maureen Potter appeared as a fairy in a pantomime with Jimmy O'Dea, then Ireland's foremost comedian. Her subsequent take-off of Alfie Byrne, the Lord Mayor of Dublin, brought the house down. In 1951, the Abbey Theatre burned down and the Abbey theatre company took a lease on the Queen's for sixteen years. The theatre closed in 1969 and was demolished in 1975.

Below: Photographed in the 1960s, Macken Street marks the end of the Westland Row parish. (Photo: Dublin City Council). Left: The Gilbert Library was completed in 1909 and named for an influential Dublin historian. (Photo: Dublin City Library). Far left: The Asgard II before she sank in the Bay of Biscay

St Andrew's Resource Centre, Pearse Street

THE POET'S REBELLION
One of the more notable Victorian buildings on Pearse Street is a former Catholic primary school that is now headquarters of the influential St Andrew's Resource Centre. With its' yellow and red-brick façade, the two-storey building could feasibly serve as a location for 'The Tudors'. Completed in 1897 and designed by William Hague, it was built to look after some 1,200 children of the Docklands at the behest of Father O'Malley, PP. In 1909, Countess Markievicz and Bulmer Hobson co-founded Fianna Éireann, a para-military organisation that instructed teenage boys in the use of firearms. Eight St. Andrew's boys were selected as the first recruits. The Fianna boys would play an important role in 1916, carrying messages and firearms to rebel strongholds across the city in what, according to the school's roll books for Easter Week 1916, they rather fetchingly described as the 'Poets' Rebellion'.

THE SOCIAL SERVICE CENTRE
The school continued to operate until the 1970s when local depopulation forced its closure. Fortunately it acquired an exceptional new owner in the form of the pioneering Westland Row & City Quay Social Service Council. In 1960, there were approximately 22,500 families living in the two parishes. By 1970, the massive slum clearances of inner city Dublin meant the total population of the area had plummeted to less than 6,000. Those left behind were mainly too old to move, with a high percentage dependent on social welfare. 'It was very traumatic', recalls Betty Ashe, who was born on Pearse Street. 'The community just disappeared.'

THE MOVE TO ST. ANDREW'S
'We couldn't just watch it go on declining', says Betty. 'We had to fight back'. In 1971, a group of community activists established the Social Service Council in premises given by Trinity College on Westland Row. From here they provided the service of a social worker and a community worker, seconded from the Health Board. They also operated a day-care centre for the elderly and an Adult Education Programme (AEP). In 1985, they acquired a lease from the Archdiocese to develop the old boy's school into the Community Resource Centre. Today, some 30 senior citizens arrive at the Resource Centre every day for a bite to eat, a bit of banter and the occasional crack at winning a game of Bingo. The AEP has since proved so successful that many 'Second Chance' adults have subsequently acquired mainstream degrees as teachers, nurses, nutritionists and social workers.

THE SOUTH DOCKS FESTIVAL
They also set up a Job Centre which sought to provide work for the large numbers of unskilled workers left in the parish after the clearances. In 1987, they started the South Docks Festival, inviting all the businesses in the area to become a Friend of the Festival for £25 (€32). This Obama-style money-raising campaign greatly increased contact between the Job Centre and the various Friends. In the early days, local businesses tended to be small and middle-sized firms - architects, engineers and such like. When the Docklands Authority arrived on Sir John Rogerson's Quay, there was a marked shift towards big business. The Job Centre urged those on file to seize the opportunity to better their education and go for the high-end jobs. The SDF is now in its 21st year and Betty Ashe has just about lost count of the number of people whom they have secured jobs for in that time. The can-do attitude at St Andrew's has been vital. 'The Holy Spirit was watching down upon us', concedes Betty.

A NEW AUTHORITY
During the 1980s, the Centre was instrumental in establishing the Grand Canal Trust which sought to bridge the gaps between the public sector, the private sector and the local community. The GCT's objective was to lobby local politicians and attract investment to the area. The body provided considerable inspiration to the Social Agenda of the Docklands Master Plan, published in 1997. That same year, the Authority acquired the 25-acre Gasworks site and the redevelopment began speedily. Suddenly things were beginning to play in the favour of the Pearse Street community.

THE KEYS TO INTEGRATION

'The changes have been dramatic', says Betty of the 11 years that have passed since then. 'But most people are agreed they're for the better'. One of the Centre's greatest challenges has been to ensure there is integration between the old residents, the new dwellers and the businesses scattered across the cityscape. 'The people who have lived here for generations wanted to know what was happening around them', says Betty. Another concept was the Docklands Business Forum, a sort of Chamber of Commerce, at which the community are invited to hear the various businesses explain just what it is they actually do. Education has also been pivotal to the success of the social regeneration programme.

SILVER-SURFERS

Today, the old school corridors are lined with black and white photographs of life in the old days. One wall is given to photos of the great theatres, picture houses and ballrooms of the inner city, the Queen's, the Hippodrome, the Metropole. The classrooms have been converted into function rooms and are frequently used by government departments for discussions of green papers and budget estimates, as well as the local polling booth. Downstairs, the cradle-to-grave Resource Centre now also boasts a childcare centre, a youth centre, a computer training centre and a cyber café where 'silver surfers' like 86-year-old Betty Dempsey can stay in email contact with relatives overseas. The Resource Centre employs 250 people, which includes 90 on FÁS-inspired community schemes. They have been careful to preserve the traditions and tales of the past through their heritage booklets. An on-going oral history campaign, spear-headed by the Centre and Trinity College Professor Ciaran Brady, will provide an insight into how the regeneration programme has impacted the lives of local people. In 2008, the St Andrew's Resource Centre won a prestigious Pride of Place award for best community facility in Ireland.

Above: The St Andrew's Resource Centre was built as a school in 1897. Below: Betty Ashe and Dolores Wilson accept the Pride of Place 2008 award from President Mary McAleese.

The Hibernian Marine School

Walking along Sir John Rogerson's Quay today, one can see two riverine heads poking out of a brick wall of the Poggenpohl Design House near Lime Street. These heads, sculpted by Edward Smyth and salvaged from Carlisle Bridge, mark the original site of the Hibernian Marine Society's School 'for the Children of Decayed Seamen'. Also known as the Marine Nursery, this was amongst the first major buildings to appear on the Quay. It was built between 1770 and 1773 and designed by either Thomas Cooley or Thomas Ivory. At the time, the foot road to Ringsend ran directly alongside it. The School was a hefty structure, all stone – 91m(300ft) at front and back, 167(547ft) on the west, 193m(633ft) at the east. The expense of the building amounted to £6,600 and was paid for by the Irish Parliament.

The grant-aided Hibernian Marine School was designed to educate and maintain up to 160 boys, the sons of sea-farers who lost their lives or became otherwise impoverished while serving with the Royal Navy or Merchant Navy. Once admitted they were given a nautical uniform and taught reading, writing, arithmetic and navigation. At the age of fourteen, these boys were then apprenticed to masters of merchant vessels or sent on board Royal Navy ships. The number of pupils peaked at 120 in 1799 with a low of just fifteen in 1845.

Much of the building was destroyed by fire in 1872 and the school was relocated to Merrion Street and ultimately became the present-day Mount Temple Comprehensive School in Clontarf. The original building became commercial premises but gradually disappeared.

Right: The Marine School was captured on canvas by James Malton in his 1796 painting, 'Marine School, Dublin, Looking Up the Liffey'. Malton seems to have caught the Quay at low-tide on a relatively quiet day with perhaps 20 ships on the water. Next page: Looking north across the outer basin of the Grand Canal Dock, the Alto Vetro building rises in front of The Tower, a Victorian sugar refinery now run as an Enterprise Centre by IDA Ireland. (Photo: Arco Ardon).

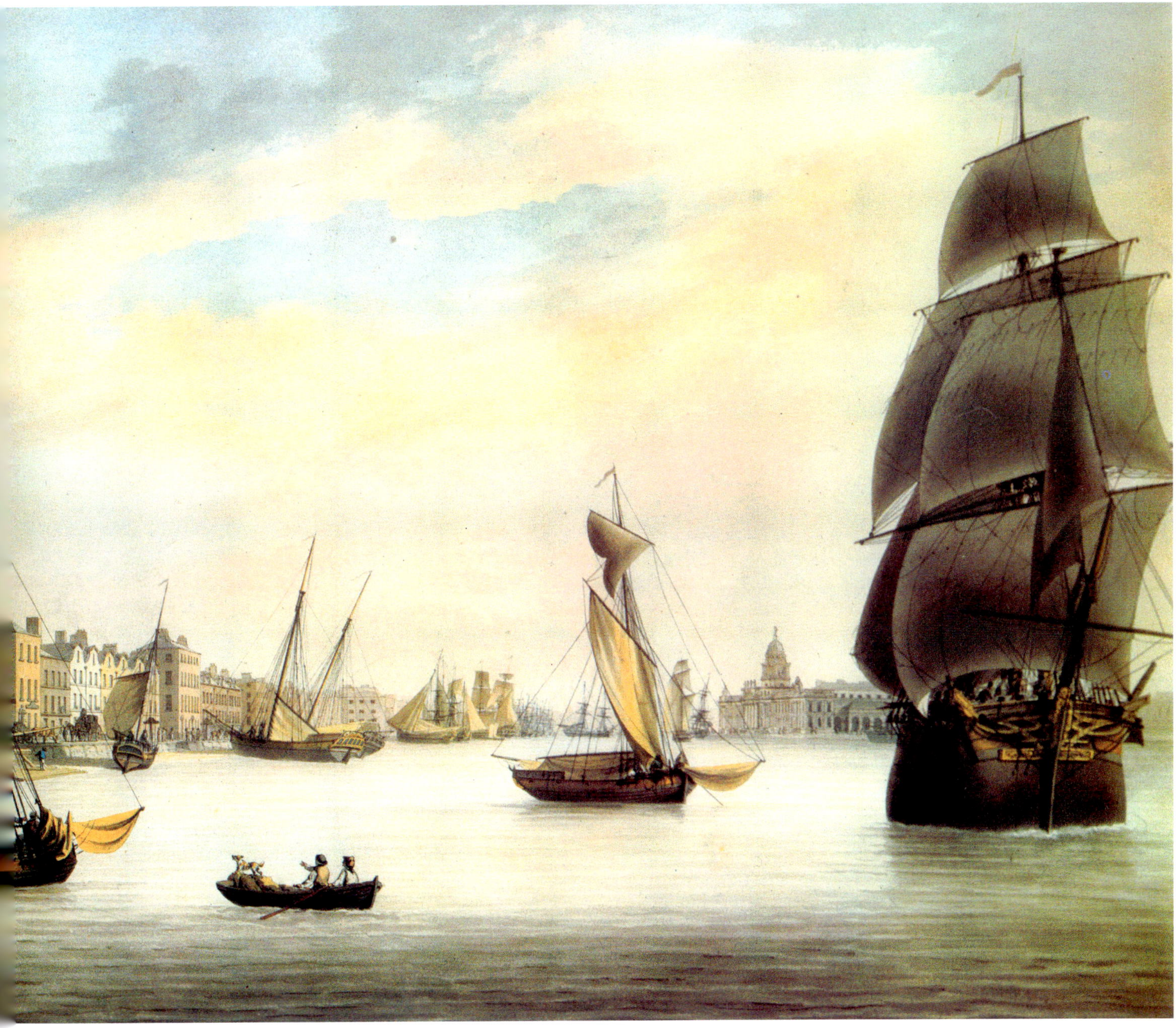

Sir John Rogerson

A MYSTERIOUS ORIGINAL

The founding father of the Dublin Docklands was arguably Sir John Rogerson, a wealthy merchant, ship-owner, property developer and sometime Lord Mayor of Dublin. Those who knew Rogerson described him as 'an Original'. Remarkably little has yet been published about the man; he receives no mention in *The Oxford Companion to Irish History* (2007). Indeed, if it were not for the unexpected evolution of the Docklands since 1988, there is every chance that all trace of Sir John would have disappeared into the murky past from which he emerged. His rise was not unlike that of his contemporary, William 'Speaker' Connolly, although even in the Speaker's case, we at least know who his father was. We do not know when or where Rogerson was born. As a merchant he was apparently as well known in London's Lombard Street as he was in the Dublin Tholsel, so perhaps he was a pure-bred Londoner. He was certainly living in Dublin by 1674 when listed as one of the first parishioners to attend the new church of St Andrew's, just off Dame Street. Among the other parishioners were Sir John Temple and Sir Maurice Eustace, for whom Temple Bar and Eustace Street were named. The young Rogerson must have also taken a keen interest in what St. Andrew's parishioner Major Henry Aston had to say in regard to his actions, circa 1680, in reclaiming and developing the river around present day Aston Quay.

FROM ALDERMAN TO KNIGTHOOD

During the latter days of Charles II's reign, John Rogerson emerged as one of the leading Aldermen in Dublin's Assembly, the group charged with overseeing the City's trade. In 1684, Alderman John Rogerson was one of the 152 members granted land on Dublin's northside in the Assembly's ill-fated North Lotts project. In June 1693, Rogerson was knighted by Henry, Viscount Sydney, Lord Deputy of Ireland. The following December, he was elected Lord Mayor of Dublin. During this time, he was given a lease of land in the vicinity of the Council Chamber near the mouth of the Poddle. He undoubtedly noted the ingenious way in which Jacob Newman, a previous owner of the Poddle, had successfully reclaimed six acres (2.5 ha) at the heart of the young city.

THE LEASE

Little is known of Rogerson's activities between 1694 and 1713, save for his brief ownership of some riverside property in Cork, the acquisition of the Poddle mouth and an association with King's Hospital secondary school in Dublin. He was appointed Sheriff of Dublin from 1707-8 and represented both the City of Dublin and the borough of Clogher in the Irish Parliament. In 1713, Sir John secured a lease from his colleagues in Dublin Corporation for the fee farm estate rights to approximately 133 acres of sand-swept marshland on the south bank of the Liffey channel, otherwise referred to as 'the Strand betwixt Lazy Hill and Ringsend'. Also known as 'Rogerson's Ground' or the 'South Lott's', this grant contained all the land bounded by the Liffey, the Dodder and modern Bath Avenue, including the 'old Steyne coast' of Grand Canal Street, Denzille Street, Sandwith Street and Creighton Street. There was also a narrow strip of land just east of the Dodder, bounded by the spit of Ringsend. In 1717, work began on the river-wall of Sir John Rogerson's Quay, a massive project which Sir John privately funded. A good deal of this wall was completed by the time of Sir John's death in 1724.

PRIVATE LIFE

Sir John Rogerson's wife Elizabeth was the youngest daughter of Emmanuel Proby of St. Gregory, London. Her grandfather, Sir Peter Proby, was Lord Mayor of London in 1622. Her mother Mary was the daughter of John Bland, a London merchant. The Rogersons lived in 'The Glen' or 'Glasnevin House', a country residence just outside the village of Glasnevin, where Sir John built the church. He was succeeded by his only son, John Rogerson, Chief Justice of Ireland for 14 years from 1727 until his death of fever in 1741. Justice Rogerson was succeeded by his son, also John, who died in 1785, leaving his considerable fortune to various orphanages and charities in Dublin, and 'the residue of his estates' to the Protestant charter schools of Ireland. Justice Rogerson bestowed generous dowries upon his daughters. His eldest daughter, Elizabeth married Abraham Crichton - or Creighton, subsequently 1st Baron Erne of Crom Castle, and was mother to the 1st Earl Erne. The family is recalled by the names of Erne Street and Creighton Street off City Quay.

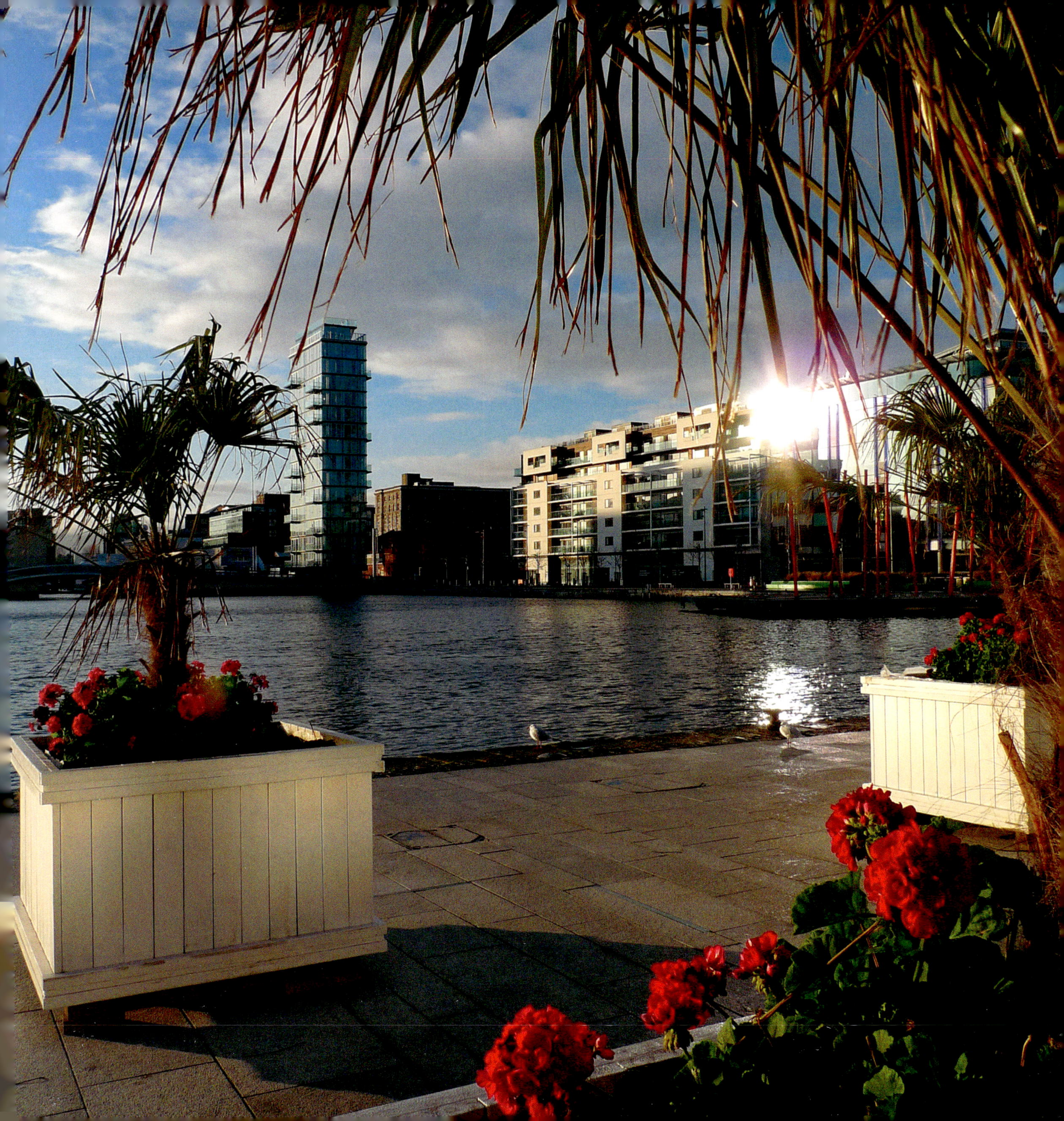

The Gasometer (1934 – 1993)

For many years the skyline of the southern docks was dominated by the 252ft high Gasometer. It stood on the corner of Cardiff Lane and Sir John Rogerson's Quay, right where the legal firm of McCann Fitzgerald now have their offices in the building known as Riverside 1. Built in Hitler's Germany and designed by Maschinenfabrik Augsburg-Nürnberg, the Gasometer's purpose was to store gas for the Alliance and Dublin Consumers' Gas Company. Completed in 1934, it had a capacity of 3 million cubic feet. This landmark – and seamark - was demolished in 1993. It would possibly have been felled earlier but for the arrival of two Peregrine Falcons who took to nesting on its roof.

A bold plan to paint it up as a pint of Guinness did not come through and down it came. The late 'Sea Scout' Skipper Dick Vekins built a miniature Gasometer using some of the original corrugated sheets salvaged during the demolition. This can now be seen in the St Andrew's Resource Centre on Pearse Street. 'Anyone can have a Gasometer', says Betty Ashe, 'but they can't have one made from the original'.

Below: Looking up Sir John Rogerson's Quay towards the Gasometer in the 1980s. (Photo: Dublin Public Libraries). Next page: A sample of the coal covers that Dubliners walk upon daily, made by foundries in the Docklands, down which coal were poured during the 19th and 20th centuries to ensure vital heating and cooking fuel supplies.

TONGE & TAGGART
LIMITED
SOUTH CITY
FOUNDRY
WINDMILL
LANE
DUBLIN

CAST AT
SOUTH CITY
FOUNDRY
41 BISHOP ST

Sir John Rogerson's Quay

ROGERSON'S GROUND

Sir John Rogerson's Quay runs for exactly half a mile along the southern banks of the River Liffey, beginning by the Seán O'Casey Bridge on City Quay and culminating at Britain Quay. In July 1713, Sir John gave notice of his intention to 'very speedily take the Strand' in what the late JW de Courcy described as 'possibly the most significant privately funded development project in the history of the Liffey'. This was the first speculative quayside development of the 18th century. Wooden or brushwood tracks may have already provided some form of access across the slobs. It's also likely that there were riverside fish traps and weirs, laid upon the muddy flats since man first settled in these parts. At any rate, the new wharf commenced when a series of wooden piles were driven into the sand to embank the river between 'the anchor-smith's shop and Ringsend point'. Two parallel stone-walls were then built behind the piles, and the space between them was filled with rocks, gravel and sand dredged from the river. The dredging simultaneously deepened that part of the river channel. The walls themselves were constructed with large stones shipped from Clontarf by John Vernon. Sir John and Vernon subsequently became embroiled in a legal battle when the former accused the latter of fobbing him off with a considerable quantity of undersized stones. Vernon huffily dumped these stones into the river just off the Quay and they were proving 'a great nuisance', scratching the hulls of 'every ship and gabbard that passed'. Eventually the City stepped in and removed them at their own cost.

It is not known if or when Sir John ever felt compelled to smash open a bottle of champagne and celebrate the opening of his Quay. One suspects a few lively nights down at The Fountain, said to have been built in 1718 and thus the first building on Sir John Rogerson's Quay. The Fountain Tavern may have had to wait a while before it had any seriously regular customers. Sir John Rogerson's Quay was not an immediate success. In the first half of 18th century, Ireland's trade was hardly booming. The island's available resources were still extremely thin after all the warfare of the previous century. The ships that loaded on Sir John Rogerson's Quay were probably exporting agricultural products such as salt beef, pork, butter, hard cheese and, latterly, grain. Undoubtedly a good deal of the ships that arrived from afar carried fine French wines for the thirsty elite.

THE SOUTH LOTTS

The marshy strand behind the Quay was divided into allotments and called the South Lotts. Sceptics derided the commercial value of the South Lotts which, like the North Lotts across the Liffey, were prone to flooding in storms. Dubliners frequently bathed in these flood-waters, while some budding entrepreneurs cultured oyster beds there. In 1759, Gabrielli Ricciardelli painted 'A View of Dublin from the Sea'. He depicts the Quay as a roughly surfaced strip, peppered with people and horses. The land behind it consists of water-logged marshlands and a meadow of haystacks.. In the 1760s, the quay was thronged with Dubliners craning their necks to see the first light shine from the brand new candle-lit lighthouse at Poolbeg. In 1792, the Duke of Leinster managed to sail his ship across the South Lotts and land safely at Merrion Square. This came about when part of the wall collapsed, allowing 'a dreadful torrent' to break through into 'the lower grounds, inundating every quarter on the same level as far as Artichoke

Above: Tom O'Brien's Ferryman Pub claims to have been built in 1780, at which time the quay walls were again repaired. If so, it was the most easterly building on the Quay for many years. Neither Faden's map of 1797 nor Bligh's surveys of 1800 – 1803 indicate any other developments any further east along the Quay. (Photo: Dublin City Council)

Road' (Grand Canal Street). Communication with Ringsend and Irishtown came to a halt; 'the inhabitants are obliged to go to and fro in boats'.

HAMMOND'S VIEW

Joseph W. Hammond gave a rather buoyant description of how the Quay might have been in 1796 in a paper read to the Old Dublin Society in 1942. He envisioned 'a pleasant suburb' with 'a touch of glamour and romance … enlivened now and then by the passing of military patrols in their scarlet and buff uniforms, the sinister press gangs swaggering with muskets or cutlass, and the boys of the Marine School in their dark blue jackets and white ducks. Florid topers in the brandy-fumed taverns looked out over their tankards at the spreading canvas of ships going by and the only sounds on the air were the cry of the gull and the curlew, or the refrain of sailors at the capstan. Time there went by ship's bell or the bugle and drum of the Marine School. Nightfall brought forth the mellow strains of the violin or the notes of a harpsichord from behind closed shutters and bolted doors, and the only sounds outside were the steady tramp of the patrol, and an occasional call of 'Halt!' or the scurrying patter of the press gang after a pedestrian who had changed his mind and turned back'. Press gangs were certainly on the prowl. In November 1793, for instance, over 100 seamen were reportedly 'pressed' from vessels in Dublin Port to serve in His Majesty's Royal Navy.

VICTORIAN TIMES

By 1860, the quayside comprised a long row of buildings and yards, occupied by a miscellany of 'shipping agents, shipbuilders, makers of ropes, sails and pumps, bakers of ships' biscuits… side by side with vintners, grocers and timber yards'. Paddle steamers, coal ships and grain barques frequently berthed alongside the quay but it was in a somewhat dilapidated state. This was the departure point for Irish holiday makers bound for the Isle of Man for over 120 years between 1846 and 1968. The Dublin Gas Company were also headquartered here in an early incarnation of the gasworks that so utterly dominated this landscape from the 1860s until the arrival of natural gas in the 1980s. Between 1870 and 1888, the Port engineer Bindon Blood Stoney and contractors such as William J. Doherty rebuilt nearly 1,219m (4,000ft) of quay wall between Creighton Street and Great Britain Quay, as well as deepening the river channel by 7m (23ft). Dublin Port was now able to offer waters deeper than most harbours in the world and Sir John Rogerson's Quay boasted 1.2km of that much sought after berthage. The lands directly south of the quay were duly made available for warehousing and industry. They were soon smothered in chemical works, coke furnaces, abattoirs, tar-pits, timber yards, foundries and gasworks. Such works were the epitome of a booming industrial city in Victorian times. It did not matter that one's lungs were being choked so long as the skyline was commanded by factories, smokestacks, bridges and railways.

THE HAILING STATION

The quayside was certainly quieter during the 20th century, not least from 1919 when the Gas Company coal-boats that once unloaded here relocated to the Grand Canal Docks. In 1934, the western end of the quay became the setting for the famous MAN Gasometer which towered over the river until demolished in 1993. During the 1940s and 1950s, one of the best known sounds along the South Quays was the voice of Mr Robinson bellowing out instructions from the salmon pink South Hailing Station on the corner of Sir John Rogerson's and Britain Quay. From here, all incoming ships were advised which berth they were to proceed to. The three-bay, one-storey Hailing Station was built in 1907 and stood for 100 years. As well as being vital to the direction of traffic along the South Quays, it was also a place where dockers could learn of ship arrivals and possible work. From 1916 to 1948, a time ball was located on the Station so that mariners could correct their chronometers, an essential task for estimating longitude at sea. Each day the time ball was released at 1pm GMT (Dublin Time having been replaced by GMT on 1st October 1916). The release of the ball was controlled by astronomers at Dunsink Observatory who determined time accurately by observing the transits of stars. Over the years the Hailing Station became abandoned and vandalised. By the time the Docklands Authority took over the area, it was utterly derelict. The Authority arranged for its preservation by record, before it was finally demolished in 2007 to make way for redevelopment.

FOREIGN SHIPS & BANANA BOATS

Sir John Rogerson's Quay beholds the North Wall Quay with the dazzling windows of the Convention Centre, Dublin, and the old red-bricks of the Railway Hotel directly opposite. It was from here that the schoolboy James Joyce recalled watching a graceful Norwegian three-master sail up the Liffey. During the International Eucharistic Congress of 1932, the Dutch East Indiaman, *Marnix van Sint Aldegonde* berthed along the quay. She was one of 63 vessels, including a dozen ocean liners and 13 cross-channel passenger ships, which docked in Dublin that week. When foreign ships like these came in to berth, the quayside filled with curious Dubliners. Flirtatious women riding High Nellies, inquisitive shysters tumbling out of pubs, and an avalanche of children, all jostling to see what the cargo and crew were composed of. If the crew looked suitably gullible, the dockers would swindle the unfortunate visitors by buying their goods with old Sweepstake tickets, which they passed off as Irish currency. When the banana-boats came in, the children would race alongside, down to City Quay, catching bananas thrown through the sky by genial sailors. The navvies on the American coalboats that moored along Britain Quay sometimes showered them with chewing gum and cigarettes. The old Dublin Corporation ferry used to pull in by the steps, upon which young boys fished for whiting, or 'joeys' as they were known. Many women were employed at Britain Quay, gutting and packing fish, and making nets and sails. Conway Shipping operated a useful store here. Other women worked for the Dublin Trawling Company's ice and cold storage plant around the corner on Benson Street.

EARLY IN THE MORNING

There were plenty of early morning pubs in the area. Smith's Pub was on the corner of Sir John Rogerson's Quay, opposite where the Diving Bell stands today. This later belonged to Joe Kelly, a landlord who used to call time by firing a shotgun into the ceiling. Kelly's was also known as the 'Foreign Exchange' after all the international sailors who gathered there. It was particularly celebrated for its vodka. Young lads seeking the price of a pint would go looking for bits of copper that had fallen off the trucks and bring them down to Mickey Mazlim's Rag Shop on Rath Row.

PLAYING BALL

Football has always been strong in the area. One of the bigger clubs was St Andrews, founded in 1906. The Club competed in Junior football competitions but was disbanded just before the 1916 Rising when many players joined Peader Mackens. The Shamrock GFC was founded in 1887 in the Denzille (Fenian) Street district but failed to survive the Parnell split. This short-lived Hillside Club was founded in 1893 and based in Westland Row. During the Second World War, young fellows often went down to play football on Sir John Rogerson's Quay. 'If you hit the Gasometer, you'd have to run for your life'. Sometimes they'd play wearing gas masks. 'What a joke they were!', recalls one former mask-wearer. 'There is no way they would have saved you'. On the night the North Strand was bombed, they watched the flames light the sky from the windows. On account of so many boats being torpedoed, the docks came to a virtual standstill during the war. Many dockers served with the Merchant Navy.

SIR JOHN ROGERSON'S QUAY TODAY

Sir John Rogerson's Quay has been utterly transformed in the past decade. Where once dockers and sailors were on the prowl, now the streets are full of young city slickers, pram-pushing mothers and foreign tourists. Where once there were six pubs, now only The Ferryman remains. The dusty timber yards, gasworks and warehouses have been replaced by hotels, office blocks, high-rise apartments and public spaces. Many who work here now are employed in this burgeoning legal quarter, by firms such as Matheson Ormsby Prentice, Beauchamps, Dillon Eustace and McCann Fitzgerald. The latter has its impressive offices on the very site of the old Gasometer. Also here is the headquarters of the Dublin Docklands Development Authority, who purchased the entire quay as part of the 25-acre Gasworks site in 1997.

By 2012, there will be almost 6,000 children under the age of 15 living in the Docklands area. As part of their bid to promote the Docklands as a quality family-friendly quarter, several children's amenity parks are being designed. 2009 sees the opening of the 1.5 hectare (3.7 acre) Chimney Park, located behind Sir John Rogerson's Quay at the base of the historic red brick chimney which gives the park its name. This innovative children's playground area was designed by Snug & Outdoor, working closely with children, schools and community representatives to establish just how they would like to use Chimney Park. A climbing structure made from plasticine by children from City Quay primary school will be incorporated into the actual playground.

Running east of the Docklands Authority's offices to Benson Street are three new high-rise apartment blocks. Another park to the rear is being built on a theme drawn from the film '*Willy Wonka & the Chocolate Factory*'. This European-style park will help generate the idea that this really is an area in which adults and children can enjoy living. The old timber yard at Cardiff Lane is now given over to the Maldron Hotel, the Ivory Building, Whitaker Square and the new offices of the Economic and Social Research Institute, co-founded by TK Whitaker.

Far Left: Three generations of docker families gather on the quayside during the 1970s. (Photo: Dublin City Council). Left: Sir John Rogerson's Quay today with the famous diving bell on the waterfront. (Photo: Cathal Furey)

The Diving Bell

Strolling along Sir John Rogerson's Quay, one is apt to be so caught up in the shimmering developments of this new horizon as to miss a huge salmon pink wrought iron yoke shaped not unlike a sink plunger. And indeed, plunging is to the fore for the origins of this peculiarity.

Mankind has been fantasising about living underwater ever since Noah got the tip off about the Flood. By 1690, Edmund Halley - he of the Comet – had devised a diving bell capable of remaining submerged for long periods of time. The principle was much the same as when you plunge a glass, mouth down, into a bucket of water and it fills with air. In Halley's bell, there was sufficient air for a man to be safely contained within and sent underwater. The only problem was that, with increasing pressure, air compresses and so, as the bell sank deeper, its occupants invariably went ga-ga or died. In 1783, Charles Spalding, a Scotsman who ran a sweetshop in Edinburgh, arrived in Dublin Harbour with a bell of his own creation. It boasted a very long leather tube designed to reach the surface, with an air pump attached, to ensure a supply of fresh air. Unfortunately Spalding died showing off his invention when his signal ropes became entangled, but the stage was set for the new age in diving bells.

The diving bell on Sir John Rogerson's Quay was designed by Bindon Blood Stoney, the improbably named Chief Engineer for the Port and Docks during much of the Victorian Age. (See page 102). It was built in Drogheda by Thomas Grendon & Co and completed in 1866. The bell was used to create the North Wall Extension and the Alexandra Basin. A team of six men would climb the ladder on the 38ft (11.5m) high funnel, pass through an airlock and then climb down into a 400 sq ft chamber which was just about high enough for a man to stand. From here the men were able to level the riverbed in preparation for the laying of the 350-ton prefabricated super-blocks that form the North Wall Extension. It was unpleasant, claustrophobic work. The chamber was often unbearably hot and the pressure was particularly tortuous for anyone with a cold; ears frequently bled and many men never recovered. Stoney's bell continued to be used for repair work in the Docklands until 1958. Joe Murphy, the last foreman to work the Bell, secured it for the southside campshire. In 1999, St. Andrew's Resource Centre restored it as a millennium project, with funding from the Docklands Authority, Dublin Port Co., The Nautical Trust and FÁS. This definitive relic will remain on the campshire at Sir John Rogerson's Quay, providing an intriguing link between the history of a working docklands and the ongoing developments.

The Samuel Beckett Bridge

Bridges should always be magnificent, conjuring all the possibilities brought on by the connection of two sides. Plans for a bridge across the Liffey from Sir John Rogerson's Quay to the North Wall have been in motion at least since a 1939 proposal by Abercrombie, Kelly & Robertson. With the ongoing success of the Docklands during the 1990s, so came increasing demand for a new crossing at Macken Street, about halfway between the Seán O'Casey Bridge and the East Link.

Dublin City Council subsequently commissioned world-renowned Spanish architect Santiago Calatrava Valls to create the new bridge. The Zurich-based designer also built the James Joyce Bridge further upriver. His other projects include the Chicago Spire for Dublin businessman Garrett Kelleher and the future train station – World Trade Centre PATH Station - at Ground Zero in New York City.

The new 394ft bridge will be cable-stayed, with a curved, inclined steel pylon. This pylon houses a rotation mechanism that allows the structure to open for maritime traffic. The bridge will have four traffic lanes with cycle tracks and footpaths on either side of the bridge. The bridge is named for Samuel Beckett, the Dublin-born writer and Nobel Prize winner whose uncle was responsible for building many of the terraced houses in the South Lotts. It will be completed by 2010.

Below: A simulated image of the Samuel Beckett Bridge, evoking a harp lying on it's side.
Left: Bindon Blood Stoney's diving bell within which the men who built the quaysides once worked upon the river floor.

Chapter Five
Grand Canal Docks

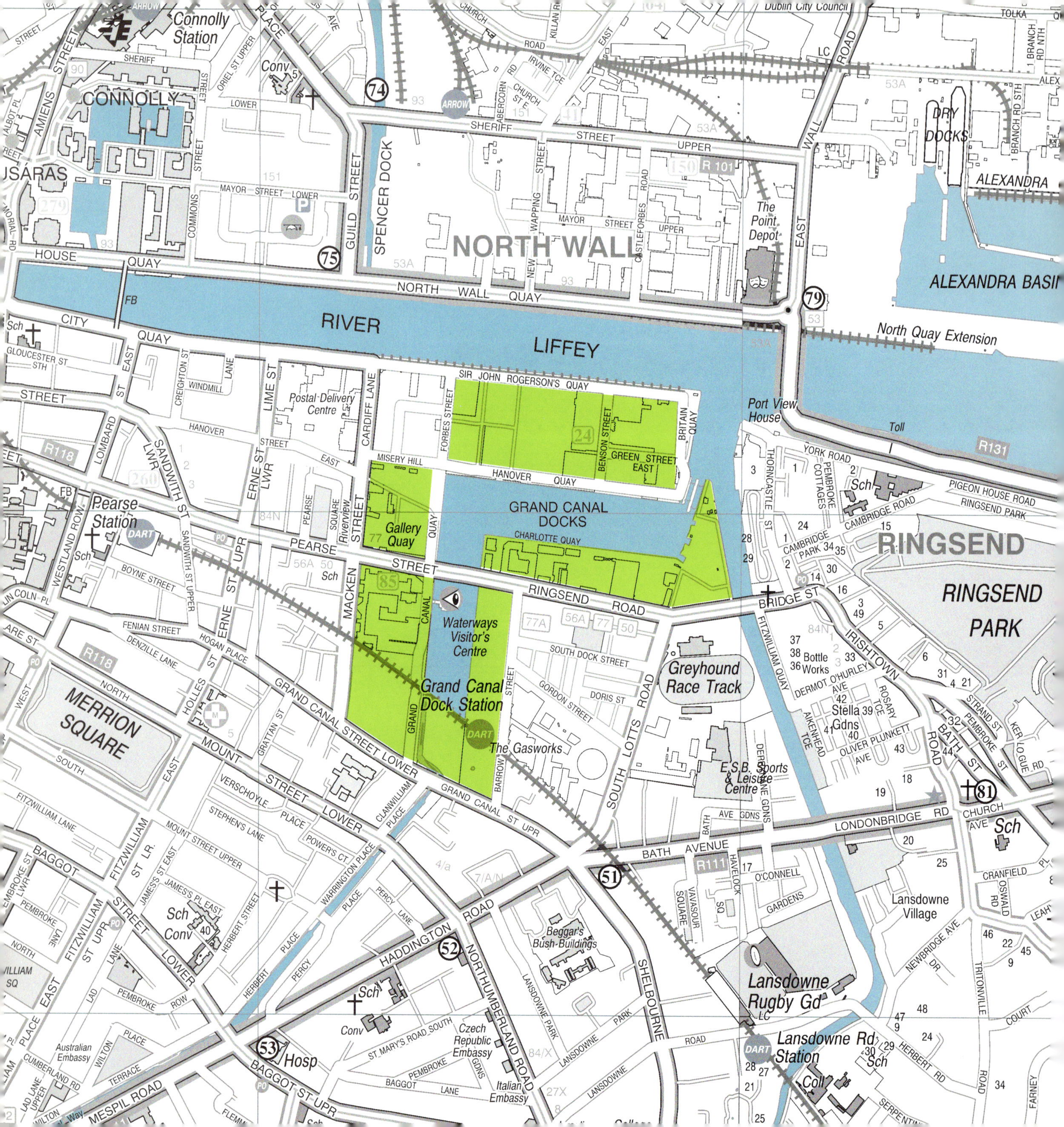
Connolly Station
CONNOLLY
BUSARAS
NORTH WALL
RIVER
LIFFEY
HOUSE QUAY
NORTH WALL QUAY
CITY QUAY
SHERIFF STREET UPPER
MAYOR STREET LOWER
MAYOR STREET UPPER
SPENCER DOCK
GUILD STREET
The Point Depot
ALEXANDRA BASIN
ALEXANDRA
DRY DOCKS
North Quay Extension
Toll
Port View House
SIR JOHN ROGERSON'S QUAY
Postal Delivery Centre
HANOVER QUAY
GRAND CANAL DOCKS
CHARLOTTE QUAY
Gallery Quay
MISERY HILL
BENSON STREET
GREEN STREET EAST
BRITAIN QUAY
Pearse Station
PEARSE STREET
RINGSEND ROAD
Waterways Visitor's Centre
Grand Canal Dock Station
The Gasworks
RINGSEND
RINGSEND PARK
BRIDGE ST
IRISHTOWN
Greyhound Race Track
E.S.B. Sports & Leisure Centre
Bottle Works
MERRION SQUARE
GRAND CANAL STREET LOWER
MOUNT STREET LOWER
LONDONBRIDGE RD
BATH AVENUE
Lansdowne Village
Beggar's Bush Buildings
Lansdowne Rugby Gd
Lansdowne Rd Station
HADDINGTON ROAD
NORTHUMBERLAND ROAD
SHELBOURNE ROAD
Czech Republic Embassy
Italian Embassy
Australian Embassy
MESPIL ROAD
BAGGOT ST UPR
Hosp
FITZWILLIAM ST LR.
PEMBROKE ROAD
PIGEON HOUSE ROAD
RINGSEND PARK

When the Grand Canal Docks opened in 1796, they were the largest docks the world had ever known. Within a few decades, they were in decline, their fall prompted by changing technology and the arrival of the railways. The elegant quaysides became the exclusive demesne of the Dublin Gas Company whose ever-eroding mountains of black coal and ash grey coke spilled across the landscape. While bakers and millers worked their magic along the southern banks of the inner basin, chemical factories, tar pits, bottle factories and iron foundries belched across the skyline.

By the 1960s, the Grand Canal Docks were almost completely derelict. The nadir was probably 1987 when Hanover Quay was simply deemed too poisonous to sell. Extraordinary developments have happened since including the complete remediation of the area, the construction of untold millions worth of real estate and the arrival of several thousand enthusiastic new residents. The Millennium Tower, Hanover Quay and the Alto Vetro building particularly stand out. The waters are now the preserve of canoeists, windsurfers and the occasional shower of young fellows leaping off McMahon Bridge. The Viking Splash Tours provide a suitably noisy disruption throughout the day. Swans are also frequently to be seen splashing across the water. The quaysides have been restored and converted into attractive campshires. Grand Canal Square promises to be one of the great landmarks of 21st century Dublin, combining big name architecture and landscape design. Indeed, there is much about the Grand Canal Docks project to inspire optimism in these uncertain times. It's a shimmering example of how, if you really push for something and secure the support of the central government, you can greatly improve the environmental, social and economic outlook of even the most downtrodden area.

Grand Canal Docks - Streetwise

Sir John Rogerson's Quay - Named for a former Lord Mayor of Dublin who privately funded the construction of the original wall on which the quay now stands.

Artichoke Road - Known as Grand Canal Street since 1791, this early name arose when John Villiboise, a Huguenot settler, built a house here in 1736 and grew artichokes in his garden.

Asgard Road - A new road, named for the gaff rigged ketch, now owned by Harry Crosbie, upon which Erskine Childers sailed into Howth in 1914 with a cargo of German guns for the Irish Volunteers. The State-owned sail-training ship *Asgard II* was a major feature in the Docklands before it unexpectedly sank in the Bay of Biscay in 2008.

Benson Street - Built in the 1840s but not named until 1895, the street probably remembers Richard Benson who, along with Luke Gardiner, appears to have acquired much of the Rogerson estate by 1796. Another contender is the engineer Sir John Benson, Ireland's answer to Brunel, knighted at the Great Industrial Exhibition of 1853. The old stores facing the Fitzwilliam Quay apartments are scheduled for a mixed residential and commercial development.

Blood Stoney Road - Named for the celebrated engineering genius, Bindon Blood Stoney, who rebuilt Sir John Rogerson's Quay in the 1880s.

Britain Quay - First built in 1727 and named for the island of Britain which it faces, the quay was completed during the Grand Canal Docks project of the 1790s. In 1865, Stoney re-faced the quayside so that it could cater to the increasing numbers of steamships that moored here. The quay is now the designated location for the 140m high U2 Tower.

Butler's Court - The entrance to Benson Street is named after Butler's Chocolates who were formerly located here, but also recalls the Butler family, Dukes of Ormonde, who once received the duties on all wine imported into Ireland

Charlotte Quay - Like Charlotte Bridge, this was named for Princess Charlotte, daughter of the Prince Regent, who married Leopold, King of the Belgians, but died in childbirth in 1817. She was named for her grandmother, Charlotte of Mecklenburg, wife of George III.

Forbes Street - Probably named for George Forbes, the Lord Mayor of Dublin in 1720 and a key player in the South Lotts allotments.

Green Street - The rather elaborate limestone warehouses here were formerly icehouses belonging to the Dublin Steam Trawling Ice and Cold Storage Co. Ltd. In 1940, the company's ship *Leukos* was rounding the Donegal coast when attacked by a German submarine. The *Leukos* and her crew of 11 were lost. The Irish Seamen's Relatives Association maintains that the *Leukos* had attempted to ram the U-38 as it threatened some nearby British trawlers.

Horse Fair Road - Named for a horse-fair said to have been held in the South Lotts in the 18th century.

Hanover Quay - Named for the family of George I, Elector of Hanover, who was invited to Britain by the Protestant elite in 1714 to secure the throne from the Jacobites.

Maquay Bridge - The first of the Grand Canal bridges was named for George Maquay, director of the Grand Canal Company and one of the founding members of the Ballast Office.

MacMahon Bridge - Named for Seán MacMahon (1894–1955), Captain of 'B' Company, Third Battalion, under Eamon De Valera in Boland's Mills in 1916. In September 1922, he succeeded General Mulcahy as Chief of the General Staff in the Irish Free State.

Right: The L-shaped Grand Canal Docks lie just east of the River Liffey. The red and green swathes of the Martha Schwartz-designed Grand Canal Square can be seen at the bottom left of the docks. All the land between the docks and the Liffey formerly belonged to the Dublin Gas Company but is now extensively developed into 21st century office and apartment blocks. (Photo: Peter Barrow)

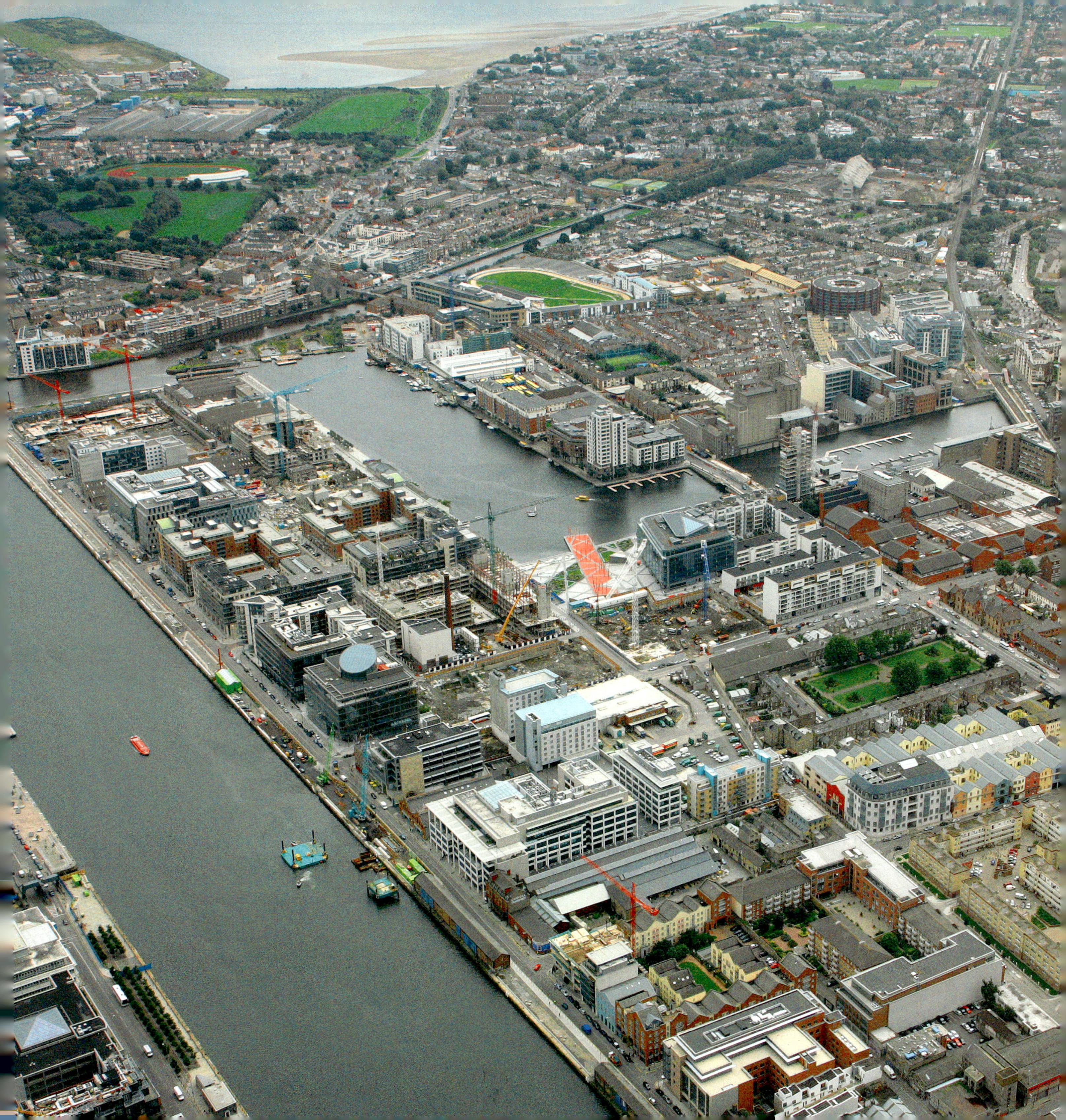

Grand Canal Docks

THE GRAND CANAL

The 1780s and 1790s marked one of the busiest construction periods in the history of Dublin. Such enterprise was undoubtedly boosted by the fact that, from 1782 until 1800, the island's Parliament operated with a considerable degree of independence from Westminster. This effectively enabled projects like the new Custom House to be fast-tracked. That said, there was nothing particularly quick about the Grand Canal. The idea of a canal link between Dublin and the River Shannon had been voiced as far back as 1715 but did not commence until 1757. By 1768 an enormous amount of money had been spent on the scheme but it was still eons away from completion. In 1772, a group of noblemen and merchants established the Grand Canal Company which, assisted by public subscription, would bring the canal across the Bog of Allen and complete the job. In 1790, the Company began work on a new circular line to run around the outskirts of Dublin City.

THE GRAND CANAL DOCKS

In 1791, the Grand Canal Company purchased 24.5 acres of duck-filled sloblands in the South Lotts. Here they would create the largest docks the world had yet seen. The project was supervised by Edward Chapman, whose father William Chapman devised the scheme along with William Jessop, the greatest dock engineer of his day. The contractor was John McCartney, knighted by Lord Camden at its official opening in 1796. It cost over £112,000 and provided the City with its first purpose-built docking facilities for sea-going vessels. Variously known as the Grand Canal Docks, the South Docks and the Ringsend Docks, the new L-shaped harbour comprised two large deep-water basins (or 'floating docks') and three dry (or 'graving') docks, accessed by two ship locks and a barge lock. These were bordered by 2000 yards of new quayage - Britain Quay on its western entrance, Hanover Quay along the northern side, Charlotte Quay directly opposite, and Grand Canal Quay along the most westerly flank. A single-lane lifting bridge ran across the two basins, where McMahon Bridge stands today, connecting New Brunswick Street (now Pearse Street) and Ringsend Road. A new 3.5 mile canal of seven locks, known as the Circular Line, was simultaneously constructed between the Grand Canal harbour at Portabello and the southern end of the new Docks. This ultimately provided barges with direct access from the Liffey all the way to the Shannon, with stops at the towns and villages along the way. The first vessels to complete the journey from the Shannon to the Grand Canal Basin arrived in July 1804. The Docks were also connected via the Barrow Navigation to Athy, Carlow and Waterford.

THE GRAND OPENING

At 11 o'clock on the morning of St George's Day (23rd April) 1796, the Earl of Camden, Lord Lieutenant of Ireland, and his Secretary Pelham, sailed in through the eastern lock on board Sir Alexander Schomberg's yacht. They were met by a royal salute fired by artillery stationed along Hanover Quay. Twenty vessels 'of considerable size' then entered the basin, each likewise saluted, followed by a large number of small craft, barges and handsomely decorated pleasure boats. A thousand of 'the principal nobility and gentry' were gathered along the quays. His Excellency came ashore approximately where Gallery Quay now stands, formally opened the new docks and addressed the crowd before everyone headed 'into a breakfast prepared in tents'. The event was captured on canvas by William Ashford in a painting called *The Opening of Ringsend Docks*.

THE THREE LOCKS

From the northern dock, three handsome granite lock gates opened on to the River Liffey, right beside its' confluence with the River Dodder. These were named for the three most recent Lord Lieutenants - Camden, Buckingham and Westmoreland. The Camden was big enough for a contemporary warship to pass through, while, adjoining Britain Quay, the Westmoreland was suitably narrow for barges. The operation of these gates was supervised by a lock-keeper who lived in an adjacent house, rebuilt in the 1940s.

Above: 'The Opening of Ringsend Docks, 1796' by William Ashford (1746–1824)

THE GRAVING DOCKS

Three 'commodious' graving docks were constructed in the basin, close to the entrance locks. These were ostensibly for the building and repairing of commercial ships and barges belonging to the Grand Canal Company but other vessels were also built and fixed here. The Dublin Dockyard Company operated it as a small-scale business until 1881. From 1913 to 1963, the docks were used by the Ringsend Dockyard Company (known as McMillan's). Between 1925 and 1939, they built most of the 48 steel motor barges used by the Grand Canal Company. They also made barges for Guinness, Odlum Mills and other companies. The graving docks area is presently being redeveloped by the Docklands Authority, Waterways Ireland and the local community, bringing another neglected waterfront area back into focus. Although the three docks were filled in during the 1960s, two have recently been excavated. One is to be restored as a Dry Dock and the other will become a key water feature in a new apartment scheme. The *Naomh Eanna*, a much beloved old Aran Islands Ferry, is moored behind the Bus Garage in the Outer Basin nearby, and is home to the windsurfing gurus of Surfdock.

A SHORT RUN

The cutting edge Grand Canal Docks were destined to enjoy a short period of prosperity. The Act of Union, which closed the Irish Parliament and brought Dublin's Golden Age to a halt, was partially to blame. The rival Custom House Docks built on the northside of the river also presented a major challenge. But there was also the fact that the new merchant ships were simply too big, a fact compounded by the heavy silting which occurred at the mouth of the Dodder, hindering the use of the outer harbour. In 1815, the channel leading into the Docks, known as the Ringsend Gut, was dredged and deepened but it was already obvious that the sea-locks leading into the Grand Canal Docks were too small and took too long to open. (The Custom House Docks experienced precisely the same problems in the 1830s.) Bigger ships continued to berth along the riverside quays. This included the valuable coal importation business of the Dublin Gas Company, which owned a huge tract of land between Hanover Quay and Sir John Rogerson's Quay. Nonetheless, large warehouses and flourmills sprung up along the handsome quaysides. In January 1847, with the famine well underway, several vessels were reported to be in the Grand Canal Docks, 'discharging cargos of foreign wheat, corn and other produce' into canal boats from where such urgently needed supplies 'were forwarded to the interior'. But with the advent of the railway at this same time, the inland waterways were in decline, and the Grand Canal Docks with it.

Right: The Alto Vetro building is one of the exciting new landmarks of the Grand Canal Docks. (Photo: Arco Ardon)
Left: From 1915 until 1943, the lock-keeper at the Grand Canal Locks was Paddy 'Sonny' Byrne. Born in 1869, his father was a deep-sea diver who drowned at sea. From 1893 until the outbreak of the Great War, Sonny was master of the Aja, a pleasure vessel that ran along the Grand Canal between Dublin and the Shannon for Mr. Sankey, 'the Guv'nor', one of the owners of the Grand Canal Company, and his guests. Sonny was subsequently appointed lock-keeper until he retired. He was offered a residence in the Lock-Keeper's cottage beside the locks but his wife Anne was so frightened their baby daughter might toddle into the water she refused to live there. Instead they lived above Kitty Whelan's drapery shop, Cullen's, in Thorncastle Street, Ringsend, opposite St. Patrick's Church, where the pharmacy is now located. Sonny died in 1953.

Grand Canal Quay

All activity within the Grand Canal Docks was supervised by the Basin Captain. He resided in a two-storey house by McMahon Bridge (formerly Victoria Bridge) on Grand Canal Quay. In a stunning display of what you can do with a very small space, this house was recently replaced by the Alto Vetro building, a crisp, delicately proportioned 16-storey glass-fronted apartment block, designed by Shay Clery Architects and completed in 2008. It looks rather like a very tall chest of drawers, with all the drawers neatly pulled out. A particularly fine view of this building can be obtained from the *MV Cill Airne* anchored along the North Wall Quay. Directly behind Alto Vetro is the Enterprise and Technology Campus purchased by Trinity College in 1999. According to the 1911 Census, this site formerly comprised a distillery, an abbatoir and a timber yard that ran to Macken Street (then Great Clarence Street). It's principal building, The Tower, was built as a sugar refinery by the renowned theatre architect, Alfred Derbyshire and engineer Sir William Fairbairn. It was later occupied by the Hammond Lane foundry, which specialized in making manhole covers, galvanised baths, aluminium buckets (for slops) and enamel buckets (for freshwater). In 1978, IDA Ireland (Industrial Development Authority) bought the Tower, preserving and restoring it as the centrepiece of their new Enterprise Centre. The restoration won a Europa Nostra award in 1983. The Tower is now a Design and Craft Centre and continues today under the auspices of Trinity College.

A small campshire runs from Alto Vetro to the Waterways Visitor Centre. Built in 1993 for the Office of Public Works, this white metal-clad Modernist cube on stilts is nicknamed 'The Box in the Docks'. Further south along the quay stands a cut-stone Victorian barley store or malthouse, built by Guinness in 1886, with a basin frontage of 100 yards. This may have replaced Brown's Flour Mills, the second largest in the city, which was totally destroyed by fire in February 1885. In 1995, the malthouse was redeveloped by TJ Cullen & Co into The Malting Tower, comprising two five-storey office buildings and seven studio apartments. The well-regarded Bridge Bar & Grill (formerly Frank's Restaurant) operates at ground level in a space that famously shudders whenever trains cross the Docks via the Grand Canal Railway Bridge. At the southern end of Grand Canal Quay stands the Treasury Building, designed by Henry J Lyons and completed in 1990. This is actually a reconstructed and re-clad version of the wonderfully functionalist Boland's Bakery built here in 1948 to a design by Belfast architect John Stevenson. The Bakery was notable for the giant lettering and a dramatic, wine-coloured curved wall, now replicated at the end of Macken Street. The 12ft high bronze figure climbing up Treasury's main wall was prophetically called '*Aspiration*' and sculpted by Rowan Gillespie, who also created the life-sized Famine sculptures by the Custom House.

Grand Canal Street & Maquay Bridge

GRAND CANAL STREET

In 1736, a Huguenot settler named John Villiboise obtained a lease from Lord Fitzwilliam on some marshland just east of Merrion Square. He built a house and planted a crop of artichokes in his garden. The street beside his house subsequently became known as Artichoke Road and remained so until 1791 when, in honour of the new inland waterway, it was renamed Grand Canal Street. One of the first major buildings here was Sir Patrick Dun's Hospital, a much respected medical school that operated from 1815 until its closure in 1986. The Hospital was named for Sir Patrick Dun, President of the Royal College of Physicians of Ireland from 1681 to 1706, who fought alongside William III at the Battle of the Boyne. The concept was simply to enable young medical students to watch more experienced Professors at work and many outstanding surgeons, nurses, anatomists and other medicine men learned their trade here. Countess Markievicz died in one of the hospital's public wards in 1927. In 1998, Sir Patrick Dun's became the national centre for civil marriages and today you can see beautiful brides and dashing grooms leaping into stretched limousines parked outside an average of five times a day, six days a week.

MAQUAY BRIDGE

The first stone bridge running across the Grand Canal Street lock was completed in 1796 and named after the banker George Maquay (1758 - 1820), a director of the Grand Canal Company. Maquay (sometimes Macquay) was one of the members of the Ballast Office who orchestrated the sale of Pigeonhouse Harbour to the Admiralty. In 1819, he and Leland Crosthwaite commissioned surveyor Francis Giles to assist George Halpin in building the North Bull Wall. Maquay's son John Leland Maquay junior (1791-1868) was a founder of the Pakenham & Maquay bank of Florence. When the bridge was replaced by the present steel and concrete bridge, the road was widened, the winches substituted and the balance beams of the lower gates removed.

'On Wednesday evening, a man was perceived taking a parcel out of the Grand Canal, near Maquay Bridge, by two gentlemen of the attorneys' infantry, who seized him, and upon examining the parcel, found it to contain eight well executed steel pikes, carefully made up in hay' – *The Cumberland Pacquet*, Tuesday, 14th August 1798

THE TRAMWAY TWINS

In 1906, an earthquake on the San Andreas Fault sent a violent shockwave into San Francisco and brought the city crashing down. Amongst the many casualties of that disaster was the San Francisco tram, then considered the best in the world. The ill-wind blew to Dublin whose tram system, electrified since 1901, duly succeeded San Francisco as the most highly rated on the planet. In that same year, William Martin Murphy, Dublin's fantastically wealthy press baron and tram magnate, oversaw the completion of two steel generating stations by the Grand Canal Docks. Known as the Tramway Twins, these stations were financed by Murphy's Dublin United Tramway Company and capped by two 60ft high steel chimneys. Murphy later gained notoriety leading Dublin's employers against James Larkin's trade unions in the lead up to the 1913 Lock-out, during which he closed the Clontarf and Shelbourne Road tram sheds. The steel chimneys became redundant with the Shannon Scheme of 1932 and were demolished in 1943 by Hammond Lane.

THE CATS AND DOGS

Grand Canal Plaza, designed by Burke-Kennedy Doyle, stands the other side of Maquay Bridge from the Treasury Building. Built in 1999, this occupies the site of the old Dublin City and County dog pound, a home for starving cats and 'other forsaken or mistreated animals'. The Society for the Prevention of Cruelty to Animals were headquartered here from 1886 to 1992. By chance this author discovered a stray called 'Horsebear' on these very same cobbled streets in 2005, now under the care of a diligent nephew. The inner Grand Canal basin alongside which these luckless beasts slept was consequently nicknamed the 'Cats and Dogs'.

Bolands Mill

During the 19th and early 20th century, the Boland family ran one of the most popular bakeries in the city. The Bakery was located where the Treasury Building stands today at the southern end of the Grand Canal Docks, and became famous as De Valera's headquarters during the Easter Rebellion of 1916. The flour and grain used to make the bread was kept within three huge industrial Gotham-like silos of reinforced concrete. Built in the 1940s, these still tower over the skyline between the water and Barrow Street. On the north side of these silos stands a rather austere six storey cut-stone Victorian storehouse, known as the Adelaide Building, with many of its 250 wooden windows facing across Charlotte Quay. Some of the old wooden hoppers and milling machines remain within. An ancillary kiln and dock mills lie further south along the basin by the railway bridge.

The Boland's horses were known to carry weights of up to a ton and a half of flour from the quayside to the bakery. Each horse made an average of 16 such trips a day. The horses were given the next day off, a move perhaps encouraged by the fact that the SPCA were headquartered next door. In 1984, Boland's Mills, then in receivership, were acquired by the IAWS Group. It was subsequently sold to developer Seán Kelly of Benton Properties and it is likely to form part of a major development in the near future.

Between 1946-48 Boland's Mills, then Dublin's largest flour mills, went on strike. The only people who had bread were those who could make it themselves, or the various organizations of the Catholic Church who handed it out in rations to the poor. Such desperate times prompted Dublin author James Plunkett to write Janey Mary, a short story about a five year old girl sent out by her mother to beg for food. In the mad scramble for bread she is crushed by a mob and left for dead, only to be saved by an Augustinian priest'.

Below: The eastern front of the inner basin is dominated by the silos and storehouses of the Boland's Bakery. (Photo: Arco Ardon)

The Boland's Garrison Of Easter 1916

THE CHIEF REFLECTS

When Éamon de Valera stepped down as President of Ireland on June 24th 1973, one of his first stops was at Boland's Bakery, now the Treasury Building, at the southern entrance to the Grand Canal Docks. This was where de Valera had gained his first real revolutionary experience a staggering 57 years earlier. During the Easter Rising of 1916, known locally as 'the Poet's Rebellion', the young mathematician made his name as the last of the rebel Commandants to surrender to the British.

SECURING THE DOCKS

Shortly after noon on Easter Monday 1916, de Valera and approximately 100 members of the Third Battalion stormed the Boland's premises and told all the bakers working there to take a half-day. Both the mill and bakery had been identified as vital strategic locations. Control could enable the rebels to prevent British reinforcements crossing the two bridges over the Grand Canal Docks, as well as the bridge by Lower Mount Street. They would also provide a key vantage point over the railway lines running between Sandymount and Westland Row, and the main road between the port at Kingstown (Dún Laoghaire) and the city centre.

Having secured Boland's, de Valera sent a sizeable detachment of Volunteers to set up an outpost in Westland Row railway station. The men quickly ripped out the railway tracks on the Kingstown line to prevent troop trains getting too close. De Valera established his own headquarters in the dispensary beside the bakery. He ordered the removal of essential parts from the gas works and the electricity supply station in Ringsend, thus cutting off the gas supply and immobilizing the electric trams. Some men were sent to Mount Street Bridge and others to cover the entrance to the British Military Barracks at Beggars Bush. Due to a lack of manpower, de Valera was unable to organize scouting parties and he was thus unaware that the Barracks were in fact virtually empty.

THE BATTLE OF MOUNT STREET

Two days later, some 2,000 British troops came marching up Northumberland Road from Dún Laoghaire, en route to oust the rebel leaders from the General Post Office on O'Connell Street. As these two battalions of Sherwood Foresters approached Mount Street Bridge, they came in for a big surprise. De Valera had surveyed the Westland Row and Grand Canal district in the weeks preceding the Rising. He had considered the military possibilities and now his planning was to pay off.

The Volunteers at Mount Street Bridge secured perfect positioning for a cross-fire ambush. The Forresters walked into a death trap. Their attempts to charge the rebels were utterly suicidal. In a battle that ultimately lasted from noon to 8pm, 234 British officers and men were killed or wounded, marking almost half of the total British Military losses for the whole week of the Rising. Only four Volunteers were killed in the same battle.

During the early part of the action, Mick Malone slipped down to the battalion HQ in the Bakery and warned de Valera that they needed a fast firing weapon urgently. The bespectacled Commandant unbuckled his own Mauser, handed it over with 400 rounds of ammo and said 'Sorry I cannot do more for you'. When the superior British firepower eventually overwhelmed the Volunteers, Malone was among the four killed in the final assault. A Memorial to the slain Volunteers stands by the bridge today; there is no such record of the unfortunate Forresters who perished.

THE SIEGE

The following day, the British gunboat *Helga* sailed up the Liffey and began shelling Boland's Bakery and Mill. A second naval gun was taken ashore from the *Helga* and set up in Percy Place. De Valera deftly neutralized the danger by flying a rebel flag from a nearby distillery, which attracted much of the subsequent shelling. An interesting memo survives, written by de Valera to the British intelligence officer, urging that permission be given to provide food and water to the 90 van horses used by the Bakery. With the British Army now firmly focused on the rebels in the GPO and the Four Courts, there was no concerted assault on the Boland's Bakery area. By the Friday, the rebels at Boland's had seen little action. All week they expected a major assault by the British but it just didn't happen. One night, de Valera and some men slipped out to a nearby railway embankment where they silently watched the city burning to the west.

RELUCTANT SURRENDER

The garrison held out until Sunday when Nurse Elizabeth O'Farrell of Cumann na mBan, the women's auxiliary of the Irish Volunteers, brought news of the general surrender. She handed de Valera the order signed by P.H. Pearse. At first de Valera thought this was simply a British ploy to coax his men out. When he was finally convinced the order came from Pearse, he ordered all arms held by the Volunteers to be put out of action lest they be of use to the enemy. No Volunteer was willing to carry the white flag of surrender so a Red Cross worker was persuaded to hold it while de Valera's vice-commandant, Joseph O'Connor, marched the men out.

Flanked by British soldiers, the rebels made their way to Grattan Street where the order was given to 'ground arms'. It galled de Valera to see the local people coming out from their homes to offer cups of tea to the British soldiers while ridiculing the Volunteers for their actions. When the British led de Valera out from the Mills, he murmured to the crowd outside: 'if only you had come out, though armed with hay forks only'.

As with all battalion commandants, Commandant de Valera was tried by court martial and sentenced to death. However, the shocking executions of the main ringleaders earlier in the week had such a marked effect on public opinion that de Valera's death sentence was commuted to penal servitude for life. Contrary to popular belief, his US citizenship was not used in his favour and he himself made no claims on that basis.

Although his garrison did not see anything like as much action as those in the city centre, de Valera's men racked up a high tally of enemy casualties. Indeed, by dint of their defence of Mount Street Bridge, the heaviest casualties inflicted on the British Army that week were by the Irish garrison stationed in Boland's Mills.

Above: Commandant Éamon de Valera stands outside Bolands Mills shortly after his surrender to the British Army.

Charlotte Quay

When ships first arrived through the sea locks into the Grand Canal Docks, they were greeted by Hanover Quay on the starboard side and Charlotte Quay on the portside. The latter was named for Princess Charlotte, the daughter of the Prince Regent, born just a few months before the Grand Canal Docks were officially opened in 1796. Her parents had actually just separated but she remained second-in-line to the British throne until her death during child birth in 1817. Had she lived, she would have succeeded George IV to become Queen of the United Kingdom. Her death was mourned nationally on a scale similar to that which followed the death of Diana, Princess of Wales, in 1997.

Today, Charlotte Quay is perhaps best known as the location of the slender white 16-storey Millennium Tower (below right), the tallest residential building in Ireland, designed by O'Mahony Pike.

A hundred years ago, this corner-block site was occupied by a 'travelling crane' and Eckford's Chemical and Manure Works, with the Dock Milling Company and King's Glass Bottle Factory nearby. Silica sand for the Bottle Factory came up the coast from Courtown Beach in a small ship, the *Mary Anne*, and was unloaded at the quay. The *Mary Anne*'s crew then rowed back up the Liffey, seeking fresh cargo to bring back down to Wexford.

In 1886, King's became the stage for the fledgling Irish Socialist League's first victory over the bosses. When the employers attempted to enforce a wage reduction, nearly 300 finishers, blowers and gatherers from Dublin's three bottle factories went on strike. The employers responded with a lock-out. A compromise was reached days later and the workers at the Ringsend Bottle Factory and Campbell's factory in the North Lotts returned to work. However, the Charlotte Quay factory remained closed and the Kings dispatched their manager to Sweden to recruit an alternative workforce. He returned with a force of 25 Swedish bottle-workers and 47 dependents who knew nothing about the strike. They were quickly met by Fritz Schumann, a heavily built Danish Marxist and one of the most active members of the Socialist League in Dublin. The Swedes were horrified to learn about the lock out and immediately downed tools. For the next few months, they lived in shoddy makeshift homes along Charlotte Quay, nicknamed 'the Scandinavian Colony', supported by the Dublin Trades Council. At length, the Kings were forced to back down and compensate the Swedes for bringing them to Ireland under false pretences. This verdict was arguably the Socialist League's greatest hour in Dublin. It was also useful for Schumann's aims of uniting the workers of the world. The following October, he successfully urged his London colleagues to host the inaugural congress of the International Union of Glass Bottlemakers.

By 1908, the Wallace Brothers, ship owners and coal importers, had extensive wharfs and bunkers along the quay, just east of where the Millennium Tower is today. Their steam-crane was said to have been 'faster than anything once it got going'. Wallace's horses, stabled nearby, were trained to carry cartloads of two tonnes of coal and covered the Ballsbridge circuit. One of their ships, *Ringwall*, achieved a degree of fame when it rescued the 250 passengers and crew from the B+I ship *Munster*, which was mined in Liverpool Bay in 1940.

During the 1990s, the Irish Nautical Trust and Duchas combined forces to landscape, plant and pave most of Charlotte Quay in a scheme short-listed for the RIAI Triennial Gold Medal 1998/99/2000. The project was a bold statement of intent as to how one could convert a hitherto rundown wasteland into one of the most prestigious addresses in the city. The quayside now hosts miscellaneous pleasure-boats, both inland and seagoing, accessible by a series of jetties along the Promenade.

General Seán MacMahon Bridge

The modern fixed span MacMahon bridge is the fifth bridge to have been constructed over the Grand Canal Docks in just over 200 years. For much of that time, this has been the unofficial border crossing between the communities of Ringsend and Westland Row. "Going over the brudge' was how we used to call it', recalls former docker Bart Nolan.

The first bridge was a wooden bascule or lifting bridge, the Brunswick Bascule, constructed with the original Docks project in 1791, deemed to be 'the best [that] the science of the day provided'. In 1857, this was replaced by an iron swing bridge, named the Victoria Bridge after the Queen. A new Victoria Bridge opened in 1901 and provided a direct link for electric trams to run from Nelson's Pillar through to Sandymount via Ringsend. In 1927, a schooner called *Cymric* was waiting for this bridge to raise so it could move to the inner basin when a gust of wind suddenly thrust its jig-boom into a passing tram. Nobody seems to have been injured.

The fourth bridge was opened by President Éamon de Valera in 1963 and named MacMahon Bridge after General Seán MacMahon (1894–1955) who served alongside de Valera at Bolands Mill in the Easter Rising. MacMahon led B-Company of the 3rd Battalion of the Dublin Brigade of the Irish Republican Army from 1916 to 1921. He was later Chief of Staff to the Free State Army from 1922 - 1924. The name 'Victoria Bridge' was discreetly transferred to the new railway bridge at the south end of the Grand Canal Basin which now carries CIE's southbound services and the DART.

The 1963 creation was a steel single leaf bascule bridge, not unlike the Scherzer Rolling Lift Bridges on the North Quays. Although nominally a lifting bridge, it was welded shut after heated complaints from local residents about the noise of buses and trucks rattling across.

In 2005, Dublin City Council commissioned a new MacMahon Bridge. Designed by Paul Arnold Architects and completed in 2007, it consists of a cantilevered structure over the existing Quay Walls, ensuring the full 90m length causeway provides adequate width for two traffic lanes and two bus lanes. Its outer elliptical stainless steel, glass-clad arches have been known to double as diving boards for some of the fearless youngsters of the parish. The new bridge does not open but an extra 40cm headroom was secured for navigation, bringing it in step with the minimum air draught height requirements for the Grand Canal.

Below: The present bridge was completed in 2007 but follows the course of a wooden lifting bridge built across the docks in 1791. (Photo: Arco Ardon). Left: The Millennium Tower occupies the site of a bottle factory where Swedish workers once operated. (Photo: Cathal Furey).

The Coalmen

MODERN COALSCAPE
There is a wonderful moment in JP Donleavy's book *The Beastly Beatitudes of Balthazar B*, when the enchanting Balthazar is sent galloping down the 'the wet gleaming cobble stones' of the quays, 'by all the long rusting sides of ships'. His flight was prompted by a surprise encounter with 'an old grey bewhiskered face … staring and mad', clasping a lump of coal in one hand by a bunker on Misery Hill. Fifty years ago, every available space along the South Quays seems to have been occupied by coal-yards. Between Sir Isaac Butt Bridge and Sir John Rogerson's Quay there were six coal merchants. At least another four were based by the Grand Canal Docks. The companies who ran them were household names across the city. Tedcastle's, Heiton's, Doherty's, Sheridan's, Wallace's, Murphy's, JJ. Carroll's, S.N. Robinson, P. Donnelly and so on. Buildings we know today as the Millennium Tower, Gallery Quay, Hanover Reach and Educo-Gym are all built on former coal yards.

THE COAL HORSE
Perhaps the most familiar sight on any given street in this area was a horse with a cart full of coal trotting along the cobbles. 'Everybody in the area had a horse then', says retired docker Bart Nolan. 'There was nothing but horses. A horse was your security. If the horse didn't die, you wouldn't die'. Tedcastle's were the first to motorize their fleet after the Second World War and so began the extinction of the Docklands horse.

GANGERS & BUTTON-MEN
In the morning, the skinny, gravelly-voiced dockers would gather for the 'Read' between The Ferryman and The Gasometer, where McCann FitzGerald is today. If you got the call up to dig coal, then off you set to meet the coal-steamers coming in, perhaps along Sir John Rogerson's Quay, or Charlotte Quay. As the ships arrived, quick thinkers threw their cigarette boxes into the hold to book their spot. It was the fellow down at the bottom of the coal pile who had the hardest job, shovelling the nuggets up into the tub, inhaling the sickly stench of tar through the morning mist. 'The Number 7 shovel was the most important thing a man could have', says Bart. When he began digging coal in JJ Carroll's yard in his youth, his father advised him to work with a slow stroke and make sure the shovel was full every time. 'Done right, the shovel could hold a stone of coal'. The men dug all day, and night if need be, working with a small paraffin light, known as a 'duck'. Their hands frequently bled raw with coke cuts; their lungs congested by coal dust. Dockers were hard men but there was always a solid sense of wit. 'I don't recognize this court', said a docker standing trial for being drunk and disorderly. 'Are ye political?', enquired the judge warily. 'No', the docker replied, 'I mean you must have painted it since I was here last'.

TUCKER TIME
At 12:30pm, the hooter would sound for lunch 'and there'd be a rush of men, like ants, running home for the grub … the smell of their clothes was truly diabolical'. One of the best-known North Wall coal-diggers was Tucker Lynch, born in Railway Street and reckoned to be the only Afro-American in the inner city. The story runs that he had to sport a bright red scarf around his neck so that his mother could identify him from the other diggers when she brought him his tea and sandwiches. Tea was a rarity in those times although occasionally, the crane-drivers would genially boil a billy-can of water in their steam engines and provide fresh tea for the lads.

THE FINAL JOURNEY
Tedcastle's led the way into the future with the acquisition of two steam-driven George Arrow cranes. These would lift a full tub onto a waiting horse-drawn lorry, known as a 'bogie', bound for the coal yards. In later times, the coal was shovelled directly into a hopper that ran up and down Gallery Quay, where the trees are now. The coal was then sacked before it's penultimate journey by horse and dray, or lorry, to households across the southern suburbs. Sometimes it was taken by bellmen, private street traders, with a horse or donkey. A lucky coal-man would just have to pour the coal down a ground level chute. It certainly can't have been fun heaving those 8-stone bags up eight flights of stairs to the top floor of a four-storey Georgian home.

THE TARA STREET BATHS

Some bogies ran down fixed tracks along the South Quays and connected to the gas works at Hanover Quay. The ghost of this narrow gauge tramway can still be seen in places today. At the gas works, the coal was taken to the coke ovens or purifier and burned. 'You could smell anyone who worked with the gas a mile away', recalls Sonny Kinsella. 'There wasn't too many of them who had baths'. Indeed, one of the few options for cleaning yourself was to go to the Public Baths and Wash Houses down at Tara Street. Bart shivers at the memory. 'You'd stand and wait for the fellow to turn on the tap but you wouldn't know if it'd be hot or cold. And if you gave out, they wouldn't let you in the next time'.

NOWHERE TO RUN

After the steamers and lorries and dockers had gone, local children came scampering in to gather as many stray nuggets as they could for the family fireplace. But you wouldn't want to be caught. 'If the police saw you, that was it', chuckles Bart. 'There was nowhere to run. How are you going to get away with a bag of coal on your back and them on the bike?'

Below: Coal arriving in from the Welsh mines is shovelled by hands into buckets and then carted to the coalyards by narrow gauge railway. (Photo: Dublin Port Company Archives)

Hanover Quay Gasworks

'Now I walk back again. To look at these great walls of blackened bricks. The gas works. Sooty grime and fire in there through these bars. Dark shadows. Men moving with their lighted end of cigarettes' –
The Beastly Beatitudes of Balthazar B, JP Dunleavy.

HANOVER QUAY

When Hanover Quay was first built in 1800, all that separated it from the River Liffey were the walls of Sir John Rogerson's Quay and a sizeable acreage of marshland sprinkled with the occasional apple tree. By 1876, the area was dominated by two industries, flour-milling and gas production. Bottle-making, sugar refining and the manufacture of chemical fertiliser were also increasingly notable. Much of the land was owned by the Dublin Gas Company who effectively divided it into three lots. Diners at the Riva and Ely hq restaurants are eating amid the ghost of a huge Coke Works where an extraordinary amount of imported coal was burned in order to provide Dubliners with the benefit of gas. A timber yard ran down the westerly flank of Cardiff's Lane to Sir John Rogerson's Quay (where the Gasometer was pitched in 1934). Directly east along the waterfront stood a vast tar works, from whose pits the stinking coal-tar was unloaded onto iron barges. A Corn Store occupied the eastern frontier by Britain Quay, with easy access to the entrance locks. Behind these were the Chemical Works of Misery Hill, where coal-burning by-products such as chemical manure, guano and sulphuric acid were manufactured. Harry Crosbie's waterside house was a Guinness barley store, housing all the sacks of barley that came in from the countryside on Grand Canal barges. In 1864, a conservationist called Brophy lowered a barrel of freshwater containing healthy live salmon into the water along Hanover Quay. They died within two minutes. When he cooked one of the salmon, it tasted of gas. This was not perhaps the most auspicious era for the quarter mile long quay named in honour of the Royal House of Hanover, but the manufacture of coal-gas was always going to be dirty work.

A BIT ABOUT COKE AND GAS

During the 17th and 18th centuries, vast tracts of woodland across Britain and Ireland were felled to provide timber for ships, industry and housing. As wood became a scarcer commodity, so the entrepreneurs turned to an alternative source of energy, coal. Coal on its own is a non-runner as a household or industrial fuel – it's far too smoky and full of sulphur. However, in the 17th century, a breakthrough came when someone baked coal in an airless oven at an intensive heat. The result was that all the coal's smoke-making properties vanished – specifically water, coal-gas, and coal-tar – leaving a rock hard, highly porous substance of smokeless fuel, or coke. Hence, coke became the main energy force driving the Industrial Revolution in Britain. In the late 18th century, scientists worked out how to extract both gas and tar from the coal, as well as coke. They also discovered that the extracted coal-gas (or town gas) could itself serve as a fuel, particularly for lighting street-lamps.

DUBLIN'S FIRST GAS-LIGHT COMPANY

Stroll any of the smart streets of Dublin today and you will see the elegant manhole covers down which the coal was poured for each individual household. Ireland does not have a lot of coal. Hence we've been importing it since at least 1665 when it ranked as third in a list of Irish imports from England. In 1720, Jonathan Swift urged Dubliners to 'burn everything English except their coal' which, remarkably, became one of the slogans of the Economic War with Britain in the 1930s. In 1820, the Dublin Gas-Light Company was established by a parliamentary act. This empowered 29 commissioners, headed up by the Duke of Leinster, to oversee the lighting of the streets and squares of Dublin. A notable stipulation of the act was that 'the refuse be not permitted to run into the river Liffey'. Judging by the ill-fated salmon alluded to above, this proviso was somewhat overlooked.

THE ALLIANCE & DUBLIN CONSUMERS' GAS COMPANY

In 1866, the Dublin Gas-Light Company and four other private gas companies were formally amalgamated into the Alliance & Dublin Consumers' Gas Company. Sixteen years earlier, Henry Shaw's Dublin Directory noted the company had works at 40 and 41 Sir John Rogerson's Quay. The Alliance & Dublin —more usually known as the Dublin Gas Company— was very quickly at the forefront of gas production, storage and distribution throughout the city. Indeed, it dominated Ireland's coal-gas market for the next 100 years. From 1889, they had the monopoly on public and private electric lighting throughout the southside. The implications of the Coal-Gas Age were enormous. Industrial production accelerated at an unseen pace. The eyes of many a tycoon gleamed with the realisation that these bright gas-lights could enable their unfortunate minions to work nightshifts too. The well-to-do could subscribe to have gas piped directly to their houses; manholes from this era can be seen on the city streets today. Gas quickly became the preferred fuel of Dublin's middle class, particularly for their gas cookers and stoves. The streets also became safer, enabling people to feel more at ease socially, while the ability to read and write by night provided a huge boost to education.

RELOCATING TO ROGERSON'S QUAY

The Dublin Gas Company originally had its principal wharfage along the quaysides of the Grand Canal Docks. Here, the colliers from Liverpool delivered the increasingly large quantities of coal required. There was also an abundance of water, an important raw material in the coke-making process. When the company's coal requirements increased, it transferred wharfage operations to Sir John Rogerson's Quay, which was better placed for larger coal ships. By the 1880s, gas-related structures dominated the South Lotts landscape from the Barrow Street Gasometer to Sir John Rogerson's Quay. The Gas Company horses were stabled down at the Benson Street end of Hanover Quay.

THE CHEMICAL AGE

By-products from the gas, such as coal tars and ammonia, provided a vital ingredient for both the dye and chemical industry. Chemical factories emerged in the South Docks during the 1870s and 1880s. Parents and children with respiratory problems such as asthma were actually encouraged by their physicians to come and breathe in these soothing sulphur fumes. A short term remedy perhaps. The major factories were Morgan Mooney & Co, William Jos, Kane & Son, and W.H. Goulding Limited. Morgan Mooney specialized in fertilizer, acid manufacturing and animal feed. Its site was later acquired by Kilsaran Concrete. Kane & Son, which made saltcake (sodium sulphate), sulphuric acid and bleaching powder, was founded by John Kean, a 1798 rebel who mastered chemistry while in exile in France. He later changed his name to Kane and his son, Sir Robert Kane, was one of the most eminent chemists of the Victorian Age. Goulding's made their fortune from chemical manure, with a focus on sulphuric, hydrochloric and nitric acids.

THE GAS COMPANY'S COAL SHIPS

As the demand for British coal increased across Ireland, so the Grand Canal Docks became an increasingly convenient location for the coal importers to maintain wharfage. It was not just useful for customers in South Dublin but also for accessing clients all along the Grand Canal and Barrow Navigation. In 1918, the large dry dock was filled in and the ground leased to Heiton's as a coalyard. Two of the graving docks were also filled in and taken over by the Gas Company. During the First World War, it became extremely difficult to maintain the vital coal supply from Britain. In 1916, the Alliance & Dublin Gas Co. purchased their own ship, the 440-ton *Ard Rí* followed by the 400-ton *Braedale*. The *Ard Rí* still docked off Sir John Rogerson's Quay but the slightly smaller *Braedale* was able to slip through the Grand Canal Locks and directly access the company depot. In 1920, the company purchased a new ship, the 460-ton *Glenageary* which was tailormade to access the 150-metred long Camden Lock and so brought the Dublin Gas Company right back into the Grand Canal Docks.

From 1919 to 1968, the Gas Company had its coal depot on the site of present-day Gallery Quay and Grand Canal Square. The *Glenageary* ultimately became the flagship of a successful fleet of four raised quarterdeck steamers, the others being the *Glencullen*, the *Glencree* and, from 1946, the *Glenbride*. With a normal crew of 11, these steamers brought coal from Liverpool to the Grand Canal Docks, a journey of between 16 and 18 hours. They operated on a clockwork system so that there were always two at sea, one loading in Liverpool and one unloading in Dublin. During the summer months, when only light coal supplies were needed, the fleet was chartered out to carry other cargos on the seas. During the Economic War of the 1930s, the *Glencullen* collected its coal from Rotterdam. Harry Gilligan bestowed considerable praise on the masters and crew of these coal steamers for braving the German bombers during World War Two, just to ensure Dubliners got their gas. The steamers were frequently bombed and strafed by machine-guns but amazingly survived the war with just two crew members injured. These hearty voyagers were unique amongst seamen at this time in that they were responsible for their own meals. 'On the other ships they'd feed you', says Sonny Kinsella. 'But these boys would be over and back in a day and had to bring their grub with them'.

50 YEARS AGO

Fifty years ago, the Hanover Quay landscape was a frenetic if unhealthy blend of agriculture and industry. Along its eastern front were the stations and furnaces of the gasworks. Then came the Hammond Lane foundry and Donnelly's coal yards where Dublin author Eamon MacThomas used to work. During the 1940s, the Gas Company also received the occasional load of 'bog-ore', carried by horse-drawn barge, via the Royal Canal, from Co Westmeath by James Leech and his son Willy. Harry Crosbie's house was owned by David Popplewell's Leinster Dyers, making the most of the rainbow of colours made from coal gas and coal tar. The coal merchants and salt manufacturers Flower & McDonald stabled their horses just to the right. Another large grain store stood alongside Britain Quay, behind the ice stores and Gas Company stables. The warehouses beside the tar-pits became a Raleigh Ireland factory but burned down in the 1970s. All the quaysides of the Grand Canal Docks were full of steam-grab cranes and black steel-hulled colliers.

THE END OF INDUSTRY

The coal-gas industry continued to prosper through the first half of the 20th century as more and more appliances became gas-operated, such as fires, cookers, refrigerators, washing machines, central heating and air conditioning. Its nemesis was electricity and, by 1960, most of Ireland had an electricity supply. From the 1950s, the British coal trade was also affected by new and better coal, first from America, then from Poland, and later by the petro-chemical industry. But coal-gas was now being derided as 'nasty, smelly, dirty and dangerous'. The coalmen were also reeling as mechanization made their careers increasingly redundant. In the 1940s they'd watched as lorries replaced horses. Before long they were to be replaced by forklift trucks and hydraulic cranes. And then came containerisation. In 1961, mechanized grabs mastered the art of lifting coal out of ships' holds. By the 1970s, unemployment was rampant as more and more of the Port's employees were laid off.

DISCOVERY OF NATURAL GAS

Córas Iompair Éireann closed the Grand Canal in December 1959. The Dublin Gas Company's coal-steamers were withdrawn from service when the company converted to oil in 1968. (The *Glencullen* and the *Glenbridge* have been spotted in the past 10 years, operating off the coasts of Dubai and France respectively). Three years earlier, a further death-knell was sounded for coal-gas with the discovery of natural gas in the North Sea. In 1971, an off-shore well struck lucky and hit upon Ireland's first indigenous reserve of natural gas off Kinsale Head. By the late 1970s, the entire energy market was in turmoil. Oil prices were doubling and quadrupling. The coal gas industry was imploding, leaving many small private companies in dire financial straits. In 1976, a number of these beleagured companies were coralled into the semi-state Bord Gáis Éireann, charged with building a natural gas infrastructure across the island. Part of the new strategy involved a 240km natural gas pipeline from Kinsale to Dublin, completed in 1983. The arrival of natural gas in Dublin effectively bankrupted the Dublin Gas Company and its assets passed to Bord Gáis. This included the 25-acre Gasworks site in the Grand Canal Docks.

Below: The SS *Glencullen* and SS *Glenageary* anchor off present-day Grand Canal Square in very icy conditions; Victoria Bridge (now rebuilt as MacMahon Bridge) and Boland's Mills can be seen at back left. Right: The SS *Glencree* arrives in the Grand Canal Docks laden with coal for the Dublin Gas Company. Above right: By 1981, the skyline of Sir John Rogerson's Quay and the Grand Canal Docks was dominated by buildings associated with the Dublin Gas Company. Here we can see the East Link Toll Bridge is under construction in the foreground. (Photos: Fantasy Jack).

Renaissance of the Grand Canal Docks

THE SALE
There were suggestions from as early as 1987 that the Dublin Gasworks could be converted into a vibrant, multi-cultural residential and commercial zone. However, the plan was put on hold as the soils were deemed irreparably contaminated. The Hammond Lane foundry and Donnelly's Coalyard were closed down. The ice stores and stables were abandoned. Kilsaran Concrete took over where Morgan Mooney once stood. The largest brownfield site in Ireland lay virtually derelict until 1997 when Bord Gáis placed the vast bulk of their Dublin operations up for sale, including all the lands between Sir John Rogerson's Quay and Hanover Quay, as well as the present day site of Grand Canal Square. Under the terms of the Act that created them, the Docklands Authority were entitled to purchase all lands owned by semi-state bodies that were deemed to be of a non-operational nature. The Gasworks more than adequately fitted that description.

PURCHASE & REMEDIATION
In the face of considerable opposition, the Authority purchased the 25-acre site for IRL£17 million in November 1997, the same month their Master Plan was published. The Authority accepted responsibility for remediating the site and subsequently spent circa IRL£50 million on the clean up. However, they were satisfied that whatever they spent would be recovered in the long run because it was likely every single acre on the site would be worth at least IRL£10 million. Parkman Consultants identifed the chemical composition in the soil, including cresol, toluene, xylene, ethylbenzene, ammonia, benzene and napthalene. Carefully monitored by the Environmental Protection Agency, a bentoninte wall measuring 8m deep and 2km long was erected to contain the site. The whole area was then excavated to a depth of 4m. All groundwater, once remediated, was pumped out, via a sewer, into a treatment works. Most soil was treated on site, but over 134,000 tonnes of material was removed. The most hazardous soils were shipped to Europe and burned off; some was later used for road building. In December 2002, the site was given a clean bill of health by the EPA. The Docklands Authority had the green light to give planning permission for 180,000 square metres of intensive office and residential developments in the area.

MAKING GOOD ON THE GRAND CANAL DOCKS
The cost of the purchase and remediation was IRL£65 million. By 2003, each acre was valued at circa €14 million. The whole area was very much undeveloped with the exception of Harry Crosbie's splendid waterfront property and U2's nearby Sound Studio. The Authority held fortnightly meetings to see how they could best convince the public that this area was now safe and friendly. The Docklands Authority has since generated well over €200 million in land sales from the site. This was a tremendous breakthrough, enabling them to play the role of developer, including the creation of the public space of Grand Canal Square (which surely no private developer could have afforded) and to fund so many other initiatives. The Grand Canal Docks also has the advantage of being extremely accessible for both cars and pedestrains. Fast-forward to the present day and few could possibly believe that Hanover Quay occupies the very same land as that poisonous, coal-infested, ash-splashed horror of old. The most memorable development is the tinted apartment block of Hanover Quay itself, which scooped the RIAI's Best Housing Award for designers O'Mahony Pike in 2007. Beside this, the old tar works has become the site of Long Boat Quay, with a EuroSpar and Milano's Restaurant at ground level. On the right, the old Corn Store has been replaced by a large glass fronted pavilion apartment and office block known as the Hanover Reach Waterfront. At ground level, the quay is now home to restaurants Riva and Ely hq, as well as the Urban Retreat Gallery, run by the Cill Rialaig Project.

Right: The red poles of the Martha Schwartz designed Grand Canal Square echo some of the taller buildings in the Grand Canal Docks, such as the Millennium Tower on the right. (Photo: Eugene Langan)

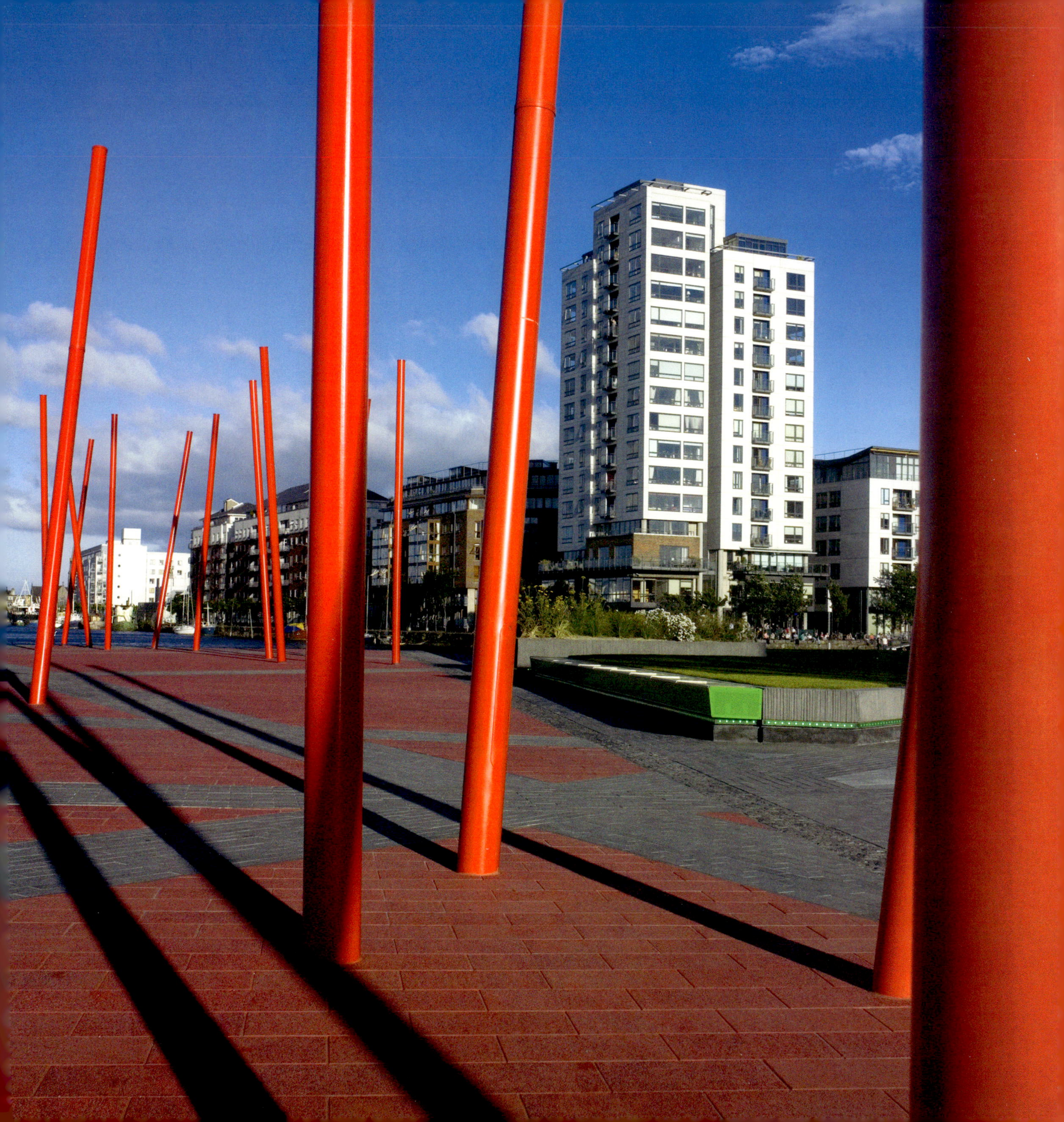

Grand Canal Square

THE CONCEPT
One of the greatest advantages of the Docklands Authority purchasing the old Gasworks site along Hanover Quay was that they could now have a proper shot at playing the role of developer. A major part of the Docklands Authority's ethos concerns the social regeneration of the area within their remit. Constructing a landscape of shimmering new high-rises undoubtedly regenerates the physical landscape of an area but it amounts to naught if the thousands of new workers and residents within have nowhere to play. Public spaces are vital to urban environments, particularly outdoor parklands and squares.

The main part of Grand Canal Square officially opened on June 17th 2007 with an open-air theatre performance by a collection of giant stilt walking butterflies. Due to be completed in 2009, the 2.54-acre Grand Canal Square has set a new standard for public squares in Ireland, with three landmark buildings and a striking sculpted landscape. The square is set to host many spectacular events in the coming decades.

THE CRACKED GLASS SQUARE
In 2005, the Docklands Authority presented just over half an acre of the former Gasworks site to Martha Schwartz Partners and gave them the go-ahead to convert the space into a bright, creative and visually inspiring public square. The Docklands Authority also took the unusual step of allowing the landscape architects' design to become the key component in defining the whole area. The principal designer was Shauna Gillies-Smith, based in Boston, Massachusetts. On-site drawings and liaisons were carried out by Dublin-based Tiros Resources while the project was managed by the Martha Schwartz studio in London. Gillies-Smith chose a concept known as 'Cracked Glass', which basically amounts to a seemingly random interplay of multi-dimensional lines. Two swards of red and green criss-cross the site. The green is soft and low, created by marshy grasses, rich perennials and flowering bulbs. The red 'carpet' is cantilevered over the dock and up to the entrance of the Libeskind theatre. This dramatic effect is created by a combination of sparkling resin-bonded coloured glass and red pick-stick lighting columns. The pick-sticks evoke childhood memories and appear to have been scattered in a willy-nilly manner, whilst simultaneously echoing and indeed embracing the towering candy-striped chimneys of Poolbeg. They also reflect the solitary relic of the Gasworks era, an old redbrick chimney standing nearby. By night, the Speirs and Major lighting elements conjure a particularly magical effect as the red and green LED clusters glow through the damp maritime air and dance with the glitter of the power station lights beyond.

The €8 million project was among the most innovative landscape design projects ever undertaken in Ireland. There is good reason to believe that it has pioneered a new perception of landscape usage in Ireland, namely of using the actual landscape as art. Functionality is never far away either; some benches double as ventilation ducts for the car park below. The coloured paving and lighting scheme is already recognizable the world over. Every day, hundreds of people sit and sprawl upon the solid granite blocks running along the water's edge and the apple-green metal benches along the planters. Skate-boarders and roller-girls are perpetually whizzing across the red and green carpets. The Square lives and breathes. This was the location for the annual Analog Festival, an arts festival commissioned by the Docklands Authority. In July 2008, Grand Canal Square hosted the Analog with performances by Hal Willner's Rogue's Gallery, a surreal gathering of 'brigands', as well as the likes of Tim Robbins, Lou Reed, Shane McGowan, Neil Hannon, The High Llamas and novelist Jonathan Coe. In August 2008, the Square marked the start of the 900km Tour of Ireland for 93 international cyclists.

CHEQUERED SQUARES & THE LIBESKIND THEATRE
Grand Canal Square is enhanced by three outstanding new buildings, two by big name international architects and one by the home-grown team of Duffy Mitchell O'Donoghue. The latter certainly threw down the gauntlet when they launched the ever-changing multi-coloured glass block of No.1 Grand Canal Square as the first building completed on the Square. Its glazing slowly changes colour as the day progresses, from cold blue to deep orange.

On the northside is the chequered 5-star Giltedge hotel, designed by Portuguese architect Manuel Aires Mateus, with interiors by the

Galway-born designer Philip Treacy. The Mateus concept was that the hotel would look like it had been 'excavated from a seven storey rock'. The east side running towards Misery Hill is commanded by the imposing, glass-faced 2,200-seat Grand Canal Theatre, the performing arts centre designed by acclaimed American architect Daniel Libeskind. Developed by Chartered Land, the theatre is owned by property developer Harry Crosbie and will be run by Live Nation. Broadcasters Gay Byrne and Gerry Ryan, who are both trustees of the theatre, laid its foundation stone on 20th June 2008. Libeskind's portfolio includes the Jewish Museum in Berlin, the Imperial War Museum in Manchester and the ongoing reconstruction of the World Trade Centre site in New York.

Below: Amongst the highlights of the Analog Festival 2008 in Grand Canal Square were performances by Neil Hannon and Tim Robbins (above right) and Lou Reed (right). (Stage Photo: Colm Mullen)

U2 – A Docklands Band

With album sales exceeding 140 million and 22 Grammy Awards in their trophy cabinet, U2 have provided a most remarkable soundtrack for many who have walked this planet over the last 30 years. They are, without doubt, a Dublin band. From a rather tenuous historical perspective, their bond with the Dublin Docklands goes back to the 1770s when the Hibernian Marine School was built on Sir John Rogerson's Quay. During the 19th century, the Marine School was relocated and renamed, ultimately becoming the Mount Temple Comprehensive School in Clontarf. And it was at Mount Temple that, in 1976, schoolboy Larry Mullen Jr posted an ad on the school bulletin board looking for musicians to join his band. As Mullen put it, 'it was "'The Larry Mullen Band" for about ten minutes. Then Bono walked in and blew any chance I had of being in charge'. Among the others who signed up were Adam Clayton and Dave 'The Edge' Evans. On Saint Patrick's Day 1978, U2 won a talent show in Limerick that set them on the road to fame and fortune. Their debut single *Three* was released the following year.

One of U2's proudest Docklands moments came in July 1982 when, taking some time out from their long *October* tour, they performed a free and unannounced gig on the rooftop of the Sheriff Street community centre. This was at a time when not even the Gardai dared go to Sheriff Street and the mood was somewhat ominous from the outset. An inebriated woman stumbled off the rooftop and had to be carted away. The tour manager advised band and crew to abandon the event. Sensing that a cancellation might entail a riot, both band and crew voted to play on. Slowly but surely U2 managed to woo the crowbar-toting crowd. Bono later recalled how a docker, 'who looked six feet wide, just walked onstage and stood in front of me. 'Let's twist again like we did last summer', he said. 'Play it'. The whole crowd quieted - this was the confrontation: were we chicken or not? I must admit, I was chicken. I just stopped the show and started to sing, no accompaniment, 'Let's twist again, like we did last summer...' And I looked at the crowd, and all the kids, the mothers, fathers, the wine and whiskey bottles in their hands, started singing and dancing. And the guy smiled'.

Just up Sheriff Street was the sorting office where Bono's father, the late Bob Hewson was employed. Bob did not retire from his job until the year U2 played their first Croke Park concert, declaring rock 'n' roll to be 'too noisy and overpaid'. Bono wrote *Sometimes You Can't Make It On Your Own* in tribute to Bob, who passed away in 2001. The video was filmed on Sheriff Street on a cold December morning. Bono sang the entire song live, without a cut. Director Phil Joanou described it as 'the best single-take performance that I have ever had the honor to film - incredibly powerful'. The song debuted at No. 1 on the UK Singles Chart and won 'Song of the Year' at the 2006 Grammy Awards.

When based in Dublin, the band members' preferred turf has traditionally been the Grand Canal Docks. Indeed, look carefully at the album cover for *October* and you will see those very docks just behind the band. Many of their videos were also made in the Docklands. In *Gloria*, the band play upon a barge moored in the middle of the Grand Canal Basin. One of the their favourite haunts was the snug of the dearly lamented Docker's pub on Sir John Rogerson's Quay where they were frequently to be found huddled around frothy pints of Guinness. Their recording studio was in an old stone warehouse on Windmill Lane behind the pub. U2 recorded or completed eight of their studio albums in Windmill Lane, including *War* which debuted at No 1 in the UK in 1983, and *The Joshua Tree*, which was then the fastest-selling album in British chart history. By 1994, they were primarily operating out of a stylish new studio on Hanover Quay, designed by architect Felim Dunne, where all subsequent albums have been recorded or finished.

In 2001, the Hanover Quay studio came under threat of a demolition order but still survives to the present day. In 2003, the band announced plans to relocate its recording studio to a new skyscraper, the U2 Tower, to be sited on Britain Quay close to where the old Hailing Station once stood. Work on the 120m-high U2 Tower will commence after 2011.

Right: The Docklands Authority appointed Geranger Limited to develop the U2 Tower, a residential tower featuring the band's egg-shaped recording studio, or pod, at the very top. The tilted design is by London-based architects Foster and Partners.

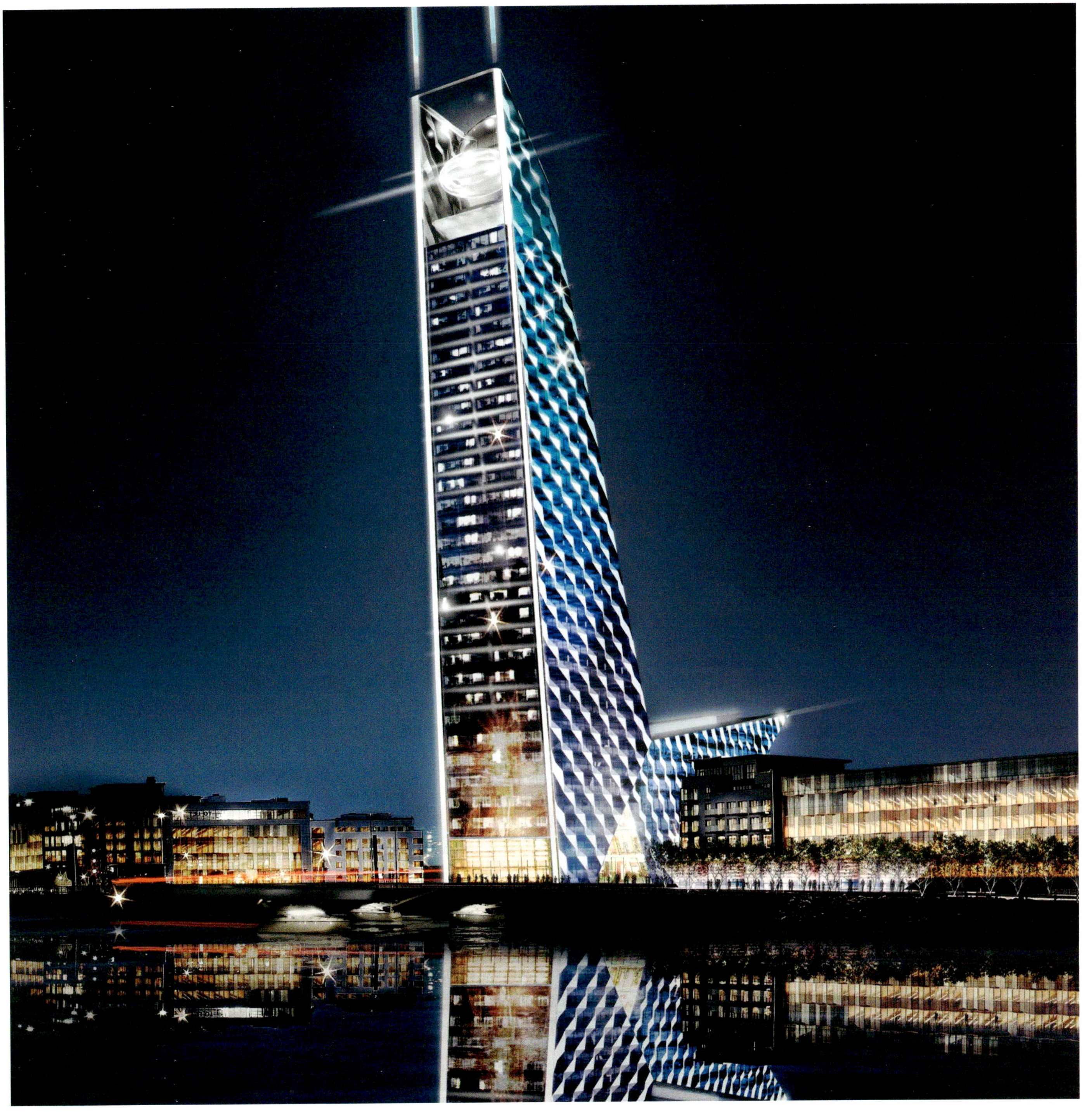

Chapter Six
Ringsend & Poolbeg

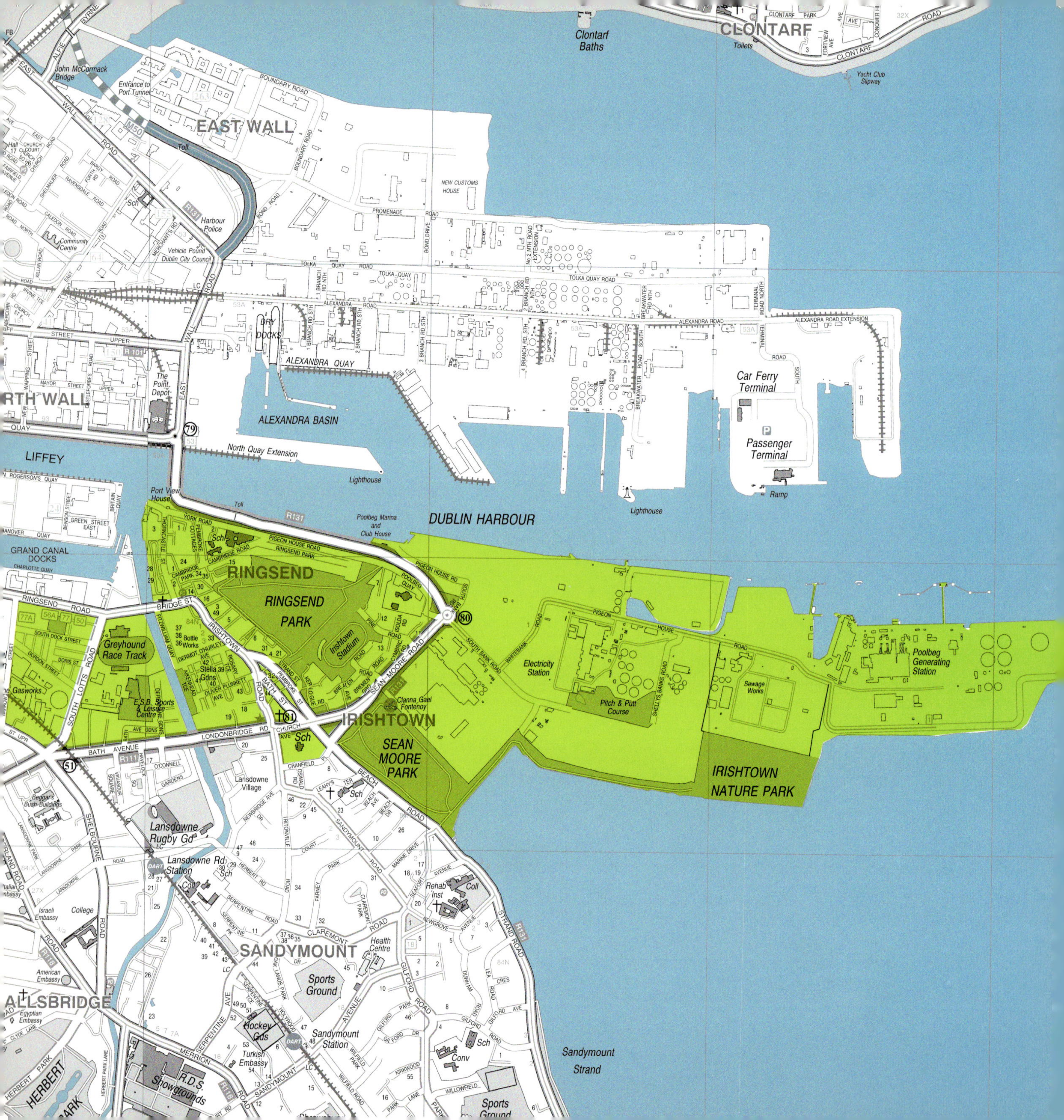

CLONTARF
Clontarf Baths
EAST WALL
John McCormack Bridge
Entrance to Port Tunnel
Harbour Police
Community Centre
Vehicle Pound Dublin City Council
NEW CUSTOMS HOUSE
TOLKA QUAY ROAD
ALEXANDRA ROAD
ALEXANDRA ROAD EXTENSION
DRY DOCKS
ALEXANDRA QUAY
ALEXANDRA BASIN
North Quay Extension
Lighthouse
Car Ferry Terminal
Passenger Terminal
Ramp
The Point Depot
LIFFEY
Port View House
Toll
Poolbeg Marina and Club House
DUBLIN HARBOUR
GRAND CANAL DOCKS
RINGSEND
RINGSEND PARK
Irishtown Stadium
PIGEON HOUSE ROAD
Electricity Station
Pitch & Putt Course
Sewage Works
Poolbeg Generating Station
Greyhound Race Track
Gasworks
E.S.B. Sports & Leisure Centre
Bottle Works
Stella Gdns
IRISHTOWN
SEAN MOORE ROAD
Clanna Gael Fontenoy
SEAN MOORE PARK
IRISHTOWN NATURE PARK
LONDONBRIDGE RD
BATH AVENUE
Lansdowne Village
Beggar's Bush Buildings
Lansdowne Rugby Gd
Lansdowne Rd Station
Israeli Embassy
American Embassy
Egyptian Embassy
Rehab Inst
SANDYMOUNT
Health Centre
Sports Ground
Hockey Gds
Sandymount Station
Turkish Embassy
R.D.S. Showgrounds
BALLSBRIDGE
HERBERT PARK
Sandymount Strand
STRAND ROAD

Not unlike East Wall on Dublin's northside, Ringsend has a long history of independent thinking. Its' origins as part of the extensive Fitzwilliam family estate are still evident from the older street-names of Thorncastle, Thomas and Pembroke, while Cambridge Road and York Road recall a subsequent allegiance to the Crown. Ringsend's golden age was the 18th century when all packet-ships from England anchored at the Pigeonhouse, despatching considerable business through the village en route to Dublin City. Ringsend duly developed into one of the largest working class Protestant communities in Ireland, and prospered through a herring fishery, salt-works, iron-works, glass-factory and various ship-building and rope-making enterprises. It even had its own suburb, the largely Catholic enclave of Irishtown.

However, when the packet-ships were transferred to Howth in the early 19th century, the once fashionable seaside resort went into decline. The last vestiges of the Protestant age are to be found in the names of the charming red-bricked terraced streets of South Lotts – Gordon, Hastings, Ormeau, Hope and Joy. In 1898, the nationalists secured control of the Pembroke Urban District and began to redevelop the area, with terraces and avenues named for Saints, Popes and the centenary of Catholic Emancipation. Many houses and groves were later named for Republican heroes who perished in the fight for independence – Ennis, O'Rahilly, Whelan. The roads off Seán Moore Road recall the various ships and colliers sunk by the Germany Navy in World War Two.

Today the village where James Joyce was 'made a man' by Nora Barnacle is on the cusp of a new dawn. The ambitious plans for Poolbeg will see the entire peninsula converted into a nature and waterside parkland with a backbone of mixed development. Ringsend will inevitably play a major role in this evolution but is sure to retain its old world charm. In the land of Ruairi Quinn, the residents are extremely proud of their past, with its curious mix of Protestantism, docker ethics and football. Both Shelbourne FC and Shamrock Rovers were founded here while the Poolbeg Yacht & Boat Club has lately completed a 100-berth marina. The Dodder remains surprisingly dangerous and is prone to flash-flooding, such as that experienced during Hurricane Charlie in 1986 and again in 2002. At low tide, the mud flats are exposed along the banks so that gulls and the occasional oystercatcher can be seen foraging through the brown seaweed.

Ringsend & Poolbeg - Streetwise

Aikenhead Terrace - Named for the Protestant-born Mother Mary Aikenhead (1787-1858) who founded the Roman Catholic religious order, the Sisters of Charity, to help counter malnutrition and fever.

Barrack Lane - In 1865, Colonel Henry Lake's constabulary left from a small Victorian barracks that stood here to arrest nightdress-clad James Stephens and other Fenians at their villa hideaway nearby. Colonel Lake subsequently became Chief Commissioner of Police.

Bath Avenue - Opened in 1792 and probably named for the bathing establishments on Irishtown Strand to which it was connected by a rough lane built across what was then an expansive salt marsh.

Beggars Bush - Before the Dodder bridges and Grand Canal Docks tamed the area, Beggars Bush was a treacherous marshland crossed by a handful of rough tracks and wooden bridges. It was also a notorious hang out for highwaymen and beggars.

Bremen Road - Named for a ship of the Cork Steamship Company which famously rescued Dutch seamen in 1940, but was sunk by Junker bombers in 1942.

Cambridge Road - Named in 1863 after Prince George (1819–1904), 2nd Duke of Cambridge, grandson of George III, and Commander-in-Chief of the British Army for 39 years from 1857 to 1895.

Caroline Place - Named for Caroline of Brunswick, the 'Injured Queen of England'. Husband George IV prosecuted her for divorce after an alleged affair with dance instructor Bartolomeo Pergami. She collapsed and died shortly after George's Coronation. She was most probably poisoned.

Celestine Avenue - Named for Pope Celestine who sent St Patrick to Ireland.

Chapel Avenue - Named for a small red-brick Catholic chapel that survived the Penal Laws but vanished during the 1990s. In 1791, Father Peter Clinch, the popular young Parish Priest of Donnybrook, Irishtown and Ringsend, was killed by an accidental blow to his jaw from an oar.

Clonlara Road - Named for a steamship built in 1926 for the Limerick Steamship Company. It survived the carnage of Almeria Harbour in 1937, only to be torpedoed and sunk with eleven lives lost in 1941.

Cymric Road - Named for the steel schooner that speared the tram at MacMahon Bridge and was lost on a voyage to Lisbon in 1944 with eleven lives.

Dermot O'Hurley Lane - Formerly known as Watery Lane and River view Avenue, this was renamed in 1954 in memory of the Archbishop of Cashel who was tortured and strangled on Gallows Hill in 1583.

Derrynane Gardens - Laid out as part of the 'Centenary Estate' project in 1929, 100 years after Catholic Emancipation, and named for Daniel O'Connell's ancestral home in Caherdaniel, Co Kerry. Also laid out in 1928-9 were Bath Avenue Gardens, O'Connell Gardens and the Malone Gardens.

Fitzwilliam Street - Named for Richard Fitzwilliam (1745-1816), the 7th and last Viscount Fitzwilliam.

George Reynolds House - Named for a local silversmith and Gaelic Leaguer who held Clanwilliam House during the battle of Mount Street and was killed shortly before the house went on fire. This was previously Alexandra Terrace, home to one of the famous Bartlett 'Tar Bay's'.

Isolda Road - Named for the Irish lights tender sunk within Irish territorial waters off Coningbeg by aerial bombing in 1940 with the loss of six lives. Another *Isolde* was launched in 1953.

Kerlogue Road - Named for the motor-driven coaster, owned by the Stafford family of Wexford, which rescued the crew of the *Bremen* after it was sunk in 1942.

Kyleclare Road - Named for the Dundee-built merchant ship owned by the Limerick Steamship Company and torpedoed by a U-boat, with 18 lives lost, on returning from a coal delivery to a power station in Lisbon.

Leukos Road - Named for the Dublin Steam Trawling Company's trawler torpedoed off the Donegal coast by a German U-boat in 1940 with a loss of eleven lives.

London Bridge - The name of a wooden bridge that crossed the unruly River Dodder, built in the first years of the 19th century as a link between the Beggars Bush Barracks and St Matthew's Church in Irishtown. The present three-span masonry arched bridge was installed in 1857. The river wall between London Bridge and New Bridge was considerably strengthened in 2007 and 2008.

Margaret Place - Built circa 1860, this was apparently renamed after Margaret Pearse (1857–1932), mother to the rebel leaders, Patrick and Willie Pearse. She served as a TD in Dáil Éireann in 1921 and is credited with co-founding Fianna Fáil.

Oliver Plunkett Avenue - Named for the Blessed Oliver Plunkett, Archbishop of Armagh, framed and executed for alleged complicity on a plot to kill the king. He was canonised a saint in 1975.

O'Rahilly House - The house on Thorncastle Street was named for Michael Joseph O'Rahilly, the tempestuous Kerryman who became the only leader of the Easter Rising to die in action.

Pine Road - Named for the *Irish Pine*, an American built ship on charter to Irish Shipping Ltd, torpedoed on an Atlantic run in 1942 with the loss of 33 men.

Pembroke Street - At the heart of Irishtown, named for the 11th Earl of Pembroke, who succeeded to 'the principal portion of the property of the 7th Viscount Fitzwilliam' upon the latters' death in 1816.

Philomena Terrace - Named for Saint Philomena, a young Greek princess said to have been martyred in the 4th century.

Rope Walk Place - Recalls the tarred hemp cables that were once stretched and twisted here to make ropes for rigging. There were many such 'rope walks' all over the docklands. Each one needed to be 100 yards long to wind a single rope.

Rosary Terrace - Named for the well-known prayer associated with Marian devotion.

Seán Moore Road - The main access road to the East Link Bridge is named for Seán Moore (1917 – 1986), the long-serving Fianna Fail TD and former Lord Mayor of Dublin. Born in Ringsend, he served as Government Chief Whip to Charles Haughey in 1979.

Seapoint Terrace - Once the location of Mr Murphy's 'Conniveing House' and ladies baths, attended by Wolfe Tone's wife in 1790.

Shamrock Avenue - Birthplace of the Shamrock Rovers Football Club.

Shelbourne Road - Laid out in 1832 and named for Henry Petty FitzMaurice, Earl of Shelbourne and later Marquess of Lansdowne. A kinsman of both the Pembrokes and Fitzwilliams, he served as Britain's Chancellor of the Exchequer and Home Secretary, advocating the abolition of slavery and the emancipation of Catholics.

Stella Gardens - This development of 183 small houses was opened in November 1916, designed by George O'Connor and named for Stella O'Neill, daughter of energetic Nationalist councillor Charles O'Neill, Chairman of the Pembroke Urban District Council.

Strasbourg Terrace - Built in 1871 and probably named by disgruntled Huguenots for the French city on the Rhine captured by Bismarck's Prussian army that year.

Sydney Place - Named for Sidney Herbert (1809–1861), 1st Baron Herbert of Lea, the half-Russian friend of Florence Nightingale who served as Secretary of War during the Crimean debacle. Sydney Parade, Herbert Place and Herbert Street are also named for him.

Thomas Street - Named for Thomas, 4th Viscount Fitzwilliam of Merrion, a Catholic outlawed in the 1690s for supporting King James II. His son Richard, 5th Viscount, conformed in 1710.

Thorncastle Street - Named for a castle on Merrion Road whose rampart was protected by thorn bushes. The castle came into the possession of the Fitzwilliams who held a vast estate running from Dundrum to Ringsend to O'Connell Bridge.

Veronica Terrace - Named for the kindly lady who wiped the face of Jesus while He was carrying his cross.

Whelan's House - Named in memory of Patrick Whelan (1893–1916), a local man and active Gaelic Leaguer killed by crossfire on the railway line by Boland's Mill during the Easter Rising.

York Road - Named for Prince Frederick, Duke of York, second son of George III and founder of the military college of Sandhurst. He is probably best known as the inspiration for the nursery rhyme, 'The Grand Old Duke of York'.

Right: The Poolbeg peninsula effectively runs from the confluence of the Dodder and Liffey rivers out to the Pigeonhouse chimneys, with the Great South Wall extending east into the Irish Sea. The twin towns of Ringsend and Irishtown occupy the near-ground while a series of parks, nature reserves, sports arenas and beaches evoke the possibilities of the great outdoors. (Photo: Peter Barrow)

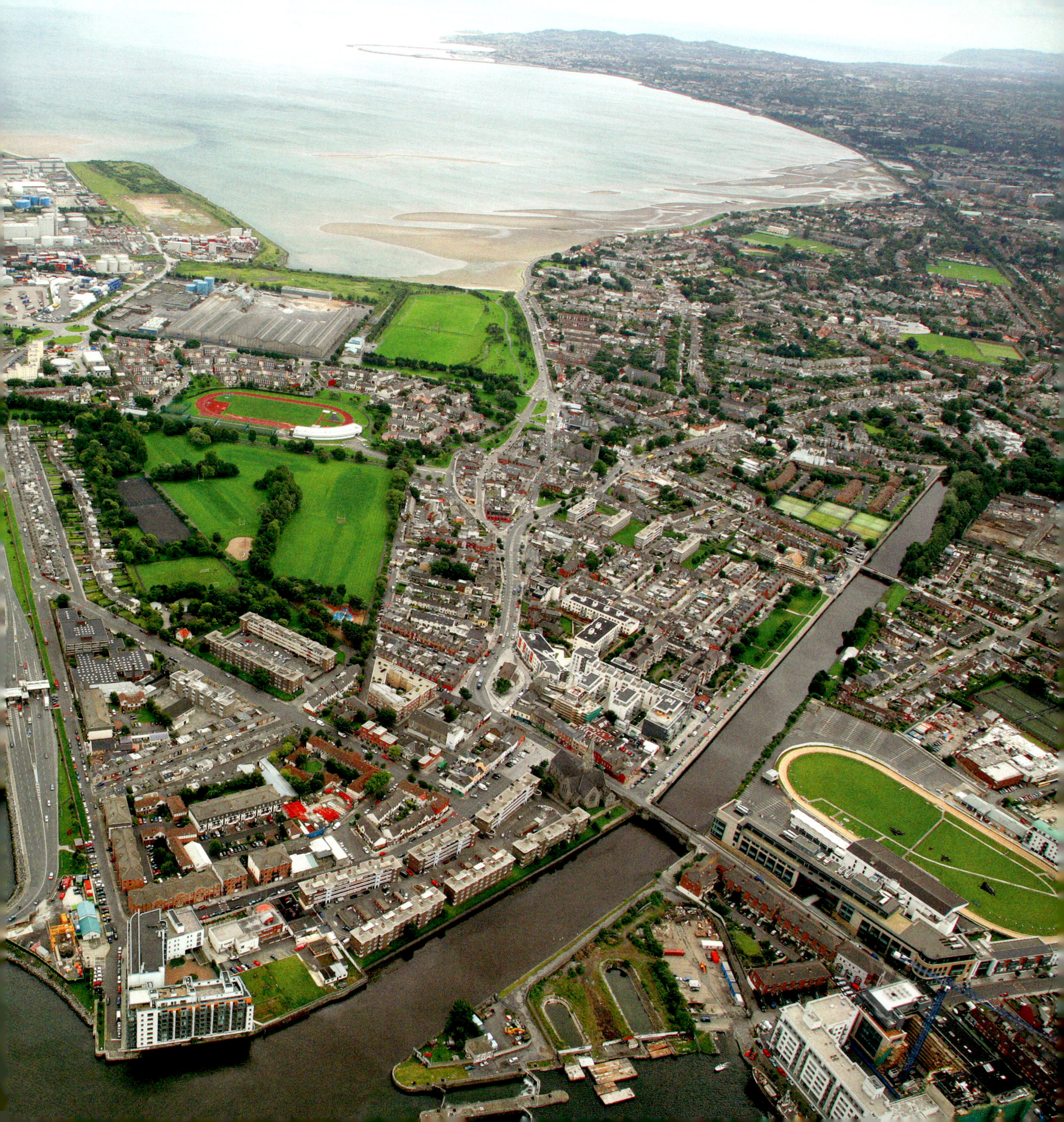

The South Lotts - Streetwise

The South Lotts originally referred to 51 plots of reclaimed land, located directly behind City Quay, which were sold to the highest bidder in 1723. In time, the term was applied to a considerably wider and less definable area. For the purpose of this section South Lotts concerns those lands bordered by Barrow Street, Ringsend Road, South Lotts Road and Grand Canal Street. Some jokingly refer to this as 'No Man's Land'. Others call it 'Googleland'. But for many who live there, this is simply South Lotts.

Barrow Street - The street was created using hard earth dug out from the nearby Grand Canal Docks and named for the river to which the Grand Canal was connected via the Barrow Navigation in 1790. The street's best known buildings include the headquarters of Google's European operations and The Factory where U2 put the polish on many of their albums. Grand Canal Station occupies the former site of the Dublin & Wicklow Railway Company yard.

Doris Street - This was probably part of the scheme built by Samuel Beckett's uncle James Beckett in the first decade of the 20th century. It may have been named for a celebrated gilder who lived here.

Gerald Street - Probably named for Samuel Beckett's uncle Dr Gerald Beckett (1884-1950), Wicklow County Medical Officer and sometime president of Greystones Golf Club. Gerald's brother James built the cottages.

Gordon Street - Named for Charles George Gordon (1833–1885), aka General Gordon of Khartoum. In 1860, he personally supervised the burning of the Chinese Emperor's summer palace in Peking for which he became known as 'Chinese Gordon'. In 1900, *Thom's Directory* noted that construction was underway for 28 small houses on the street. By 1902, another 28 were under construction.

Hastings Street - Named for the family of Francis Rawdon Hastings (1754-1826), 2nd Earl of Moira and, from 1817, Marquis of Hastings. This County Down man served with distinction against the American rebels in 1771 and went on to become commander of all the British forces in India. He sided with Wilbeforce against slavery and successfully annihilated several pirate nests on the coasts of Oman and Kuwait. In 1819, he purchased Singapore.

Howard Street - Probably named for Howard Beckett, son of William, brother of Gerald and James, and uncle of Samuel Beckett the playwright.

Ormeau Street - Recalls the names of Belfast's oldest municipal park and the name may be a nod to the Belfast residents who moved to the area.

Penrose Street - Possibly named by Ringsend glassworkers after George and William Penrose who founded the Penrose Glass House in Waterford in 1783. The company later became Waterford Crystal.

Ringsend Road - The No. 2 Dublin Bus garage was formerly the Ringsend Permanent Way Yard used to store all the tracks, poles and wiring required for maintenance of the tramway system. In 1929, the operation transferred to Donnybrook.

Somerset Street - Probably named for the 12th Duke of Somerset (1804–1886), a staunch opponent of Gladstone's Irish policies. His wife was a granddaughter of the playwright Richard Brinsley Sheridan.

South Dock Street - Named for the 'South Docks', otherwise known as the Grand Canal Docks.

South Lotts Road - Dates to at least 1721 when a road was built linking Britain Quay through South Dock Road to Artichoke Road (now Shelbourne Road and Grand Canal Street). The redbrick terraced houses along the northern end were built by Samuel Beckett's uncle James between about 1890 and 1910. The houses at the southern end date to 1930. This is also home to the Shelbourne Park Greyhound Stadium.

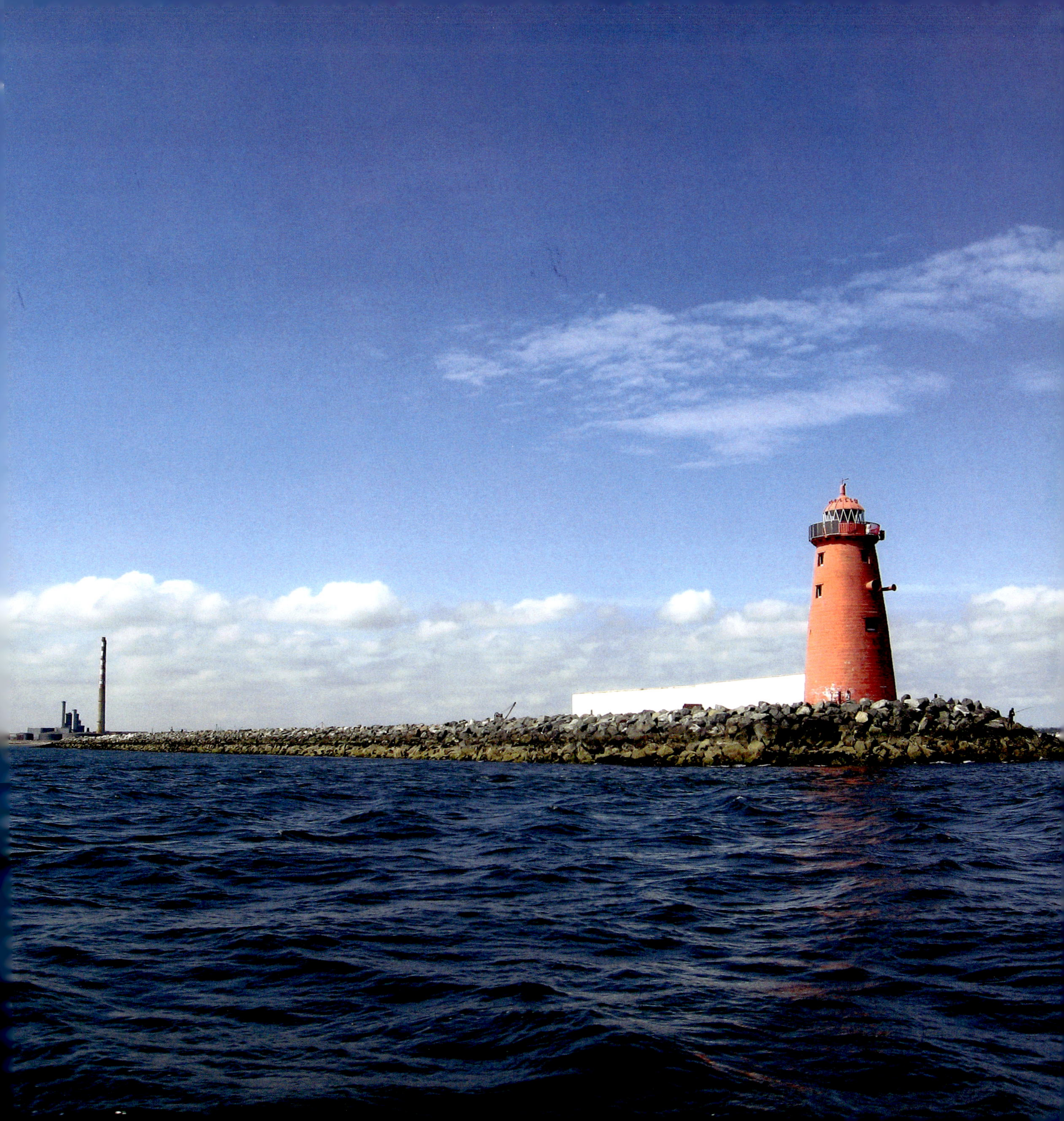

The Early Years

DERIVATION OF RINGSEND

In 1841, the British essayist Edward Mangin claimed the name Ringsend was simply 'an absurd corruption of Wring Sand, the proper name of the suburb'. When respected writers say things like that, you tend to believe them. However, Mangin was talking claptrap. In 1859, Richard Stephen Charnock quoted an old Dublin pilot called 'old Jemmy Walsh' who remembered seeing ships moored between Sir John Rogerson's Quay and Ringsend with 'their ropes run through the rings of the wooden piles on the river'. Where these rings came to an end, Charnock explained, is the place we now know as Ringsend. Alas, Charnock is also talking gobbledygook. The origin of the name is considerably more ancient than the rings of Sir John Rogerson's Quay. It is a simple corruption of the Irish expression *'Rinn-abhann'*, meaning ' the end point of the tide' or 'the end spit of the land'.

THE FIRST BUOY

Before the reclamation of Poolbeg and the South Lotts, Ringsend was an isolated dry spit that rolled out to the Irish Sea, frequently washed by the tidal waters of the Liffey and the marshy streams of the River Dodder. Humans have been fishing these shallow waters and tidal flats for over a thousand years. The spit was a well-known landmark for approaching ships in medieval times. In 1566, Dublin merchant Gerald Plunkett, guardian of *The Book of Kells*, placed a series of buoys, or perches, along the spit by Poolbeg, signalling the start of a new age for the harbour. Some years later, the Tudor elite built a fortified outpost on the Green Patch, a small parcel of land between the Salmon Pool and Poolbeg, which remains dry at high tide. Faced by the constant threat of an Armada invasion from Europe, they were determined to keep watch over any dispossessed Irish chieftains tempted to set sail for Spain or France in pursuit of military assistance. In those times, few heavy merchant ships would dare cross the treacherous Dublin Bar. Trade ships tended to dock in Dalkey Sound and send their cargo overland along the coastal road to Donnybrook. However, the Green Patch did serve as a useful staging post for some ships to unload goods onto lighters and rafts in the estuary. By 1600, though by no means perfect, Ringsend had superseded Dalkey as the main deep-water port for Dublin. A thriving fishing industry brought large numbers of merchants and coopers to the village known locally as 'Raytown' until recent times. In 1620, the customs and excise commissioners built a fort approximately where the Caroline Row entrance to Ringsend Park is today. Two years later, two entrepreneurs, Edward Gough and James Sedgraw, attempted to establish a herring station in Ringsend but came up against strong opposition from the influential King family of Clontarf.

THE FITZWILLIAMS

As an independent Liberty, Ringsend paid no taxes to the City of Dublin and enjoyed its own jurisdiction. During the late 16th century, the spit was granted to Sir Thomas Fitzwilliam of Merrion Castle, Vice-Treasurer of Ireland in 1559. In 1629, Charles I elevated Sir Thomas's grandson to the peerage as Baron Fitzwilliam of Thorncastle and Viscount Fitzwilliam of Merrion. At about this time, he began to lay the foundations for present day Thorncastle Street, Fitzwilliam Quay and Moryon (Merrion) Street. In 1666, Charles II granted the 2nd Viscount Fitzwilliam a vast estate in Dublin, including present-day Ringsend, Donnybrook, Baggotsrath, Merrion, Simonscourt and Dundrum. The Fitzwilliam family retained ownership of this estate until 1816 when, in the absence of any sons, the 7th Viscount bequeathed the property to his cousin, the 11th Earl of Pembroke. As a young man, the 7th Viscount had fallen in love with a local barmaid. His horrified father packed him off on Grand Tour and married the barmaid to another man. The desolate 7th Viscount vowed never to marry, thereby ensuring the complete extinction of his entire line and title.

CROMWELL IN RINGSEND

The 1640s were one of the most miserable decades Europe has ever known. If you weren't wiped out by a troop of marauding soldiers, you would probably succumb to famine or disease. Or maybe you'd simply be strung up on a tree for believing in the wrong version of God. If there were any trees left, that is. A civil war had raged across

Above: The Great South Wall was one of the greatest engineering feats of the 18th century. (Photo: John Wallace)
Previous Page: The Poolbeg lighthouse was built in 1768. It was reputedly the first lighthouse in the world to operate on candlepower. It was re-designed and re-built into its present form in 1820. (Photo: John Wallace)

Ireland since 1641 leaving untold thousands dead. In 1646, the English Parliament despatched its commissioners to Ringsend to negotiate a peace settlement with the Confederates. The failure of these talks ultimately prompted Oliver Cromwell to take action and bring the Irish Confederates to heel. On 15th August 1649, an armada of 35 ships sailed into Ringsend with Cromwell at their head. Henry Ireton landed two days later with a further 77 ships. The combined fleet carried 8,000 foot-soldiers and 4,000 cavalry, as well as a large train of artillery, battering rams, wagons and other vitals. In his memoirs, Ludlow recalled how the men-of-war and other ships moored in Ringsend rang a loud peal in celebration of their safe arrival. It is believed that Cromwell himself landed close to the Thorncastle Street - York Road junction. A nearby flight of steps leading down to the river, known as Cromwell's Steps, was buried beneath the new approach road to the East Link Toll Bridge. Upon disembarking, Cromwell met with senior civil and military officers in Ringsend. Here he received full details of their resounding victory over the Confederates at the battle of Rathmines twelve days earlier. However, the Ringsend garrison, commanded by Lieutenant-Colonel Philip Ferneley, were badly mauled by a detachment of Lord Ormonde's soldiers shortly before the battle. Cromwell despatched men to take Viscount Fitzwilliam's home at Baggotsrath and convert it into a garrison. A new bridge across the Dodder and a fortress for 70 men was also built at Ringsend. Less than four weeks after his arrival, Cromwell's army stormed Drogheda.

SLOBS AND FLEMINGS

Before the Pigeonhouse harbour was created, all the cross-channel packet ships from Holyhead landed at Ringsend. Indeed, it was one of the busiest ports on the east coast of Ireland. However, regular flooding made human settlement on the Ringsend spit virtually impossible. In 1670, for instance, a colossal flood swept in over Ringsend as far as Trinity College destroying many frail, timber-built houses in low-lying areas. The embanking of the Liffey and Dodder rivers between 1711 and 1725 had a profound effect on the landscape. Not only was the Liffey now navigable for bigger ships, and its quays more accessible, but a large amount of the surrounding sloblands was also made available for development. The reclamation had its origins in a Royal directive of 1672 when, anxious to prevent Dutch ships plundering English merchant ships in Dublin Bay, London dispatched Flemish engineer Sir Bernard de Gomme to survey the Dodder and Liffey rivers. De Gomme proposed an embankment on the bay's southside and a vast pentagonal fortress, to be built on a 30-acre site just south east of Merrion Square. The fortress was never built but work on the South Wall commenced in 1717.

SHOVELS AND KINGS

On Good Friday 1690, a curious naval battle took place just off the Ringsend coast. A Jacobite frigate was attempting to flee to France in the wake of James II's defeat at the Boyne. It was intercepted off Poolbeg Harbour by the *Monmouth*, a yacht commanded by the memorably named Sir Cloudesley Shovel. The two vessels fired upon each other but the *Monmouth* won the day, killing seven of the frigate's crew and obliging the rest to jump overboard. Perhaps the most important aspect of the engagement was that James II, the increasingly despairing monarch, was in Ringsend at the time and witnessed the whole damned thing.

IRISHTOWN

In 1660, Ringsend registered a population of 59 persons of English and 21 persons of Irish descent, while the adjoining village of Irishtown had 23 English and 75 Irish. This supports the theory of John Pentland Mahaffy, Provost of Trinity, that Irishtown came into existence when Oliver Cromwell's son and heir Henry Cromwell ordered all native Catholic Irishmen to withdraw from the metropolis of Dublin. However, Irishtown was also something of a suburb of Ringsend, built as the fishing community expanded into a populous village. Today, it is almost impossible to distinguish between the two, although Seapoint House is deemed to be a useful 'border' mark.

Right: The Pigeonhouse chimneys have been one of the most distinctive landmarks of Dublin since they were built in the 1970s. (Photo: Monika Hinz)

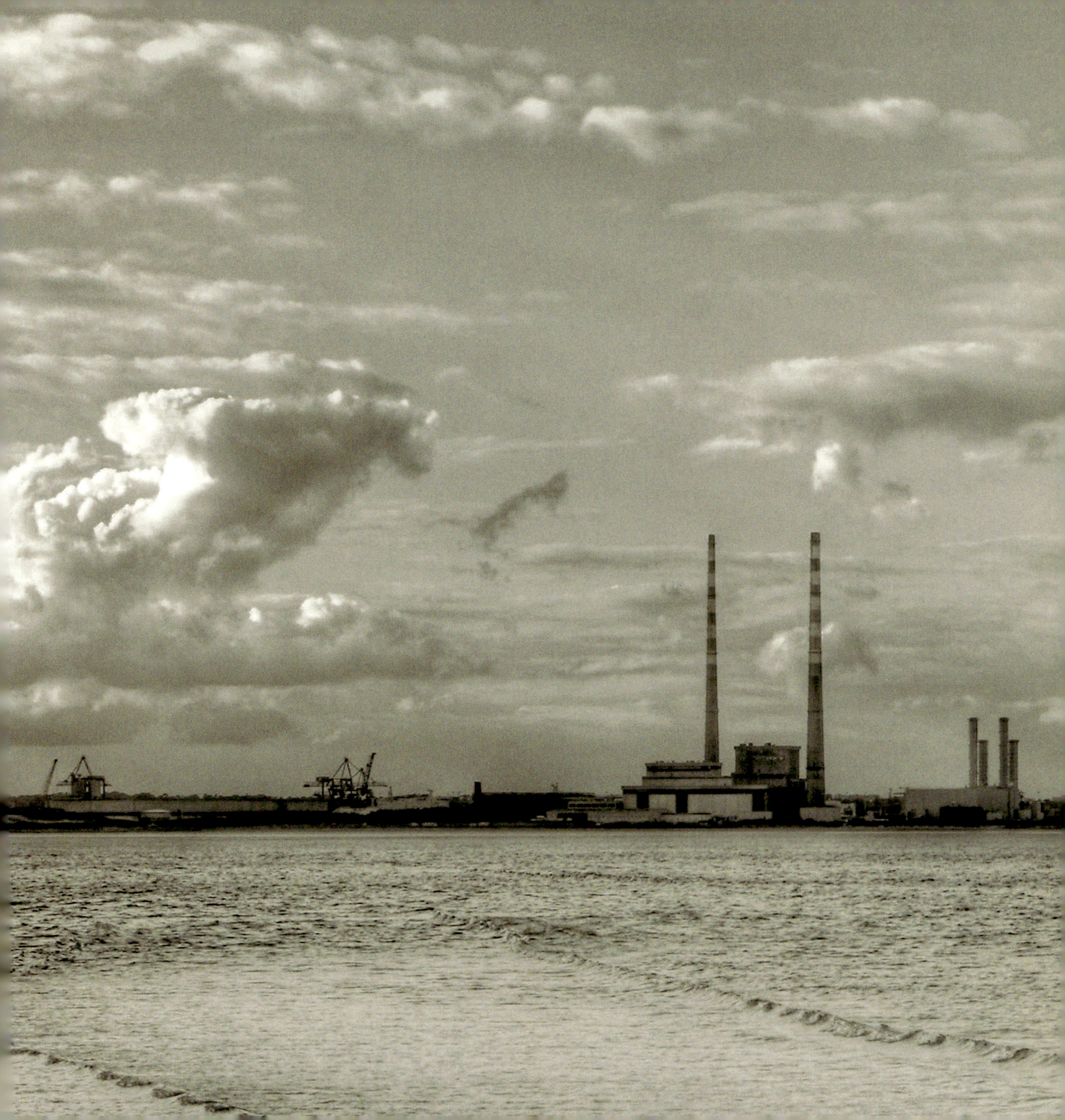

The Great South Wall

Sometimes humanity doesn't pat itself on the back and say well done. We're always achieving awesome things. In Victorian times, much extraordinary work was achieved by the sheer strength of hordes of men physically building something as monumental as the Great South Wall. Layer upon layer of thick granite rock, it was one of the most remarkable and best constructed breakwaters of its kind anywhere in the world. The South Wall extends from Ringsend for nearly three and a half miles into Dublin Bay and measures 32ft (9.7m) wide at the base, tapering to 28ft (8.5m) at the top. It was designed to shield the river channel from the massive breakers that swooshed in during stormy tides, clogging the riverbed with its shifting sands.

Work commenced on the wall in 1717. Lighters were employed to deepen the riverbed and the enclosing of the ground on the south side of the river began. By 1731 there were wooden piles all the way to the Green Patch where the Pigeonhouse was later built. Many ships were fatally hurled against these piles during 18th century storms. In the 1740s, engineers began rebuilding and extending the wall as far as Poolbeg, using wooden cases filled with rocks and gravel from Blackrock. The new wall not only provided vital channel protection but also allowed for a wide roadway to be built to the fishing village of Ringsend, and from there to the City.

In 1766, the Ballast Office built two new wharfs at either side of the South Wall where ships could berth and so the Pigeonhouse Harbour was born. The Poolbeg lighthouse was completed two years later. It originally stood alone out at sea but a wall was then built back inland from the lighthouse to connect with the existing causeway, a feat completed in 1796 under the direction of Viscount Ranelagh. In 1820, George Halpin redesigned the lighthouse as the present-day handsome red gem.

Today, the South Wall offers a much-treasured 40-minute stroll all the way to the Poolbeg Lighthouse. Catfish and seals, herons, terns, curlews, cormorants and Brent geese are all to be seen. So too are the tiny black guillemots who inhabit the cracks along the side of the wall and occasionally set sail, looking like bathtub ducks, with their jet black feathers, bright orange feet, red beaks and perfect white circles on their wings. The cold, clear waters that crash against the rocky ballast and sometimes sweep over the pier are the same waters in which members of the Half-Moon Swimming & Water Polo Club, founded 1898, are apt to practice freestyle swimming. Rusty ladders clamber up the licheny walls beside their white-washed clubhouse where canons stood in former times.

From the Half-Moon to the Lighthouse, the wall is of a markedly better quality, benefitting from a major restoration in 1982. From here, one can marvel at the gliders of Howth and Clontarf, the kite surfers of Dollymount Strand, the Bull Wall bobbing beneath the water. Aside from the heather-clad hills of Howth, the northern view is so flat you can sometimes hear the airplanes taking off from Dublin airport. Looking south one beholds a stunning panorama from the Dublin Mountains and the Sugar Loaf to the steeples of Dun Laoghaire, then north past the RTE mast in Donnybrook to the candy-striped chimneys of Poolbeg. On the eastern horizon, bulky frigates are spread between the billowing sails of yachtsman out for a leisurely summer evening race. In the distance, one hears the fog-horn of the approaching ferry from England.

THE ABDUCTION OF AN HEIR

In April 1728, James Annesley, the 13-year-old son of the late Lord Altham, was abducted at the Ormond market, thrown into a boat and taken to a ship in Ringsend and sailed out past the South Wall. From Ringsend, the heir to the house of Annesley was taken to North America where he was held as a slave for 13 years. This wicked deed took place in full view of the boy's uncle Richard who subsequently declared him dead and claimed the title of Lord Altham. A celebrated court case ensued when James finally escaped and returned to Ireland. However, he was unable to raise sufficient funds to prosecute his uncle and ultimately predeceased him.

Above: The Great South Wall was built to block the great waves of the Irish Sea from piling up the sandbar at the entrance to Dublin Bay. (Photo: Micahel Ryan)

Ringsend Cars

For a long time, the only way across Ringsend Bridge was in a horse-drawn rickshaw known as a 'Ringsend Car'. Before the reclamation of the South Lotts, the land between Lansdowne Road and City Quay was a large salt-marsh over which the 'mingled waters of the Dodder and the sea' swept twice a day. Ringsend Cars were specifically designed with wide-rimmed spoke wheels that enabled these carriages to cross the one-mile of wet sands that lay between the Bridge and Lazar's Hill (Townsend Street).

As well as being a practical vehicle, Ringsend Cars were highly treasured by 17th century boy-racers. On 15th May 1665, *The Intelligencer* reported on a race attended by the Duke of Ormonde.

'We have here upon the Strand several races, but the most remarkable are by the Ringsend coaches (which is an odd kind of carriage) … There were a matter of 25 of them, and His Excellency the Lord Deputy bestowed a piece of plate upon him that won the race; and the second, third and fourth were rewarded with money. It is a new institution and likely to become an annual custom, for the humour of it gives much satisfaction, there being at least five thousand spectators'.

Amongst those almost certainly in attendance at this race meeting was an entrepreneurial Huguenot nobleman, Rene De La Mezandiere. That same year, the Duke of Ormonde awarded him the monopoly on Dublin's hackney and sedan chair service. Part of his brief was bringing passengers and freight from Ringsend to the City. However, judging by one contemporary account of De La Mezandiere's coach, perhaps it is not surprising that the business had fizzled out by the 1670s.

'It was wheel-barrow in fashion, only it had two wheels not much bigger than a large Cheshire cheese. The horse that drew this princely pygmy chariot, I at first mistook for a over-grown mastiff, but viewing him narrowly, found him the extract (by his shape) of a Scotch hobby… I fancied myself to be some notorious malefactor drawn on a sledge to the place of execution'.

A more generous passenger was London bookseller John Dunton who journeyed to Dublin to promote his trade in the 1690s. He described the two-wheel Ringsend car as a 'perfect' vehicle, with 'a seat for three passengers raised crossways' to the back. Nonetheless, he noted that the seat was covered with 'a cushion of patchwork suggestive of a beggar's coat' while the journey across the sands jolted his sides so much that he was 'in purgatory' until they reached Lazar's Hill. Dunton estimated that there were more than 100 such cars 'plying for hire' at this time. One wonders how many of Dublin's present-day taxi drivers descend directly from the Ringsend charioteers.

Whatever travellers thought, the Ringsend Car was a survivor. In his 1753 epistle '*Mr Warburton*', the Drury Lane actor Theophilus Cibber referred to the driver of a Ringsend car 'as furiously driving through thick and thin, bedaubed, besplashed and besmeared'. At this time, they were known as 'noddy' cars for their habit of oscillating back and forth. The noddy was succeeded by the jingle and, later still, the jaunting car. Both of these were in use for some time after the Act of Union. Indeed, when all the nobility duly abandoned Dublin, the Duchess of Gordon complained there were now only two titled men who frequented her soirees at the Castle - Sir John Jingle and Sir John Jaunting Car. Remarkably, Ringsend Cars were still strutting their stuff in 1862, when the *Illustrated Dublin Journal* quoted Lady Morgan's reference to Dublin as 'the most car-drivingest city in the universe'. Ringsend Cars, the author continued, were 'the rudest specimens of these peculiarly Irish vehicles… consisting of a seat suspended on a strap of leather which supported the entire weight of the company between shafts and without springs'.

Above: Now a popular place for walking dogs, Irishtown Strand was a favoured haunt of the Ringsend Car drivers in the 17th and 18th centuries. (Photo: Karim Heredia)

Ringsend's Golden Age

By 1730, Ringsend was a village on the rise. It boasted a well-established, largely Protestant community, comprising 'officers of the Port and seafaring men'. The wealthier inhabitants drank in the King's Head Tavern, ate Poolbeg oysters in The Good Woman, and fresh cockles and shrimps in The Sign of Highlanders. They travelled the 3km journey to and from Dublin City by Ringsend Car. (See page 226). From 1703, the Protestants had their own church, St. Matthew's, built on the old shore of Irishtown Lough. The Catholics also had a small chapel that managed to survive the penal clampdown. The village was still cut off from Dublin by the wet sands and constant floods but any sense of isolation must have been tempered by the constant presence of merchants and travellers. For the entire 18th century, Pigeonhouse Harbour was the main packet station for the boats that came from England, laden with post, commercial missives, government directives and goods. As all such incoming traffic passed through Ringsend, the community prospered. The merchant's horse-carts carried a regular supply of useful produce - apples and cheese, copper and silk, lead and coal.

A lucrative indigenous industry commenced when an English undertaker established a salt works. Shortly afterwards, John and William Clarke founded an iron-works for the manufacture of steam-engines, machinery, iron boats and 'utensils of various kind'. Messrs Bunit and Simpson employed local women to pluck and sell the delicious Poolbeg oysters at the markets in Dublin. The strand at Irishtown was at one time noted for its cockles and shrimps, but after the severe winter of 1741, known as 'The Hard Frost', the shrimps completely disappeared. The herring fishery also employed a good number while many more were recruited to build ships and make ropes and sails. Some boat-builders, such as the Huguenot families of du Moulin and Beckett, later turned to house-building.

In the 1750s, Ringsend was hailed as one of the most beautiful, clean and healthy environs of Dublin, with vines trailing up the walls of its high-gabled houses, handsome orchards and well-stocked gardens that bloomed in the maritime air. During the summer months, it was a popular seaside resort. Gentlemen raced horses and cars along the charming strand. When tempers flew, they met for duels near Londonbridge. In 1727, a curious ballad was published entitled '*Warning to Concolds - A New Ballad on the Whipping-Club Held at Rings- End*'. Presumably some of its club members were the same well-to-do ladies and gentlemen who came to avail of the famous sea-baths at Seapoint Avenue. The Cranfield baths were said to have been the first hot sea-water baths in Ireland.

The turning point for Ringsend may have been the collapse of yet another 'Ringsend Bridge' in 1782, swept away during a rainstorm that 'continued for 14 hours with a violence that was truly alarming'. Ringsend, said one visitor, resembled a town that had 'experienced all the calamities of war [and] been sacked by an enemy'. A new bridge was begun in 1786 but destroyed by another bad storm the following year. A basic timber bridge was erected in 1789 and miraculously stayed up 14 years. The bridge was essential. The only alternative routes to Dublin were a hearty trek north to Ballsbridge on the Dalkey to Dublin highway or a wade across the marshlands. Between 1785 and 1796, Councillor Vavasour reclaimed the Dodder delta and laid a useful new road across these marshes, about where Bath Avenue runs today. The construction of the Custom House at this time was another positive, bringing the city business closer to Ringsend.

In 1802, the new British Parliament changed the tariff rates on glass in an early indication of what a terrible, terrible mistake it was for the Dublin Parliament to vote itself out of existence. As the Ringsend glass-works reeled, local confidence was not improved when the floods yet again swept away Ringsend Bridge. A new bridge was built in its place and named for Princess Charlotte, the baby daughter of George IV. That is the same arched granite bridge that we know today. It features an unusual strengthening feature whereby its ellipse curves unbroken through the abutments and under the channel of the river itself to form a complete elliptical ring. This ingenious concept ensures good hydraulic flow conditions under the bridge in times of flooding.

Above: St Patrick's Roman Catholic Church in Ringsend was designed by J.F. Fuller, District Architect for the Irish Ecclesiastical Commissioners from 1862-1870. (Photo: William Murphy)

The Tale Of The Pidgeons

As the sun slowly glided across the Dublin mountains in the autumn of 1786, Mary Pidgeon sauntered out of the kitchen carrying another platter of succulent Poolbeg oysters for the top-hatted gentlemen seated at the table. The sea was rougher than it had been for some days but otherwise it was business as usual for the Pidgeon family restaurant. Little did Mary know that there would soon be a murder most foul in this very house.

Today, the Pigeonhouse is the name by which the Poolbeg ESB plant is best known. Built in the 1970s, the two chimneys of the power station rise like giant barber-shop poles to dominate the Dublin skyline for miles around. Ask anyone why the Pigeonhouse is so-called and 9 out of 10 will understandably suggest a connection to our portly feathered friends. Such an answer would be wrong.

Situated approximately 1.5km east of Ringsend on the Poolbeg peninsula, the Pigeonhouse takes its name from an enterprising fellow called John Pidgeon who lived here in the 18th century. Quite where Mr Pidgeon came from is unclear but the surname may well derive from the French interpretation of LittleJohn, aka "Petit Johan".

In 1761, Mr Pidgeon was appointed caretaker for a new storehouse built by the Ballast Office. This lonesome structure stood on the northern edge of the windswept Poolbeg peninsula, overlooking the small and rather inefficient harbour where the mail-ships coming from England and Wales anchored. To the east was the Great South Wall, a mile and a half of solid granite built to protect Dublin Bay from the waves that rolled in from the stormy Irish Sea.

The storehouse to which Mr Pidgeon was assigned started life as a wooden storage depot for equipment used during the building of this phenomenal wall. In time, the Ballast Office converted it into a more homely structure, with eight rooms downstairs and a large loft above. Mr Pidgeon's duties included making sure the fire in the Poolbeg lighthouse was constantly lit, keeping an eye out for French or Spanish enemy ships, and providing a bed for those caught out in the bad weather.

To care-take such an isolated location would have driven a bachelor insane. Fortunately, Mr Pidgeon was a married man. Moreover, when Mr and Mrs Pidgeon moved to their new residence, they brought with them their feisty young son, Ned, and two beautiful daughters, Mary and Rachel.

Mr and Mrs Pidgeon were a resourceful couple. It occurred to them that the passengers who disembarked from the packet-ships were frequently greener than the lichen-stained South Wall. In rough weather, the journey across the sea from Holyhead could take up to three or four days. Mr Pidgeon wondered whether a drop of rum or brandy might not be appreciated by such exhausted voyagers?

It also occurred to the Pidgeons that the South Wall itself was generating a considerable volume of visitor traffic from well-to-do gentlemen interested in this pioneering maritime work. Sometimes these curious chaps arrived on horseback or in the rickety horse-drawn carriage that came from Dublin City. On calmer days, especially Sundays, they sailed their yachts in from Dun Laoghaire (then Kingstown) and Howth. Surely, said Mrs Pidgeon to Mr Pidgeon, such adventurous souls would appreciate a cup of tea and a bite to eat.

Before long, the Pidgeons had converted their coastal home into one of the most popular restaurants in Dublin, providing their customers with cockles, shrimps and oysters, pots of tea and the occasional tankard of stout, rum or whiskey. Mrs Pidgeon and her lovely daughters gamely served up the food and beverage, while Mr Pidgeon and Ned took their esteemed guests on guided tours of Dublin Bay Wall, transporting them in a small, brightly coloured rowing boat. The storehouse quickly became known as 'Pidgeon's House', subsequently corrupted to the Pigeonhouse, and its owner found himself 'on the fair road to fortune'.

This was the Dublin of Grattan's Parliament, a Golden Age for many in the city. People were coming from all across Europe to marvel at the construction of the new Georgian skyline, dominated by such impressive buildings as the Custom House and the Four Courts. Some wanted to see the college where Jonathan Swift, Oliver Goldsmith and Edmund Burke honed their literary skills. Others wanted to enjoy the theatre and music that played upon the streets where Handel's Messiah was first performed a generation earlier. But whatever their purpose for visiting Dublin, few of those who sailed in or out of Dublin would not have paused at the Pigeonhouse for a quick tipple.

However, life at the Pigeonhouse was not all crumpets and tea. Luckless emigrants headed for England were sometimes captured and press-ganged into service with the Royal Navy. The coaches coming from Dublin City were occasionally attacked and plundered by 'desperate banditti armed with swords and pistols'. Smugglers were often at large, awaiting darkness and fog so they might sail into Dublin Bay and unload their contraband without watchmen like John Pidgeon alerting the army. There was also a constant threat of invasion from France. Indeed, when the last of their guests departed and the cold, dark night settled upon the Poolbeg peninsula, the Pidgeon family must have felt more than a pang of isolation and fear.

It was on one such dark and foggy evening in 1786 that life for the Pidgeons took an abrupt turn for the worse. Four strangers arrived at the door claiming to be in distress. The Pidgeons gallantly let them in, only to find themselves under attack. Ned and the girls came galloping down from the loft to defend their parents. During the ensuing scuffle, Ned's hands were badly slashed by a sword. The raiders grabbed everything they could find, smashed a hole in the Pidgeons' boat and fled into the night.

When they heard the terrible news, the Pidgeon's regulars immediately organized a collection to buy them a new boat. However, the event had shaken the family very badly. Mr Pidgeon died soon afterwards, possibly from injuries received during the attack. All to soon he was followed Ned who never recovered from his wounds. Destitute and distraught, Mrs Pidgeon was also soon dead, leaving the two girls to fend for themselves.

There was, however, a happy ending of sorts. One evening Rachel and Mary, still living at the family home, sailed to the rescue of an Americans ship wrecked in a storm off the South Wall. As well as the captain, they saved a wealthy widower from Philadelphia and his three-year-old son. The Pidgeon girls provided the unfortunate trio with 'blankets, food and warmth', and looked after them until they were fully recovered. The American subsequently fell in love with Mary and proposed to her. The sisters duly emigrated to Philadelphia where Rachel also struck lucky and found a husband. Whether either sister had any children or not is presently unknown.

Below: The Pigeonhouse Fort was built in the 1790s as hotel to service passengers sailing to and from Holyhead on the packet ship that moored in the nearby dock.

The Pigeonhouse

THE PIGEONHOUSE HOTEL

In 1787, the year after John Pidgeon's death, the Ballast Office built a new building on the site. Its first residents were Francis Tunstall, the new Inspector of Works, and Patrick O'Brien, the new caretaker. Mr O'Brien and his wife continued the Pidgeon tradition of serving refreshments. In 1793, the Pigeonhouse Harbour was completed, with a new hotel, as well as the Half-Moon Battery, a three-gun platform, built along the South Wall to protect ships from privateers. According to a contemporary account, the hotel boasted 25 chimney pieces – 14 of black stone, nine of Kilkenny marble and two of mountain stone.

THE LONG COACH

Although never brilliant, the Pigeonhouse Harbour served as a Packet Station for the Holyhead ships and enabled passengers to disembark at the Pigeonhouse quays. From here guests were transported to and from Dublin City in a 'Long Coach', a half hour journey in a rickety carriage capable of 'holding 16 inside passengers and as many outside, with all their luggage'. A passenger on this Long Coach in 1810 likened his journey to an 'earthly purgatory' on board Noah's Ark, 'the clean and the unclean' together, everybody crammed together and smelling of seasick. It was, concluded the author, 'no bed of roses'.

Below: A sentry stands by the gate to the Pigeonhouse Barracks in 1881. Right: The Holyhead ferry sails in past the Poolbeg Lighthouse. (Photo: Michael Ryan).

PLUCKING THE PIGEONS

For those stomach-churned and exhausted passengers arriving at the Pigeonhouse, the Customs was not always a pleasant start. They became prey for what the initiated knew as 'Plucking the Pigeons'. In 1806, for instance, Sir Charles Hoare complained bitterly how, in addition to paying standard duty at the Customs depot, he was obliged to pay no less than 12 different officers at the Pigeonhouse before he could proceed on his journey. Hoare's remarks evidently caused a stir for, by 1810, Nathaniel Jefferys praised the Customs for 'giving as little trouble as possible to persons frequently fatigued by a tedious passage and seasickness'.

"On Friday morning 27 poor haymakers attending at the Pigeonhouse in order to be put on board ship for England, were seized by a press-gang and put on board a tender - the commander of the press-gang telling them at the same time that if they were able to mow hay, they could have no objection to mow the enemies of their country, and they should have passage, diet, &c., gratis."

The Dublin Chronicle, 3rd August, 1790

HOTEL BARRACKS

Following the 1798 Rebellion, the government requisitioned the hotel as a military stronghold. The 'Hotel Barracks', as Captain Bligh called them in 1800, remained an army base for nearly 100 years. The Pigeonhouse Fort was built partly as a repository for State papers, bullion, and other valuables in time of disturbance, and partly for the defence of the Port against attacks from either land or sea. Work was soon to commence on the 15 Martello Towers that would ring Dublin Bay.

EMMET & THE PIGEONHOUSE FORT

The Pigeonhouse barracks were one of the chosen targets for attack during Robert Emmet's ill-fated rebellion of 1803. Educated at Trinity

College, the 24-year-old Protestant revolutionary was determined to reinvigorate the spirit of rebellion that had been so miserably crushed in 1798. Amongst his friends was the timber merchant Thomas Brangan. Over the course of 1802, Brangan's horse-drawn carts conveyed two or three wagon-loads of pikes, hidden inside hollow beams of timber, to a secret depot in Irishtown. This presumably included a weapon of Emmet's invention - a folding pike, fitted with a hinge, which could be concealed under a cloak. On several occasions when the tide was out, Brangan and Emmet walked across the strand to plan an assault on the Pigeonhouse Fort. Indeed, the rebellion was supposed to begin at the Pigeonhouse. However, on 23rd July, another arms depot exploded prematurely. With the authorities alerted, Emmet gave the nod and the rising erupted on the streets around Dublin Castle. In Irishtown, Brangan and his men awaited the signal to attack – a rocket was to be fired into the sky. It never happened. Appalled by the murderous violence of his supporters, Emmet had called off the rising. Brangan went on the run, abandoning his wife and four children, and made his way to Portugal. He became a Captain in the 3rd Regiment of the Irish brigade, served gallantly in the Peninsula War and was killed in a duel in 1811.

ON THE DEFENSIVE

After Emmet's rising of 1803, an armoury and a guardhouse were built to command the road from Ringsend. 24-pounder guns were installed and trained upon the river mouth. The War Department also built soldiers quarters', stores, batteries, a magazine and tanks for fresh water. Two defensive gateways were constructed along the South Wall, protected by trenches cut into the paved surfaces and crossed by windlass-operated drawbridges. In 1814, the Government formally purchased the hotel and other buildings from the Ballast office.

A CLOSE CUT

In December 1821, the Marquis of Wellesley arrived at the Pigeonhouse Fort amidst heavy rains to take up the Viceregal office. His voyage had been delayed by three days. As he disembarked, he was informed that he had missed a procession of 'the broad-cloth weavers of the Liberty', who, accompanied by a golden fleece and a flag inscribed 'The Sons of Jason welcome the Marquis Wellesley', had gathered along the South Wall to pay him homage.

A DECAYING VILLAGE

Ringsend's greatest blow came in 1813 when the main packet-ship station was transferred from the Pigeonhouse to Howth (and later to Kingstown). The average duration of the passage from Pigeonhouse to Holyhead was 18 hours. From Howth it was only 12 hours; seven hours when steam packets were introduced. Pigeonhouse harbour continued as an occasional landing place, especially for the Liverpool packets. Although still technically available for guests, the Pigeonhouse Hotel was now an officer's quarters. When the Duke of Dorset passed away in 1815, some 200 'carriages of the Nobility and the Gentry' escorted his coffin to a waiting ship at the Pigeonhouse. The following year, Lord Blayney counselled his readers that Ringsend had become 'a vile, filthy and disgraceful looking village'. Things had not improved by 1836 when Samuel Lewis described it as 'mean and dilapidated ...

having fallen into decay since the discontinuance of its extensive salt-works'. The iron-works, glass-works and distillery were also struggling, although a chemical laboratory was still operational. Irishtown, says Lewis, was in a 'less ruinous condition'. In 1832, a new Protestant Male School was built by St Matthew's Church. There was also a new Almshouse for Widows, and a dispensary to fend off the onslaught of cholera. On 10th January 1839, a devastating hurricane ripped through Dublin, blowing down part of the steeple of Irishtown church which collapsed through its' roof. During the Great Famine, the community were able to sustain themselves through local fish and the importation of Indian corn by Sidney Herbert. Also here in these times were the 'Tar Bay's', fisher-folk from Brixham and Torbay in Devonshire, who settled in Ringsend at the suggestion of the Rev Henry Francis Lyte. The Trinity College educated hymn-writer was a frequent visitor to Ringsend in his youth. He is best known for the haunting words of 'Abide with Me', written just two weeks before his death in 1847.

PIRATES IN DUBLIN BAY

One dark evening in October 1829, Samuel Bartlet, one of the Ringsend 'Tar-bays', was out fishing in Dublin Bay when three large boats abruptly hove into view and came alongside him. Upwards of 40 pirates then swung onto the boat, knocked Bartlet down with a paddle and threatened to throw him overboard. Somehow Bartlet managed to escape but the 'ruffians' successfully plundered his vessel of all fish, before cutting up his nets, destroying his gear and hurling everything into the sea.

THE *TIMES* TRAGEDY

By 1850, the old Revenue Barracks at the Pigeonhouse had become the fort hospital. The location of some form of medical centre made sense given the high number of ships that seemed to collide in the foggy estuary. In June 1853, Dr Gilburn, the resident physician, and Colonel Savage of the Royal Artillery, were faced with a particularly horrific tragedy when a boiler on board the *Times* screw steamer exploded just as the vessel was passing the Fort. This instantly scalded many of those on board, humans and livestock, creating an utterly appalling scene. At least eight people were killed. The steamboat had been built just 18 months earlier for the Dublin & Liverpool Steam Packet Company.

ACTION STATIONS!

It is said the Pigeonhouse soldiers were never called upon to fire their guns in anger, save to intimidate the hundreds of thousands who gathered across the bay in Clontarf for Daniel O'Connell's Repeal of the Union monster meeting. For the most part, the Fort was simply a training barracks from which 21-gun salutes were fired for Royal births, weddings and deaths. When the Pigeonhouse batteries rang, they were generally answered by the firing of a rocket from the Phoenix Park barracks and a salute from any men-of-war anchored off Dun Laoghaoire (Kingstown). However, the Fort was placed on high alert during the Fenian troubles of 1866 and 1867. One commentator was Charles Dickens who alarmed the authorities with an eloquent description of just how easy it would be for rebels to conquer Dublin. What, he asked, would happen if half a dozen men simply surprised and gagged the sentry? The following year, Dickens returned to the Fort and declared that 'some military harlequin had come with his wand and touched the place', renewing the stockades and outposts, refurbishing the guns and drawbridge. In 1868, the Barrack Report registered a full complement of 13 officers, 242 non-commissioned officers and men (none married), six horse officers and six troop horses.

THE ARMY RETREAT

In the 1880s, there were still sentries guarding the Fort's portals, armed men tramping around its courtyards and salvoes of artillery resounding from the batteries. During the land agitation of December 1880, a storeship called *Staveley* arrived direct from the Royal Arsenal at Woolwich and unloaded 20,000 rounds of buck shot and a huge number of trenching tools, lanterns, candles and matches for the use of the army in Ireland. However, the soldiers garrisoned at Pigeonhouse were not summoned into battle that time either. The Fort gradually lapsed into disuse. In 1897, it was sold to Dublin Corporation for £65,000. The army retained, in perpetuity, a right of way through the precinct for their troops. The fort was never used for military purposes again although, during the Great War, it was identified as a landmark the German Navy might feasibly attempt to control.

Above: In the summer of 2008, over 2,500 shivering souls gathered on the South Wall to take up acclaimed American photographer Spencer Tunick's challenge to bare all for art. Passengers on the incoming ferry from Holyhead were greatly surprised by this early morning fáilte.

Captain William Bligh

CAPTAIN WILLIAM BLIGH

'Mutiny on the Bounty' is one of those epic films that gets remade every generation. It tells the tale of the stubborn Captain Bligh and his good friend and second-in-command, Fletcher Christian. During a long voyage through the South Seas, Bligh's increasingly tyrannical behaviour alienates him from the crew to such an extent that Christian is obliged to orchestrate a mutiny. Bligh and his cronies are cast aside but somehow make it all the way back to England in a rowing boat, where the Captain is promptly court-martialled for losing control of his ship. Throw in some beautiful Tahitian women and you're guaranteed box office gold. The earliest version was filmed in 1916. Clark Gable and Charles Laughton went head to head in 1935. Marlon Brandon and Trevor Howard did it in 1962. Mel Gibson and Anthony Hopkins did it in 1984. A brand new version is sure to be headed your way sometime soon.

One thing none of these films mention is that Captain Bligh played a key role in shaping Dublin Bay as we know it. Born in England in 1754, he cut his cloth sailing the South Seas on board the *Resolution* with Captain James Cook when he was 18-years-old. *The Bounty* incident took place in 1787. Captain Bligh was honourably acquitted at the court-martial three years later. In 1800, the Captain was sent to Dublin to survey and sound the bay and estuary. He deduced that most shipwrecks in Dublin Bay were caused because the ships carried too little cable and tackling to guarantee safe anchorage in stormy sea conditions. One of his solutions was to strengthen the South Wall from the Poolbeg Lighthouse to the Half Moon Battery. These improvements began shortly after Bligh's report was submitted. In 1803, he published an extremely accomplished map showing the bay in fine detail, along with his proposed improvements. The Bull Wall has also sometimes been erroneously attributed to him. Bligh's work in Dublin helped earn him the Fellowship of the Royal Society. In 1805, he was appointed Governor of New South Wales, Australia, where he faced another mutiny and was imprisoned by the mutineers for two years. He returned to England afterwards. In 1814, he was appointed a Rear Admiral and later Vice Admiral. He died in 1817 and was survived by six daughters.

The *Ouzel Galley*

THE *OUZEL GALLEY*

In the autumn 1700, Dublin society was greatly shocked to see an Irish merchant ship called the *Ouzel Galley* sail brazenly up the Liffey. Everyone had presumed the ship either 'lost at sea' or captured by Algerian pirates. She had sailed out of Ringsend five years earlier under the command of Captain Eoghan Massey. Her destination was the port of Smyrna in the Ottoman Empire. By 1698, there had been no word from the ship for three years. As such, the shipowners had already cashed in on the insurance policy and several of the crews' wives had remarried when the *Ouzel Galley* mysteriously reappeared with her full complement of crew and a valuable cargo of spices, exotic goods and piratical spoils.

Captain Massey explained that they had indeed been captured by Algerians while returning home. These brutes had obliged the Irishmen to participate in numerous piratical raids on merchant vessels plying the lucrative Mediterranean shipping lanes. The *Ouzel Galley* finally managed to escape while her captors were engaged in a drinking binge. And, as luck would have it, her hold was full of pirate booty when she took off. Many doubted the truth of the Captain's tale. The ownership of the *Ouzel*'s cargo certainly became a matter of dispute. As plunder, it could not be legally divided. A panel of eminent merchants was assembled to consider the case. They concluded that the ship's owners and insurers should be properly compensated. All monies remaining after this were to be set aside as a fund for the alleviation of poverty among Dublin's 'decayed merchants'.

Founded in 1705, the Ouzel Galley Society was designed as a permanent arbitration body to deal with similar shipping disputes. It became 'a magnet for men of ambition and ideas' and was regarded as a notably liberal and non-sectarian society. Many of its members were either Catholics or dissenters. In 1761, the Society became the 'Committee of Merchants' which, in 1783, became the Dublin Chamber of Commerce.

RINGSEND

(after reading Tolstoy)

Oliver St. John Gogarty

I will live in Ringsend
With a red-headed whore,
And the fan-light gone in
Where it lights the hall-door,
And listen each night
For her querulous shout,
As at last she streels in
And the pubs empty out.
To soothe that wild breast
With my old-fangled songs,
Till she feels it redressed
From inordinate wrongs,
Imagined, outrageous,
Preposterous wrongs,
Till peace at last comes,
Shall be all I will do,
Where the little lamp blooms
Like a rose in the stew;
And up the back garden
The sound comes to me
Of the lapsing, unsoilable,
Whispering sea.

Above: Captain Bligh, painted from life, by J. Russell. (Photo: National Maritime Museum, London). Left: *The Ouzel Galley*, forefather of the Dublin Chamber of Commerce.

The Pembroke Township

TRAMS AND RESEVOIRS

By the 1860s, there was a growing demand among Irish tenants to have a greater say in the administration of the areas in which they lived. In 1863, an Act of Parliament established the Pembroke Township, essentially comprising Baggotrath, Donnybrook, Sandymount, Ringsend and Irishtown. This was to be administered by an Urban District Council who would provide for 'lighting, paving, sewage, draining, cleansing, supply of water and otherwise improving and regulating the township'. One of these elected commissioners was the architect Edward Henry Carson, father of the Ulster Unionist leader. The Earl of Pembroke retained a paternalistic control over the township. In 1868, a reservoir was constructed in the Rathmines Township at Glennasmole which considerably tamed the Dodder. In the early 1870s, a horse-drawn tramline was laid through the area connecting Nelson's Pillar with the Martello Tower at Sandymount.

THE ORIGINS OF RINGSEND PARK

Cholera had long been a problem in Ireland but, in 1869, both Ringsend and Irishtown were badly hit by a typhoid epidemic. In 1873, Lord Pembroke offered a site on the South Wall for the building of a temporary hospital – or lazaretto - where cholera sufferers arriving in Ireland could be quarantined before they headed into the city. The military at the Pigeonhouse Fort strongly objected, despite – or perhaps because of - the fact they did not have their own freshwater supply and several soldiers had already perished of cholera. In 1879, when typhoid threatened the exclusive residential area of Raglan, Clyde and Elgin Roads, the Pembroke UDC decided to take action. Lord Pembroke reinvested much of the estate rental income in a major overhaul of the drainage, sanitary and water supply systems on the Pembroke estates. Between 1878 and 1881, the Rathmines and Pembroke townships completed a huge drainage project. Untreated sewage was then discharged through a station on Londonbridge Road down a 1.8m diametre pipeline and into the Liffey estuary at the penstock house just east of the Pigeonhouse. A stable sandbank was built over the open drain which, together with some reclaimed land, became a public park known as the Southern Intake. In 1897, the Corporation began developing a metropolitan sewage system for Dublin, which opened in 1906. For many decades, the residual effluent continued to be dumped east of the power station, while the sludge was taken out by boat and dumped in a line extending due east of the Baily lighthouse. In 1900, the Earl of Pembroke leased these lands to the Pembroke Urban District Council (UDC) who converted it into a recreation park. Before long, Ringsend Park, as the area is known today, had its own pitches for football, hockey and GAA, as well as lawn tennis, croquet, bowling and cricket.

The time that Julius Caesar tried to land down at Ringsend,
The coastguards couldn't stop them, so for the Dublins they did send
And, just as they were landing, lads, we heard three ringing cheers:
'Get back to Rome like blazes - here's the Dublin Fusiliers'.
The Dublin Fusiliers - Molly Maguire

FISHING LESSONS

In 1893 the Earl of Pembroke opened a technical and fishery school in Ringsend. He presented the site as a gift, along with a £4000 donation. This came at a time when steam trawlers were revolutionising the fishing industry and it was essential for the community to learn the latest techniques. When the Earl died two years later, his coffin was covered in wreaths from all over Ringsend – from boat-owners, fishermen, the teachers, the poor and the parish priest

NEW HOMES TO GO TO

Lord Pembroke also provided money for the development of the Pembroke Cottages, the first of a major series of housing developments for workers in the area. After the 1898 Local Government Act, the Unionist domination of the Pembroke UDC dissipated. One of its new nationalist leaders was Councillor Charles O'Neill who initiated a massive house-building campaign shortly before the outbreak of the First World War. By 1908, some 269 new artisan dwellings had been built in Pembroke, many of them in the South Lotts. Each house featured modern sanitary services. That same year, the village of Ringsend was divided along Ringsend Road with the south portion falling to the Pembroke UDC and the north to Dublin Corporation. A further 85 houses were built in the wake of the 1911 election when the Nationalists won control of the Pembroke UDC. The main architect was Edwin Bradbury while the builder was James Beckett, uncle of Samuel Beckett the playwright, who lived on the nearby Riverside. The leading businesses located here at this time included the Ringsend Dockyard, Alexander Hull's Building and Joinery Works and John Kellett's 'Shamrock Peat Company'.

THE LIFFEY TUNNEL

In 1925 the Liffey Tunnel was designed to carry water and electricity across the Liffey from Thorncastle Street to the North Wall. Built by McAlpine's, the 831ft(253m) long tunnel carries a 24" main as well as a 15" pressure sewer and power cables through the riverbed. Twenty-five of the 70 workers employed on the project suffered from the bends.

Up until the 1960s, Ringsend continued to be something of a suburban village. Many of the houses in South Lotts were built by Samuel Beckett's uncle in the early 20th century. (Photos: Dublin City Council).

The Ringsend Gasholder

SAMUEL CUTLER & SONS

In 1996 property developer Liam Carroll purchased the 7.8 acre gasworks site from Bord Gáis for just over €10 million. The subsequent development included Gordon House on Barrow Street (where Google are now head-quartered), 600 apartments and, most notably, the 'Ringsend Gasworks'. This landmark structure, or Gasholder, has dominated the South Lotts skyline since 1885 when installed for the Alliance & Dublin Consumers' Gas Company. The decorative wrought iron frame was made by the London firm of Samuel Cutler & Sons, based at the Providence Ironworks in Millwall on the Isle of Dogs. When completed, the Gasholder was one of the largest moving metal structures in the world.

THE CANARY EFFECT

Gas explodes when it comes into contact with oxygen. That made traditional gas-holders dangerous. However, the Cutler design ensured no air could get in. As the volume of gas went up and down, a sub-roof rose and fell within the structure, ensuring the holder never had space for anything except gas. Even if a little gas escaped, through a slipped tile perhaps, there was never enough air in the mix to make it explosive. As with the coalmines, a caged canary was kept in the void between the two roofs to monitor gas leakage. Canaries are particularly sensitive to toxic gases and if their whistle gave any sign of distress, that was a clear signal that conditions were unsafe and that the gasholder should be evacuated. An external lift ran up the outside of the structure, providing access to the roof. Many a cameraman has scaled these heights to capture a ferry coming in to the North Wall.

MODERN TIMES

Architects O'Mahony Pike oversaw the subsequent transformation of the Victorian gasholder into a nine-storey apartment block. This rather skilful evolution was carried out by Daninger and Fabrizia, subsidiaries of Zoe Developments. Now known as 'The Gasworks', the 210 apartments were built as a cylindrical block within the original wrought iron, while the exterior was fully restored and repainted. The block was clad with a structurally bonded glass façade system to achieve reflections of both the gasholder frame and the sky. The building may be converted into a 520-bedroom hotel, which would make it one of the largest hotels in Ireland.

In Irishtown there live's a girl
Fairer than the flower I'm wearing.
Rose Donohue all fresh and new,
And I love her past all caring
And there she goes, my Ringsend Rose,
In God's garden there's none rarer.
And there she goes, my Ringsend Rose,
Dublin Town has seen none Fairer.

Ringsend Rose, Pete St. John

Above: The original Victorian gasholder on South Lotts Road was converted into a cylindrical nine-storey apartment block by O'Mahony Pike. (Photo: Gerry O'Leary).

Ringsend Sport & Community

FOOTBALL TURF

Football has long been one of Ringsend's greatest passions. One of Ireland's earliest clubs was the Pembroke Club, founded by bottle blowers from Ringsend in the 1890s. They started work half an hour early at 5:30am in order to finish at lunchtime on Saturdays so they could play football in the afternoon. Today, locals play ball in the Seán Moore Park, South Dock Park and the ESB Sportsco. The area is the birthplace of two of Ireland's greatest clubs, Shelbourne FC and the Shamrock Rovers, as well as some celebrated 20th century players. In 2004, the Docklands Authority helped renovate the old stadium in Ringsend Park into 'Irishtown Stadium', complete with a floodlit 400m athletics track and five floodlit, all-weather, five-a-side football pitches.

SHELBOURNE FOOTBALL CLUB

Shelbourne FC was founded in a Ringsend pub in 1895 by seven men who tossed a coin beneath the Bath Avenue DART bridge to establish the club name. Heads for 'Shelbourne', tails for 'Bath'. Home games were initially played on a patch of wasteland (M'Lady's Field) near Lansdowne Road. The club quickly made its presence felt by reaching the Leinster Senior Cup final in 1896. Ten years later, Shelbourne beat Belfast Celtic 2-0 to become the first Dublin team to win the Irish League final. The *Evening Herald* reported on tar barrels and bonfires blazing across Ringsend and Sandymount that night as the Irish Cup was paraded around the district. The following year Shelbourne played Bohemians in a charity match that raised more than £100 for the building of a new Catholic Church in Ringsend.

SHAMROCK ROVERS FOOTBALL CLUB

Ireland's most successful football club was founded at 4 Irishtown Road in 1901. The second meeting took place around the corner on Shamrock Avenue and so the name was born. In 1905 the Ringsend men won their first piece of silverware when crowned County Dublin League winners. Shamrock Rovers, also known as 'the Hoops', have won more FAI Cups (24) and leagues (16) than any other Irish club.

VAL HARRIS (1884–1963)

Valentine 'Val' Harris was an Irish footballer who played Gaelic football for Dublin and soccer for, among others, Shelbourne, Everton and Ireland. A consummate Gaelic footballer, he won honours at club level with Ringsend GAA team Isles of the Sea and, in 1901, won an All-Ireland medal with Dublin. He successfully switched codes to soccer and, in 1906, he captained Shelbourne when they won the Irish Cup finals. He remains the clubs most capped player. In 1913 he captained the first Ireland team to beat England. In 1939 he coached Shelbourne to their first victory in the FAI Cup.

BOB FULLAM (1897–974)

Bob Fullam was a Ringsend docker who was so good with his feet that he became the 'Golden Boot' of his generation. He played for Shelbourne FC from 1918 to 1921, winning the Irish Cup in 1920, before transferring to Shamrock Rovers. His temper frequently got the better of him, such as during the inaugural Free State Cup final in 1922 when he was banned for the start of the following season. Despite this, he finished up top scorer of 1922 with 27 goals in 22 games. He twice played for the Irish Free State, scoring the country's first ever international goal against Italy at Lansdowne Road in 1926. 'Give it to Bob' duly became a Dublin catchphrase.

JIMMY DUNNE (1905–1949)

Legendary striker Jimmy Dunne was one of the first Irishman to figure prominently in the English League. During the 1930–31 season, the Ringsend man scored 41 league goals for Sheffield United, including a hat-trick of headers against Portsmouth. He was also a dual internationalist and played for both Ireland teams - the FAI XI and the IFA XI. Idolised by Irish fans, he played for Arsenal during the 1930s before finishing his career at Shamrock Rovers. In 1949, he died suddenly of a heart attack aged just 44. His son Tommy played for Shamrock Rovers while his nephew Christy Doyle played for the Republic of Ireland.

DERMOT J. GALLAGHER (BORN 1957)

The Ringsend-born referee was one of the best-known arbitrators in England's Premier League, officiating at 378 games between 1992 and his retirement in 2007. The last Premier League fixture that he refereed was a 2-2 draw between Liverpool and Charlton Athletic in May 2007. He was also a FIFA referee from 1994 to 2002. In 2008, Gallagher was the official referee for The Legends on ITV.

CLANNA GAEL FONTENOY GAA CLUB

The Fontenoys were founded in 1887 at 20 Bath Avenue. They took their name from the small Belgian town of Fontenoy where, in 1745, the Irish Brigade led the French army to a famous victory over the British and Dutch forces. The Gaelic Football team did not have such an auspicious start. In their first ever match, they scored the first point but didn't score again and were hammered by 1-15 to 0-1. The hurling team were in motion by 1901 when the 'Freeman's Journal' advised members to meet at their practice grounds at Londonbridge Road. The first game played at Ringsend Park took place on 14th May 1910. Today, the Ringsend men are the only GAA club inside Dublin 4, and also field intermediate football, hurling and camogie teams, as well as 22 juvenile teams. Their new flood-lit grounds at Seán Moore Park opened with a senior football challenge match between Dublin and Monaghan in March 2008.

RINGSEND HEROES

On November 29th 1927, Calvin Coolidge, President of the United States, presented gold medals to two Ringsend men serving on the British steamer *Olyeric*. J. Dullin of Pembroke Cottages and A. Weafer of Stella Gardens were singled out for 'their bravery on the high seas when rescuing two children, passengers and crew of the American schooner *Valkyria*' a year earlier.

THE COMMUNITY

In 1989 the old Hammond Lane foundry on Thorncastle Street was converted into the Ringsend and Irishtown Community Centre, now one of the chief focal points of the village, both for newcomers and for those whose families have lived here for many long generations. The Centre's provisions include crèche facilities, computer training, a daycare centre and lessons in karate, drama and dancing. Indeed, the Centre's Collide Dance Academy were the All-Ireland IDTA Hip-Hop and freestyle Champions of 2008, while the Under 16s won the Classical Ballet category at the National Dance Awards 2008. The Ringsend Community Training Centre focuses on helping the marginalised, disadvantaged and single parents to discover their potential and, wherever possible, to return to education and training and so find employment.

Above: Ringsend also has a strong tradition of rowing, with two clubs, St. Patrick's and Stella Maris, located here and the annual Ringsend Regatta. Dublin University Boat Club also traces its origins to Ringsend where it was founded as the Pembroke Club in 1836. Supported by the Docklands Authority, the Poolbeg Yacht & Boat Club have completed a state-of-the-art 100-berth marina (right) at the foot of the towering stacks of Poolbeg Power station. The club's busy calendar includes an 18-race sailing series in Dublin Bay every summer. (Photo: Cian Gallagher).

Park Life

IRISHTOWN NATURE PARK

Between 1948 and 1978, the southern half of the Pigeonhouse precinct was used as the Irishtown Tip Head. This created a sizeable artificial hillock which today forms the basis of Irishtown Nature Park. A new sewage treatment plant was installed within this park in 1985 and caters to most of the sewage from south Dublin. The park is now a surprisingly wild and rugged refuge for birds, wild flowers, insects and the occasional white-chested stoat, with many a Sunday walker looping around its heath.

SEÁN MOORE PARK

During the 1980s, Seán Moore Park was the only recreational public space available within the Dublin Docklands. Originally called Sandymount Beach Park, this extensive park was given to the people of Sandymount in 1980 by Dublin Port Company. It was to be held in fee simple, in perpetuity, in trust by Dublin City Council for the public. In 1987, the park was renamed after Ringsend born Fianna Fáil politician, Seán Moore (1917 – 1986). This reclaimed parkland is already a haven for flora and wildlife, with numerous species of birds foraging in the damp mosses. Large gatherings of Brent geese and the occasional peregrine have been spotted here in the evenings. A substantial bank was constructed along the eastern front as a defence against the wintry gales. Some of the park has been fenced off by the Clanna Gael Fontenoy GAA club for their new, flood-lit all-weather pitches.

DRAGONS & TRAVELLERS

The last moments of Leonard Abrahamson's acclaimed 2004 movie *'Adam and Paul'* were filmed against the backdrop of Irishtown Nature Park. Seán Moore Road provided the setting for Perry Ogden's award-winning 2005 film *'Pavee Lackeen: The Traveller Girl'*. The Poolbeg power station and the Pigeon House Hotel doubled as a futuristic London for the €70 million dragon flick, *'Reign of Fire'*. Directed by Rob Bowman and starring Matthew McConaughey and Christian Bale, this sci-fi turkey is presently the most expensive film ever shot in Ireland.

The Irish Glass Bottle Factory

In 2006, the 25-acre Irish Glass Bottle Company site on Seán Moore Road was purchased for €412 million by Becbay Ltd, a consortium consisting of private developers and the Docklands Authority. The Docklands Authority are currently preparing a draft planning scheme for 100 acres of the Poolbeg peninsula, including the IGBC site. In preparation, an urban design framework has been prepared by West 8 Urban Planners in collaboration with a large multi-disciplinary team headed by Urban Initiatives. This follows an earlier framework plan for the area by acclaimed urban planners DEGW for Dublin City Council. The concept is to deliver a sustainable mixed-use development, including social and affordable housing. There is also to be a major emphasis on nature and landscape, maintaining and extending the existing parklands and beaches, and developing cutting edge amenities. Becbay Ltd are carrying out remediation work on the site, including decommissioning of plant, demolition of buildings and the removal of approximately two metres of underlying soil material. These works are expected to be complete by December 2009.

The Irish Glass Bottle Factory site lies next to the 12-acre (4.9 ha) South Wharf site owned by Liam Carroll's Fabrizia Developments. This formerly belonged to the late Henry Herbert, 17th Earl of Pembroke (1939 – 2003), an unconventional aristocrat who made his name directing 'Emily', an erotic movie with Koo Stark, as well as two rock documentaries about Otis Redding and Jimi Hendrix, and a number of episodes of 'Bergerac' in the early 1980s. In 1969, the 17th Earl inherited the Pembroke estates from his father. He sold the Poolbeg Peninsula, comprising all the land between Ringsend Park and the lighthouse, to the Dublin Port and Docks Board for £300,000. In 1972 the Board sold 12 acres of this land to the IDA for £600,000. Eight years later, those same 12 acres were sold at a loss of £50,000 to Allied Irish Bank who planned building a Sports and Social Club on them. In 1988, AIB abandoned the club concept and sold the site for a cool £24 million.

Left: The beach alongside Irishtown Nature Park. Below: An aerial photograph of the Poolbeg Peninsula indicates plenty of green space along the southern shore.

Poolbeg Power Station

THE POWER HOUSE

The Pigeon House Road today runs east of Ringsend Park and Seán Moore Park through a strangely romantic industrial belt. Much of this peninsula has only been reclaimed in the past forty years. The topography looks not unlike the inside of a wireless with the occasional pink wallflower, yellow dandelion or burst of white bindweed to represent nature. Giant cylinders, electricity depots and brash fences rise up from the earth. Baby blue NTL cranes heave giant Maersk Sealand and Triton containers onto rusty freight ships that rub alongside merchant ships, yachts and schooners. ESB and Bord Gáis workers alight from misty morning buses and walk to work in Poolbeg. The industrial origins stretch back to 1899 when Dublin Corporation secured the Pigeonhouse Fort from the army and began work on a new building for 'extending and improving the electrical lighting of the city'. The scheme was designed to supply '100,000 lamps of eight-candle power' while 412 new arc lights were to be installed on the streets. In 1903, the Corporation transferred its electricity generating operation from Fleet Street to the Pigeonhouse. Over the next ten years, demand grew from 763kW to 5,150kW. In 1927, the Electricity Supply Board was established and the Corporation ceased generating electricity. During the Emergency years 1939 – 1945, Pigeonhouse and the Ardnacrusha hydro-electric power station on the Shannon attempted to supply the whole country. However, the quality of the coal arriving at Pigeonhouse wharf was apparently so poor that grass could be seen growing upon the nuggets. In 1949, the ESB built a new oil-fired generating station on the North Wall. Pigeonhouse Station was nonetheless developed to reach an installed capacity of 95,000kW in 1952. In 1955, the ESB built another new station in Ringsend, powered by either coal or oil.

NO TOAST FOR ME

An early symbol of troubles ahead came in September 1906 when the Improvements Committee of Dublin Corporation brought a large number of guests on a short cruise down the Liffey on board the Corporation steamer *Shamrock* to view the new drainage works at the Pigeonhouse. Among those on board were a number of Sinn Feiners, headed up by Alderman Thomas Kelly. On boarding the steamer at Custom House Quay, Kelly went to the stern where the traditional red flag of the merchants' ship was flying, with the Union Jack quartered upon it. Using a large clasp knife, he cut the strings and threw the flag into the river. The incident created 'a very painful sensation' while Mr Kelly explained that he had cut down the flag because it was an insult to his nationality. Alderman Kelly was still present for the lunch, along with the Lord Mayor, the Attorney General and the Lord Lieutenant's Under Secretary. When a toast was raised to 'The King', Kelly and his friends shouted 'We won't drink to it' and stormed out. A stunned *Times* correspondent wrote of the incident under the heading 'Disloyalty in Dublin'.

POOLBEG GENERATING STATION

In the 1960s a new red-brick power station was built in the lands of Pigeonhouse precinct. Officially called Poolbeg Generating Station, it is today widely known as the Pigeon House. It is also one of the icons of the Dublin skyline on account of its thermal station chimneys, rising like barber shop poles from the water. These are among the tallest structures in Ireland and are visible from most of Dublin city. Number 1 chimney is 207.48m (680ft 9in) high. Number 2 chimney is 207.8m (681ft 9in) high. Fuelled by either oil or natural gas, the first two 120MW units of the Poolbeg plant officially opened 1971. These units both have turbo-alternators manufactured by Brown Boveri and 'drum type' boilers by Fives Penhoet, France. A third 271MW unit was added in 1978, with a turbo-alternator manufactured by Alsthom, France, and a 'once through' type Boiler by MAN Germany. The Pigeonhouse itself was decommissioned in 1976. Today magpies, kestrels, sparrow-hawks and racing pigeons swoop from the roof of the old hotel and through the grimy windowless power station.

THE NEW QUAYS

During the late 20th century, the Port and Docks Board built a further three new Liffey-side quays in the precinct west of Poolbeg station. South Bank Quay was designed to handle container traffic and for roll on / roll off traffic. Coal Quay was for the importation of coal. At the western boundary of the precinct, the Ringsend Station of 1955 has a coal conveyor gantry that spans across Pigeonhouse Road. The Poolbeg station's oil storage tank extends the original Green Patch eastwards to meet the remnant of the Shelly Banks strand that still separates it from the White Bank.

Right: The Irish Sea laps onto Sandymount Strand with the Pigeonhouse chimneys in the distance. (Photo: Monika Hinz). Below: Irishtown Strand is a popular stretch for dog walkers. (Photo: Michael Ryan). Far Below: Dublin Corporation's generation station was built alongside the Pigeonhouse Fort in the 1890s. (Photo: Fantasy Jack)

Dublin Docklands Development Authority

BOARD MEMBERS:

Mr. Dónall Curtin
Mr. Brendan Malone
Ms. Catherine Mullarkey
Mr. Niall Coveney
Mr. Mark Griffin
Ms. Sheila O'Donnell
Ms. Niamh O'Sullivan

COUNCIL MEMBERS:

Mr. Liam Whelan
Mr. John Boylan
Mr. Enda P. Connellan
Cllr. Tom Stafford
Cllr. Emer Costello
Ms. Margaret Sweeney
Mr. Charlie Murphy
Ms. Geraldine O'Driscoll
Mr. John Tierney
Mr. Niall Grogan
Mr. John Henry
Cllr. Aodhán Ó Ríordáin
Cllr. Kevin Humphreys
Cllr. Daithi Doolan
Mr. Willie Dwyer
Ms. Dolores Wilson
Ms. Denise Brophy
Ms. Betty Ashe
Mr. Seánie Lambe
Mr. Malcolm Alexander
Ms. Oilbhe Madden
Ms. Fionnuala Rogerson
Ms. Deirdre Scully
Mr. Colm Treanor
Mr. Gerry Fay

COMMUNITY LIAISON COMMITTEE:

Mr Dónall Curtin, Chairman
Ms. Betty Ashe
Mr. Willie Dwyer
Mr. Gerry Fay
Mr. Seánie Lamb
Ms. Oilbhe Madden
Mr. Charlie Murphy
Ms. Geraldine O'Driscoll
Ms. Dolores Wilson

PAST CHAIRMEN:

Mr. Donal O'Connor (2007-2009)
Mr. Lar Bradshaw (1997–2007)
Ms. Dervilla Donnelly (1992 – 1997, CHDDA)
Mr. Seamus Páirceir (1990 – 1991, CHDDA)
Mr. Frank L. Benson (1986 – 1990, CHDDA)

Paul Maloney
Chief Executive of the Docklands Authority since 2005.

Peter Coyne
Chief Executive of the Docklands Authority (1997-2005).

Lar Bradshaw
Chairman of the Docklands Authority (1997–2007).

Acknowledgments

An enormous amount of people showed great kindness and support for this project. It is clearly a subject that people feel passionate about, not least my beautiful wife Ally who has frequently had her dreams interrupted as I holler loudly in my sleep about the lousy fate of the poor Pidgeons and the price of coal. I would particularly like to thank the team at Montague Publications for all their help and good cheer, particularly that rock of calm, collected visual brilliance, Michael Swoboda. Carmel Smith and Loretta Lambkin have shown immense patience, humour and attention to detail in the creation of these pages since the outset. Nick Coveney and Jane Williams provided me with a most useful retreat on more occasions than I can possibly remember. For taking the time to colour in the background, I take my hat off to Betty Ashe, Owen Binchy (Nascadh), Lar Bradshaw, Gerry Browne, Peter Coyne, Niall Dardis (Dublin Port), Betty Dempsey, Terry Fagan, Sonny Kinsella, Seánie Lamb (Inner City Renewal Group), Gus MacAmhlaigh, Paul Maloney, Joe Mooney, Bart Nolan, Paul O'Brien (paulobrien.eu) and Bill Taylor. Colleen McFadden and Grainne Clarke tackled the proof-reading with admirable tolerance and zest. Any subsequent faults are mine, not theirs.

Thanks also to: Agnes Alvite, Daphne Barrow, David Bedlow, Alice Boyle, Kevin Bright, Tony Brennan, Mary Buckley (Norma Smurfit Library), Andrew Bunbury, Claire Byrne, John Callanan, Garrett Casey, Liz Casey (Bord Gáis), Catherine Cavendish, Dr. Mary Clark (Dublin City Archives), Howard Clarke, Art Cockerill, Michael Corcoran, Ron Cox, Harry Crosbie, Jessika Creedon, Aileen Cummins, Gemma Curry, Brenda Daly, Brendan Delany, Gillian Davidson, Dermot Desmond, Brendan Dinneen. Brian Donovan, Siobhan Duran, Dermod Dwyer, Willie Dwyer, Eneclann Ltd, Sam Field Corbett, Allen Foster, Michael Fox, Kieran Frost, Maureen Fryer-Kelsey (Mills and Millers of Ireland), Charles Funke, Cian Gallagher, Peter Goble, Joan Gordon, Fred Hammond, Brian Hand, Mette Boye Hansen, Jim Hargis, Laura Harty, John Heueston (IFHS), Andrew Hewat, Tom Hulton, Paul Hutchin (map master), Roisin Ingle, Hugo Jellett, Arthur Johnson, Art Kavanagh, Michael Kavanagh (MVK Architects), Mary Kelleher, Gerry Kelly, Jed Kelly, Rosa Kende, Liam Kenny, Patrick King, Clodagh Kingston, Erin Leitzes, Pat Liddy, Marcel Lindsay, Rosalyn Long (Live Nation), Camille Lynch, Criostoir MacCarthaigh, Séamas Mac Philib, Michael Purcell, Fiachra McCarthy, Jennifer McCormack, Paul McGowan, Tim Magennis, Ronan Maguire, John Maher, Siobhan Marlow, John Martin, Paul McCann, Mary McMahon, Andrew Moore, Helen Mumby, Charlie Murphy (Irish Nautical Trust), John Murphy, Colm Murray (Heritage Council), Isabella Rose Nolan, John Nolan (Walls), Annette Nugent, Mícheál Ó Cionna (Liffey Ferry), Roland O'Connell, Carol O'Connor (An Taisce), Des O Murchu, John Onions, Aodhan O Riordain, Peter Pearson, Michael Pike, William Paterson, Derek Patterson, Dave Pennington (LNWR Society), Jason Popplewell, Roger Quarm, Ruairi Quinn, TD, Charlie Raben, Stan Ridgeway, Eibhlin Roche, Erica Roseingrave (Bus Éireann), Angel Sanchez, Jessica Slingsby, Francis Taylor, Simon Thornton (Chadwick's), Cait Tutty, Margaret Ward, Susan Walsh, Bill Webster, Derek Whelan (IWAI), Karim White, Trevor White and Dolores Wilson.

PHOTOGRAPHS

For contemporary photographs I take a heartfelt bow to the following: Arco Ardon, Peter Barrow (aerial photos), Stu Carroll, Ronan Conroy, Nathalie Márquez Courtney, Maurice Frazer, James Fennell (jamesfennell.com), Cathal Furey (RedAgenda.com), Charles Howarth, Derek Head, Karim Heredia, Monika Hinz, Kami Kami, Richard Kelly, Baz Keogh (bazkeoghshow@hotmail.com), Eugene Langan, Brian Lawlor (cover image), William Lawlor, Michael Moran, Colm Mullen (info@colmmullen.ie), Donal Murphy, William Murphy (streetsofdublin.com), Henriette Gran Myreng, Gerry O'Leary, Luca Rocchini, (lucarocchini.com) Michael Ryan, Damian Scott, Carlos Jiménez Soriano, John Wallace (johnwallacephotography.com) and the Dublin Camera Club.

Other photographs came from private collections or were generously sent in by interested parties such as Paddy Curtis, Aiden McCabe, Charles Friel, Fantasy Jack Palance, Ray Peacock, Anne Ingle, Dublin Chamber of Commerce, Dublin City Public Libraries, Dublin City Council, Dublin Port, the Industrial Heritage Association of Ireland (steam-museum.com), the Institution of Civil Engineers, the John Osman Collection (www.photographs.ie), the National Archives, the Guinness Archive Collection, the National College of Ireland, the National Gallery of Ireland and the Railway Preservation Society of Ireland (steamtrainsireland.com),

Bibliography

While it would be remiss of me to leave out the word 'Google', or indeed the fantastic archival resources of *The Irish Times* and *The Times*, the following manuscripts have been invaluable.

MAIN SOURCES

Adams, R: Protest by Pupils, (Falmer Press, 1991)

Ball, F.E. A history of the county of Dublin (Dublin, 1902)

Beresford Ellis Peter: A History of the Irish Working Class (Pluto Press, 1996)

Blacker, Rev. Beaver H: Sketches of the Parishes of Booterstown and Donnybrook (1860)

Blake, Raymond: In Black and White: A History of Rowing at Trinity College Dublin (Dublin University Press, 1991)

Blayney, Andrew Thomas, Baron, 1770–1834. Sequel to a Narrative of a Forced Journey through Spain and France, as a Prisoner of War in 1810 to 3; Including Observations on the Present State of Ireland, &c. (London, 1816).

Byrne, Kevin: East Walls Schoolboy Strike 1911 (East Wall Festival Brochure, 1975).

Casey, Christine: 'Dublin: The City Within the Grand and Royal Canals and the Circular Road' (Architecture, 2005).

Casey, Christine: The Buildings of Ireland: Dublin (Yale University Press, 2005)

Charnock, Richard Stephen: Local Etymology: A Derivative Dictionary of Geographical Names. (Houlston and Wright, 1859)

Clerkin, Pau: Dublin Street Names (Gill & Macmillan, 2001)

Cox, Ronald C: Bindon Blood Stoney – Biography of a Port Engineer (Institution of Engineers of Ireland, 1990).

Cox, Ronald C. & Gould, M.H.: Civil Engineering Heritage: Ireland (Thomas Telford Publishing, London, 1998).

Cox, Ronald C: "John Purser Griffith 1848 - 1938: Grand Old Man of Irish Engineering' - paper presented on 5th October 1988 to a joint meeting of the Civil Division and the Heritage Society of the Institution of Engineers of Ireland.

Corcoran, Michael: Our Good Health - A history of Dublin's water and drainage (Four Court Press, 2005)

Cosgrave, Rev. Dillon: 'North Dublin' (1909)

O'Carroll, Derval, & Fitzpatrick, Seán: 'Hoggers, Lords and Railwaymen - A History of the Custom House Docks, Dublin' (Custom House Docks Heritage Project, 1996)

D'Alton, J.D: 'The History of Drogheda: With Its Environs, and an Introductory Memoir of the Dublin and Drogheda Railway' (J. D'Alton, 1844).

Dawe, Gerald, & Mulreany Michael: The Ogham Stone: An Anthology of Contemporary Ireland (Institute of Public Administration, 2001)

De Courcy, J.W: The Liffey in Dublin (Gill & Macmillan, 1996)

Duncan, Mark, with Eoin Kinsella and Paul Rouse, National College of Ireland _ Past, Present, Future (The Liffey Press, 2007).

Dunton, John: The Dublin Scuffle (1699) with an introduction by Andrew Carpenter (Four Courts Press, 2000).

Fagan, Terry (ed), The Forgotten Women (North Inner City Folklore Project 2008).

Farmar, Tony: Heitons – A Managed Transition (A & A Farmar, 1996)

Ferguson, Paul (ed.): The A to Z of Georgian Dublin: John Roque's Maps of the City in 1756 and the County in 1760 (Harry Margary, 1998).

Fraser, Murray: John Bull's Other Homes: State Housing and British Policy in Ireland, 1883-1922 (Liverpool University Press, 1996)

Garnham, Neal: Association football and society in pre-partition Ireland. (Belfast: Ulster Historical Foundation, 2004).

Gately, Alan: Tearaways (Vanguard Press, 2006).

Gilbert, Sir John T: A History of the City of Dublin (Dublin, 1885).

Gilligan, H.A: 'A History of the Port of Dublin' (Gill & Macmillan, 1988)

Glin, Knight of, with James Peill, James Fennell, Dara McGrath: Irish Furniture: Woodwork and Carving in Ireland from the Earliest Times to the Act of Union (Yale University Press, 2007)

Grigg, R.: The origins and significance of the school strikes in south Wales, 1911, The Local Historian, vol.33 no.3 (August 2003).

Head, Richard: The English Rogue, Described in the Life of Meriton Latroon, a Witty Extravagant; Being a Compleat History of the Most Eminent Cheats of Both Sexes (Mead & Co, New York, 1928)

Hoare, Sir Charles: Tour in Ireland, Monday, 23rd June, 1806 (W.Miller, 1807)

Hudson, Thomas N: 'Admiral William Brown - Master of the River Plate' (Libris, 2004)

Hylton, Raymond: Ireland's Huguenots and Their Refuge, 1662-1745: An Unlikely Haven (Sussex Academic Press, 2005).

Jefferys, Nathaniel: An Englishman's Descriptive Account of Dublin (Cadell and Davies, 1810).

Johnson, Norman: The Great Northern Railway (Ireland) In Colour (Colourpoint Books, 2005).

Judges, A.V: Key Writings on Subcultures, 1535-1727: Classics from the Underworld (Routledge, 2002)

Kilfeather, Siobhán Marie, with Terry Eagleton, Dublin: A Cultural History (Oxford University Press US, 2005).

Laffan, Michael: The Resurrection of Ireland: The Sinn Féin Party, 1916-1923 (Cambridge University Press, 1999)

Lane, Fintan: The Origins of Modern Irish Socialist, 1881-1896 (Cork University Press, 1997)

Liddy, Pat: Secret Dublin: Lincolnwood, Illinois (Passport Books, 2001)

Madden, Richard Robert: The United Irishmen, Their Lives and Times (J. Madden & co., 1846).

Maddox, Brenda, Barnacle. Nora: The Real Life of Molly Bloom (Houghton Mifflin Books, 2000)

Magennis, Tim: 'Where are the Barges Now?' (Inis na Mara 2003/2004).

Mangin, Edward: The Parlour Window: Or, Anecdotes (E. Lumley, 1841)

McManus, Ruth: Dublin, 1910-1940: Shaping the City & Suburbs (Four Courts 2000)

M'Cready, Rev. C.T: Dublin Street Names: Dated and Explained. Dublin (Carraig Books, 1892)

McDonald, Frank: The Construction of Dublin (Gandon Editions, 2000)

Moore, Niamh: 'Dublin Docklands Reinvented - The Post-Industrial Regeneration of a European City Quarter' (Four Courts Press, 2008)

Murphy, David: 'Ireland and the Crimean War' (Four Courts, 2002).

Neary, Bernard, The Candle Factory: Five Hundred Years of Rathbone's, Master Chandlers (Lilliput, 1999).

O'Brien, Paul, Flexman, Oliver & Dickie, Steven: New Chronica Dublin (Open Mute 2007).

O'Connor, Ulick: A Terrible Beauty is Born (Hamish Hamilton, 1975)

Quinn, Ruairi: Straight Left - A Journey in Politics (Hodder Headline, 2005).

Patterson, EM: The Great Northern Railway (Ireland) (Oakwood Press, 2003).

Pelly, Frank: Founding Father of the Irish Lighthouse Service (F Beam, 2004-2005 edition)

Plunkett, James, Strumpet City (Arrow Books, 1978)

Robins, Joseph: Custom House People (Institute of Public Administration, 1980)

Rolt, LC, Green and Silver (Allen & Unwin, 1949),

Ryan, Philip B: The Lost Theatres of Dublin (Badger Press, 1998).

St. Andrew's Heritage Project, 'Along the Quays and Cobblestones - Folklore of the South Docks Community' (Saint Andrew's Resource Centre, 1992)

St. Andrew's Heritage Project, 'Dublin's Diving Bell – A History' (Leinster Leader, 2003).

St. Andrew's Heritage Project, 'Journeys from the Steyne - An Historical Portrait of the Westland Row / City Quay Community' (Saint Andrew's Resource Centre)

Skempton, A.W: A Biographical Dictionary of Civil Engineers in Great Britain and Ireland (Thomas Telford, 2002).

Stone, Norman: Europe Transformed 1878 – 1919 (Fontana Press, 1985)

White, Gerry, O'Shea, Brendan & Younghusband, William: Irish Volunteer Soldier 1913-23 (Osprey Publishing, 2003)

Wright, Rev GN: An Historical Guide to Ancient and Modern Dublin (1st edition).

2008 New Irish Architecture 23, AAI Awards 2008, Gandon Editions, Provosts Stable

O'Donoghue, Jo, Seán McMahon & Maeve Binchy: Brewer's Dictionary of Irish Phrase & Fable (Cassell, 2005)

A Social and Natural History of Sandymount, Irishtown and Ringsend (Community Services, 1993)

MAPS & SURVEYS

A Survey of the City Harbour Bay and Environs of Dublin on the same Scale as those of London Paris & Rome / by John Rocque Chorographer to his Majesty with Improvements & Additions to the Year 1773, by Mr. Bernard Scale.

Dublin City Map Dublin: ERA-Maptec Ltd., 1992.

1911 census map. Map showing Boland's Bakery on Grand Canal Street. (Ordnance Survey, 1:2,500 (25 inches to mile), Dublin, sheet XVIII,

Ordnance Survey Ireland. Dublin City and District Street Guide. Phoenix Park, Dublin: Government of Ireland, 2002.

Ordnance Survey Ireland. Dublin City Centre Street Atlas. Phoenix Park, Dublin:

REPORTS & JOURNALS

The Pembroke Estate Papers are readily available to the public by personal visit to the public Reading Room of the National Archives in Bishop Street, Dublin 8.

Dublin Journal: The Illustrated Dublin Journal a Miscellany of Amusement and Popular Information by the Most Eminent Writers. (Dublin: Duffy, 1862).

The Improvement of Dublin Harbour, Charles A. Stanuell, Esq. Read, January 19th, 1912.

'The Architects' Journal' (1919).

City bridges over the Liffey: present and future. Mallagh, Joseph J., Institution of Engineers of Ireland Transactions, 1938–1940, 65–66, 225–253

The Liffey Bridges, from Islandbridge to Eastlink: A Historical and Technical Report. IDA, Dublin, 1987.

Gateway – The Brewery Council Community Journal Vol 2, No 3 (Oct – Dec 1990), Mike Lawlor (ed).

'Some notes on Charles Wye Williams, his family, their life and times', Hazel Smyth, Dublin Historical Record, 49:1 (1996)

Historic Buildings in Spencer Dock, Franc Myles, France and Margaret Gowen, Tuesday, 15 August 2000 from www.mglarc.com

A Report on Dublin's bridges by Michael Phillips and Albert Hamilton: Proceedings of the Institution of Civil Engineers, Bridge Engineering 156 (December 2003).

Partridge, D: When the Kids were united (BBC History Magazine, September 2003, pp.24-26)

Project history of Dublin's River Liffey bridges, M. Phillips and A. Hamilton. Proceedings of the Institution of Civil Engineers, Bridge Engineering 156, December 2003 Issue BE4.

The Liffey Bridges, from Islandbridge to Eastlink: A Historical and Technical Report. IDA, Dublin, 1987.

UPDATES

For updated information about the Dublin Docklands and the contents of this book, visit www.dublindocklands.ie and www.turtlebunbury.com